Early Plastics

Early Plastics

Perspectives, 1850–1950

Edited by

Susan Mossman

Leicester University Press
London and Washington

in association with

**SCIENCE
MUSEUM**

London

First published 1997

Leicester University Press
A Cassell Imprint
Wellington House, 125 Strand, London WC2R 0BB

PO Box 605, Herndon, VA 20172

Science Museum
Exhibition Road, London SW7 2DD

British Library Cataloguing-in-Publication Data

A Catalogue record for this book is available from the British Library.

ISBN 0 7185 0020 2

Library of Congress Cataloging-in-Publication Data

Early plastics : perspectives, 1850–1950 / edited by Susan Mossman.
    p. cm.

    Includes bibliographical references and index.
    ISBN 0-7185-0020-2 (hardcover)
    1. Plastics—History.   I. Mossman, S. T. I. (Susan T. I.)
TP1116.E27   1996
668.4'09—dc20

        96–5736
        CIP

Typeset by Ben Cracknell Studios
Printed and bound in Great Britain by Martins The Printers

Contents

List of Colour Plates

1. Jewellery from the Jesse Collection, *c.*1910–50.
2. Assorted natural plastics objects of tortoiseshell, horn and amber.
3. Gutta percha inkstand, *c.*1851.
4. Collection of shellac Union Cases, mirrors and seals, *c.*1860–80.
5. Group of Bois Durci objects, including two furniture plaques and four wall plaques, *c.*1850–70.
6. Group of rubber objects, both natural and vulcanised, dark and coloured, *c.*1600–1951.
7. Parkesine (cellulose nitrate) objects made by Alexander Parkes, *c.*1862.
8. Group of cellulose nitrate (Celluloid) objects.
9. Xylonite and Ivoride objects made by Daniel Spill & Company.
10. Group of cellulose acetate objects, *c.*1880–1910.
11. Casein button books with the trade names Erinoid and Lactoid.
12. A group of phenolic (dark) and cast phenolic (brightly coloured) objects, showing the range of objects that could be made, *c.*1910–59.
13. Fada radio with outer casing made of catalin, USA, *c.*1940.
14. A range of domestic ware made from thiourea-urea-formaldehyde and urea-formaldehyde, 1930s–50s.
15. Warerite doors and laminated office surfaces from the Bakelite Limited Factory, 1936.
16. Polyethylene objects showing samples of the first pound and first ton of polyethylene, dated to 1936 and 1938 respectively.
17. A range of acrylic objects from the late 1940s onwards.
18. Polystyrene and urea-formaldehyde domestic ware.
19. Catalin plastics reference guide, 1945.
20. Advertisement for Alkathene from *Good Housekeeping*, 1956.

List of Figures

Foreword

No one today doubts the technical, economic and social importance of plastics. In less than 150 years (depending on how you define the term), plastics has grown from an insignificant 'backyard business', often bringing bankruptcy in its wake, to a gigantic industry whose products are an essential part of modern living.

The basic history of most other raw materials, such as timber, clay and natural fibres, is lost in antiquity. We shall never know the name of the first person to smelt iron or shape clay into a pot. All we can do is to recognise that such moments were seminal in human history. Plastics are different – and more fortunate. Thanks to their more recent history, we are able (albeit with controversy) to acknowledge the contributions of specific people. With that said, much remains to be discovered and recorded.

Not surprisingly, the success of plastics has resulted in an immense literature on the subject. Topics such as the chemistry, physics and manipulation of polymers are covered in all major languages. What is much less well documented is one of the subjects covered in this book – what might be called the social history of plastics.

The authors, specialists in their own fields, have combined to produce a detailed account of the key factors which influenced the demand for plastics up to the 1950s. It is particularly gratifying to have on record both the observations of the late Dr Morris Kaufman – the doyen of plastics historians – and details of the remarkable collection of polymeric artefacts housed in the Science Museum, London.

'Plastiquarians', as we call ourselves, will find much of value and interest in these pages.

Percy Reboul
Chairman, Plastics Historical Society

Acknowledgements

This book has had a long gestation period and many people have contributed at various stages. First I wish to thank my co-authors, Roger Newport and Mark Suggitt, for contributing their chapters and for their patience and good humour throughout. I am grateful to Mrs René Kaufman, who generously gave permission for the publication of the chapter written by her late husband, Dr Morris Kaufman. The book has been written under the aegis of the Science Museum, with the support of Dr Robert Bud. Other colleagues who have made significant contributions to its completion are Peter Bailes, Marc Foden, Jane Insley, John Liffen, Dr Peter Morris, Anna Rundle and Francesca Riccini, as well as my former colleague, Ann Carter. David Exton provided the colour plates of objects from the Science Museum's Plastics Collection. I have also benefited from the advice of Dr Derek Robinson and from the encouragement of Heather Mayfield, Anna Hodson and Giskin Day. Outside the Science Museum, John Morgan, Percy Reboul, Colin Williamson and Ann Morgan of the Plastics Historical Society Committee have given me considerable support and assistance in the final stages of this book, for which I am most grateful. A final thanks is due to David Jones of the Suffolk Record Office.

Disclaimer

All efforts have been made to obtain the copyright of the images used. Any enquiries should be addressed to the Science Museum.

Susan Mossman
The Science Museum, London
1 December 1995

1 Introduction

Susan Mossman

What Are Plastics?

Plastics can be defined in a number of ways. There is the common dictionary definition as a material 'capable of being moulded'. In March 1926, an American trade magazine, *Plastics*, defined the word 'plastic' as: 'The property of a substance by virtue of which it can be formed or molded into any desired shape, as opposed to non-plastic substances which must be cut or chiselled'. The definition of plastics as a material was:

> any material that by its nature or in its process of manufacture is at some stage, either through heat or by the presence of a solvent, sufficiently pliable and flowable, in other words plastic, so that it can be given its final shape by the operation of molding or pressing. [Du Bois 1972: 1–2]

More philosophical definitions of the meaning of plastics are discussed by Colin Williamson, who also gives the precise date, 1951, when the word 'plastics' was formally recognised by the British Plastics Federation and the British Standards Institute (Williamson 1994: 3ff). This may be regarded as an affirmation of the increasing importance of the plastics industry at this time.

In the 1990s John Brydson, an eminent polymer scientist, defined plastic as a material which can be moulded or shaped into different forms under pressure and/or heat (Brydson 1991).

Chemically, plastics are polymers, that is substances composed of long chains of repeating molecules (monomers) made up predominantly of carbon and hydrogen atoms, which under the right conditions join up into chain structures. For example, polyethylene is a polymer of ethylene (Diagram 1). In addition to carbon and hydrogen, oxygen, nitrogen, chlorine, silicon and other elements may be found in some polymers.

Early plastics pioneers did not understand the structure of plastics. Indeed, this subject was a matter for heated debate in the early twentieth century, as is discussed later. We are fortunate in possessing a better understanding of the structure of plastics in the late twentieth century.

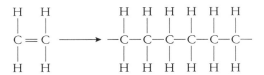

Diagram 1 Ethylene is polymerised into polyethylene

Certain plastics are known as thermo-plastic materials; examples include Celluloid, polyethylene and polystyrene. These plastics set into a certain shape, but if reheated can flow into another. This is due to their molecular structure, which consists of long chains of molecules held together by weak intermolecular forces.

Thermo-plastics may be contrasted with other plastics known as thermo-setting plastics or thermosets, which include phenolic plastics, commonly known as Bakelite. Once moulded into a shape, thermosets remain in that form, and cannot normally be changed by further heating. At a molecular level, a two-step polymerisation process eventually causes their molecules to form a three-dimensional structure with cross-linked bonds which do not break down on heating. At very high temperatures they will break down irreversibly.

Plastics can also be classified in another way as condensation or addition polymers (Nicholson 1991: 5ff, 14). In forming condensation polymers such as nylon 6,6, a small molecule, usually water, is lost during the reaction (Diagram 2).

Hexamethylenediamine   Adipic acid

$$nH_2N(CH_2)_6NH_2 \quad + \quad nHOOC(CH_2)_4COOH \longrightarrow$$
$$HN_2[(CH_2)_6NHCOO(CH_2)_4CO]_n + (n-1)H_2O$$

Diagram 2   Nylon 6,6   Water

In an addition reaction, such as that for producing polyvinyl chloride from the monomer vinyl chloride, an unsaturated (double-bonded) monomer breaks its double bond to form a molecule which can then bond with other monomers (Diagram 3).

$$nCH_2 = CHCl \longrightarrow [-CH_2 - CHCl -]_n$$
vinyl chloride   Polyvinyl chloride

Diagram 3

Type of Plastics	Name	Main Period of Use
Natural	Amber	*c.*2000BC - now
	Horn	*c.*2000BC - now
	Tortoiseshell	*c.*2000BC - now
	Bitumen	*c.*2000BC - now
	Rubber	AD1736 - now
		(in the Old World)
	Papier mâché	1772 - now
	Gutta percha	1843 - *c.*1945
	Shellac	1850 - 1950
	Bois Durci	1855 - 1880s
Semi-Synthetic	Vulcanite	1839 - 1970
	Cellulose nitrate (Celluloid, Parkesine)	1862 - 1980
	Viscose rayon	1892 - now
	Casein (casein-formaldehyde)	1899 - *c.*1970
	Cellulose acetate	1928 - now
Synthetic	Phenol-formaldehyde (Bakelite)	1910 - now
	Cast phenol-formaldehyde	1928 - 1960
	Thiourea-urea-formaldehyde	1928 - 1940
	Polyvinyl chloride (PVC)	*c.*1930 - now
	Polystyrene	*c.*1930 - now
	Urea-formaldehyde	*c.*1931 - 1940
	Ethyl cellulose	1935 - now
	Melamine-formaldehyde (laminates)	1935 - now
	Polymethyl Methacrylate (Acrylic, Perspex)	1935 - now
	Polyamide (Nylon)	1938 - now
	Polyethylene	*c.*1938 - now
	Polyurethane	*c.*1939 - now
	Polyester fibres (Polyethylene terephthalate, Terylene)	1941 - now
	Glass-fibre-reinforced plastics (fibreglass)	1942 - now

Table 1   The chronology of plastics, *c.*2000 BC–*c.*AD 1950

Plastics can now be tailored for almost any purpose by a suitable choice of monomers, or by combining with other materials to form composite plastics which are an increasingly important part of the plastics industry today (Table 1).

Plastics are often thought of as a recent phenomenon, despite their long history. Amber, horn, tortoiseshell, bitumen, shellac, gutta percha and natural rubber are all naturally occurring materials which have been used and moulded into many different shapes for centuries, and are regarded as natural plastics. Throughout the nineteenth century, natural plastics continued to play a minor role in industrial manufacture, with all but amber destined to make significant and substantial contributions at different times. The methods used to mould natural plastics such as horn (for example, heating and pressure moulding) were later very successfully adapted to fabricate the semi-synthetic and later entirely synthetic plastics.

In the second half of the century, semi-synthetic plastics were developed to provide substitutes for natural materials such as ivory, which were becoming scarce. In the 1850s the first true plastic was invented in Birmingham by Alexander Parkes and given the name Parkesine, the precursor of Celluloid. Ivory, coral, tortoiseshell and jet were very effectively imitated by the cellulosics (such as Celluloid), casein and hard rubber (Vulcanite). What we now call plastics (principally mouldable organic materials) have served a variety of purposes during their history.

Early in the twentieth century, these materials were joined by the first fully synthetic plastics, phenolics, which were advertised by their inventor, Leo Baekeland, as materials of a thousand uses and supplied in the form of resins, moulding materials and laminated sheet materials. Plastics, as a generally identifiable group of materials, began to take on characteristics of their own – they were lighter than metal, with good electrical properties, and capable of being shaped by various moulding techniques and mass produced.

By the 1930s many more plastics had been created and popular interest was growing, so the Science Museum held an exhibition to show the plastics of the day, aimed at industry and the market rather than the general visitor. It was so popular that its closure had to be postponed twice. Exhibits included ornate lampshades and even a room entirely made and furnished with plastics, with walls of black phenolic and orange-coloured urea-formaldehyde laminates (described as Bakelite and Beetle laminate in the reports of the time). The curtains were made of cellulose acetate silk, and the floor covering, 'a new cellulose material … recently placed on the market', was identified by an article in *The Times Trade and Engineering Supplement* as 'Grenolin' (*The Times* 1934).

Although it was industry that benefited substantially from the plastics of the 1930s, the public were also fascinated by plastics, in particular the most modern colourful ones made of urea-formaldehyde and turned into bright picnic sets and almost unbreakable crockery. Plastics in the 1930s were new and exciting.

The development and expansion of plastics continued before, during and particularly after the Second World War, and by the 1950s their place in the market was firmly established and ever-expanding.

Plastics and People

In 1900 a typical middle-class family would encounter few plastics items as they went about their daily business. Perhaps the women would wear Celluloid combs in their hair, or carry Celluloid evening bags (Figure 1). If in mourning, they might wear artificial jet jewellery made of Vulcanite,

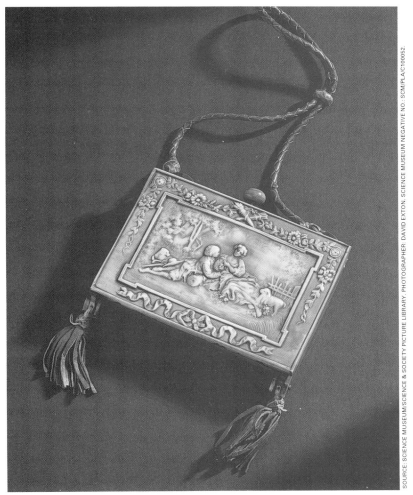

Figure 1 Cellulose nitrate handbag, with moulded design and leather strap, 1920s (cat. no. 410).

have Celluloid or casein cosmetic boxes and use Celluloid-backed brushes and mirrors. Children's dolls might have Celluloid heads. Smokers might use Vulcanite Vesta matchboxes (Figure 2) (cat. no. 215). All the family would be eager to listen to the new-fangled shellac gramophone record: only eleven years old in 1900. They might well wear Celluloid collars or cuffs. Artificial fibres were still in their infancy, although artificial silk and the new viscose fibres were causing some excitement.

Natural plastics such as gutta percha (related to rubber) had already been in use for half a century for insulating underwater cables as well as for a variety of mouldings. Semi-synthetic plastics such as Vulcanite had been adopted for a variety of uses, from denture plates to ear trumpets and early electrical equipment (Figure 3). Ten years later, phenolic plastics known principally as Bakelite were developed, and proved vital

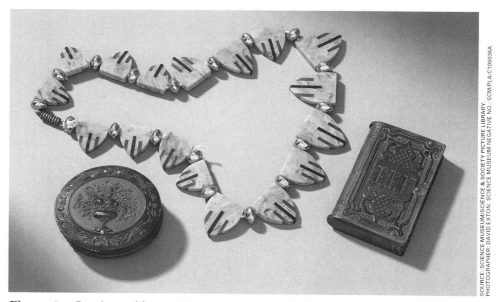

Figure 2   Casein necklace, 1930s (cat. no. 608), shellac Union Case, *c.*1860 (cat. no. 39) and 'Feu' Vulcanite Vesta match box, *c.*1890 (cat. no. 215).

Figure 3   (opposite) These ear trumpets in gutta percha are an example of the close relationship which plastics have had and continue to have with the human body, 1850s.

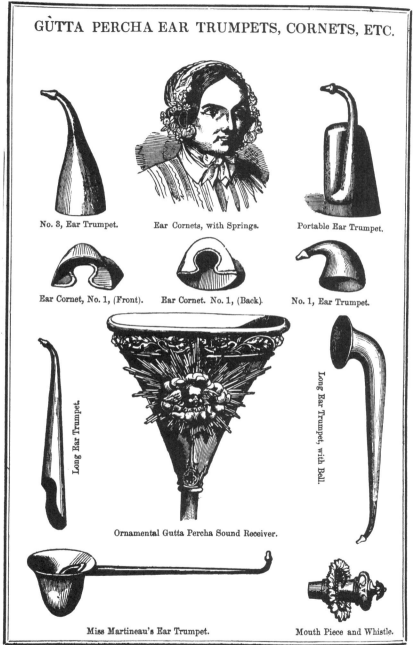

GÙTTA PERCHA EAR TRUMPETS, CORNETS, ETC.

No. 3, Ear Trumpet.   Ear Cornets, with Springs.   Portable Ear Trumpet.

Ear Cornet, No. 1, (Front).   Ear Cornet. No. 1, (Back).   No. 1, Ear Trumpet.

Long Ear Trumpet.

Ornamental Gutta Percha Sound Receiver.

Long Ear Trumpet, with Bell.

Miss Martineau's Ear Trumpet.

Mouth Piece and Whistle.

64   The Gutta Percha Company, Patentees.

during the First World War because of their excellent electrical insulating properties. They appeared in a variety of electrical fittings, laminates, resins, lacquers and eventually the familiar black telephone, as well as the very practical thermos flask and a variety of ashtrays, cigarette boxes and clocks (Figures 4 and 5). They were even used to make car dashboards. Another material, cellulose acetate, was used in liquid form as dope to coat the fabric covering the bodies of early aeroplanes.

The inter-war years saw dazzling innovations in the field of plastics. The properties of phenolics were not forgotten, but new plastics – thiourea- and urea-formaldehydes – were invented which not only possessed the excellent temperature-resistant qualities of phenolics but could be made in an amazing variety of colours. The 1920s and 1930s saw new materials such as urea-formaldehyde, which, under trade names such as Beetle, appeared in light, bright, swirling colours and were made into very attractive picnic sets. Plastics laminates such as Formica and Warerite came into being and revolutionised kitchens: away with the old wooden draining boards and wood or stone surfaces; in with easily cleanable laminates, which were often made to resemble the old wood or marble worktops. These were the new plastics celebrated in the 1933 Plastics Industry Exhibition at the Science Museum (Figure 6).

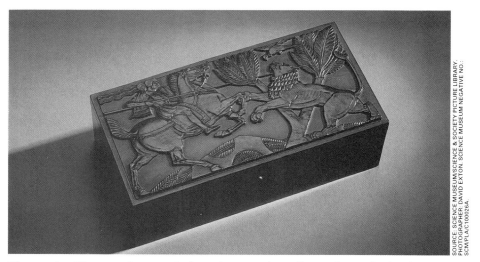

Figure 4   Cigarette box made from brown phenolic, trade marked 'Elo Ware' 1930s (cat. no. 700).

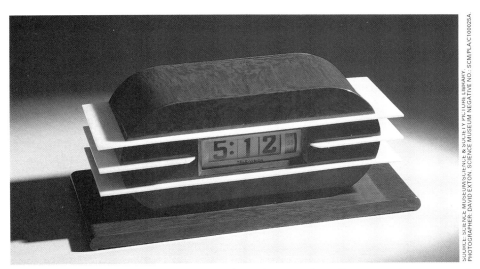

Figure 5 Electric digital clock, made from brown phenolic, *c.*1930 (cat. no. 726).

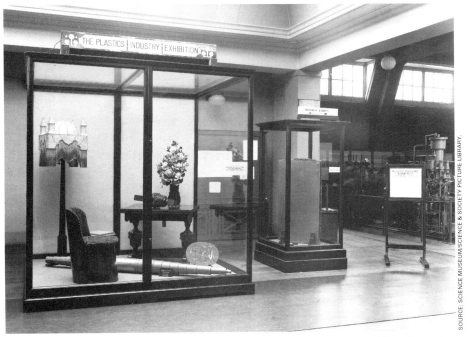

Figure 6 Cases from the Plastics Industry Exhibition, 1933, held at the Science Museum, London.

Following the work of Wallace Carothers, the 1930s saw the development of nylon, famous mainly as the wonder material for stockings. Polyethylene and polystyrene were also developed and shaped into a variety of wares, both domestic and industrial. In 1937 the manufacturers, ICI, thought that the 'outstanding quality of polythene was unquestionably in its electrical properties' (ICI 1939: 87), and the material went on to play a vital role in insulating cables (particularly for radar) during the Second World War: 'On the invasion of Normandy in June 1944 a number of polythene insulated telephone cables for use at radio frequencies were laid across the channel' (ICI 1944–5: 239). Most of the newer plastics became almost totally unavailable to the general public at this time, since manufacture was confined to producing goods for the war effort.

Manufacturers of plastics such as ICI were understandably concerned about future markets for their products in the change from military to domestic use after the war ended in 1945. Interest soon picked up; polyethylene, for example, became a major success story, and by 1953 was a familiar name to the public, being used for a variety of everyday objects, notably the washing-up bowl and baby baths. Later, in the form of films and bottles, it was to become a vital packaging material.

Plastics took off in a big way after the Second World War, as evidenced by the Daily Graphic Plastics Exhibition held in London in association with the British Plastics Federation in November 1946. This exhibition was also most popular, and was visited by Queen Mary herself. By 1953 ICI could say that the word 'plastic' itself had come 'to have a more honourable meaning in the household' (ICI 1953: 196).

For over a century until the 1950s, plastics had been developing slowly. As late as 1950 the *British Plastics Yearbook* listed only 25 categories of plastics material, and nearly half of these were semi-synthetic or naturally occurring. Since then there has been an explosion in the number of plastics being developed, until today plastics are very precisely tailored for specific uses, be they for sports equipment (such as the finely honed modern ski) or medical uses, as in the valves used in open-heart surgery and for limb replacement. Such is the variety that developments in plastics since 1950 would need a book to themselves to explain the extraordinary multiplicity of materials and uses.

Collecting Plastics

People and museums collect plastics for many different reasons. Social historians collect plastics for what they can tell us about the society we live in: how we use plastics to eat with, in our clothes, and even in our leisure activities; to what extent plastics play a role in our everyday lives. Social historians have to consider all these issues as well as explore the ways that people perceive plastics and how they have influenced and changed our lives. In addition, such historians may contemplate the production side: in what conditions were these items produced? What were the conditions for the workers? Did it affect their health? Were skilled or unskilled workers required? Often, plastics are collected in association with other items which reflect some aspect of society, and the emphasis is on their role in people's lives and people's attitudes towards them.

Students of design look for different qualities in plastics. They might ask exactly what this material is: how may it best be used? Can it be adapted for specific purposes? Does it have special qualities that make it the best material for a particular use? Is it visually attractive, and/or hard-wearing? Is it more easily manufactured into objects than other materials? What is the cost of an object made of plastic and how many were produced of a specific kind – is it rare? Are there associations with a famous designer, and is the design of the object evocative of or formative for its period?

Others investigate plastics from a different point of view and want to know when the first plastic was invented: from where did it develop and how did plastics develop further? How are plastics made and from what materials? How successful were the pioneers of plastics and why did some of them fail?

Plastics may be collected almost incidentally, when they form part of an object collected for other reasons.

The Science Museum's Early Plastics Collection

The Science Museum, London, began to collect plastics in 1884 when a plaque of Thomas Hancock in vulcanised rubber (dated to *c.*1840) was put on inventory (transferred from the Patent Office). Today the collection numbers 1059 items dated up to *c*.1959, acquired for their importance in the development of plastics materials and in the machinery used to produce them. The collection is listed in the catalogue later in this book, with duplicate items grouped together under single entries, and a selection of the objects are illustrated in the plates. They include specimens of Parkesine, widely regarded as the first plastic, dated to the mid-nineteenth century and the precursor of Celluloid, as well as other important examples of early synthetic fibres such as viscose and rayon.

Within the main collection, the Museum holds two discrete groups of plastics, in total numbering 631 objects, collected up to about 1970 by John Jesse and Roger Newport (the latter is one of the contributors to this work), and acquired by the Museum in 1979 and 1980 respectively. The Jesse collection contains plastics items of design importance, including masterpieces such as the cellulose acetate 'cherry' box made by the Parisian workshops of René Lalique, and a variety of ornate cosmetic boxes from the workshops of Eduard Marco Fornells, an Andorran craftsman who worked for Lalique before setting up his own business. It also contains a selection of plastics jewellery (Plate 1). The Newport collection covers a range of early plastics materials from natural via semi-synthetic to synthetic pieces, with rare examples of natural plastics such as Bois Durci and shellac.

The Science Museum collection of early plastics is representative, and is rich in certain areas such as Parkesine, gutta percha and casein. An active interest is maintained in the acquisition of early plastics items. Most of our collecting in this area is done by acquiring items and archives from the manufacturers or descendants of the inventors of the various plastics. We also have a keen interest in other collections of plastics, notably the Baekeland Archives at the Smithsonian Institution in Washington, DC, and in historic centres of the plastics industry, notably Oyonnax in France and the National Plastics Center in Leominster, Massachusetts.

Plastics are also to be found within many of the Science Museum's other collections, notably telecommunications, electronics, space technology, aeronautics and medicine.

There is a growing number of private collectors of plastics. They range from specialists who collect mainly in a particular field, such as early plastics or a specific plastics material (for example Bakelite), to those who are more varied in their tastes. Early plastics radios are now very collectible, particularly the notable phenolic examples made by the Ekco factory. Another favourite is Bandalasta Ware, the thiourea-formaldehyde plastic often made into multicoloured fruit bowls and other domestic ware. Some enthusiastic collectors cover the whole field: if it is plastic, they collect it. They may travel all over the country to find bargains which can be proudly displayed at specialist meetings. Many are members of the Plastics Historical Society, set up in 1986 under the aegis of the London-based Plastics and Rubber Institute, now affiliated to the Institute of Materials.

The Authors

In defining the public perception and acceptance of plastics, the role of the designer is at least as important as that of the scientist. Roger Newport, who has written the chapter on 'Plastics and Design' with particular reference to industrial design, is a lecturer on art and design and brings his expertise to bear on this aspect of the subject. He is also a major collector of plastics from whom the Science Museum has acquired a technologically significant collection of plastics, known as the Newport Collection.

Mark Suggitt, who has written the chapters on 'Living with Plastics' and 'Working with Plastics', is a social historian by training. He has used valuable documentary and oral history material to write an account of how people lived and worked with early plastics. His contribution combines a summary of what is already known with the results of new research, concentrating on the early Celluloid industry in Britain.

The late Morris Kaufman was acknowledged as an expert on the history of plastics; his book *The First Century of Plastics* (1963) is essential reading for those interested in the origins and development of plastics. At the time of his death in 1988, he was working on a book on the plastics industry, under the aegis of the Science Museum, of which he was a fellow. It has been possible to include part of his unfinished manuscript in this book as the chapter on 'Other Technologies and Plastics'. Dr Kaufman's contribution gives a wider perspective on the world in which the plastics industry was born and grew, and points to the influence of plastics developments on the new electrical, automobile and telecommunications industries.

Susan Mossman is a curator at the Science Museum, London, and has worked on the Museum's collection of plastics. She discusses the technological development of plastics from the nineteenth to the mid-twentieth century, based on a study of the 1059 objects in the Museum's collection of early plastics, and on archive material concerning Parkesine and polyethylene. The collection is described in the catalogue section and illustrates aspects of the history and technology of plastics up to the 1950s. This arbitrary cut-off point includes the exciting developments of plastics immediately before, during and after the Second World War, and gives an indication of the plethora of plastics which were to develop immediately after this period.

A complete history of the development of plastics is outside the range of this study, which is necessarily selective. The authors offer insights from the study of previously unpublished archive material and oral history. This tempers the artefact analysis with historical perspective, and contributes a human element to those pioneers who developed the earliest plastics.

Other excellent studies of plastics include the monumental work by Sylvia Katz, *Plastics: Designs and Materials* (1978), the extensive account of the chemistry of plastics by John Brydson (1982) and more detailed accounts of specific plastics such as that of PVC by Morris Kaufman (1967).

This book provides a fresh insight into certain aspects of plastics as well as a detailed reference catalogue for the curator and collector of plastics. It also aims to put the first century of the plastics industry into the context of society, science and aesthetics, using the richness of the Science Museum's collection of plastics as a guide.

2 Perspectives on the History and Technology of Plastics

Susan Mossman

From Coal to Oil

The earliest plastics, apart from the natural ones, were made partly from natural and partly from artificial substances. They are known as semi-synthetic plastics and include cellulose nitrate (known as Celluloid) and casein-formaldehyde (based on milk).

The earliest cellulosic semi-synthetic plastics were the products of mixtures of natural materials such as cellulose (from cotton), which was reacted with nitric acid and then mixed with solvents and plasticisers from a number of sources such as vegetable oils, camphor and alcohol. Synthetic early plastics – phenolic- and urea-formaldehydes – were made from the by-products of the gas and coke industries, which also produced constituents of polyvinyl chloride (PVC) and polystyrene. The ethyl alcohol produced from molasses gave ethylene to form polyethylene.

The change to oil came during the 1930s in the USA, spurred on by an increasing need for the products of the petroleum industry, both for petrol and, by the late 1930s, for the olefin ethylene from which polyethylene is produced. Britain's first oil cracker designed specifically for the plastics industry came on stream in 1942 at the behest of British Celanese, mainly to produce acetic acid for cellulose and vinyl acetates (ICI Plastics *c.*1964: 76). The petroleum chemicals industry has continued to grow, expanding rapidly after 1950, although Europe has not fully adopted oil for the plastics industry in all cases, and coal and now natural gas still play a part in providing raw materials for plastics.

The earliest plastics were produced by adapting techniques used to work other natural, mouldable materials such as rubber and horn. They were often heated and pressed into moulds, carved or extruded (that is, pressed through holes in dies to produce tubing or fibres). Calendering was another process used with thermo-plastics: in this, softened plastic is pressed through rollers to produce flat sheeting. Extrusion and calendering are still used today to produce tubing and sheeting. Other processes include injection moulding, compression moulding, blow moulding, thermo- (vacuum-)forming and rotational moulding. Dip moulding was also used to mould PVC in the 1940s. Many of these processes are discussed by Roger Newport in his chapter on 'Plastics and Design'. Reference to particular moulding processes is only made here when they have a special significance for a certain material.

The Chronology of Plastics

Plastics are discussed in roughly chronological order from the middle of the nineteenth to the middle of the twentieth century (see Table 1, p. 3).

Natural Plastics

Natural plastics (Plate 2) appear in many forms and were used in the most ancient civilisations. The ancient Egyptians moulded amber, a fossilised resin from trees, into items such as jewellery. Another natural product, horn, has had a long period of use: it was used as windows in lanterns, to make knife handles, spoons, moulded boxes, drinking cups and horns, and in the eighteenth century as a substitute for glass. The use of horn has been discussed extensively elsewhere by Hardwick (1981) and Williamson (1994: 3ff.) Perhaps one of the most important applications of horn was in the manufacture of combs, particularly between 1770 and 1880. There is a remarkable collection of decorative combs in both horn and plastics in the Musée du Peigne et des Plastiques in Oyonnax, France. This was a centre for the horn-comb industry and then developed into a plastic-comb-manufacturing centre. Many techniques which were traditionally used to form objects of horn, such as pressing into flat sheets and moulding into simple shapes, were later adapted to shaping semi-synthetic plastics.

Gutta Percha

Gutta percha (Plate 3), a relative of rubber, comes from trees of the genus *Palaquium,* which is native to Malaysia. Gutta percha is dark brown and

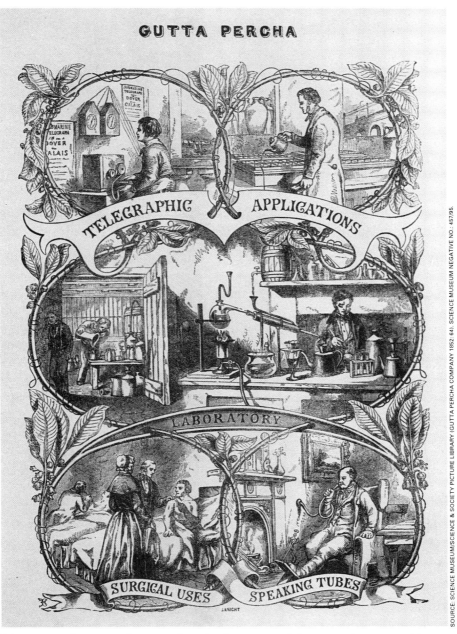

Figure 7   Gutta percha was advertised as a material appropriate to a wide range of tasks.

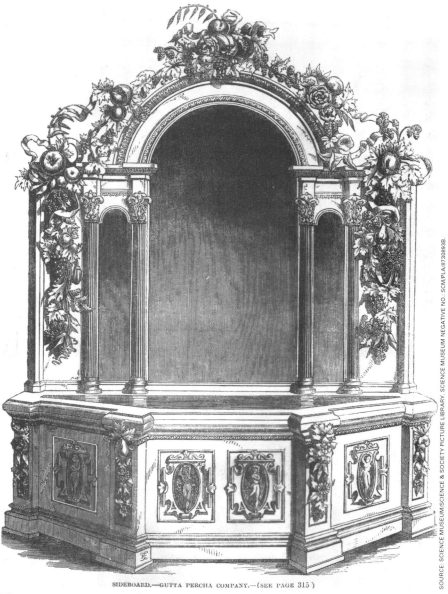

SIDEBOARD.—GUTTA PERCHA COMPANY.—(SEE PAGE 315.)

Figure 8   Engraving of a gutta percha sideboard exhibited at the Great Exhibition in 1851. Unfortunately this was not a successful use of this material as it was reported that the pendulous fruit on the top of the sideboard cracked and fell off. Taken from the *Illustrated London News* 1851: 313.

can be shaped by softening over heat and pressing into cold moulds, or alternatively by extrusion.

Henry Bewley set up the Gutta Percha Company with Charles Hancock in 1845, although they traded under their own names until 1846 (Telcon 1950: 12). In 1845 Bewley adapted equipment already used for the extrusion of rubber so that it could produce gutta percha tubes, which, in 1851, were used to cover the first submarine cable between France and England. Gutta percha possesses excellent insulating properties, and so was ideal for this purpose. Wire insulated with gutta percha was also laid across the Hudson River at Fort Lee in August 1849 for the Morse Telegraph Company. Many submarine cables were to follow, a highlight being the first transatlantic cable, which was successfully laid at the second attempt by the *Great Eastern* in 1866 (Telcon, 1950: 62ff).

The uses made of gutta percha were many and varied (cat. nos. 16–37) (Figure 7). A pictorial catalogue of gutta percha mouldings from the Gutta Percha Company is held by the Science Museum Library (Science Museum inventory no. 1984-1101) and shows a variety of gutta percha mouldings ranging from coats of arms to cherubs. There were some problems with the large architectural mouldings, which tended to be brittle and break off. A gutta percha sideboard was exhibited at the Great Exhibition of 1851, but unfortunately the elaborately moulded and pendulous fruit fell off (Figure 8). Indeed, gutta percha mouldings from the 1850s onwards are now very fragile and are often cracked and broken.

The extrusion process had its origins in early nineteenth-century devices used in Italy to produce pasta, and was adapted to produce rods and tubes of gutta percha and Vulcanite; today it is also used to produce plastic bags. The plastic granules are fed into a hopper and melted. The melted plastic is extruded through a die, producing a tube of plastic which is then flattened, wound up and sliced into bags; the cutting process leaves one end open, the other heat-sealed.

Shellac

Shellac (Plate 4) is the refined secretion of the lac beetle, which lives on certain trees in India, Burma and Thailand as well as to a lesser extent in other Asian countries. Harvested since ancient times, mainly as a cottage industry, shellac became particularly popular in the latter half of the nineteenth century for moulding into a variety of different shapes. It could be mixed with a number of different fillers such as wood flour and slate dust, and then pressed into heated moulds. When the moulds cooled, the object was released. Shellac has the advantage of being able to reproduce a fine level of moulded detail and was used for such purposes as decorative mirror backs and gramophone records.

In 1854, an American, Samuel Peck, patented a technique for combining:

> gum shellac and woody fibers or other suitable fibrous material dyed to the color that may be required and ground with the shellac and between hot rollers so as to be converted into a mass which when heated becomes plastic so that it can be pressed into a mold or between dies. [United States Patent (USP) 11758, 1854: ll. 20–7]

He then used his new mouldable 'natural plastic' to make Union Cases, which were popular as holders for the photographic equivalents of the period, known as daguerreotypes (polished and silvered copper plate) and ambrotypes (glass collodion positives) (cat. nos. 38–45). Such cases were necessary, as otherwise these forerunners of the photograph faded in the light.

Union Cases were usually decorated with geometric patterns produced with a rose lathe. However, on occasion inspiration was taken from famous paintings of the day, such as John Vanderlyn's *Landing of Columbus* (located in the Rotunda of the Capitol Building, Washington, DC). This was exceptionally large at $7\frac{3}{8}$" × $9\frac{3}{8}$"; Union Cases were usually much smaller, at $3\frac{3}{4}$" × $3\frac{5}{16}$" or less. The designs were the work of very skilled die engravers; a detailed study of these has recently been published (Krainik and Krainik 1989). Examples of the most elaborate types of Union Case are held by the National Museum of Photography, Film and Television in Bradford. By the 1870s, advances in photography such as paper prints made Union Cases superfluous.

Shellac was also moulded into decorative items such as mirrors and letter seals, which could be ochre in colour (cat. nos. 47–113). Shellac's ability to pick up intricate detail also meant that it found another valuable use in the manufacture of the earliest 78 r.p.m. gramophone records in 1897. The composition of shellac records remained fairly constant for fifty years, consisting of *c.*15 per cent shellac resin and 85 per cent ground slate and carbon black. The advantages of shellac for records were only superseded in 1948 by those of the vinyl copolymer record (a copolymer of vinyl chloride and vinyl acetate) developed by Union Carbide under the trade name 'Vinylite'. This material was less brittle and more flexible than shellac, with reduced surface noise and finer detail (Mitchell 1993: 14ff). However, it too has been largely replaced by the polycarbonate compact disc.

Bois Durci

Bois Durci (Plate 5) is a plastic-like substance invented by a Frenchman, François Charles Lepage. He patented it in Britain in 1856 (British Patent (BP) 2232), and described it as: 'a new composition of materials which may be employed as a substitute for wood, leather, bone, metal and other hard or plastic substances'. Bois Durci is a form of wood pulp moulding made from sawdust (from a hardwood such as ebony or rosewood) mixed with egg or blood albumen. The sawdust can be mixed with 'any vegetable, mineral or metallic powders' and the albumen with 'any other

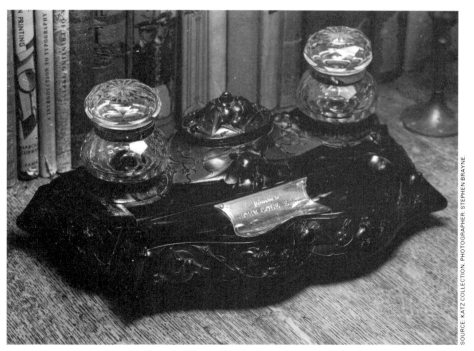

SOURCE: KATZ COLLECTION. PHOTOGRAPHER: STEPHEN BRAYNE.

Figure 9   Bois Durci inkwell, 1872, from the collection of Sylvia Katz.

glutinous or gelatinous substance'. Lepage soaked the powder in albumen diluted with water, then dried it and compressed it in a steel mould under steam heat and pressure.

The resultant mouldings showed a fine level of detail (cat. nos. 124–129). Bois Durci was apparently only produced between 1855 and the late 1880s, and most often appears in the form of commemorative plaques, for example of Napoleon and contemporary heroes such as John Cobden and Richard Bright. These are frequently stamped with the trade name 'Bois Durci' as well as the trade mark of a feather, which appears beneath the moulded head. Desk equipment such as inkwells (Figure 9) and pen trays were produced in the material, as well as ornamental plaques for furniture and doors (Williamson 1988: 8; Societé du Bois Durci n.d.).

India Rubber

Natural rubber (Plate 6) has a long history of use. The Peruvian Indians used it in a variety of ways. For example, they turned it into waterproof shoes (the earliest galoshes) and into rubber balls, with which they played a traditional game known to us from both folk tales and archaeological evidence. There is a rubber ball from a Peruvian child's grave dated to about 1600 in the Science Museum's collections (cat. no. 131). Rubber first came to the attention of the Western world after Columbus's second voyage to Haiti in 1493. However, it did not come into wide use in Britain until the late eighteenth century, when it began to be used by draughtsmen as erasers (Coates 1987: 15).

In its natural state rubber is malleable and does not withstand heat or cold adequately, becoming sticky in heat and rigid in cold, but, as with many other natural mouldable materials, the nineteenth century saw major experimentation and modifications to this substance. In addition, machinery was developed or improved to produce a variety of rubber goods, and was later used to produce plastics.

Two British men, Charles Macintosh (1766–1843) and Thomas Hancock, and an American, Charles Goodyear, were key figures in these developments. Macintosh and Hancock worked together as a chemist and a mechanical engineer respectively. Macintosh found that coal-tar oil was a good solvent for rubber, producing a solution which, when coated between two fabrics, resulted in a very satisfactory waterproof material. This was used to make double-texture waterproofed cloaks which

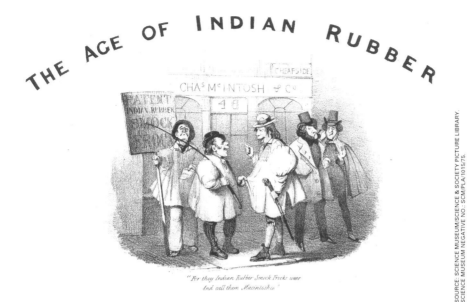

Figure 10 'The Age of Indian Rubber', a cartoon illustrating early attitudes to India Rubber, *c.*1830 (cat. no. 135 pt. 1).

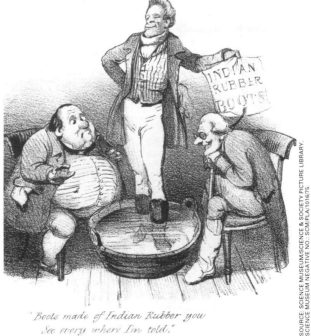

Figure 11 'Boots made of Indian Rubber you see everywhere', a cartoon illustrating the wonder aroused by this new material, *c.*1830 (cat. no. 135 pt. 2).

became known as Macintoshes (cat. no. 135) (Figures 10 and 11). However, it was the development of Vulcanite (hard rubber) which was to turn rubber into an extremely useful and resilient material.

Semi-Synthetic Plastics

Vulcanite (Ebonite)

Vulcanite (Plate 6) is a semi-synthetic plastic (also known as ebonite or hard rubber in the USA) made of rubber hardened with sulphur. Within a year of each other, Thomas Hancock in Britain (1843) (Figure 12) and

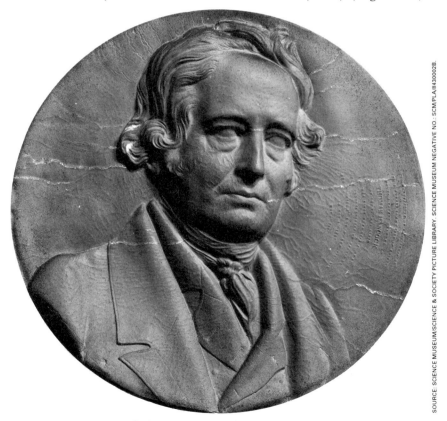

SOURCE: SCIENCE MUSEUM/SCIENCE & SOCIETY PICTURE LIBRARY. SCIENCE MUSEUM NEGATIVE NO.: SCM.PLA/8430002B.

Figure 12   Portrait of Thomas Hancock (1786–1865) in vulcanised rubber, *c.*1843 (cat. no. 130).

Charles Goodyear in the USA (1844) patented methods for the vulcanisation of rubber (BP 9952; USP 3633). An illuminating note written by Alexander Parkes in his copy of Hancock's memoir (now in the Science Museum Library) suggests that Hancock may have obtained his idea for the vulcanisation of rubber from Goodyear in the first place, although indirectly through the good offices of his friend, Brockedon, who had met Goodyear and been given a strip of hardened rubber. Parkes wrote: 'he [Hancock] must always have on his mind Goodyear, for to him alone is the invention due as first in America' (cat. no. 130), and proceeded to annotate Hancock's memoirs with comments emphasising that Goodyear invented the process first! Eventually he is moved to comment: 'This discovery was made first by Goodyear in America and not by Hancock. Justice must be done to Goodyear.' Unfortunately this was not the case, as Goodyear died in poverty without realising the benefits of his invention.

The American plastics historian John DuBois firmly states that Goodyear was the inventor of the vulcanisation of rubber (DuBois 1972: 14). The catalogue attached to the rubber exhibition held at the Science Museum in 1934 equally firmly names Hancock as the inventor. On balance, although Hancock patented Vulcanite first, Goodyear deserves the accolade as he invented vulcanised rubber in 1838.

Hancock developed a number of pieces of machinery to manufacture rubber articles, including his masticator (cat. no. 180). Hancock explained his process as follows:

> I now saw my course straight before me; my experiments had shown that the rubber and sulphur must first be blended ... by rollers and masticators; the blended material could be reduced to a state of solution by any of the usual solvents, or to a state of dough, and spread on cloth by the machinery of my previous patents for waterproofing, or on sized cambric for sheets. Blocks of the masticated compound could be pressed into moulds and cut into sheets, and into every variety of form and size that the new uses of the 'changed' rubber might require; ... ordinary cut sheets of pure rubber in the form they came from the knife, or made up into other forms, could be immersed in a sulphur bath, and changed to any required degree, from the softest and most elastic up to a state of hardness similar to horn, and capable of being wrought with carpenters' tools, or turned like ivory and ebony in a lathe. [Hancock 1857: 104ff] (Figures 13 and 14)

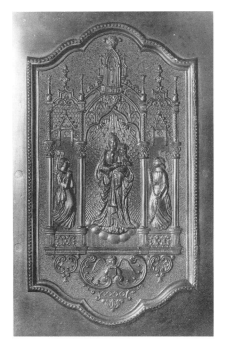

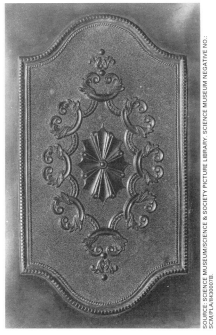

Figure 13   Two early vulcanised rubber mouldings, decorated with moulded gothic design, made by Thomas Hancock, *c.*1840 (cat. no. 137 pt. 2).

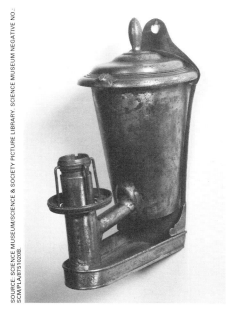

Figure 14   Vulcanising lamp made and used by Thomas Hancock, *c.*1843 (cat. no. 230).

Hancock called this substance Vulcanite after the god Vulcan, who, in Roman mythology, worked with heat and sulphur. Vulcanite may be regarded as the first truly semi-synthetic plastic, since it is made from a natural material, rubber, which has been chemically altered, its composition and properties being changed by the addition of sulphur under controlled conditions. It was popular for items such as dental plates, Vesta matchboxes and pen holders (Plate 6). Vulcanite spoons are also known.

Imitation jet jewellery was made in Vulcanite, too, and was very popular for mourning wear after the death of Prince Albert. The material is characteristically black in colour, but when mixed with white and red pigments produces a pink substance, which could be made to resemble gums for false dentures (cat. nos. 227–228).

Cellulose-Based Plastics (CN, Parkesine, Xylonite/Ivoride, Celluloid)

The drive for the semi-synthetic plastics such as cellulose nitrate (CN) (Plates 7 and 8) came from the need to find good substitutes for natural materials such as ivory or tortoiseshell which were becoming increasingly rare and/or expensive. A shortage of material for billiard balls (made of ivory until the mid-nineteenth century) is often cited as one of the main causes, but its significance may have been overstated.

Christian F. Schönbein, a Swiss-German chemist, is said to have discovered cellulose nitrate in 1845 in the kitchen, when he spilled some nitric/sulphuric acid and wiped it up with his wife's apron. When put to dry in front of the fire, the cloth (presumably cotton) disappeared in a puff of smoke! On 27 February 1846 he communicated his finding to Michael Faraday: 'I have of late made a little chemical discovery which enables me to change very suddenly, very cheaply and very easily common paper in such a way as to render that substance exceedingly strong and entirely waterproof'. He wrote again on 18 March 1846: 'To give you some idea of what may be made of vegetable fibre I send you a specimen of a transparent substance which I have prepared from common paper. This matter is capable of being shaped into all sorts of things and forms' (Kahlbaum and Darbishire 1899: 155).

Alexander Parkes (Figure 15), an Englishman living in Birmingham, learned of Schönbein's work and experimented with the material,

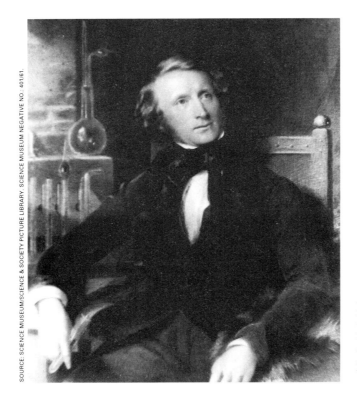

SOURCE: SCIENCE MUSEUM/SCIENCE & SOCIETY PICTURE LIBRARY. SCIENCE MUSEUM NEGATIVE NO.: 401/61.

Figure 15   Alexander Parkes (1813–90), inventor of the first semi-synthetic plastic, as a young man, by A. Wivell Junior, 1848.

producing cellulose nitrate from nitric acid, sulphuric acid and cellulose (derived from sources such as cotton). The cellulose nitrate was mixed with vegetable oils and small proportions of organic solvents, giving a mouldable dough which he christened Parkesine and displayed in a variety of colours and forms at the International Exhibition of 1862 (cat. nos. 234–318). He received a bronze medal for his accomplishment, and a silver medal when he exhibited his discovery at the Paris Universal Exhibition in 1867. Both these medals are now in the Science Museum's Coins and Medals Collection (Science Museum inventory nos.1970-587 and 1970-588). Some Parkesine objects were produced from dough which had been softened by heating and then pressed into moulds; others were hand-carved; certain pieces were inlaid with mother-of-pearl or metal wire; while other pieces were extruded. Parkes himself was an expert in wood carving, painting and modelling (cat. nos. 263–265, 309).

He was quite capable of either hand-carving Parkesine or of making the moulds from which the elaborately decorated repeated pieces were pressed.

Parkes launched the Parkesine Company Ltd in April 1866, with a capital of £10,000, some of which was his own money. However, following initial optimism, the company failed to become a commercial success and went into liquidation in 1868, perhaps because Parkes had committed himself to producing Parkesine too cheaply, using inferior materials which resulted in a poor product subject to shrinkage and warping. In addition, the product had great limitations due to its flammability, although it was relatively easy to produce.

Parkes signed over his patent rights in 1869 to the Xylonite Company (Hackney Archives 1869) which had been set up in the same year. This company tried to make money out of Parkes's invention, which was renamed Xylonite. The Xylonite Company produced items made of Xylonite and Ivoride (imitation ivory) ranging from billiard balls to knife handles as well as imitation coral (cat. nos. 320–326) (Plate 9). Daniel Spill, who had been Parkes's works manager, had an initial role in the Xylonite Company which is unclear, but he appears to have been involved in its setting up, and then acquired the rights to the company in 1873. Spill was no more successful than Parkes in his business venture (Hackney Archives 1873). Some of his problems seem to have been of a financial nature, as documents show that in 1874 he had to mortgage both patents and premises (Hackney Archives 1874).

An American, John Hyatt, was also experimenting with cellulose nitrate, and experiencing the problems with flammability already suffered by Parkes and Spill. Concerning the manufacture of billiard balls by his Albany Billiard Ball Company, Hyatt wrote: 'In order to secure strength and beauty only colouring pigments were added, in the least quantity.' As a result, the billiard balls were coated with a film of almost pure gun-cotton (cellulose nitrate). Hyatt went on to say:

Consequently a lighted cigar applied would at once result in a serious flame and occasionally the violent contact of the balls would produce a mild explosion like a percussion guncap. We had a letter from a billiard saloon proprietor in Colorado, mentioning this fact and saying that he did not care so much about it but that instantly every man in the room pulled a gun. [Hyatt 1914: 158–9]

A more stable product was needed. The breakthrough came in 1870 when Hyatt patented his discovery of the fact that camphor made an excellent solvent for cellulose nitrate (USP 105338), the title of his related 1870 patent being: 'Improvement in treating and moulding pyroxyline' (another name for cellulose nitrate). He called his product 'Celluloid', and this is the name which is most commonly used today for products based on cellulose nitrate. In the same year he set up the Albany Dental Plate Company. By 1872 the name of the company had changed to the Celluloid Manufacturing Company, and it became an enormous commercial success for Hyatt and his brother, Isaiah Smith Hyatt.

Spill was most unhappy with the Hyatts, claiming they had infringed his patented processes. Lengthy litigation resulted, in which Parkes gave evidence on behalf of the Hyatts. After an initial success, Spill finally lost the battle; he died from diabetes in 1877.

In the meantime, Hyatt had made significant advances in the machinery used for the production of Celluloid. He had already benefited from that developed for natural plastics: namely Samuel Peck's screw press, Hancock's masticator, Bewley's extruder and Real's hydraulic press of 1816. He also used Hancock's slicer of 1840 to make Celluloid sheets by slicing thin sheets from large moulded blocks. However, Hyatt also:

> sought the services of a practical engineer to collaborate with him in the design and construction of proper machinery for manufacturing his material and the various articles that might be made therefrom. The engineer engaged was Mr Charles Burroughs, the founder of the Burroughs Company. [DuBois 1972: 42]

Burroughs designed specific tools and machinery for the manufacture of Celluloid, including the 'stuffing machine', which produced Celluloid 'in the form of a bar, sheet or stick'. This was then machine finished (USP 133,229, 1872). The 'stuffing machine' is considered to be the precursor of the modern injection moulding machine.

Burroughs had other inventions to his credit, including the compression sheet-moulding press and the hydraulic planer which sliced Celluloid slugs into thin sheets. The 'Burroughs Blowing Press' made Celluloid tubes or sheets expand to fit the contour of the mould, and was an early example of blow moulding (DuBois 1972: 45).

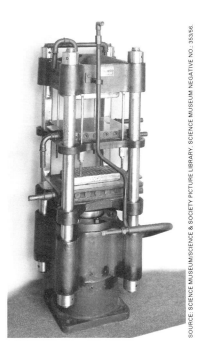

Figure 16   Pilot plant for cellulose nitrate manufacture. Block press size 8, working load 38 tons, made in 1948 by Tangyes Ltd, Birmingham (cat. no. 517).

New evidence has come to light in the form of letters and diaries which reveal that Parkes not only continued his work on cellulose nitrate after the collapse of his company in 1868, but was also fully aware of the importance of camphor as a solvent for Celluloid (Mossman 1994). He had assigned his patents to the Xylonite Company in 1869 and had undertaken that he would: 'not at anytime hereafter during the continuance of the ... Letters Patent ... be engaged as principle partner Agent Manager or Workman in any Manufacture ... of compounds or materials containing Xylodine [cellulose nitrate]' (Hackney Archives 1869). When Parkes's patents expired, his diaries reveal that in 1881 he returned to the problem of nitrating cellulose. In September 1881 an entry records another recipe for solvents and camphor: 'by this addition the bulk is increased to 7 gallons when camphor goes in to increase the bulk of this celluloid' (Williamson 1989: 8). Parkes and his brother Henry set up the London Celluloid Company Ltd in 1881 (PHS 1881: 3). Unfortunately this company collapsed very rapidly (Goldsmith 1934: 54). During his lifetime, Parkes failed to obtain the recognition he deserved as the true inventor of Celluloid.

The Science Museum's plastics collection includes a cellulose nitrate block press with a working load of 38 tons (cat. no. 517) (Figure 16). This was part of a pilot plant for cellulose nitrate manufacture. Although it was made in 1948, by Tangyes Ltd of Birmingham, the form was largely unchanged from the machinery which had been in use at the company for over sixty years. This particular machine was used for preparing small quantities of Xylonite sheet for sampling. In addition, the collection contains a number of pilot machines made by various companies, including Baker-Perkins and Burroughs, for the manufacture of Celluloid, and acquired from BIP Plastics (cat. nos. 513–520).

Celluloid was used to make a range of objects from the 1870s onwards (cat. nos. 327–512), including articles of apparel such as collars (cat. nos. 411–412) and cuffs and corset clasps (Plate 8 and Figures 17–22). It was also widely used to make cosmetic boxes and dental plates, although perhaps this was an infelicitous use considering the reports made by cigar smokers of exploding dentures (Brown 1994, p. 5). One of the most

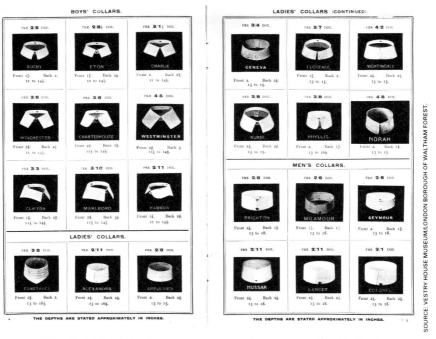

Figure 17   British Xylonite Company catalogue entry for Xylonite (cellulose nitrate) collars and cuffs, 1 January 1911.

CELLULOID CORSET CLASPS.

SIDE AND DRESS STEELS.

PERSPIRATION PROOF.   ELASTIC.   DURABLE.

In introducing these Improved Corset Clasps, &c., let us call your attention to some of the points of the superiority over all others heretofore in use.

1st.—THE INTERIOR IS FINELY TEMPERED CLOCK SPRING STEEL.

2d.—THE EXTERIOR IS CELLULOID.

3d.—THE COMBINATION OF THE TWO UNITES THE STRENGTH OF THE STEEL WITH THE RUST-PROOF QUALITIES OF THE CELLULOID.

4th.—THE TROUBLE OF RIPPING OUT AND SEWING IN THE STEELS EVERY TIME CORSETS ARE LAUNDRIED BECOMES UNNECESSARY AS THESE STEELS NEED NOT BE TAKEN OUT FOR THAT PURPOSE.

5th.—THEY ARE WARRANTED NOT TO RUST AND THUS STAIN THE CORSETS OR OTHER GARMENTS.

6th.—THEY ARE THE BEST STEELS IN EVERY PARTICULAR EVER OFFERED.

SOLD BY ALL DRY AND FANCY GOODS DEALERS throughout the country.

SOURCE: KEITH LAUER. SCIENCE MUSEUM NEGATIVE NO.: 558/95.

Figure 18   American printed advertisement card for Celluloid corset clasps, *c.*1885. Side one.

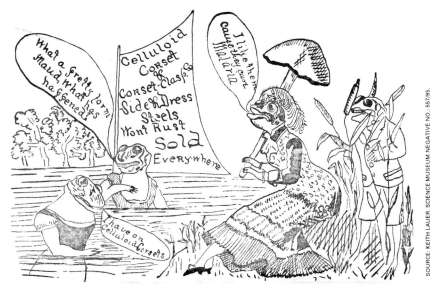

SOURCE: KEITH LAUER. SCIENCE MUSEUM NEGATIVE NO.: 557/95.

Figure 19   American illustrated advertisement card for Celluloid corset clasps, *c.*1885. Side two.

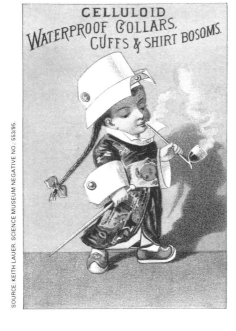

Figure 20 (left) American illustrated advertisement card for Celluloid waterproof collars, cuffs and shirt bosoms, *c.*1885. This shows how they can be worn even while smoking, despite Celluloid's flammability!

Figure 21 (below left) American illustrated advertisement card for Celluloid waterproof collars, cuffs and shirt bosoms, *c.*1885. This shows how they can be worn while fishing, due to being waterproof.

Figure 22 (below) American illustrated advertisement card for Celluloid waterproof collars, cuffs and shirt bosoms, *c.*1885, extolling their multiple virtues; reverse of Figure 21.

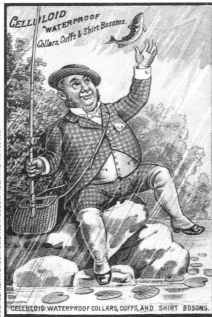

CELLULOID
(WATERPROOF LINEN,)
COLLARS, CUFFS AND SHIRT BOSOMS.

The following will commend the use of these goods to all who study convenience, neatness and economy. The interior is fine linen—The exterior is Celluloid—the union of which combines the strength of Linen with the Waterproof qualities of Celluloid. The trouble and expense of washing is saved.

When soiled simply rub with soap and water (hot or cold) used freely with a stiff brush. They are perspiration proof and are invaluable to travellers, saving all care of laundrying.

ADVICE

In wearing the turn-down Collar, always slip the Necktie under the roll. Do not attempt to straighten the fold.

The goods will give better satisfaction if the Separable Sleeve Button and Collar Button is used.

Twist a small rubber elastic or chamois washer around the post of Sleeve Button to prevent possible rattling of Button.

To remove Yellow Stains, which may come from long wearing, use Sapolio, Soap or Saleratus water or Celluline, which latter is a new preparation for cleansing Celluloid.

GOODS FOR SALE BY ALL DEALERS.

DONALDSON BROTHERS, FIVE POINTS, NEW YORK.

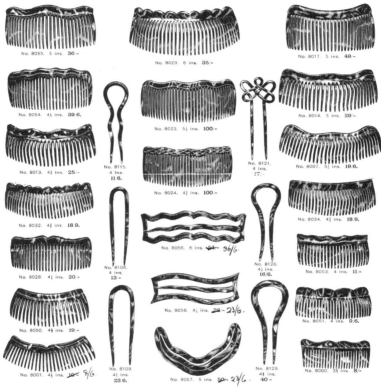

Figure 23   British Xylonite Company advertisement for Xylonite (cellulose nitrate) combs, 1904.

THE HALEX RANGE

The Halex range includes seven patterns of tooth-brushes, a dental plate brush and the new Halex shaving brushes. The toothbrushes and the dental plate brush are available in six colours—Ruby, orange, lemon, green, tortoiseshell and ivory. Each tuft of bristles is immovably fixed in the head by a nickel silver wire anchor, barbed so that it can never come out.

HALEX No. 1 *Child's size*
Well spaced for quick draining and drying. Three rows of bristles. Medium only.
Price 9 – a dozen.

HALEX No. 2
Popular size. Improved pattern. Four rows of bristles, shaped concave serrated. Medium and hard.
Price 12/– a dozen
—the best 1/– brush on the market.

HALEX No. 3
Specially designed neck and handle for reaching back molars. Three rows of bristles. Medium and hard.
Price 15/– a dozen.

HALEX No. 4
A toothbrush for hard service. Four rows of firm bristles, well spaced for quick drying. Medium and hard.
Price 18/– a dozen.

HALEX No. 5
A prophylactic pattern. Specially designed for women. Three rows of bristles. Medium and hard.
Price 21/– a dozen.

HALEX No. 6
A prophylactic pattern for men. A long-lasting brush, with large masculine handle. Four rows of bristles. Medium and hard.
Price 24/– a dozen.

HALEX No. 7
Soft *outer* bristles to give gums gentle massage. Stiff *inner* bristles to give teeth thorough cleansing. Four rows of bristles.
Price 21 – a dozen.

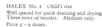

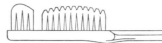

HALEX DENTAL PLATE BRUSH
Five rows of unbleached bristles specially shaped to suit the dental plate.
Price 30/– a dozen.

HALEX SHAVING BRUSHES
Non-porous, well-weighted handle, free from fussy crevices where dried soap could collect. Sterilized in our own factory. Knot bound with silver wire and set in its socket with lasting security.

Pure Badger. *Red Ring.*
(Price 180/– a dozen.)

Stained Hog. *Blue Ring.*
(Price 60/– a dozen.)

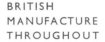

BRITISH
MANUFACTURE
THROUGHOUT

THE BRITISH XYLONITE CO. LTD.
HALE END, E.4

All prices quoted in this list are less 33⅓% trade discount.

HALEX BRISTLES DON'T COME OUT

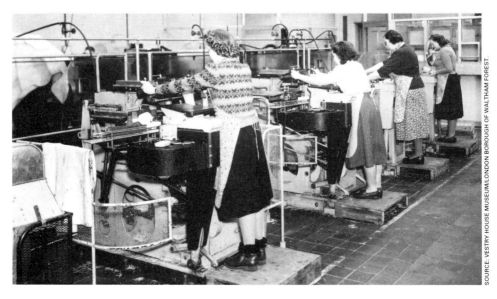

Figure 24 (opposite above) The Halex range of cellulose nitrate toothbrushes made by the British Xylonite Company Ltd, Hale End, *c*.1935.

Figure 25 (opposite below) Women working with brush-filling machines at Halex Ltd, Walthamstow, *c*.1935.

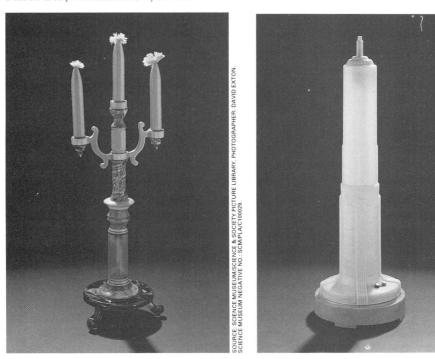

SOURCE: SCIENCE MUSEUM/SCIENCE & SOCIETY PICTURE LIBRARY. PHOTOGRAPHER: DAVID EXTON. SCIENCE MUSEUM NEGATIVE NO.: SCM/PLA/C100029.

SOURCE: SCIENCE MUSEUM/SCIENCE & SOCIETY PICTURE LIBRARY. PHOTOGRAPHER: DAVID EXTON. SCIENCE MUSEUM NEGATIVE NO.: SCM/PLA/C100023A.

Figure 26 (above) Ornate candelabrum of various multicoloured plastics, possibly cellulose nitrate, with three imitation candles and wicks and cast phenolic stem, early twentieth century. Probably French (cat. no. 332).

Figure 27 (above right) Cream and amber Cellulose nitrate lamp modelled after the beacon on the Empire State Building, with fluorescent tube, made in USA by the All-Lite Manufacturing Company, Chicago, Illinois, 1938 (cat. no. 333).

important uses was in the manufacture of combs (Plate 9 and Figure 23). Other applications included toothbrushes and electrical light fittings (Figures 24–7).

Robert Friedel (1978) has examined the markets for Celluloid in America and shown how, in varying forms, and in particular as collars, cuffs and combs, Celluloid became very popular in the late nineteenth century. However, it lost a lot of ground in the 1920s with the coming of the short bobbed hairstyle, resulting in a much reduced market for hair combs.

Cellulose Acetate (CA)

The flammability of Celluloid remained a problem, although during the Second World War this property was turned to advantage when Celluloid fire-leaves were thrown from planes over Germany (a foretaste of napalm) (Glover 1981). One solution was cellulose acetate (Plate 10), which had a low combustibility.

Cellulose acetate was first prepared by the French chemist, Paul Schützenberger in 1865: he heated cotton with acetic anhydride in closed tubes at 130–40°C. Techniques were gradually refined for controlling acetylation under less severe conditions. In 1910 the Dreyfus brothers (Henri and Camille) made cellulose acetate photographic film.

Cellulose acetate was first produced on an industrial scale in the form of dope (cellulose diacetate) dissolved in acetone and used to coat the fabric wings of aeroplanes during the First World War, replacing the dangerously flammable cellulose nitrate lacquers. Dope is produced by acetylating cellulose to triacetate and treating it to produce diacetate. When war ended, more cellulose acetate was being produced than was required. In 1918 cellulose acetate rod, sheet and household products such as lampshades were being made. The sculptor Naum Gabo (who had already worked with cellulose nitrate sheet) also used cellulose acetate sheet in his work. Cellulose acetate was used as a substitute for glass in preference to cellulose nitrate due to its lack of flammability, and had applications such as car-window interlayers and goggles. It was produced in a mouldable powder form in 1929, using the injection moulding process developed by Dr Arthur Eichengrün.

Those in the industry always hankered after Celluloid as it could produce far more beautiful effects, such as mother-of-pearl and tortoiseshell. Cellulose acetate was used to make utility buckles and toys, and, in 1931, the extraordinary 80-metre high Helicoidal Tower at the Paris International Exhibition (Katz 1978: 50). The Andorran craftsman Eduard Fornells used cellulose acetate to produce early, elaborately moulded cosmetic boxes in his Editions Fornells range (cat. no. 529) (later replaced by urea-formaldehyde).

Cellulose acetate was the only plastic of note which was injection moulded until after the Second World War. However, this is now the most common process used to shape plastics.

Injection moulding (Figure 28) had a forerunner in the machinery developed by Burroughs and Hyatt to produce Celluloid, although the injection moulding of Celluloid was always hazardous. Dr Arthur Eichengrün produced an injection moulding machine in 1921 in Germany, and the first commercial production injection moulding machines were made in 1926 by Wallace Eckert and Professor Karl Ziegler.

The injection moulding process entails melting the polymer in a cylinder and injecting it into the mould where it sets. In the case of thermo-plastics, the mould is at a temperature lower than that at which the plastic sets. With thermosets, the mould is heated to a degree which ensures that the thermo-setting plastic hardens by cross-linking. The mould is then opened and the moulding removed. The Science Museum possesses an example of one of the earliest injection moulding machines, dated to about 1935 (cat. no. 1054). This process was originally hand

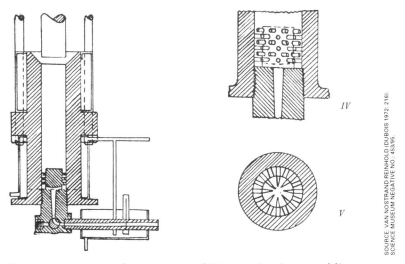

SOURCE: VAN NOSTRAND REINHOLD (DUBOIS 1972: 216).
SCIENCE MUSEUM NEGATIVE NO.: 453/95.

Figure 28 The patent drawing for the original Hyatt injection moulding machine, patented in 1872. Hyatt's injection moulding experiments with cellulose nitrate were extremely hazardous because of the flammability of the material.

operated, but fully automated 36-oz injection moulding machines with hydraulic rams were in existence by 1939.

Cellulose acetate had an important impact on synthetic fibres, and these are discussed below.

Cellulose-Based Fibres

The concept of synthetic fibres is not modern. Robert Hooke in his *Micrographia,* published in 1665, commented that:

> A pretty kinde of artificial Stuff I have seen, looking almost like transparent Parchment, Horn, or Ising-Glass ... And I have often thought, that probably there might be a way found out, to make an artificial glutinous composition, much resembling ... that Excrement, or whatever other substance it be out of which, the Silk-worm wire-draws his clew. (Figure 29).

By 1754, the French physicist René de Réaumur had made the following observations in his *Histoire des Insects*: 'Silk is only a liquid gum which has been dried. Could we not make silk ourselves, with gums and resins?' The idea of artificial fibres had clearly exercised human curiosity for some time before a silk-like fibre was patented by George Audemars of Lausanne in 1855. This was made from cellulose nitrate taken from the bark of the mulberry tree, mixed with nitric acid, dissolved in a mixture of ether and alcohol and mixed with a solution of caoutchouc (rubber); from this mixture, threads were drawn with steel needles. However, Audemars's process was not used commercially.

Artificial silk did not develop much further until the work of Swan and Chardonnet in the 1880s. The artificial silks produced by these two men form the earliest synthetic fibres held in the Science Museum's collections of plastics and textiles. The initial impetus came from the electrical industry and the need to produce a carbon filament of uniform size and solid texture for use in incandescent electric lamps. Various solutions had been tried but without great success. Thomas Edison made filaments from carbonized bamboo fibres, and Swan had used carbonized cotton threads parchmentised in sulphuric acid. In 1882 Weston made filaments from a solution of cellulose nitrate in ether alcohol (BP 4458/1882).

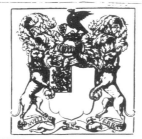

MICROGRAPHIA:

OR SOME

Phyſiological Deſcriptions

OF

MINUTE BODIES

MADE BY

MAGNIFYING GLASSES.

WITH

OBSERVATIONS and INQUIRIES thereupon.

By *R. HOOKE*, Fellow of the ROYAL SOCIETY

Non poſſis oculo quantum contendere Linceus,
Non tamen idcirco contemnas Lippus inungi. Horat. Ep. lib. 1.

LONDON, Printed by *Jo. Martyn*, and *Jo. Alleſtry*, Printers to the
ROYAL SOCIETY, and are to be ſold at their Shop at the *Bell* in
S. Paul's Church-yard. M DC LX V.

Silk, ſeeming to
be little elſe then a dried thread of Glew, may be ſuppos'd to be very
eaſily relaxt, and ſoftened, by being ſteeped in warm, nay in cold, if pene-
trant, juyces or liquors. And thereby thoſe tinctures, though they tinge
perhaps but a ſmall part of the ſubſtance, yet being ſo highly impregnated
with the colour, as to be almoſt black with it, may leave an impreſſion
ſtrong enough to exhibit the deſir'd colour. A pretty kinde of artificial Stuff I have ſeen, looking almoſt like tranſparent Parchment, Horn,
or Iſing-glaſs, and perhaps ſome ſuch thing it may be made of, which being tranſparent, and of a glutinous nature, and eaſily mollified by keeping in water, as I found upon trial, had imbib'd, and did remain ting'd
with a great variety of very vivid colours, and to the naked eye, it look'd
very like the ſubſtance of the Silk. And I have often thought, that probably there might be a way found out, to make an artificial glutinous
compoſition, much reſembling, if not full as good, nay better, then that
Excrement, or whatever other ſubſtance it be out of which, the Silk-worm
wire-draws his clew. If ſuch a compoſition were found, it were certainly an eaſie matter to find very quick ways of drawing it out into ſmall
wires for uſe. I need not mention the uſe of ſuch an Invention, nor the benefit that is likely to accrue to the finder, they being ſufficiently obvious.
This hint therefore, may, I hope, give ſome Ingenious inquiſitive Perſon
an occaſion of making ſome trials, which if ſucceſsfull, I have my aim, and
I ſuppoſe he will have no occaſion to be diſpleas'd.

Title page and part of Observation V from " Micrographia " by R. Hooke, F.R.S.
(Reproduced by Courtesy of the John Rylands Library, Manchester)

Figure 29 Page from Robert Hooke's *Micrographia* (1665) in which he comments on the possibility of making artificial silk.

In 1883 (BP 5978), Sir Joseph Swan made filaments by squirting a solution of cellulose nitrate in acetic acid through a nozzle into a coagulating liquid (alcohol). He denitrated the fibres by treating them with a solution of ammonium sulphide and then carbonised them for use in his lamps. Swan exhibited these fibres at the Society of Chemical Industry in London in 1884. A year later, fabrics crocheted by Lady Swan from these threads were shown at the Exhibition of Inventions in London under the name of 'artificial silk'. An early example is a silk handkerchief with an artificial Swan silk lace border dated to *c*.1883, held in the Science Museum's Textile Machinery collections (Science Museum inventory no. 1927-214).

Swan did not exploit his invention for textile purposes. This was to be left to a Frenchman, Comte Hilaire de Chardonnet (Figure 30). His first patent of 1884 (French Patent (FP) 165349) referred to: 'an artificial textile material resembling silk'. Chardonnet's artificial silk was based on cellulose nitrate. He began using fibres from the bark of the mulberry

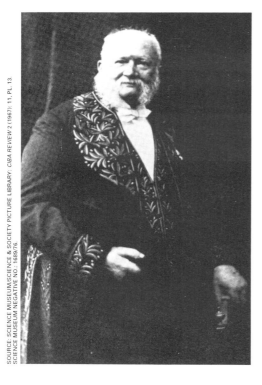

Figure 30   Comte Hilaire de Chardonnet (1839–1924), inventor of Chardonnet artificial silk.

Figure 31   Framed advertisement for Chardonnet silk (artificial silk), 1896, patented by Comte Hilaire de Chardonnet (cat. no. 545).

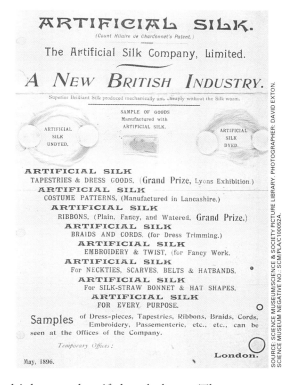

tree but later turned to cotton, which was plentiful and cheap. The cotton was treated with nitric acid, sulphuric acid and water at a temperature of 45°C for one to two hours. The cellulose nitrate formed was then dissolved in a mixture of ether and alcohol. The resulting solution was forced through a series of spinning jets (each with one tiny hole) into cold water. As the filaments entered the water they solidified initially on the outside. As they passed through the water they were stretched, and became completely solidified. This 'wet spinning' process was later replaced by the 'dry spinning' process, where the filaments were formed by the evaporation of the solvents.

The product was very attractive, causing a sensation when exhibited at the Paris Exhibition of 1889, where it gained the Grand Prix. At first it was commercially successful, and by 1891 Chardonnet's factory was producing 125 lb (56.8 kg) of 'silk' a day. However, Chardonnet silk was very flammable, as initially the thread was not denitrated. A contemporary joke suggested that the ideal present for a mother-in-law was a box of matches and a dress of Chardonnet silk (Hard 1933). The French government banned the production of Chardonnet silk in France, and Chardonnet then opted for Swan's denitration process. Unfortunately this process weakened the fibres, making them brittle. A sample card of Chardonnet silk dated to 1896 is held in the Science Museum's collections (cat. no. 545) (Figure 31).

Artificial silk was also produced at Wolston, near Coventry, 1896–1900, under the supervision of Comte Chardonnet (Science Museum inventory no. 1948-232), and a spool of artificial silk was produced by Legh Powell *c*.1885 using the zinc chloride process (Science Museum inventory no. 1936-169).

Viscose

The natural development of artificial silk was viscose rayon, a fibre originally based on cellulose acetate and eventually on cellulose xanthate. Viscose was the brainchild of two Englishmen, Charles F. Cross and Edward J. Bevan (Figures 32 and 33), and was patented by Cross, Bevan

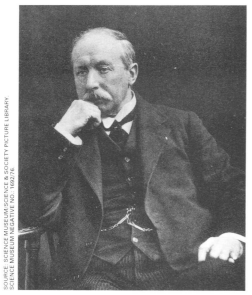

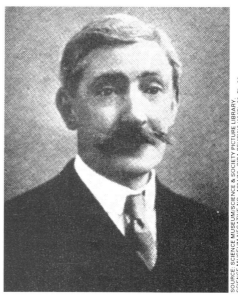

SOURCE: SCIENCE MUSEUM/SCIENCE & SOCIETY PICTURE LIBRARY.
SCIENCE MUSEUM NEGATIVE NO.: 1692/76

SOURCE: SCIENCE MUSEUM/SCIENCE & SOCIETY PICTURE LIBRARY.
SCIENCE MUSEUM NEGATIVE NO.: 1694/76. *CIBA REVIEW* 2 (1967). 22. PL. 26.

Figure 32 Charles Cross (1855–1935), inventor of viscose rayon.

Figure 33 Edward Bevan (1856–1921), inventor of viscose rayon.

and C. Beadle in 1892 (BP 8700). In essence, viscose is regenerated cellulose.

Cellulose (obtained from cotton, etc.) was treated with caustic soda. After squeezing out the excess alkali, the residue was broken up, placed in a vessel and sprayed with carbon disulphide. After 3–5 hours the resulting solution (cellulose xanthate and by-products) was dissolved in water. The solution so obtained is of a yellow colour and extremely viscous; hence the name viscose. Cross and Bevan's patent describes the methods used to remove the by-products: 'The soluble derivative of cellulose has the property of being reconverted into cellulose' by long standing, heating or treatment with oxidising agents. 'The final product obtained has all the characteristics of cellulose.'

Once it was developed as a fibre, the inventors did not exploit their discovery immediately. This was left to Charles Stearn and Charles F. Topham. Both men had worked with Swan in his development of the electric lamp. Stearn was interested initially in viscose for lamp filaments but later saw the possibilities of producing it as a textile yarn (Figure 34). In 1894 he formed the Viscose Syndicate Ltd with Cross and Bevan to produce solid viscose items, and in 1898 formed the Viscose Spinning Syndicate in an attempt to produce artificial silk. It was the work of these two groups that eventually led to viscose's commercial success.

Stearn made repeated attempts to spin viscose but failed in 1894 and again in 1897. He collaborated in this work with J. E. Criggal (Coleman 1969: 15). Further attempts were made, but the threads simply fell off the jet. Fortuitously on one occasion the solution was left, and next day it was discovered that attempts at spinning were much more successful. In 1898, by leaving the solution to stand even longer (that is, to ripen), it became possible to spin strong threads (Figure 35).

During 1898–9 Topham and Stearn devised a bath of ammonium sulphate to fix the filaments emerging from the spinneret. Topham overcame further problems relating to the spinning of the solution, devising a platinum jet with many holes: an advance on the single-hole jet. In 1900 (BP 23158) he patented the Topham box for twisting and collecting the newly spun thread in a cake form (cat. no. 584) (Figure 36). He also developed a pump for controlling the amount of viscose solution fed through the jets. This viscose was given the name 'Stearn silk' and produced commercially in 1903 (cat. nos. 565–567, 570–571) (Figure 34).

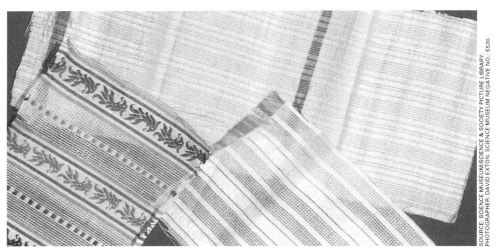

Figure 34   Three woven fabrics made partly of Stearn artificial silk (viscose rayon), 1903. Top row, pt. 1 is a cream fabric with two green stripes. Second row, left: pt. 2 is an elaborate cream fabric with stripes containing the phoenix, in gold, olive, cream and red; right: pt. 3 is a gold-striped fabric with three stripes filled with floral design (cat. no. 567).

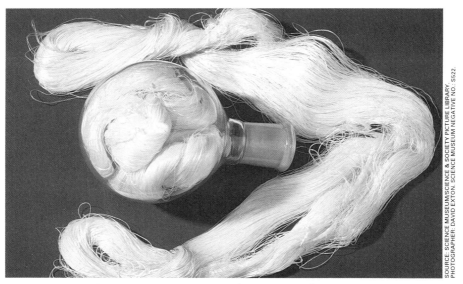

Figure 35   Earliest existing specimen of viscose artificial silk, dated 30 August 1898, in flask, from the Cross and Bevan Laboratories (cat. no. 568).

Figure 36 Later form of Charles Topham's experimental spinning box used to spin early viscose, 1901, embodying the first flexible spindle and two skeins of viscose silk wound on wooden reels, made by Topham, *c.*1903 (cat. nos. 585, 571).

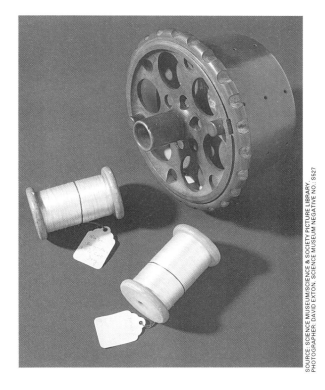

Eventually the invention began to make money for the Viscose Spinning Syndicate, and the commercial products became known as 'Rayon'. The British patents were taken over by Courtaulds in 1904, and rayon went on to become a world-wide success story.

Cellulose Acetate Fibres

Apart from early viscose, cellulose acetate was not exploited as a fibre until after the First World War. As described above, cellulose acetate (diacetate) dissolved in acetone had been used to coat aeroplane wings during the First World War. To meet the requirements, the Swiss Dreyfus brothers had been asked to set up an additional factory to produce cellulose acetate at Spondon, Derbyshire. When the war ended, more cellulose acetate was being produced than was required. Dr Henry Dreyfus led a research programme into producing artificial fibres from cellulose acetate. This was successful, and by 1921 the fibre was being marketed as Celanese. This fibre was spun in much the same way as viscose.

Casein-formaldehyde (CS, Erinoid, Galalith, Syrolit, Lactoid)

Casein-formaldehyde (Plate 11) is an early plastics material made from either milk curds or skimmed milk (protein-based). It was developed by two Germans, W. Krische and Adolphe Spitteler, at the end of the nineteenth century, and patented by them in 1899. Casein was marketed as Galalith in Germany, and initially as Syrolit (1909) and later on as Erinoid (1914) in Britain. Skimmed milk became the preferred source for casein after 1914. Erinoid Ltd produced it using the so-called dry process: the enzyme rennet was used to precipitate casein out of skimmed milk; the casein was ground to a powder, mixed with water, then, when absorbed, fed into an extruder; the extruded rods could be sliced into button blanks, pen barrels, etc., or used for moulding sheet. The sheets (produced in presses) were then stamped into their chosen form. Finally the casein was hardened by immersion in aqueous formaldehyde. The result was a material which resembled horn or bone; it could not be reworked but could be slightly shaped by hot pressing (Morgan 1989: 12ff; Erinoid n.d.) (cat. nos. 635–637).

Casein-formaldehyde can be made with a variety of colours either added during the manufacturing process or by surface dyeing, usually after polishing (cat. no. 649). It was used to make a wide variety of buttons in various colours and finishes (cat. nos. 638–639, 641–642). Fish scales were added to produce the pearlised effect found in many casein buttons (Morgan 1994). Casein is still used to make some of the more expensive buttons. It was also used for clock cases and even as veneers on early gramophones, for knitting needles and very beautiful fountain pen cases and pencil and letter holders (cat. nos. 672, 599). It was most popular in Britain in the early years of this century. Unfortunately casein warps, crazes and cracks when in contact with damp, and so has been largely superseded by machine-washable plastics such as polyesters for buttons.

Synthetic Plastics

Phenol-formaldehyde Plastics (PF, Bakelite)

Phenol-formaldehyde plastics (Plate 12 and Figure 37) were the first truly synthetic plastics. They were invented and patented in 1907 by Leo Baekeland, a Belgian-born chemist who had emigrated to the USA. By

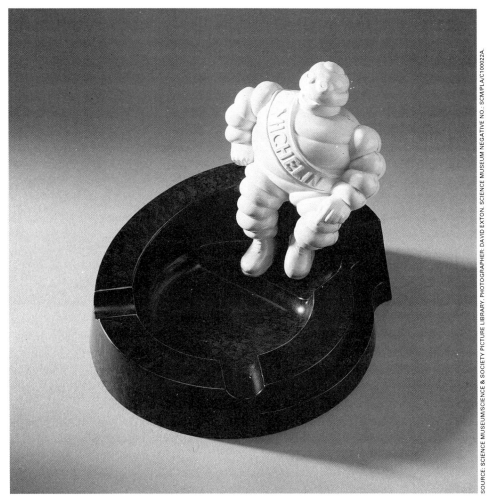

SOURCE: SCIENCE MUSEUM/SCIENCE & SOCIETY PICTURE LIBRARY. PHOTOGRAPHER: DAVID EXTON. SCIENCE MUSEUM NEGATIVE NO.: SCM/PLA/C100022A.

Figure 37 'Michelin' man ash-tray made of walnut-effect phenolic, Michelin man made of ivory urea-formaldehyde, *c*.1940s (cat. no. 709).

reacting phenol and formaldehyde (two common chemicals) under controlled conditions, Baekeland produced an amber-coloured resin which could be used on its own (by casting), to impregnate fabrics and papers to produce laminates, or combined with fillers to produce a thermo-setting moulding material. He called his material Bakelite, phenol-formaldehyde polymer (PF) or phenolic resin.

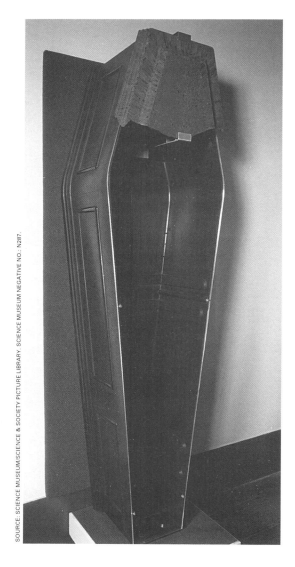

SOURCE: SCIENCE MUSEUM/SCIENCE & SOCIETY PICTURE LIBRARY. SCIENCE MUSEUM NEGATIVE NO.: N287.

Figure 38   Coffin made of Bakelite (phenol-formaldehyde), 1938 (cat. no. 777)

Baekeland's work on phenolic resins was a masterpiece of systematic scientific investigation. Products made from the resins possessed good electrical and mechanical properties which, combined with an ability to be mass produced, justified the inventor's description of his products as 'materials of a thousand uses'. One drawback was that the resin tended to darken upon heating, and filled, compression-moulded phenolic products were largely available only in dark brown, black or dark green. The moulding materials' physical properties could be amended by the inclusion of different fillers such as cotton rags, paper, mica, etc.

Phenolics are very difficult to ignite, and since they are thermosets (that is, once moulded they will not change shape on reheating) they are an ideal material for electrical components, such as plugs and insulators, and domestic appliances such as radio cases, thermos flasks and even electric hot-water bottles. However, they can be brittle and may crack if dropped.

The desirable properties of phenolics, combined with a massive growth in industries looking for such properties (including those producers of radios, telephones, electric motors and automobiles), meant an assured market, and growth was world-wide. Typical uses for the moulding materials included electrical plugs and sockets; handles for domestic products, such as saucepans and smoothing irons; radio valve bases, switches and knobs; radio cases; and electrical equipment cases.

Phenolic plastics are compression moulded. A most unusual moulded item in the Science Museum's collection is a Bakelite coffin made from imitation walnut phenolic (with a wood-flour filler), believed to be the largest moulding of its kind ever made (cat. no. 777) (Figure 38). It proved to be little more than a technological curiosity, partly because of the death of its inventor, James Doleman, in 1944 in the Second World War, and because the moulding machinery was taken over by the War Office for the war effort (Doleman 1985). Possibly also it held no attraction for undertakers, whose livelihood depended in part upon the manufacture of traditional coffins with their related jobs of woodworking and upholstery.

Compression moulding was the first plastics production process developed on a large scale, and is still used today. In the process, the material is heated in a mould and pressed into shape by a hydraulic press. This process is best suited to thermo-setting plastics, because the setting reaction takes place in the mould and the moulding can be taken out while hot. When used with thermo-plastics, the mould must first be heated to soften the plastic, then cooled, after which the moulding may be removed.

Cast Phenolics (Catalin)

Catalin (Plate 12) is the common name of cast phenolic, and was produced after 1928. It is a type of phenolic resin made without a filler, being cast at lower temperatures than the filled variety: heated for three hours at 70°C, then hardened by heating for three days at 70–85°C. Catalin was widely used in the 1930s to produce decorative mouldings which successfully resembled a variety of natural substances such as amber, jade, onyx and marble.

Fada Radios and the Carvacraft range of desk accessories are well-known examples of this material (cat. nos. 835, 827–31) (Plate 13). Less well known are the range of art deco candlesticks and cosmetic containers made of cast phenolic (cat. nos. 785–90, 792–811).

Amino Plastics

These are thermo-setting plastics obtained from mixing amines or amides with aldehydes. In this group fall the polymers known as urea- and thiourea-formaldehyde (made by reacting ammonia and carbon dioxide) and melamine-formaldehyde (with many production methods, now mainly from urea).

Thiourea-Urea- and Urea-formaldehyde (UF, Bandalasta, Beetle)
Thiourea-urea-formaldehyde polymer was discovered in 1924 by a British chemist, Edmund Rossiter, working for the British Cyanides Company; it was used to make plastics items marked Bandalasta (cat. nos. 856–857) (Plate 14). By 1929, urea-formaldehyde (Figure 39) offered improved properties. The only difference between thiourea-urea-formaldehyde and urea-formaldehyde is the substitution of one atom of sulphur in thiourea-urea-formaldehyde for an oxygen atom in one of the monomers of urea-formaldehyde (Diagram 4).

Diagram 4

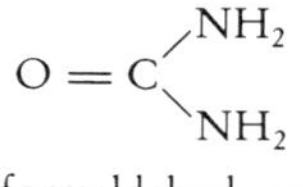

$$O = C \Big\langle {}^{NH_2}_{NH_2} \qquad\qquad S = C \Big\langle {}^{NH_2}_{NH_2}$$

Urea-formaldehyde monomer 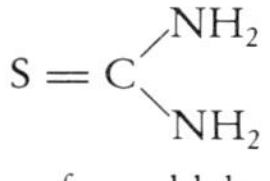   Thiourea-urea-formaldehyde monomer

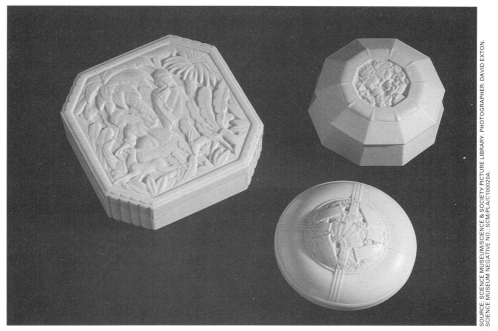

SOURCE: SCIENCE MUSEUM/SCIENCE & SOCIETY PICTURE LIBRARY. PHOTOGRAPHER: DAVID EXTON.
SCIENCE MUSEUM NEGATIVE NO.: SCM/PLA/C100020A.

Figure 39   Three examples of Eduard Fornells's designs for cosmetic boxes, made by Editions Fornells, of white urea-formaldehyde, *c.*1930. Left to right, top row: cat. nos. 866, 896, second row: cat. no. 863.

These plastics had the advantage over phenolics that they could be made in light, bright colours, but were still moisture- and heat-resistant. However, they tended to absorb water. Their development began a fashion for brightly coloured and practical picnic sets stamped 'Beatl' (later renamed 'Beetle'). These were very popular, as they did not 'taste', unlike phenolics.

Early laminates were made from paper or cloth impregnated with urea or thiourea resin. Tougher laminates such as those needed in cars were also made from phenol-formaldehyde.

In the 1933 Science Museum plastics exhibition, as mentioned in chapter 1, there was a room with walls laminated with black phenolic and orange-coloured urea-formaldehyde (described as Bakelite and Beetle laminate in the reports of the time) (*The Times* 1934).

Melamine resin was discovered by the German chemist Baron Justus von Liebig in 1834, but melamine-formaldehyde polymer was not patented until 1935, after which it was produced commercially in 1939 by the American Cyanamid Company. Melamine-formaldehyde was water-resistant, tougher than urea-formaldehyde and transparent, so that it was possible to impregnate patterned papers for surfacing decorative laminates such as Formica and Warerite. These ushered in easy-care surfaces, particularly in the kitchen. They were also used in offices such as those of Bakelite Ltd at Tyseley (Plate 15).

Polyvinyl Chloride

Polyvinyl chloride (PVC) is polymerised from the monomer vinyl chloride and can be produced in a range of hardness: from very soft to very hard.

Polyvinyl chloride has a long history. It was recorded in 1835 by the French chemist, Henri Regnault, polymerised in 1872, and made in a soft plasticised form in Moscow by I. Ostromislensky in 1912. By 1928 America's first PVC had been manufactured.

Britain did not produce PVC before 1939, but the exigencies of the Second World War forced progress, and a factory for it was built at Hillhouse by 1940. PVC played an important wartime role, with varied applications ranging from electrical insulation to acting as a replacement for rubber in aircraft, radios and electrical goods.

As mentioned above, PVC is made in different grades of hardness and rigidity. Rigid or unplasticised (UPVC) PVC is used for pipes, guttering and windows in outdoor use, and with other formulations is used to make wipe-clean wallpaper. PVC is used as a copolymer with acetate to make records (although this may not be the case for much longer) (Mitchell 1993: 14ff). Under the name 'Vinylite', as mentioned earlier, it was adopted in 1948 as the material for gramophone records, and gained the generic name of vinyl. Within five years it had largely replaced shellac due to its superior qualities.

Polyethylene (PE, Polyethene, Polythene)

Polyethylene (Plate 16) was first discovered at ICI, Winnington, on 24 March 1933 by chance, during a research programme into high-pressure

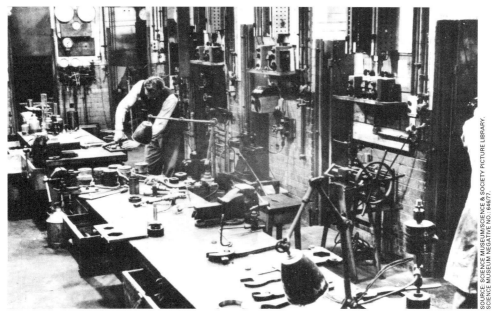

Figure 40   The Winnington research department high-pressure laboratory at ICI.

reactions of aromatics with olefins. In an experiment reacting benzaldehyde with ethylene, a leak in the high-pressure apparatus meant that more ethylene gas, which contained a small amount of oxygen, was admitted. This acted as a catalyst, converting some of the ethylene into polyethylene. The cause took a long time to establish before the experiment could be repeated (Figure 40). In 1935 Eric Fawcett announced the results of this experiment in front of a number of scientists, some from Germany, among them Hermann Staudinger. Fortunately for the future allied war effort, Staudinger did not believe that such a reaction was possible (Kennedy 1986: 66) (cat. no. 964). By 1937, ICI had developed a 9-litre reaction vessel which could produce 10 tons of polyethylene a year (cat. no. 966) (Figures 41 and 42), and in 1939 the first 100-ton-per-year polyethylene plant went into production – on the day Germany invaded Poland. From then on, for the duration of the war, all polyethylene produced was detailed for military applications (Kennedy 1986: 71ff). Polyethylene was used for the insulation of telecommunications cables and, particularly importantly, of radar cables. Tests showed that polyethylene had superior dielectric properties to those of gutta percha,

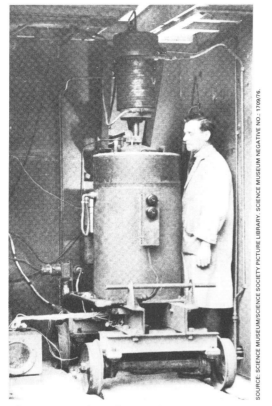
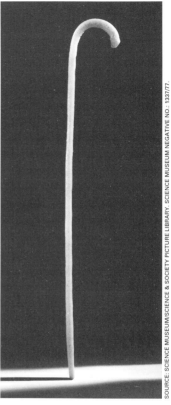

SOURCE: SCIENCE MUSEUM/SCIENCE SOCIETY PICTURE LIBRARY. SCIENCE MUSEUM NEGATIVE NO.: 1709/76.

SOURCE: SCIENCE MUSEUM/SCIENCE & SOCIETY PICTURE LIBRARY. SCIENCE MUSEUM NEGATIVE NO.: 1337/77.

Figure 41   The 9-litre polyethylene reaction vessel *in situ* at Winnington, 1937. The first ton of polyethylene was produced in this vessel by December 1938. The vessel was designed in 1936 by W.R.D. Manning and S.G. Marshall of ICI (Alkali) Ltd, Northwich (cat. no. 966).

Figure 42   Walking stick made of cream-coloured polyethylene produced in the Wallerscote Pilot Plant of Imperial Chemical Industries Ltd, England, December 1938 (cat. no. 939).

the material which had been favoured for insulation purposes until the discovery of polyethylene (Edwards 1991–2: 12; 1990: 14ff). No scientific papers were published on polyethylene until after the war. By 1942 ICI allowed the American company Du Pont to have free use of their polyethylene patents for war purposes for the duration of the war. Carbide & Carbon (now the Union Carbide Corporation), another American company, was eventually given a sub-licence to manufacture polyethylene in 1943, and soon became the world's leading producer (ICI 1942: 60).

After the war, ICI were left with something of a problem with their overcapacity for polyethylene production. Until the end of the war, they had been producing too little for the military market. After the war, they had a glut, and began to explore new uses for their product. Initially their progress was slow. Extra annoyance was provided by advertisements in American journals such as *Modern Plastics* by Carbide & Carbon which gave the impression that the Americans had invented polyethylene. The response to these came in articles in *The Times Trade and Engineering Supplement* (January and February 1945), in *British Plastics* and in other journals on the discovery, war uses and properties of polyethylene.

Markets for polyethylene were slow to come for ICI until the autumn of 1953, which:

> was notable for the successful emergence of P[olythene] as a moulding material for a wide variety of domestic articles … the name 'polythene' became entirely familiar to the general public, and indeed the success of the application in this field was such that the word 'plastic' itself came to have a more honourable meaning in the household. The pioneers of this development were G & E Equipments, Halex and E K Cole; many other firms followed suit. The articles moulded were mainly hollowware (bowls, pails, babies' baths and the like). [ICI 1953: 196]

Washing-up bowls quickly gained acceptance. Later came dolls and bottles, and, perhaps of greatest significance, the omnipresent 'plastic bag', which was to revolutionise retail marketing throughout the world.

Marketing success had been faster coming in America. Tupperware was devised there in the mid-1940s by Earl Tupper, and was made from polyethylene; it was enthusiastically marketed in America with prizes, treasure hunts and other selling techniques. Tupperware parties became an institution in both the USA and Britain, and were held in people's homes specifically to sell the Tupperware products (Clarke 1990a) (Plate 16).

The earliest polyethylene was of the low-density form produced by the high-pressure process, with typical densities in the range 0.915–0.945 g/cm^3. Low-density polyethylene is still manufactured today, but is complemented by the high-density form first produced by Professor Karl Ziegler in 1953. ICI's marketing diaries record that:

In summer of 1954 it was learnt that Ziegler had developed a new process and was able to produce high molecular weight polymers of ethylene at atmospheric pressures ... it was learnt that, by a reaction at atmospheric pressure at 50–100°C in a simple closed vessel with a catalyst dissolved or suspended in a hydrocarbon solvent, it was possible to make a very high molecular weight polythene which had greater stiffness and higher softening point but was of greater intractability by fabrication from current commercial polythene ... Advantages claimed for the process were improved properties, for some purposes, of the product and reduced costs due to the absence of high pressures and the need for high purity ethylene. [ICI 1954: 245ff]

Polyethylene produced by the Ziegler process is of medium density (*c.*0.945 g/cm^3). The more recent *Phillips Standard Oil* (Indiana) process produces very high-density polyethylenes, in the range of 0.96 g/cm^3 (Brydson 1982: 190ff; Nicholson 1991: 7ff). This is now a rapidly developing field, with new generations of polyethylene based on metallocene catalysts.

The ICI process for producing high-density polyethylene was publicly announced in March 1956 (ICI 1956: 1). High-density polyethylene (HDPE) is produced using lower pressures and temperatures than those for the high-pressure process, in combination with catalysts. In addition to being stiffer, it is more temperature-resistant than the low-density form, as well as not being flexible. The more rigid, high-density form of polyethylene is used for dustbins and stackable boxes, and has even been used in hip replacements.

Extrusion and blow moulding are two processes, used to produce bottles, which were very suitable for polyethylene. They were used by the Cascelloid Company in the 1950s to produce a variety of different shapes, including the Vinolia teddy-bear-shaped talcum powder bottle (cat. no. 961) (Plate 16). The process to make a bottle starts with extruding a small, finger-shaped piece of plastic called a parison. This piece is put in the mould and gas is injected into it, blowing the parison into the shape of the mould. Early problems were experienced with achieving a uniform thickness of the moulding, but these were resolved by varying the thickness of the parison.

Polyethylene Fibres

The earliest polyethylene fibres were made at the end of the Second World War by ICI, and a yarn called Courlene was made by Courtaulds. The immediate problem was its low melting point, which meant it could not be ironed and so was difficult to use as a fabric. Polyethylene can be used for car upholstery, and has been used for protective clothing where people are in contact with corrosive chemicals, as it is chemically resistant, not water-absorbent and not prone to fungal attack. It is also used as interlinings for collars and cuffs, and combined with cotton.

Melted polyethylene is spun through a multi-hole jet, and then solidified in cold water in a bath lying immediately below the jet. It is usual for the filaments to be drawn out to many times their original length.

Polymethyl Methacrylate (PMMA, Acrylic, Perspex, Plexiglas)

A glass-like acrylic resin was first formed by Rudolph Fittig in 1877 and developed by the German chemist Otto Rohm. It took until 1928 for Rohm & Haas to produce acrylic commercially, and at first the resin was used in coatings. The aim was to produce a transparent plastic to replace Celluloid, which yellowed in sunlight and was flammable. Rowland Hill and John Crawford working at ICI produced the harder form of acrylic in 1934 (Plate 17). ICI registered the trade mark 'Perspex' on 16 November 1934. The name was derived from the Latin verb *perspicare,* 'to see through', and the substance was sold commercially by 1936. The German equivalent was 'Plexiglas'.

Acrylic sheet, and hence Perspex, was made by heating the monomer methyl methacrylate into a heavy syrup, which was poured in between flat glass sheets (which give acrylic its highly polished surface). The glass 'cell' was then placed in an oven to complete the polymerisation process, removed and cooled, after which the glass plates were taken away. The manufacture of Perspex was difficult, as the syrup could react violently, bubbles could appear in the cast sheets, and any dust or worker's sweat had to be removed using spatulas. In the early days of commercial production in 1936, the drying room for Perspex was kept at 40 °C. The workers were weighed weekly to check any weight loss, as they were found to have lost their appetites for all foods apart from tinned fruit (Tilley 1994: 96).

Demand for Perspex grew between 1936 and 1938, as war approached, and wartime uses included the cockpit canopies of Spitfires. After the Second World War Perspex was used for various domestic purposes, such as a magnifying lens which was put in front of the earliest very small television screens (cat. no. 1001). It also had decorative applications, for example as used by the late sculptor Arthur Fleischmann (Tilley 1994: 100). Acrylic is now commonly used to make moulded bathroom and light fittings. An important medical application is in corneal grafts.

Vacuum forming (developed from thermo-forming) is a process which is used to mould sheets of thermo-plastics into a particular shape. Thermo-forming was first used with natural plastics such as horn, and then with semi-synthetic Celluloid. In this process the sheets of horn or Celluloid were shaped with heat over a form. In vacuum forming, the sheets are heated, then clamped over the mould, and the air is removed, forming a vacuum. This causes the sheet to form into the shape of the mould. Thin sheeting is formed under atmospheric pressure, but compressed air is required to form heavier-duty plastic sheet such as that found in baths.

This method was extensively developed in the Second World War in military applications such as aircraft canopies and the noses of bombers made in Perspex. It is now used to make a variety of items ranging from architectural models to spectacle lenses.

Acrylonitrile and Acrylic Fibres

These were developed during and after the Second World War. Examples include Orlon, an acrylonitrile which was developed by Du Pont, who started research in early 1940 and had progressed to the pilot-plant stage by 1945. In 1948 the resultant fibre was given the trade mark 'Orlon', and commercial production started in 1950. The acrylic fibre 'Acrilan', made by Chemstrand Corporation, was piloted in 1950 and sold to the public in 1952. Acrylic fibres form a significant part of the synthetic fibre industry today.

Nylon (PA, Polyamide)

Nylon 6,6 (polyamide) (Figure 43) was discovered in the 1930s by a team led by Wallace Hume Carothers (Figure 44). It was developed as part of a programme of fundamental research into the subject of polymerisation undertaken by the American company Du Pont, which also produced

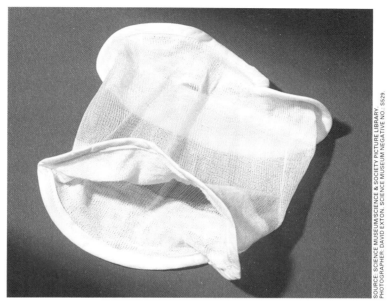

Figure 43 Sample of the first nylon knitted tubing, knitted in July 1935 from polyamide made from pentamethylenediamine and sebacic acid. Made by Du Pont Nemours Ltd, USA (cat. no. 1007).

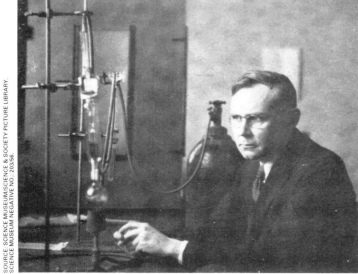

Figure 44 Wallace Hume Carothers (1896–1937), inventor of nylon.

other fibre-forming polymers (Mark and Whitby 1940). Nylon was a step forward in the understanding of polymer chemistry, as it was part of a systematic study to produce new polymers in the light of Staudinger's theory of polymers and polymerisation. Nylon (patented in 1935) is inextricably linked in people's minds with nylon stockings and Betty Grable, who was used by Du Pont to advertise their product; but its first public appearance in 1938 was in the distinctly unglamorous form of the bristles on the 'Miracle Tuft' toothbrush. The first nylon stockings were made in the USA in February 1939. In 1942 nylon was taken out of commercial production and put into war use for parachutes, tents, etc. Du Pont licensed ICI to develop nylon in Britain and the Commonwealth in 1939. British Nylon Spinners were formed by ICI and Courtaulds in 1940, but had to concentrate on wartime demands for the next five years.

Nylon was produced in various forms (cat. 1007) (Figure 43). Du Pont initially concentrated on nylon 6,6. Other types which have since proved commercially successful include nylon 6, nylon 6,10 and nylon 6,11. The different numbers are dependent on the number of carbon atoms in the nylon molecule. The particular qualities of nylon are its toughness, oil- and fuel-resistance, and low friction coefficients.

The advantages of nylon are that it is very strong but also light. It is wear-resistant and will spring back into shape, and is not open to fungal or insect attack.

Nylon is a condensation polymer; that is, during its manufacture from its constituents, it loses a molecule of water. It is thermo-plastic and so can be injection moulded, rotational moulded and extruded. In industry, nylon is used in a solid form to make gears, bearings and medical sutures. The moulded variety is very tough as well as light and, with its low coefficient of friction, it can be used for functions such as zips and curtain rails.

Polyesters

Terylene (PETP, Polyethylene terephthalate)

During his researches, Wallace Carothers also worked with polyesters (Figure 45), but discarded them in favour of polyamides, which he considered made better fibres. His research was taken further by

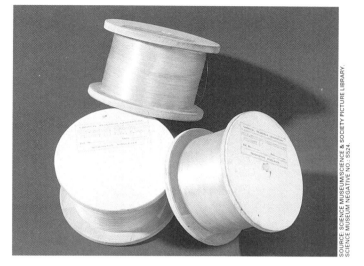

Figure 45
Three spools of
polyethylene
terephthalate
(Terylene) filaments
produced at the
Chemical Research
Laboratory,
Teddington, 1943–44
(cat. no. 1009).

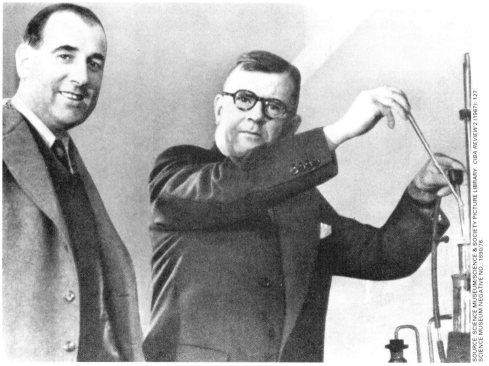

Figure 46   J.R. Whinfield and J.T. Dickson, inventors of Terylene.

J. R. Whinfield and J. T. Dickson of the Calico Printers Association in Britain (Figure 46). In 1941 they discovered the polyester later known as Terylene (polyethylene terephthalate fibre). This discovery was then exploited by ICI (cat. nos. 1009–1011).

Glass-fibre-reinforced polyester (GRP)
Glass-reinforced plastics (GRP) are made of glass fibres bound together with polyester resin. The first polyester resin (polyglycerol tartrate) was produced in 1847 by Jön Jakob Berzelius. A variety of polyester resins now exists. In essence they are condensation polymers produced by a variety of processes, including reacting a glycol with a dicarboxylic acid (Brydson 1982: 626ff; Nicholson 1991: 66ff). Examples are the Marco and Crystic unsaturated polyester resins produced by Scott Bader in 1946 (Parkyn 1953; 1994: 107) (cat. nos. 1012–1013).

Glass fibres were known to the ancient Egyptians as early as the second millennium BC, and by 1713 glass fibres had been woven (Parkyn 1994: 106). The Science Museum's Textile Machinery collection contains a remarkable banner-screen decorated with fleur-de-lys woven of glass fibre on a silk ground, and purchased in Venice in the early 1840s (Science Museum inventory no. 1944-5). This is a mixture of natural and artificial fibres, and is significant as an early example of the use of glass as a textile fibre. Glass fibres were not successfully used with resins as a composite material until the 1940s.

'Low-pressure resins' for reinforced plastics were first used commercially in 1942, in the form of glass-cloth-reinforced resin radomes for aircraft in the USA (Parkyn 1994: 107). By the late 1940s, GRP, commonly known as 'fibreglass', was in use commercially, and many of the earliest developments came in the manufacture of boat bodies. By 1947, 16-foot seaplane floats had been produced in Britain (Parkyn 1994: 108). The first car with a fibreglass body, the Corvette, was made in Detroit, Michigan in 1953. Singer Motors Limited (Birmingham and Coventry) produced a fibreglass-bodied roadster in 1954 (the Singer SMX model) – one of the first plastic-bodied cars to be produced by a British car manufacturer.

There were early problems with getting the polyester resin to set, but the problems associated with air inhibition and cold curing were solved by 1951 (Parkyn 1953: 4ff; 1994: 108ff).

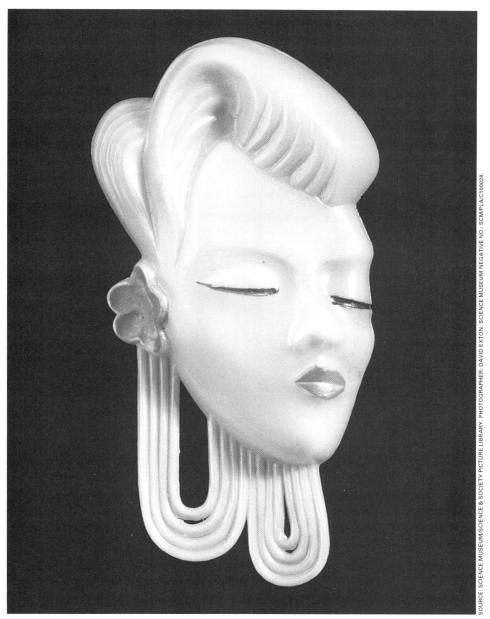

SOURCE: SCIENCE MUSEUM/SCIENCE & SOCIETY PICTURE LIBRARY. PHOTOGRAPHER: DAVID EXTON. SCIENCE MUSEUM NEGATIVE NO.: SCM/PL/A/C100028.

Figure 47   Brooch of pearlised pink polystyrene in form of a woman's head, with red flower in hair and red lips painted on, *c.*1945 (cat. no. 1016).

Apart from boats and cars, GRP was also used for corrugated roofing, for decorative mouldings, and (unsuccessfully) for window frames and baths. Furniture is often made using fibreglass, and such furniture first appeared in the 1950s. Many types of stackable moulded chair are made of fibreglass, as they are tough and fairly inflexible as well as light and convenient to move around.

Epoxy resins are also used with glass fibre to make a composite, low-pressure, reinforced moulding material. They were first developed in the 1930s by Pierre Castan, and became a commercial proposition in 1939 with IG Farben's patent concerning liquid polyepoxides (German Patent 676,117) (Nicholson 1991: 72; Brydson 1982: 666). However, the initially high cost of production of epoxy resins as compared to that of polyesters limited their use until later improvements in production methods (Brydson 1982: 667). Today they are particularly advantageous for space applications, due to their combination of light weight and excellent electrical insulating properties (Katz 1978: 149).

Polystyrene (PS)

Styrene, a derivative of benzene and ethylene, was first described by J. F. Bonastre in 1831. The polymer polystyrene (Plate 18) is manufactured from styrene; this was demonstrated to be possible by P. E. Marcelin Bertholet in 1866 (Kaufman 1963: 78). IG Farben produced polystyrene on a commercial scale in 1930 (Brydson 1982: 386), and by 1935, they were manufacturing it under the name 'Trolitul' (Katz 1978: 84). American polystyrene was on the scene by 1937 under the names of Styron (Dow Chemical) and Bakelite polystyrene (Bakelite Corporation), and was used to make electrical insulators. Polystyrene's range of colours and clarity are obvious assets, but early polystyrene soon cracked and crazed. Polystyrene is brittle, but can be strengthened by incorporating butadiene to produce high-impact polystyrene.

Early examples of toy crockery made from polystyrene are also found (cat. nos. 1023–1037), as well as jewellery (Plate 18 and Figure 47). Its optical clarity can be made use of in probes, useful in both medicine and industry. Expanded polystyrene (EPS) is a good packaging material. Due to its excellent insulating properties, polystyrene is used in houses to insulate cavity walls, lofts and under-floors.

A related plastic is acrylonitrile-butadiene-styrene (ABS). However, as it did not become commercially viable until 1948, it has been excluded from this study.

Polyurethane (PU)

Polyurethane (a condensation polymer made from isocyanates and glycols or polyols) was discovered in 1937 by Dr Otto Bayer and his team in Germany. Bayer continued to work with polyurethane, developing a variety of foams as well as coatings, glues and fibres. By the 1960s this material was being used by state-of-the-art furniture designers such as Roger Tallon, who used it for his spectacular 'Super Chair' with an 'egg-box' surface (Katz 1978: 114). Such objects are difficult to preserve, due to the tendency of polyurethane foams to deteriorate over time. Polyurethane in its various forms now has a wide range of applications ranging from coatings, packaging, padding and insulation to clothing and building materials.

The Years after the Second World War

Plastics which had been restricted due to the war (such as nylon, polyethylene and acrylic) became available to the ordinary public in the years following it. Huge queues formed when the first nylon stockings appeared in British shops after the war. Plastics such as GRP were refined, and wider access was gained to those plastics previously unavailable to the general public. The period up to 1950 set the scene for the development of many new types of plastic, gradually refined to fit their purpose. The sales figures of the British plastics industry are not recorded before 1933; however, sales more than tripled from 50,000 tons (51,000 tonnes) in 1939 to c.160,000 tons (163,200 tonnes) in 1950. Sales figures rapidly increased to 550,000 tons (561,000 tonnes) in 1960 and have continued to grow since, with the addition of many more types of plastic, as well as the 'customised' material developed for a precise purpose. It is all a far cry from the c.330 tons (c.336.5 tonnes) of Celluloid produced by the Xylonite factory in 1888 (Ashlee 1982: 112).

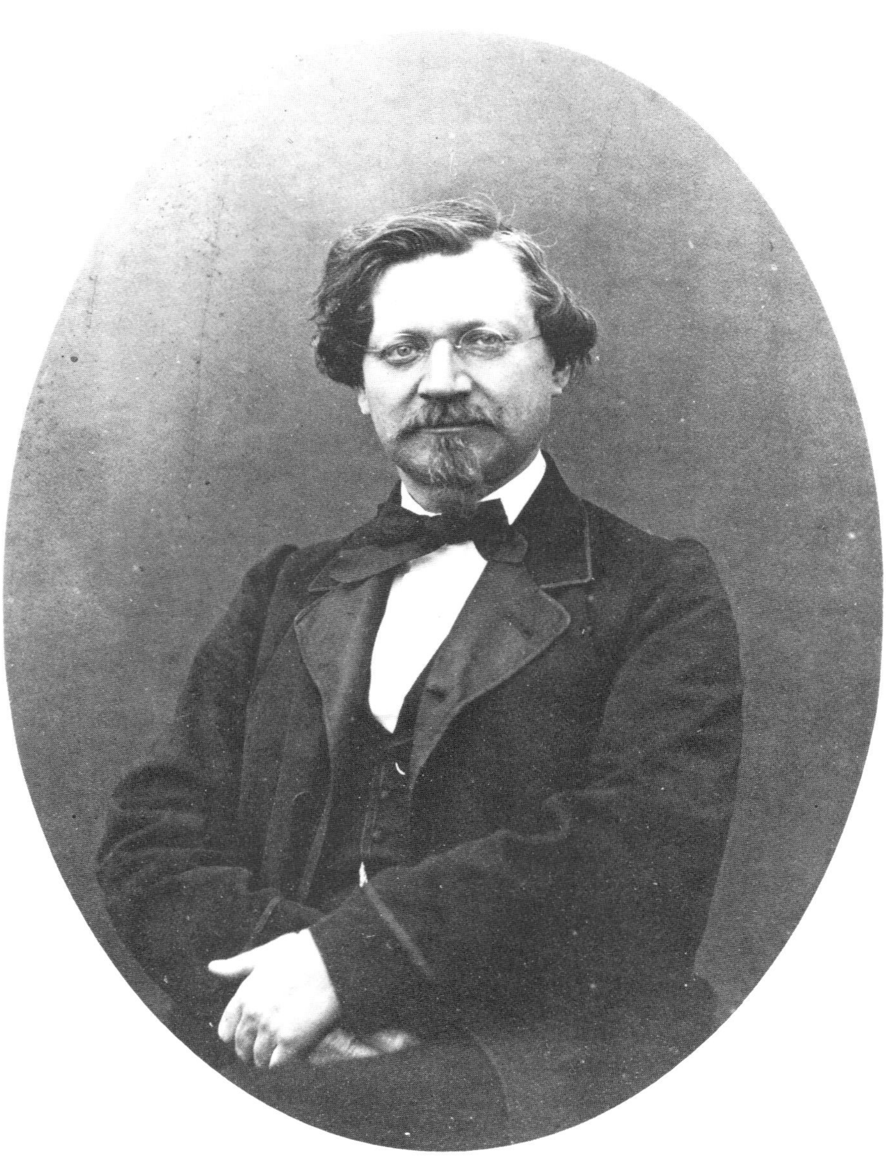

Figure 48   Professor August Wilhelm von Hofmann (1818–92). Henry Parkes studied chemistry under Professor Hofmann and was later able to put this experience to good use in his work with his brother, Alexander Parkes, on Parkesine, among other inventions.

Conclusion

The initial developments of plastics were empirical. There was no understanding of the formation and structures of polymers for the first sixty years of the industry. The idea of polymers as giant molecules was not at all understood until the work of the German chemist Hermann Staudinger, who first postulated the idea of the giant molecule in the 1920s. His theory met with opposition and sometimes even hostility from chemists of a more traditional point of view. It finally won acceptance with the work of Wallace Hume Carothers, who was given a free rein in research by Du Pont, explored various avenues including synthetic rubber, and carried on a fundamental programme of polymer research which resulted in polyamides (nylons). Staudinger's work at Freiberg in 1926 on the development and structure of polymers eventually won him the 1953 Nobel prize for Chemistry (Morris 1990: 49ff).

It can be seen that the first century of plastics was peopled by lone inventors, chemists and entrepreneurs, as well as mixtures of these three categories. The way plastics were discovered and made moved gradually from the small laboratory, domestic workshop or even kitchen to the large research and development laboratories of today's multinational chemical companies (with a few exceptions). Many of the inventions of the mid-twentieth century were the results of large research teams working together. Nylon was produced by a team at Du Pont working under the guidance of Carothers. Polyethylene and acrylic were the result of teams working at ICI, polyurethane of a team working under Dr Bayer in Germany.

Finally, it is worth focusing on three significant participants in the plastics industry during the period from *c.*1850 to 1950. They are Alexander Parkes, Leo Baekeland and Wallace Carothers. The importance of Staudinger's work on the structure of polymers has already been noted.

Alexander Parkes (Figure 15) was a British inventor who worked closely with his chemist brother Henry. His initial work on Parkesine was on a small scale and sometimes even in domestic circumstances. Henry had been a student of the famous German Professor August Wilhelm von Hofmann, prominent among the organic chemists of the era (Figure 48). Parkes relied on his brother Henry to help him with his experiments, and in some cases they took out joint patents together.

Parkes has commented: 'I gave nearly 5 years of my Extra time to Chemical Experiments assessed by my brother Henry Parkes whos[e] Chemical Kno[w]ledg[e] was allwa[y]s great value to me' (PHS N1, 1881). Despite this strong combination of an inventor and a chemist, Parkes was not a very good businessman and his commercial enterprise, the Parkesine Company Ltd, failed. It took the entrepreneurial skills of another, John Hyatt, to make a success of Celluloid: he analysed what the customer wanted to buy (combs, collars and cuffs), marketed them well and sold his products in very large quantities.

Leo Baekeland was a Belgian chemist trained in the European tradition. He was dissatisfied with the way chemistry was administered in Europe and hence went to America. In addition to being an excellent chemist, Baekeland had the advantage of being a shrewd businessman, and after relinquishing a brilliant academic career he was able to combine his gifts as a chemist with those of a marketeer of his own product, Bakelite. He had the added advantage of having sold the rights of his invention of Velox photographic paper for a fortune. He was not averse to setting up his own company when he met with difficulties in persuading established plastics manufacturers to adopt the new methods of moulding required for phenolic plastics. These are produced by placing the resin in a cold mould, heating it and applying pressure, then removing a rigid moulding. Baekeland had to set up a new company as older companies did not want to adopt these new working methods, being used to the older methods of heating the plastic until molten and then pressing it into cold moulds. He also recognised that his product would be invaluable for use in the new electrical industry, due to the good insulating properties of Bakelite, and promptly produced a wide range of electrical goods.

Wallace Hume Carothers, an American (Figure 44), was an outstanding organic chemist who also made the decision to move from a high-flying academic career to the industrial sector, where he was able to apply his very considerable skills and qualities to the entire subject of polymerisation. Carothers was hired purely for research; he was not expected to market his products as well. This was done by the marketing division of his employing company, Du Pont. His role in the production of nylon is similar to that of the team of research scientists at ICI who fortuitously discovered polyethylene. Indeed Eric Fawcett, one of the polyethylene team at ICI, had worked with Carothers at Du Pont and become a close friend. Both companies were supporting systematic research programmes; ICI into high-pressure reactions, and Du Pont into the search for condensation polymers. Unfortunately, the massive resources of Du Pont were unable to prevent a tragedy. Wallace Carothers was very highly strung and was to die by his own hand at the age of 41. He did not live to see or gain from the rich fruits of his labours.

One may see from this brief summary of their achievements that Alexander Parkes, Leo Baekeland and Wallace Carothers were truly pioneers in the first century of the plastics industry.

3 Plastics and Design

Roger Newport

Introduction

It is arguable that every manufactured product has been designed. Somebody has decided what it will be like, and taken steps to make it so. Whether it has been designed by an experienced designer is another matter. The kind of design which is principally concerned with the human factors of the product as well as technological ones, industrial design, has only been in existence for some sixty years or so. Before that, human factors had been taken care of by a tradition of making, or bespoke manufacture, or a mixture of both.

One of the principal lessons of the advent of mass manufacture was that the manufacturer was almost at once put at a distance from information about what the consumer wanted. The fact that products were purchased owed as much to their scarcity as it did to their desirability.

The profession of the industrial designer, then, was created to re-establish the vital connection between the end user and the manufacturer, and to create and develop products which satisfied both. Today, this complex task is often undertaken not by a lone designer, hoping to cope with all the facets of technology, production, marketing and consumption, but by a team in which these responsibilities are shared and staged.

During the period addressed by this book, a large number of plastics products have been manufactured by comparatively small companies, and usually without the help of an experienced designer. Plastics have been seen as substitute materials for those in short and therefore costly supply, and designs transposed rather than created – especially in the field of jewellery (Figure 49). Some plastics materials are equally suitable for craft production (Figure 50), where a market hunch can be played with much less risk. At the same time, designers have been fascinated by the demands and opportunities of the new materials, and a great deal of

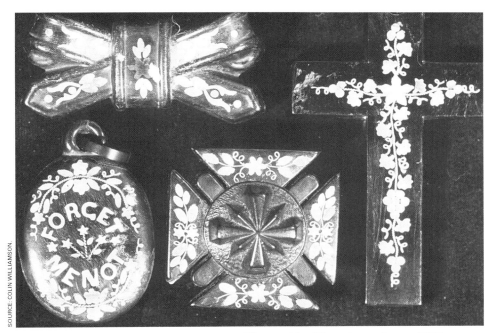

Figure 49 Horn brooches, *c.*1870. Jewellery and fancy goods suffered from severe and sometimes repeated scarcity of raw materials. Dyed horn (moulded from sheet and powder), shellac and hard rubber all substituted for jet.

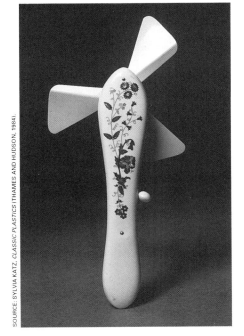

Figure 50 A French hand-powered rotary fan called 'The Zephyr', patented in 1901. The mechanism is sealed into a case, moulded from sheet Celluloid and inlaid with mother-of-pearl and engraved silver.

design work has been done for innovative companies working with the best designers of the time.

Design can be understood as the process by which the alternative possibilities for the attributes of the product, and the values they embody, are explored and decided. Because the object is not bespoke, however, consumers – whether purchasers or users – understand products in very different ways from the people who design them.

Before purchase, a product might be seen in a shop window or in use, inquired about or the subject of lunchtime gossip, and some types of product may be seen advertised on a billboard or in a magazine. During purchase, typically, additional information can be obtained from the retailer, and the object may be handled if not actually used.

After purchase, experience changes our understanding of the product. First and subsequent uses provide a set of routines and skills; cleaning, maintenance and maybe even servicing often come sooner rather than later. The object changes in character as it is used – it becomes noisier or more comfortable; the surface gets worn and probably changes colour. Information about similar products is gathered more easily once the product is not only recognised but identified; others are seen and compared; a mythology develops which labels them in popular conception as anything from 'classics' to failures. Finally, when maintenance no longer works or is not cost effective, the object is discarded, sold on, or stored against some other use or eventuality.

Three main factors are at work here for the consumer: what the products promise; what they do in terms of function and appearance; and the information which surrounds them from a variety of sources.

Designers, by contrast, can have none of these consumers' experiences with the objects they are designing. The closest they get is to use their imagination to predict possible events with more or less fidelity, and to use an armoury of techniques for testing more or less exactly whether these predictions might hold true. Indeed, the majority of consumer experiences – packaging and advertising, for example – are usually created and implemented after the product designers have completed their work.

Designers have access to detailed information about the predictable behaviour of the materials they specify; generalised information about manufacturing techniques; a specific set of manufacturing skills and machines if they are working with a manufacturer; the sales record of products previously manufactured; and informed predictions about finance and market competition. All this information, whether overtly investigated or derived from previous experience, is used at some time or other to inform the design process.

To designers concerned with human factors, the act or process of designing creates alternative ways of satisfying these conflicting requirements. They are all analysed against the designers' personal understanding and against the available objective measures of what it will be like to react to the product in a variety of ways: for example, whether it will be comfortable; what it will look like; whether is will be easy to use; whether it will be strong enough; and whether the buyer will choose it.

An advertisement in the 1945 *Plastics Catalogue* by General Electric in America put it this way:

> Styling is indispensable, in many instances, for the success of parts molded from plastics. General Electric offers a complete designing and styling service to assure more saleable merchandise and more economical manufacture. General Electric has a competent staff of industrial designers who are thoroughly familiar with modern trends and styles. They are intimately acquainted with the characteristics of plastics, permitting them to render ably new product design or to make suggestions for design improvement.
>
> Today, any manufactured commodity is dependent upon functional design for its contour and appearance. In a product fabricated of plastics, good design is vital to efficiency and economy, essential to its eventual range of usefulness. [Anon. 1945]

During the first half of the twentieth century, both the plastics industry and the design profession grew to a substantial maturity. The newly identified specialism called 'design' within industrial production was influenced by four organisations set up for the purpose. The Design and Industries Association (DIA) was founded in 1915 'to combat the unpractical influences in British design and industry' (Collins Baker 1922: 9). The Society of Industrial Artists (SIA) was founded in 1930 'to advance and protect the interests of all engaged in the profession of Design for Industry, Publishing and Advertising' (MacCarthy 1972: 105). The Council for Art and Industry (Board of Trade) was founded in 1934 'to encourage good design, especially in relation to manufacturers', and the Council of Industrial Design (CoID) by Parliament in 1944 'to promote by all practicable means the improvement of design in the products of British industry' (Dalton 1945: 1612).

The engineering institutions were mostly founded in the nineteenth century, but the engineering professions were still growing, and the Institute of Engineering Designers was established in 1946. Engineering designers were primarily concerned with the technological aspects of industrial as well as consumer and capital products, and, for this group, plastics became increasingly important for electrical insulation, bearings and complex components of all kinds.

During the period up to 1950, the group of materials we now call plastics (principally those which are not only organic but also mouldable) played several roles. Throughout the nineteenth century, natural plastics such as horn (Figure 51), bitumen, shellac (Plate 4 and Figure 2), rubber and gutta percha continued to play a minor role in industrial manufacture, with all but horn destined to make significant

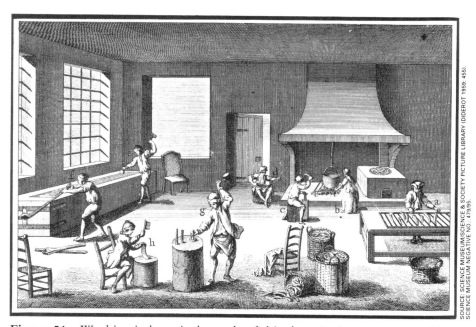

SOURCE: SCIENCE MUSEUM/SCIENCE & SOCIETY PICTURE LIBRARY (DIDEROT 1959: 455).
SCIENCE MUSEUM NEGATIVE NO.: 479/95.

Figure 51 Working in horn is the trade of this shop. Its instruments are heat, either on a grill (a) or at a fireplace (b) which softens horns; mallets, cleavers and chopping block (g, h), and most important of all a long, multi-action press (f) used to mould the softened horns into desired forms.

and substantial contributions at various times. In the second half of the nineteenth century, semi-synthetic plastics were developed to provide substitutes for materials which were scarce even then. Ivory, tortoiseshell (Figures 52–6) and jet were all variously imitated by casein, hard rubber (Plate 6 and Figure 2) and the cellulosics such as Celluloid, and imitated so well that even today it is difficult to see the difference.

Celluloid is now a trade name of the Celanese Plastics Corporation, but was used originally for one of Hyatt's companies in the USA, the Celluloid Manufacturing Company, set up in 1871. Celluloid is a generic name for all brands of cellulose nitrate or pyroxylin materials.

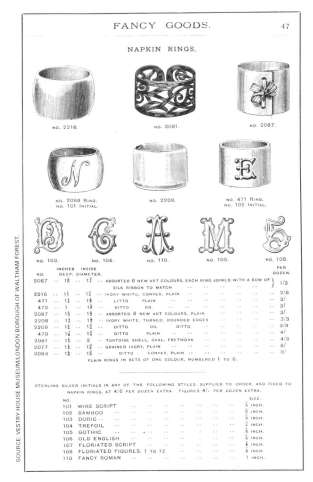

Figure 52 Fabricated napkin rings produced in yellow ivory, antique ivory, grained ivory and tortoiseshell, decorated with sterling silver initials in any one of eight typefaces. Made of cellulose nitrate, British Xylonite Company Catalogue 1899: 47.

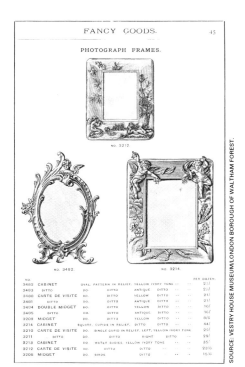

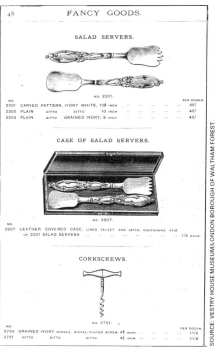

Figure 53   Blow-moulded photo frames produced in yellow ivory, antique ivory, grained ivory and tortoiseshell, made of cellulose nitrate, British Xylonite Company Catalogue 1899: 43.

Figure 54   (above right) Blow-moulded salad servers produced in yellow ivory, antique ivory, grained ivory and tortoiseshell, made of cellulose nitrate, British Xylonite Company Catalogue 1899: 45.

Early in the twentieth century these natural and semi-synthetic materials were joined by the first fully synthetic plastics (which incidentally also substituted for amber), and plastics as a generally identifiable group of materials, began to take on characteristics of their own: lighter than most metals, tougher than ceramics but not necessarily as strong; and during the 1930s, above all colourful (Figure 57). There are, however, some very important materials which do not conform to this general stereotype and which are sometimes still recognised by the public as separate from 'plastics'. This category includes Ebonite (Vulcanite) and Bakelite. Bakelite is now a trade name of the Bakelite Corporation, USA, and Bakelite Ltd, UK, but was originally used by Leo Baekeland for his

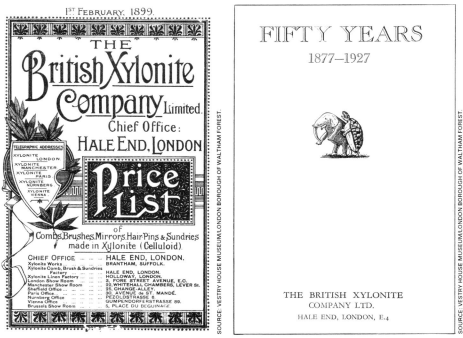

Figure 55   British Xylonite Company price list, 1 February 1899.

Figure 56   Even the trade mark of the British Xylonite Company reflected the expectation that the primary use of plastics materials was to imitate natural materials. It shows an elephant and turtle, both standing on rear legs, 1899.

General Bakelite Company, set up in 1910. Bakelite is now also a generic term for all phenol-formaldehyde materials.

Ebonite and Bakelite are characterised by their lack of flammability; the fact that they do not melt once they have been moulded (they are thermoset rather than thermo-plastic); their excellent electrical insulating characteristics; and their very dark colouring. Their colour could not be economically overcome except by painting, and this made the market introduction in the late 1920s of the brightly coloured and translucent thermoset urea-formaldehyde materials such as Beetle even more remarkable.

Even as late as 1950 (as mentioned in chapter 1), the *British Plastics Yearbook* listed only 25 categories of plastics material, and of these nearly half were either semi-synthetic or naturally occurring.

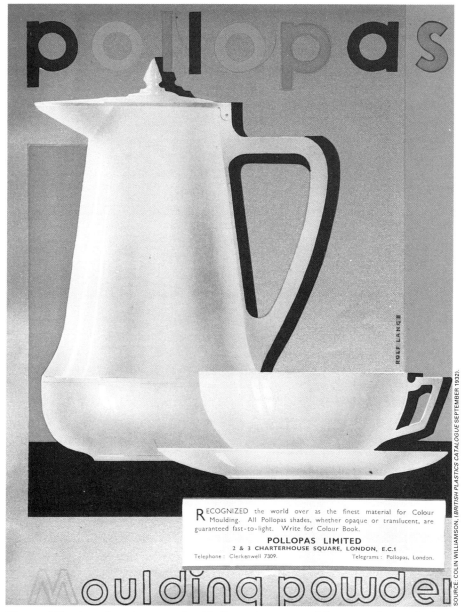

Figure 57   An advertisement for 'Pollopas' urea moulding powders, which indicates the importance of the new freedom from dark colouration imposed by the use of Bakelite and Vulcanite thermoset materials.

At the end of this period, although plastic televisions and Tupperware parties were commonplace, toys were still made mostly of cardboard, tin plate or die-cast metal. Fitted kitchens were uncommon, kitchen furniture was made of painted wood, and enamelled steel washing-up bowls had not yet all been replaced by Polythene.

Plastics comprise one group of materials which has radically changed the way manufacture happens, and therefore the way designers think about their products. They have also changed the designers' functional and aesthetic portfolio. In a world of manufacturing dominated by traditional crafts and a range of materials very different from today's, plastics were seen to have an almost universal impact.

Synthetic plastics provided alternatives: to the 'natural' plastics; to leather travel goods; to natural lacquers and semi-synthetic resins in paints, adhesives and varnishes; to enamelled steel and ceramics; and to many more. Plastics, as a range of both products and materials, have assumed a variety of roles in the context of historical change, and given rise to a variety of meanings.

Design for Production

The four considerations of market, use, materials and manufacture provide the main groups of criteria for a successful design, and the designer's job is deciding how to create alternatives and identify from them a proposal which will not only meet all the criteria, but convince others that the investment is worth while. The way this information and these facilities are managed will govern the success of the project.

Every design of consumer durables for manufacturing implies a level of investment, a level of operating costs and a rate of production for any particular manufacturer. Design, market organisation and economics dictate the rate at which the product can be consumed, and the two sets of circumstances have to match for the product to be competitive. Every new product requires investment before profit, and all product manufacturing life cycles are comparatively short in a free market, where competition soon develops for successful products and even these are incrementally improved.

Design for production includes material, process and finish selection for the design of components, and appropriate fitting and fixing processes for assembly.

Before the Second World War, plastics were used mainly for high-technology and decorative products. High-technology applications included transport, electrical goods, military equipment and mechanical engineering. Decorative goods included dressing-table and desktop accessories, clothing and fashion items (Figure 58).

The newer materials such as the ureas and vinyls were also introduced for more functional domestic goods. Rossiter of British Cyanides first produced mixtures of thiourea- and urea-formaldehyde in 1924, which were exhibited at the 1925 Wembley Exhibition (Katz 1978: 65). Beetle picnicware and tableware were first marketed in 1926. The best known of the vinyls is flexible PVC (polyvinyl chloride). Plasticised PVC was patented in 1912 (BP 6299) by Ostromislensky, but first introduced commercially at the Chicago World's Fair in 1933 by the Carbide and Carbon Corporation.

The post-war period saw the introduction of materials based on polystyrene, Polythene, polyester and epoxy. Polystyrene was first produced commercially by BASF in Germany in 1929 (than part of IG Farben), and first injection moulded in 1930 (Katz 1978: 84; Kaufman 1963: 78; Brydson 1982: 386). Dow Chemicals and the Bakelite Corporation began manufacture in 1937. Polythene is a trade name of E. I. Du Pont de Nemours for polyethylene (Katz 1984: 158). ICI first produced the material, but used the trade name 'Alketh' when they began production in 1936, later changed to Alkathene in 1942 (Wilson 1994: 72). Polythene is now a generic term for all polyethylene materials.

Whinfield and Dickson, working at the Calico Printers Association, perfected the manufacture of fibres from a linear, thermo-plastic form of polyester better known as Terylene. The US patent (no. 2,465,319) was issued in 1949 and carried an assignment to Du Pont. Epoxide or epoxy resins were developed by Germany shortly before the Second World War, but an American patent from the Ciba Company (USP 2,324,483) of 1943 was the first knowledge the Allies had of the material, which is a more expensive, chemically more resistant and stronger alternative to polyester, and a base for the adhesive Araldite (Kaufman 1963: 94).

The introduction of nylon and acrylic spanned the war after the start of commercial production in 1938 and 1934 respectively, Du Pont's

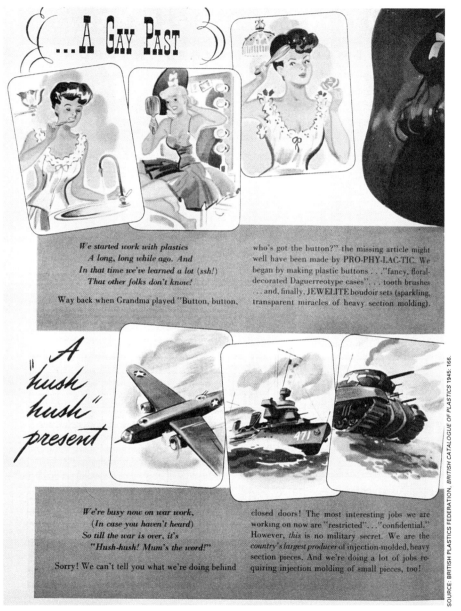

Figure 58   A 1945 American advertisement for Prolon Plastics, showing a 'past' in fancy goods, a wartime 'present' in military goods, and (not shown) a suitably 'wonderful future'.

nylon resulting from Carothers's work in the early 1930s. ICI's Perspex is perhaps the best-known trade name for the acrylic polymethyl methacrylate. ICI were granted their first patent in 1932 (BP 555,687) but did not commence industrial production until 1934 (Kaufman 1963: 87).

The primary chemical sources during this period, for the majority of these synthetic materials in the UK, were 'air, water and coal' rather than oil (*British Catalogue of Plastics* 1948: 15).

Production technologies were, of course, also changing. Originally they had been inherited from industries which used the natural plastics as their raw materials. Sheet horn and tortoiseshell were pressed, formed and fabricated for cups, combs and boxes. Amber was used as a basis for varnishes as well as hand carved into ornamental statuary. After the turn of the twentieth century, it was discovered that carved scraps of amber could also be moulded.

Shellac was similarly used as the basis for varnishes, but after Samuel Peck's American patent of 1854, it was also used to mould Union Cases, picture frames, book covers and record discs. Rubber was moulded by 1820 in the UK by Thomas Hancock, and turned into a thermoset by vulcanisation after Hancock's 1843 (BP 9952) and Charles Goodyear's 1844 (USP 3633) patents. The product, known as Vulcanite, Ebonite or hard rubber, became a significant moulding material. Gutta percha, a material similar to rubber, was extruded and moulded after Charles Hancock's patent of 1844 (BP 12,223) and used for just about everything (Figure 7), but of principal importance was its use as insulation for underwater telegraph cables (Figure 59).

With this legacy of techniques in the UK, a group of materials based on the chemical modification of cellulose, such as Celluloid (cellulose nitrate), rayon (viscose rayon), cellophane (waterproofed viscose sheet) and cellulose acetate (otherwise known as the 'non-flam Celluloid') grew in importance after Alexander Parkes's first patent of 1855 (BP 2359). Manufacturing techniques were still basic, but included injection moulding (Figure 28), which had first been patented in 1872 (USP 133,229) by Hyatt in the USA. Commercially successful machines were not available until the late 1920s, but within a very short period were fully automatic.

Injection pressure for injection moulding at this time was still provided by a piston (Figure 60) and significant changes did not occur in

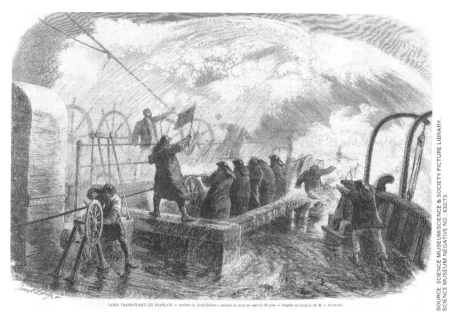

Figure 59 The *Great Eastern* attempted to lay the second transatlantic cable in 1865, but after several breaks had been successfully retrieved by grapnels and repaired, the *Great Eastern* gave up and started again. The first successful cable was laid in 1858 by the vessels *Maegera* and *Agamemnon*. The successful connection lasted only a month.

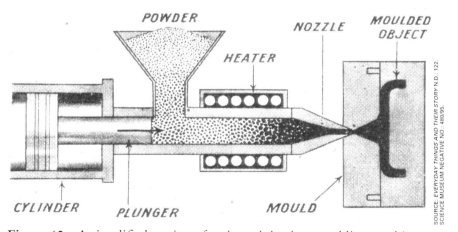

Figure 60 A simplified section of a piston injection moulding machine from the 1940s. The principle of using a reciprocating screw to provide pressure for injection moulding, which made the process commercially viable, was patented by W.H. Willert in 1956.

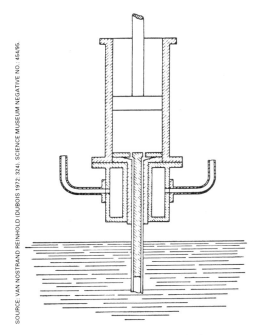

Figure 61   Section of a piston extrusion machine made by Henry Bewley for gutta percha, 1845.

commercial viability until that was replaced by the reciprocating screw in the 1960s. The principle of discontinuous extrusion with a piston providing the pressure (Figure 61) had been used in various industries from pasta to ceramics, but as a continuous process it was important too, for example, in the covering of telegraph cable with gutta percha, or the production of sizeable lengths of rubber tubing. This only became possible with a screw providing the pressure, a principle patented by M. Gray in 1879 (BP 5056).

Production machinery technology during this period was almost always available in advance of materials technology, and most of the significant developments were in the field of materials (Kaufman 1963: 101).

Dealing with the thermoset materials, which, once melted, could not be remelted, did pose a problem to moulders already familiar with thermo-plastics, even though the thermosets, starting with the introduction of Bakelite after Baekeland's initial heat and pressure patent (USP 942,699) of 1909, were available as moulding powders and fed in this form by hand directly into the moulding cavity. After this development, the principle manufacturing methods for the period were established, and Bakelite was followed by other thermosets, the ureas and melamine. In 1935, Henkel showed that melamine formed a resin in combination with formaldehyde (Kaufman 1963: 69), and, after its introduction in 1939, the ureas were replaced because of melamine's superior water-absorption and heat-resistance. Between 1923 and 1938, the turnover of the plastics industry in Britain had risen from nothing to an estimated £20m per annum, with 25,000 people directly employed (Barron 1938: 140).

Before the war, it was customary for design to take place inside the manufacturing organisation, though this was supplemented exceptionally by design consultants who worked for design-conscious manufacturers. For example, Wells Coates, Serge Chermayeff and Misha Black designed radios for Ekco (Figures 62 and 63); Raymond Loewy designed the Purma Special camera for Thomas de la Rue; Walter Teague the Brownie camera for Kodak; and Jean Heiberg a telephone for Ericsson.

Designers were also organising for their own professional benefit. The Industrial Design Partnership was set up in 1935 with Milner Gray and

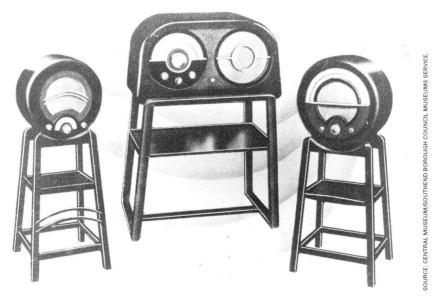

SOURCE: CENTRAL MUSEUM/SOUTHEND BOROUGH COUNCIL MUSEUMS SERVICE.

Figure 62 Display of three Ekco phenolic radios on matching stands: left to right: AC76 designed by Wells Coates, AC86 designed by Serge Chermayeff, and AD36, 1935–36.

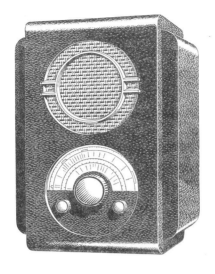

SOURCE: GLOAG 1945: 36.

Figure 63   Mains radio set, model UAW78, moulded in phenol-formaldehyde by E.K. Cole Ltd, designed by Misha Black, *c.*1937.

Misha Black, and the Design Research Unit (DRU) in 1943. Right at the end of the period, manufacturers also recognised the benefits of promoting design in a practical way. BIP (British Industrial Plastics) set up the Product Design Unit, headed by A. H. Woodfull. BIP produced Beatl thiourea, then Beetle and Scarab urea and Melmex melamine materials, and the design service was for moulders who used their materials and led by speculative work which featured in the plastics industry press (Tilson 1989: 229; British Industrial Plastics 1951, 1952).

Industrial design grew from the movement which promoted the employment of artists by manufacturing industry, but was not well known until the 1920s and 1930s, when it began to be taught as a separate subject in colleges of art (Pevsner 1937). Up until this period, the function had sometimes been taken by designers trained as architects or, more especially in America, advertising or exhibition designers. Usually, it was covered by engineers, working on drawings, who demonstrated exceptional levels of craft ability (Baynes and Pugh 1981) using water colour and pencil rather than markers and technical pens. The 'blue print' – the colour of the print from a pencil drawing on tracing paper or linen – became the term for all detailed planning.

When the designer is working directly for a manufacturer, the means of production are usually prescribed in advance and the designer can make use of the available production expertise, by incorporating those features which are necessary because of the specific nature of the production facility. The design can also be followed after its acceptance, throughout the tooling stage, and after production prototyping and production, when modifications might prove necessary.

If the designer is working for an entrepreneur, inventor or selling organisation, most of the design work may be done in principle before the production facility is identified, and without the benefit of cooperation with a specific manufacturer. After the design goes out for manufacturing tender, a further stage of development is usual.

Working in principle has a number of advantages; for example, the technology can be chosen which is appropriate to the product, to its use and to the production numbers envisaged. Most of the available plastics-processing technologies can be chosen in principle on the basis of general physical properties, production numbers, production costs and limitations of size. For example, electrical insulation could have been provided by nearly all plastics during the period, but if tracking (i.e., excessive leakage of electricity between two insulated points) did occur, then a material which had a high ignition, degradation or distortion temperature would be a considerable advantage.

Assuming sufficient sales were forecast to warrant investment in moulding tools, the thermo-setting plastics such as the phenolics could have been used after their introduction in the early twentieth century, but if they were to be moulded rather than cast, then they were only

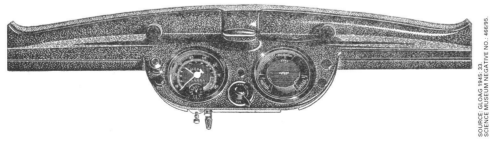

SOURCE: GLOAG 1945: 33.
SCIENCE MUSEUM NEGATIVE NO.: 466/95.

Figure 64 The fascia board of a pre-war two-litre Sunbeam Talbot. Large thermoset mouldings like this one in wood-filled urea-formaldehyde were available provided sufficient numbers were anticipated to justify the cost of tooling.

available in dark colours. Before that, Vulcanite could have been used, but similarly was only available in dark colours. If colour and resistance to tracking were important, but not moisture-resistance, then the ureas (introduced in 1925) could be chosen (Figure 64). If greater arc resistance, higher strength and lower moisture-absorption were required, then it would have to be the melamines, after their introduction in 1939.

In this way, for example, electrical insulation throughout the development of the internal combustion engine and radio communications was achieved with Vulcanite, bitumen, phenolics (Plate 12) and the amino plastics (urea and melamine). Shellac remained the only material capable of insulating some parts of radar installations throughout the Second World War.

Practical Plastics Illustrated (Smith 1947) lists six categories of plastics production processes: (a) compression moulding for the thermoset materials; (b) injection and transfer moulding for thermo-plastic and thermo-setting materials, all incidentally with ram rather than screw cylinders; (c) extrusion for both classes of material; (d) rubber-bag moulding, including autoclave moulding of flat plywood and moulded veneers, which used thermo-plastic and thermo-setting glues; (e) sheet forming, including blowing, stretching and forming, deep drawing and the use of matched hardwood moulds; and (f) laminated plastics for radio parts and gear wheels.

Some design considerations for moulding, whether by compression, injection or transfer machine, are similar. The principle is that two 'matched' steel mould halves fit precisely together, and leave between them a void which is filled with the material to be moulded. The two halves are parted after the material has set, and the moulding is removed by hand or with the aid of automatic ejection pins built into the mould.

Shapes which would make it difficult or impossible for the moulds to fit together, or impossible for them to be parted with the moulded part in place, have of course to be avoided. Much ingenuity was exercised not only in redesigning complex shapes for the moulding process, but also in reducing the cost of the mould by keeping it to two halves, with few or no extra side cores and other parts (Figures 65 and 66). Screw threads, for example, could be moulded in a number of ways. Complex moulds such as the standard telephone handset were, however, commonplace.

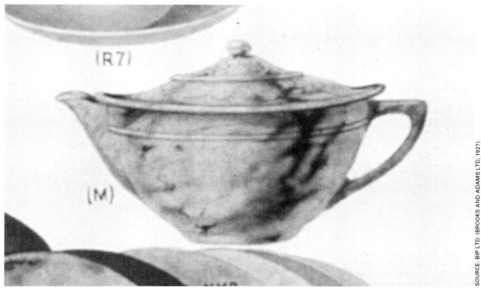

SOURCE: BIP LTD. (BROOKS AND ADAMS LTD, 1927).

Figure 65 The three-part Bandalasta teapot, redesigned for manufacture by two-part moulds. The spout is an open form and there are no undercuts. A conventional teapot form would be almost impossible to mould. The 1927 Brookes and Adams catalogue showed 12 'self colours' as well as 15 marbled colours. The three-quarter-pint patent teapot cost 9/6 – 47 new pence (Katz 1984: 45).

All the thermoset materials would have been compression moulded (Figures 62 and 63) during this period, using moulding powders, hand fed to machines with long cure cycles and costly, hard steel tools. During the 1940s, the more economic transfer moulding (Figure 67) was introduced, whereby the thermo-plastic material was melted before being introduced to the mould under pressure. This was a faster process, but the penalties for inadvertently allowing the material to harden inside the machine were obviously high.

If injection, compression or transfer moulding were too costly for the part envisaged, then the alternatives were extrusion or forming from a sheet either by blow moulding (Figure 68) or mechanical means. All these parts could then be finished, fabricated and assembled by cutting, shaping, fitting and fixing, although the advantage of a complex moulding was that it eliminated or substantially reduced the necessity for the more labour-intensive processes.

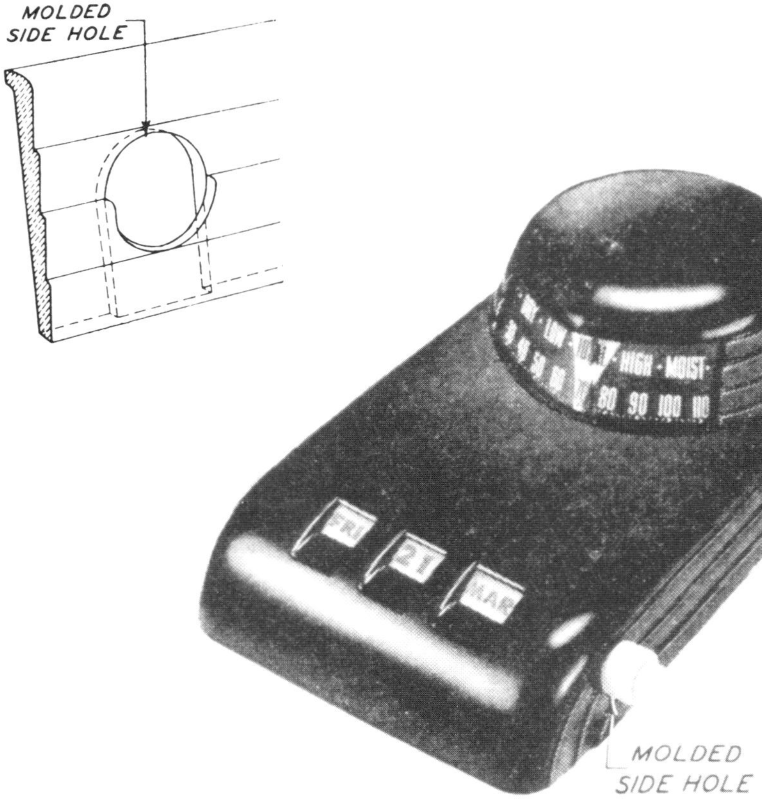

Figure 66 The 'Calendaire' designed by W. B. Petzold, USA, showing how a hole effectively at 90° to the direction of mould closure can be formed without a separate side core.

Choice of material was made on the basis of physical and chemical characteristics, and then overall sizes and thicknesses determined. The means of production were chosen first of all because of the physical limits of moulding size, and secondly because of the limitations of the moulding processes themselves, which provided the second major set of criteria for design for production.

Once the general shape of the moulding had been decided, the wall thickness depended on considerations of strength, material costs and the

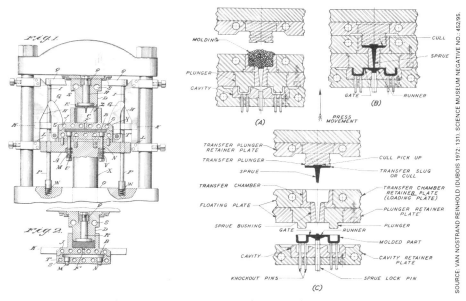

SOURCE: VAN NOSTRAND REINHOLD (DUBOIS 1972: 131). SCIENCE MUSEUM NEGATIVE NO.: 452/95.

Figure 67 L. E. Shaw's American patent for transfer moulding of 1926. This technique – consisting of melting the thermosetting powder before transferring it to the mould to solidify – cut moulding times significantly.

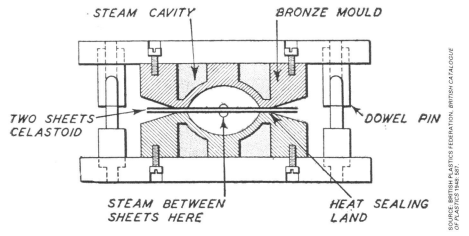

SOURCE: BRITISH PLASTICS FEDERATION, *BRITISH CATALOGUE OF PLASTICS* 1948: 587.

Figure 68 A sectional view of a two-sheet blow moulding machine, a process which has been in use since before the turn of the century, especially for moulding Celluloid into decorative objects such as small picture frames, dressing-table boxes, walking-stick handles and dolls' heads.

way the material was introduced to the void. Moulding pressures were high, and the hydraulic pressure exerted by the molten material could distort parts of the mould which were not strong enough. For example, a hole needed for a fastening might be formed by a pin fixed into the mould and bridging its two halves, but if the part of the pin exposed to material flow was too long for its thickness, then the pin would bend or break.

Compression moulding was usually accomplished with the moulding material in the form of a powder or a 'preform' tablet, introduced to a mould split horizontally, so that the moulds could be brought together using a vertical press. With this arrangement, powders of different colours could be mixed to produce mottled and multicoloured mouldings, which depended for the success of their pattern on the skill of the operator.

Design considerations for compression moulding included siting the mould ejection pins so that they did not leave a mark on the mould

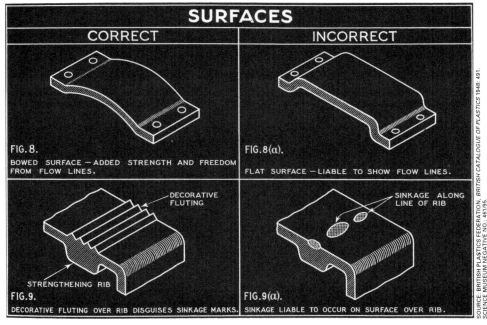

Figure 69 General hints on how to avoid unsightly flow lines and sink marks by using curved surfaces and disguising unavoidable changes in thickness.

where it mattered; using textures and patterns on the mould surface to disguise flow lines, which formed where stiffening ribs or fastenings joined a visible outer wall (Figure 69); placing the 'flash' of unwanted material (from the line where the mould halves parted) in a place where it could be cleaned off easily; keeping the flash line as smooth as possible, to aid the cleaning process (Figure 70); providing sufficient taper in side-wall thickness and draft angle to enable the mould to open easily; keeping the wall thickness as thin as possible, to cut down curing times; keeping the wall thickness as constant as possible, to reduce localised 'sink' marks and distortion; and allowing for general shrinkage, which takes place after a hot moulding is taken from the mould.

Moulded-in components were often used with compression moulding because moulding cycle times were substantial (as the material had to heat up as well as cool down), and the extra time it took, for example, to insert brass screw threads into a radio cabinet moulding was comparatively insignificant. The technique was not new, though, having been patented in 1856 (USP 14,202), the patent assigned to Littlefield, Parsons & Company and used by them for the insertion of brass hinges

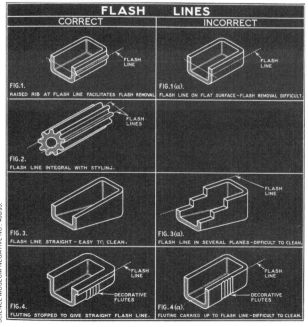

SOURCE: BRITISH PLASTICS FEDERATION, *BRITISH CATALOGUE OF PLASTICS* 1948: 489. SCIENCE MUSEUM NEGATIVE NO.: 460/95.

Figure 70 Compression mouldings required appreciable amounts of 'flash', where the mould halves came together, for the moulder to be certain that the mould was full. The flash would then need to be cleaned off, so the location of the flash line was crucial to effective cleaning.

into the shellac Union Cases of the period (Newport 1976: Catalogue, 2; cat. no. 40).

Two-colour moulding was also possible with two differently shaped mould halves, fitting a common opposite half. One colour of material was moulded and then inserted into a second mould for a second colour. This technique was used principally for decorative ware, and for high-contrast, moulded-in graphics, for example on radio dials and knobs.

Most of the general considerations for compression moulding also apply to transfer and injection moulding, but whereas a thermoset solidifies by heat, and the shrinking is almost entirely due to cooling contraction, a thermo-plastic will stay liquid as long as it is hot. This means that any variation in thickness will result in the thicker area taking longer to cool, continuing to shrink as it cools, and producing pronounced 'sink' marks. To eliminate variations in wall thickness, therefore, was even more critical than with the thermosets.

Extrusion, as described earlier, is a process whereby the material is squeezed through a shaped die in the same way as toothpaste is formed by the nozzle of a toothpaste tube. The result can be complex, but the design is confined to the cross-section, and any three-dimensional forming has to be done by subsequent fabrication. By suspending a shape in the middle of the nozzle, hollow forms such as tubes can be extruded, the principle design consideration being uniformity of wall thickness.

In the six categories of plastics production processes listed in *Practical Plastics Illustrated* (Smith 1947), plywood moulding was included in the sheet-forming section because of the extensive use of adhesives based on thermo-plastics and thermo-setting plastics, and their requirement for heat and pressure to mould and cure. The limitation of plywood lamination, however, is that it can only be formed from flat sheets in two-dimensional curves. The section on laminated plastics deals mostly with the production of laminates with thermoset materials, particularly phenolics, for subsequent cutting and machining into gears, pulleys, bearings and other parts where wear-quality is important (Figure 71).

Sheet forming includes many techniques which were very important during the period. Besides twin-sheet blow moulding, single sheets could be heated and forced into single-sided moulds under air pressure. Sheet could also be free blown, using a shaped collar. This technique was used particularly for aircraft cockpit covers (Figure 72), and required high levels of skill and closely controlled conditions. Other forming

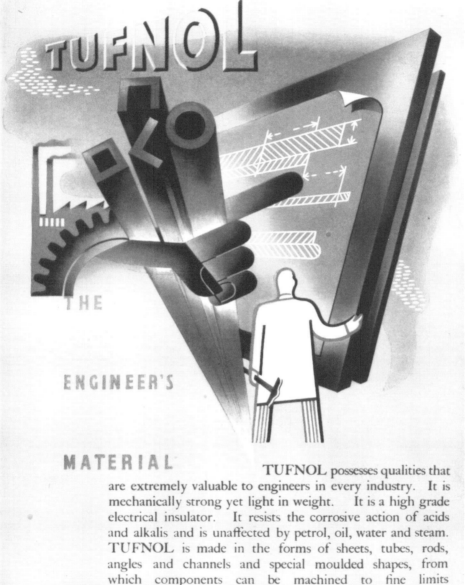

TUFNOL possesses qualities that are extremely valuable to engineers in every industry. It is mechanically strong yet light in weight. It is a high grade electrical insulator. It resists the corrosive action of acids and alkalis and is unaffected by petrol, oil, water and steam. TUFNOL is made in the forms of sheets, tubes, rods, angles and channels and special moulded shapes, from which components can be machined to fine limits with engineering tools.

Figure 71   Advertisement for Tufnol, which exemplifies the techniques of the 1940s.

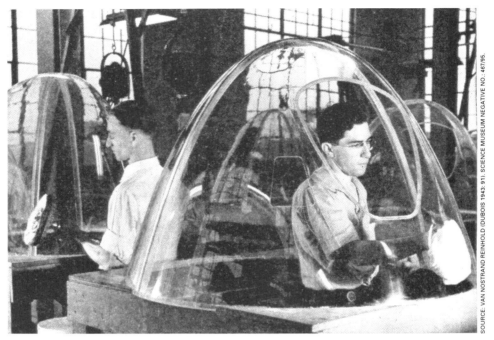

SOURCE: VAN NOSTRAND REINHOLD (DUBOIS 1943: 91). SCIENCE MUSEUM NEGATIVE NO.: 467/95.

Figure 72   The nose cones for Second World War American bombers were formed by free blowing from Plexiglass (Workers of the Writers' Program of the Work Projects Administration in the Commonwealth of Pennsylvannia 1945: 33).

techniques, such as deep drawing and mechanical forming, were derived from metal-fabrication practice.

The only other technique which perhaps was too universally applicable to be included in *Practical Plastics Illustrated* categories was casting, which for limited quantities, with particular types of casting resin, was used to very good effect – for example, Carvacraft cast phenolic desk accessories made by John Dickinson and Co. Ltd and the Catalin (cast phenolic) dashboards, window fillets and dados specified for the Park Ward-bodied Bentley 4.5 coupé shown at the 1939 Motor Show.

Notable by their absence are techniques which were common even twenty years later – vacuum forming, parison blow moulding, rotational moulding, calendering and dip moulding. Vacuum forming, as described in Chapter 2, involves generating sufficient negative air pressure to suck the softened sheet down over the mould, instead of blowing it with compressed air. Parison blow moulding is the technique of extruding a

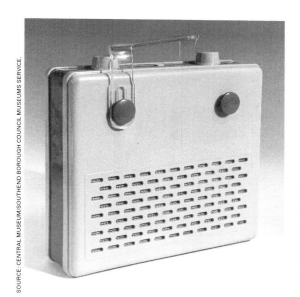

Figures 73 and 74   The Ekco Princess portable radio, designed by Wells Coates in 1948, was the first injection moulded radio. Design for assembly and colour separation was as important to manufacture as the design of the parts involved (Ray 1949: 12).

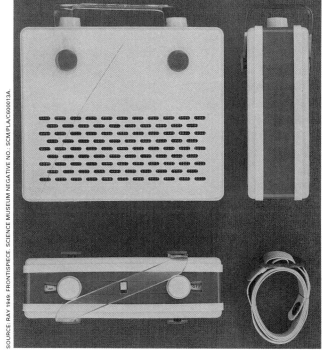

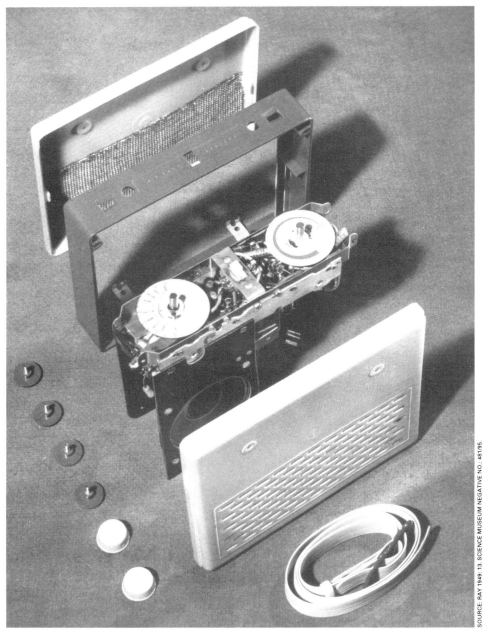

Figure 75 The Ekco Princess portable radio, in exploded form.

vertical parison or tube between the female mould halves of a blow moulding machine before inflating the parison against them. Rotational moulding heats plastics powder inside a tumbling cavity mould, which coats the surface of the mould before cooling. Sheets were made by a variety of methods depending on the material. Calendering, developed by E. Chaffee in 1833 for rubber, was a process of squeezing a plastic mass through rollers and allowing it to cool (DuBois 1972: 237). Cellulose nitrate was veneer cut or planed from a solid block, and this is one means by which it can be identified, the knife having left 'tram lines' on the back or unpolished side. Dip moulding involves heating a male mould form or component, and dipping it into a fluidised bed of thermo-plastic powder. The resulting skin can be stripped from the mould if the material is flexible enough, or left in place on the component.

Design for assembly also became more readily identifiable as economic-ally important as labour costs rose (Figures 73–5), but was not included in *Practical Plastics Illustrated* categories. This reflected the organisation of an industry where materials supply, trade moulding and product assembly were usually undertaken by different and independent companies.

Although most of the design criteria for moulding are normally presented as restrictions, the moulding techniques themselves can also be seen as providing profound new sets of design possibilities, realised by designers of a great many innovative products of the period.

Design for the Market

Marketing represents all those activities which connect the production item with the consumer. In the period after the Second World War, when shortages and rationing were the expectation, manufacturers could sell all they could make and the idea of asking customers what they wanted was seen as an unnecessary expense, as it is wherever a competitive market economy is not functioning.

Alan Jarvis commented on this state of affairs in Penguin's *The Things We See* series, and the consumer's dilemma which he describes is still not completely resolved:

> the shops of this country are filled not with mass-produced accidents, but with objects which are as they are because the manufacturers behind the

machine believe they were what their consumers wanted. Either they instructed their designers to make these things as they are because they believed them to be what the customer wanted or because they knew, or both manufacturers and designers, competing for sales, took a risk in trying something which they hoped would sell to the public.

In theory, the set up is ideal: in practice it may be the exact opposite, because the consumer has no simple way of telling the maker what he wants. The manufacturers judge the success of their designs in terms of how they sell: if the public buy shoddy, ill-designed or ugly things the manufacturers will continue to make them. On the other hand we consumers tend to take what we can find near to hand rather than do without, and the manufacturers are confirmed in their faith that we buy it because we really like it. Thus a vicious circle is set up whereby the manufacturers make what they think we want and we buy it just because it is there on the shelves. The result, of course, is an increasing indifference on the part of the makers to the quality of their products and an increasing feeling of hopelessness on our part when we go to the stores. [Jarvis 1946: 34]

The market for these goods was relatively unsophisticated, and it was understood almost through sales alone. A dominant differentiator was regional or local variations, which reflected not only taste and purchasing habit, but also the ease of collecting information and the allocation of salespeople to territories. The media of mass visual communication – the cinema, national newspapers and a small number of magazines – had yet to be joined by television and become the powerful integrative influence which arguably spawned the post-war subcultures of youth.

It is easy, therefore, to view the role of the Council of Industrial Design as representing consumers as well as educating them. R. D. Russell, writing in *Art and Industry* before *Design* magazine was published, was concerned with several aspects of design in plastics and consumers' understanding (*Art and Industry* 1948a: 149). Two inherent disadvantages, he considered, were the word 'plastics' – a 'misleading omnibus word' referring to a transient condition during the process of moulding – and the harmful premise that scientific research would provide for every need; 'plastics have somehow acquired a pseudo scientific news value'.

Among the design disadvantages, he considered, were 'the poor textural or tactile quality of many materials' and, in terms of form, that 'the very lack of limitation demands the three dimensional sensitivity of a sculptor'. He continued by asserting that an advantage in pre-war plastics tea cups and beakers was that they could be less fragile than pottery because of their thickness, but price competition had reduced the material content so that there was no longer an advantage. This polemic demonstrates a variety of consumer issues, and the role which the design establishment was taking in bringing them to public discussion.

A reply to Russell's article by S. D. Cooke entitled 'In Search of Better Plastics' was published (*Art and Industry* 1948b: 182). It confirmed that 'shoppers [were] so starved of goods … any articles of apparent usefulness were snapped up by the public with little regard to … efficiency or appearance', and went on to complain of 'the production of an assorted mass of products vaguely functional, unstudied and unplanned by untrained minds'. The article identified two principle types of goods: one made to customers' order and therefore specified and comparatively well planned, and the other produced to nobody's specification by small firms, some of which were 'not at all concerned with quality, design or colour'.

The idea of marketing includes market research, product development, pricing, packaging, distribution, advertising (Plate 19) and sales promotion; selling; merchandising and after-sales service. The areas of concern to the designer include some if not all of these, although for the designer 'the consumer' becomes a general term, within which it is necessary to distinguish between the characteristics of those involved in purchase, use, maintenance, servicing, repair and disposal. Traditionally, the focus of the industrial designer's concern has been the user, whereas the focus for the marketer has been the purchaser.

Every new design entails a new market. Although some might be very similar to superseded ones, it is very unlikely that exactly the same group of people will have two unrelated products in common. The market is also changing; consumers get more experienced and older, the inexperienced are introduced, and styles of living change.

The development of marketing as a discipline is principally one of companies' transition from production through sales to marketing orientation. Until the start of the First World War, assured markets throughout an extensive British Empire meant that a 'seller's market' predominated, and manufacturers saw themselves in terms of their production capability instead of sales capacity or customers.

Indications of change had been evident but largely ignored. Even in 1776, Adam Smith had written in *The Wealth of Nations*: 'Consumption is the sole end and purpose of all production and the interests of the product ought to be attended to, only so far as it may be necessary for promoting that of the consumer.' (Smith, 1976: 660). That sales were threatened by increasing competition is shown by the formation of the Sales Managers' Association in 1911: 'In the early years of the twentieth century, the word 'marketing' was still almost unknown … Market research was in its infancy, and budgetary control practically non-existent' (Chartered Institute of Marketing n.d.). Sales records were the primary source of information for this growing movement, and they were nowhere near accurate until semi-automatic methods of receipting were introduced. The Paragon check book was introduced in 1887 (Elias 1934: 260), and James and John Ritty developed 'Ritty's incorruptible cashier' in 1879, a recording cash register which 'curtailed inaccuracy and pilferage'. The ubiquitous paper roll was added in 1881. The Rittys' National Manufacturing Company was bought out in 1884 by J. H. Patterson, the founder of the National Cash Register Company, now known as NCR (NCR 1984: 4). The information link between consumer and producer was growing stronger.

Increasingly, information about sales was brought to bear on product development, even if the first article on 'Market Research' did not appear in *Marketing* until 1935 (Chartered Institute of Marketing n.d.). Research into purchaser motivation and behaviour now informs, among other things, price, advertising, packaging design, product graphics and the firm's reputation (Figure 76), as well as product development. The majority of the marketing effort, however, is directed towards repeat purchase of consumable products, rather than consumer durables which may only be purchased once or twice in a life time. The majority of plastics advertising during the period between the wars, for example, was therefore aimed at the plastics industry and the design profession (Figure 77), rather than the ultimate consumer. To reflect this general development in companies' orientation, the Institute of Marketing developed from the Incorporated Sales Managers' Association in 1968 (Chartered Institute of Marketing n.d.).

Late in 1950, industrial design appeared for the first time on the agenda of the British Institute for Management, under the title 'Design and its contribution towards economic production and marketing' (Davis

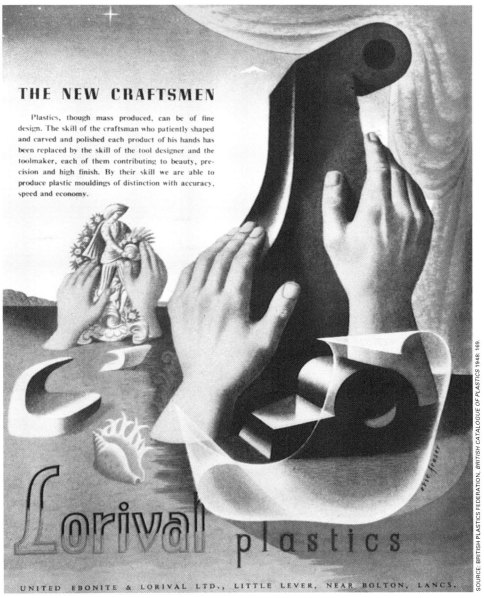

Figure 76 This advertisement attempts to confirm the place which plastics had assumed in everyday mythology. It offers reassurance that hand-craftsmanship had not been lost through mass production, just transferred from object making to mould making. It seemed that everything would eventually be achieved by the protean ubiquity of plastics.

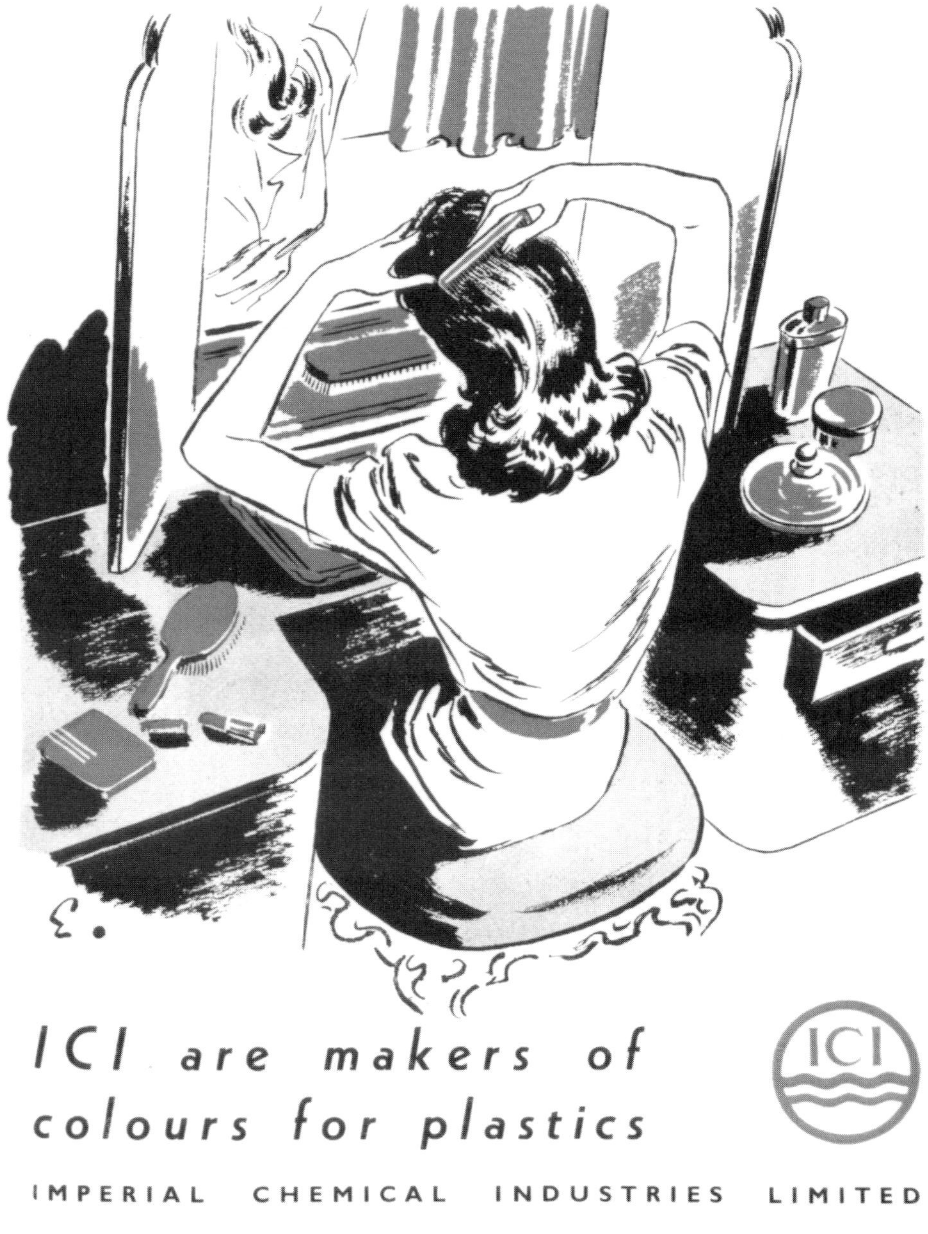

Figure 77   ICI advertising their colour pigments to trade moulders and designers in 1948.

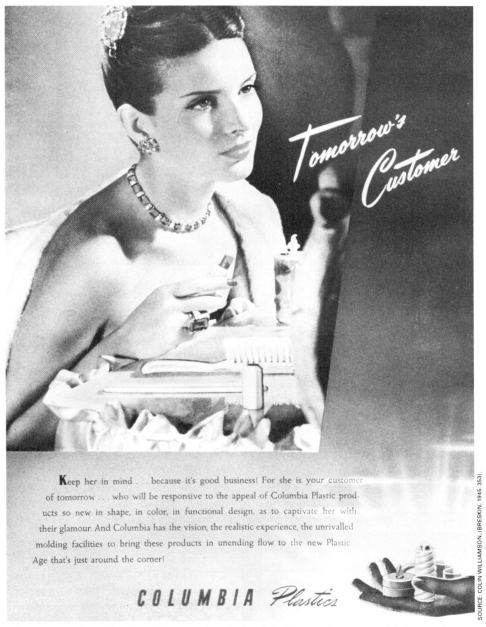

Keep her in mind . . . because it's good business! For she is your customer of tomorrow . . . who will be responsive to the appeal of Columbia Plastic products so new in shape, in color, in functional design, as to captivate her with their glamour. And Columbia has the vision, the realistic experience, the unrivalled molding facilities to bring these products in unending flow to the new Plastic Age that's just around the corner!

COLUMBIA *Plastics*

SOURCE: COLIN WILLIAMSON, (BRESKIN, 1945: 353).

Figure 78   A trade advertisement by Columbia Plastics in 1945, which says less perhaps about the 'plastic age' than about the age of marketing (Breskin 1945: 623).

1950b: 26). Here the responsibility for bad design was disputed, and ascribed variously to the public, the retailer, the fact that designers should 'get out of the back room into the board room', and the fact that engineers were not being given a more liberal education.

At the 1951 Design Congress, held by the Council of Industrial Design, on the theme 'Design Policy in Industry as a Responsibility of High Level Management' (*Design Policy in Industry* 1951), 22 speakers represented six countries, but although nearly all spoke of advertising, some of 'educating the customer' and others of 'marketing', nearly all went on to talk about selling as a post-production activity. One or two did explain, however, that marketing, sales and advertising personnel were shown new designs before rather than after they went into production (Hartley in *Design Congress* 1951).

This represented a common level of management and information organisation for the time, but there were signs of a change. One speaker asserted that 'designers must seek information as well as receive it' about customer preferences (Lee in *Design Congress* 1951), and another placed marketing at the hub of 12 functions, which included 'appearance design', 'market research' and 'product planning' (Bec Var in *Design Congress* 1951). This last speaker was director of design for the General Electric Company, USA, where manufacturing company perceptions were considerably in advance of Britain's.

The American experience was very different: having made the transition to advertising, publicity-led design and marketing before the war (Sparke 1983). Norman Bel Geddes's team for an RCA (Radio Corporation of America) radio cabinet, for example, included the design director, the technical director, an accounts executive, designers, a research technician, assistant draughtsmen and assistant designers. As the advertisement by Columbia Plastics shows (Figure 78), competition for custom in America continued throughout the war period.

Meeting the requirements of the customer is now seen as one of the prime tasks of industrial provision, and it is sometimes difficult to imagine what designing was like when the relationship between marketing, production and design was so significantly different. Meeting consumers' demands and expectations is as much a matter of information and management as it is of good design. Techniques for gathering even the most basic information, together with habits for its use, changed dramatically and irrevocably between the inception of mass production and the 'plastics age'.

Design for Use

The size of the gift market, from socks and jewellery to souvenirs, gives a good indication that the purchaser of a product and its user are quite likely to be two entirely different people. Unsuitable gifts at Christmas only highlight the diversity of motivations and value systems, and this extends throughout industrial and commercial purchasing (including capital goods from office furniture to fork-lift trucks), where the difference between purchasing and using behaviours can become institutionalised, to the detriment of efficiency and job satisfaction.

If the value systems of purchaser and user are known, then the designer can model product response to the satisfaction of the user and the commercial benefit of the enterprise, but the difference between designing for purchase and designing for use can become problematic. Does the object look as if it will withstand the use it is going to get? Does it look as if it is a quality product? How does the purchaser tell whether it is going to be reliable? Every purchaser has experience of answers to these problems, whether or not they turn out satisfactorily.

Another aspect of design which influences purchasing behaviour but only has a marginal influence on use is that of packaging. Plastics packaging was still in its infancy in the 1950s. Most consumables were repackaged at the retail outlet and as a part of the sale. Sweets were bagged; tea and coffee were weighed out and parcelled up with paper and string. Ready-packed goods were confined to chocolate bars and packets of dry goods, and few packaging materials were plastics.

For the user, however, plastics provided a range of real alternatives: tougher and lighter than ceramics and glass for picnic-ware, Beatl picnic-ware and other tableware in thiourea- and urea-formaldehyde became widely available in 1926. Plastics were cheaper than leather for shopping bags and stainproof for table cloths; tougher, more elastic and sheer for stockings; less noisy and longer-lasting than enamelled steel for washing-up bowls. ICI's polyethylene 'Alkathene' replaced enamelled steel for washing-up bowls comparatively quickly after its introduction for this purpose in 1948, even though it was more expensive at first (Plate 20).

Plastics were also cheaper for upholstery that replaced a complex construction of springs, canvas and horsehair with a foam – and which could be covered with a waterproof fabric.

The first plastic bath was moulded from acrylic in Australia in 1947 (Barrett 1982: 3), although market demand here was from the plumbers, who installed it because of its lightness and durability rather than any of the advantages to the user. The bath was moulded by N. V. Appleton Proprietary Ltd of Brisbane, Australia.

The divergence between the designer's aesthetic response and the consumer's has been exhaustively discussed since the critical debate which ensued from the 1851 Great Exhibition (of the Works of Industry of all Nations) in Hyde Park. Paul Reilly, writing in a *Design* magazine article (Davis 1950a: 12) called 'Pitfalls and Possibilities of Plastics Design', quotes Digby Wyatt criticising the 1851 Great Exhibition for 'borrowing ornaments expressive of lofty associations and applying them to mean objects', and goes on to say:

> moulding of course almost as easily provides ornament as it does plain surfaces (in terms of investment) and consequences were the same for cast iron in the nineteenth century … yet too many plastics articles on sale today are constipated little objects … and what they lack in line is wrongly assumed to be compensated for in detail.

Before and since, the meaning of beauty has occupied artists, designers and scholars, but it was not until the Second World War that even the physical diversity of users' response was codified in any useful way. The psychological response of large groups of individuals is still largely unmapped, with changes through time and across cultures of great importance to sales as well as use.

The Second World War proved the necessity of a design approach to possibly complex pieces of industrial and military equipment which were to be operated by newly trained recruits. Mistakes were identified as counterproductive if not fatal, and the size of individuals, together with the way they responded to instruments and controls, was subject to intense scrutiny. The results subsequently provided designers with a way of approaching size, control layout and product graphics decisions, which was a powerful tool in enabling them to predict user behaviour.

Although the first descriptions of human posture date from the second half of the nineteenth century, reports on industrial fatigue and aspects of workplace design were not published until the 1920s. Anatomists, psychologists, physiologists, industrial medical officers, industrial hygienists, design engineers, work study engineers, architects and illumination engineers gathered together in 1949 to coin the new word 'ergonomics' and form the Ergonomics Research Society (Murrell 1965).

Work deriving from a study of US forces personnel was first published by Dreyfus as *The Measure of Man* in 1959. In it, Dreyfus notes that the discipline started '30 years ago … [with] rules of thumb … [on] chair heights … [and] shipbuilders … had … unwritten laws about clearances' (Dreyfus 1959: 4). The work in its republished forms became a standard for designers. What it demonstrates is how individuals differ in size, and in what ways. Designing outside a tradition or a standard became more sure. Testing could be conducted with a comparatively good idea of whether the tester represented the market, in size at least.

People vary not only in size from individual to individual, but also with sex, with age and from generation to generation (Dreyfus 1959: vii). The tallest 2½ per cent of the US population were 30 per cent taller than the shortest 2½ per cent in 1959. When the wartime generation in Britain had grown up, raised through rationing on cod-liver-oil and orange juice dietary supplements, they overtook American youth in height.

A market for a product can be characterised by sex, age group, income, physical ability (Figure 3), skill and many other factors. How big the designer makes the product, and the understandability of its controls if it has any, are still vital issues, whether for users of polythene baby baths, radios, electric shavers, furniture or any other type of consumer durable. These issues were addressed at a number of levels – illustrated by the Electrical Association for Women, which published widely on user issues in the 1930s.

When the designer works for a client who is also the user, as has historically been the case with large parts of architectural and craft practices, all these issues can be addressed with relative ease and resolved to their mutual satisfaction. When an object is to be designed for a large potential market, as is the case with the great majority of plastics products, the means of addressing and resolving the issues were, and remain, much more complex.

It is difficult in hindsight to forget the enormous changes in materials, processes, information technology and design techniques which have taken place this century. Even at the end of our period, plastics were specified as 'off the shelf' instead of being designed for specific applications; production processes were limited and a lot less versatile than they are today; information about markets and users were much more a subject of speculation; and design techniques were limited to pen, paper and model making.

The current fascination with early plastics products is as much a reflection of the circumstances of their production and of the changes which have taken place in the intervening period as it is of our acquisitiveness. Our aesthetic response is perhaps much more to do with the meanings we ascribe than with our attitudes to history.

4 Living with Plastics

Mark Suggitt

In a bakelite house the dishes may not break, but the heart can.
                    [J.B. Priestley, *Midnight on the Desert*, 1937]

The quick change artistry of plastic is absolute: it can become buckets
as well as jewels.   [Roland Barthes, *Mythologies*, 1957]

Is a plastic cup less real than a china one? Nylon stockings less real
than silk? More to the point, is plastic any more fraudulent than a
stage performance? Or a poem?   [Graham Swift, *Ever After*, 1992]

'Plastic' is an emotive word. 'It's so plastic' is a phrase which is often
used to describe something insincere or phoney. Why is this so? Plastics
are now accepted as an integral part of modern life, so why are they
seldom celebrated and still denigrated?

Plastics have been viewed as products that are somehow less 'honest'
than traditional materials such as woods and metals. The result of
complicated chemical processes, they summon up images of artifice and,
more recently, pollution. This perception has continued into the 1990s,
accompanied by the increasing use of plastics in almost every sphere of
life. Until the concerns over the environment became a global issue there
was a case for saying that the very ubiquity of plastics made them almost
invisible as materials – useful, but not something to really think about.

Yet plastics are *the* materials of the twentieth century. Despite this
there has been very little research into their social history. Who made
them? In what conditions? Who bought and used them? Did consumers
notice that they were buying new materials which were replacing older
ones such as enamel ware and tin plate? In short, what is required is an
investigation into the process of acceptance – to look at how plastics
were perceived during the period between the late eighteenth century and
the end of the 1950s. What follows is a first step in examining some of
these issues, looking at the material culture and the ways in which it has
been received within the wider culture of the UK.

In order to do this we must move ahead to the end of the period under
discussion. In 1957 Richard Hoggart wrote of the changes he saw in the

working-class home of the 1950s. He was not impressed: 'Chain-store modernismus, all bad veneer and sprayed on varnish stain, is replacing the old mahogany; multi coloured plastic and chrome biscuit barrels and bird cages have come in' (Hoggart 1957: 35). It is interesting to compare Hoggart's comments with those of a very different type of Englishman, Evelyn Waugh. In his semi-autobiographical novel of the same year (*The Ordeal of Gilbert Pinfold*) he wrote: 'His strongest tastes were negative. He abhorred plastics, Picasso, sunbathing and jazz – everything in fact that happened in his own lifetime' (Waugh 1991: 14). Let us now compare this with the writings of a Frenchman, again from 1957. Roland Barthes felt that: 'Plastic has climbed down, it is a household material. It is the first magical substance which consents to be prosaic' (Barthes 1989: 106). It appears that the English saw plastics as an unwelcome aspect of twentieth-century life. The attitude seems to have crossed that equally English divide, class difference: Waugh's writing expressed his wish to see the aristocratic order remain, while Hoggart saw the traditions of working-class life becoming debased. Like J.B. Priestley and George Orwell before them, they lamented different worlds which were both passing, both in the process of being 'Americanised'.

Their remarks could be seen as reactions against some of the shoddy plastic goods on sale at the time, but there is more to it than that: there is a cultural assumption against modernity, which is still prevalent throughout British society. The long shadow of the Arts and Crafts Movement, working through the Design Council, meant that few mass-produced British products were the successful results of art and industry. This produced mainstream products which tried not to look mass-produced, and a sure way to achieve that was to make them look old-fashioned. 'Pure' plastic products had no part in this world. Dubbed cheap and nasty through the legend of the shattering plastic mac, they were used as imitations of those 'real' materials of the world of Waugh and Hoggart. Britain was out on a limb compared to European countries such as Italy and Germany, which had built up new plastics industries in the post-war period, and designed good products that gained popular acceptance.

This then is the view from the 'high ground' of published cultural indicators. It is now time to turn our attention to those people who used the stuff. It is time to go back to the beginning of our period and see how people reacted to the material, and whether they saw it as a concept as threatening as it seemed to some writers and designers.

Some of the earliest natural plastics were shaped into objects for personal use; for example, moulded horn was used for snuff and trinket boxes. Makers such as John Obrisset produced moulded lids of great delicacy and detail in seventeenth-century London. These were relatively up-market products, and it was not until the mid-nineteenth century that large numbers of British people were able to buy plastic products. Plastics did not get off to a good start with the waterproof Macintosh coat, named after Charles Macintosh, who, in 1823, dissolved rubber in naphtha and sandwiched it between layers of cloth to make them waterproof. When this cloth was made into garments they were found to be hard and brittle when cold and smelly when hot (Figure 10). Nevertheless rubber was used widely in the nineteenth century for a variety of purposes, from pipes and hoses to false teeth. This hard, 'vulcanised' rubber was produced by mixing it with sulphur. In Britain it was known as Vulcanite.

The search for new, stronger materials was vital for the continuance of the Industrial Revolution and the exploitation of the emerging markets for manufactured goods. Before the gradual success of rubber and, later, Celluloid, papier mâché was the first 'new material' to gain popular acceptance. An improved method of producing papier mâché had been patented in Birmingham by Henry Clay in 1772, and it remained popular throughout the nineteenth century. Birmingham and Wolverhampton were the major manufacturing areas. Once moulded, the surface was usually lacquered and varnished, then decorated with inlaid mother-of-pearl and painted designs. The ground was generally black. Late eighteenth-century production concentrated on trays and boxes. Papier mâché trays replaced the older material of painted sheet iron.

It is worth dwelling on papier mâché for a moment, as it is an interesting prelude to the production of the semi-synthetic and synthetic plastics. The refinements of Clay and the quality control of A. Jennens and T. H. Bettridge allowed larger items to be made out of the material. Better-quality paper was used instead of relying on pulp, which could give an unequal density (Moore 1968). The 'common method' of production used pulp and moulds, while the 'revolutionary' Clayware was more a type of pasteboard (Jones 1981).

We need to examine the reactions to this 'new' material. If his products were not totally original, Henry Clay at least marketed them well, presenting a sedan chair with papier mâché panels to Queen Charlotte and opening a shop in Covent Garden. He created the right image for the product and could boast among his customers style leaders such as Horace Walpole, who ordered pieces for his house at Strawberry Hill. Papier mâché was fashionable, and was to remain so for another fifty years. Depending on the quality of the material and the decoration, it was affordable to a broad cross-section of society. Decorative items such as trays, boxes, letter racks and snuff boxes were produced, as well as small tripod tables. Sofas, bedsteads and wardrobes were also produced, but to a lesser extent. Large panels were made for steamship saloons. An advertisement for a set of these described the effects of the decoration as 'at once chaste and gorgeous' (*Birmingham Times* 1854).

So, it can be said that papier mâché, a 'replacement' material, gained acceptance as it was seen to do some jobs better than its rivals. A product of the Industrial Revolution, it not only was accepted but achieved fashionable status. In 1851 Harriet Martineau visited Jennens and Bettridge's works and commented on the shortcomings of the old sheet iron tray:

> It was gay when new, but the colours soon flaked off in the middle ground and rusty spots broke out in the black ground. It warped and stood uneven and clattered with every jog of the table. The rim was apt to crack and leave jagged edges. [Martineau 1851]

She contrasted this with the lightness and toughness of the paper tray. Papier mâché was also an improvement on wood, as it could be japanned without fear of warping or cracking. The elaborate japanned and inlaid surface decoration disguised its origins, but papier maché was seen as an improvement and not something second rate. It was part of that nineteenth-century journey to discover new materials and processes. The demise of papier mâché came about through the production of inferior work in both material and design, and through the success of another Birmingham process: electroplating. Nevertheless, it set the scene for future developments.

There was considerable interest from manufacturers and investors in new materials which could be moulded. The nineteenth century saw the rise of a market for highly decorated goods, influenced by the increasingly popular 'gothic' styles. Moulded or cast materials could replace the costly hand-carved item. The expensive craft skill was only required once, to produce the mould or die. After that, thousands of objects could be produced for an expanding market. Die stamping was well established for metal working, and if newer, cheaper materials could be found there was money to be made for both the inventor and the manufacturer.

The tradition of fancy goods production, coupled with the search for new types of material, was part of life for the Birmingham-born Alexander Parkes (Figure 15); and Harriet Martineau was in no doubt where the future lay in 1851. She had heard of a Norwegian church built of papier mâché panels. She concluded her piece for *Household Words*, quoted above, by saying:

> At present, we old fashioned English, who haunt cathedrals and build churches, like stone better. But there is no saying what we may come to. It is not very long since it would have seemed impossible to cover 18 acres of ground with glass; yet it is done [the Crystal Palace] … it would be presumptuous to say what cannot be achieved by Science and Art, under the training of steady old Time. [Martineau 1851]

The natural plastic shellac was next to gain acceptance, especially in the form of Union Cases for ambrotype and daguerreotype photographs (Plate 4). The term 'Union Case' derives from the item's popularity during the American Civil War. Thousands of soldiers had their photographs taken, often by studios set up in the camps. The moulding process was patented in the USA in 1854, and was able to produce decorative details as sharp as those produced by die stamping in metals. Millions were made to encase the millions of portraits coming out of the studios of the USA, Britain and Europe. Such personal plastics were for the middle classes and the artisan in good times. They were certainly part of the suburban world of scones and crumpets in T.S. Eliot's 'A Cooking Egg' of 1920, up on the wall with the silhouettes, recorders of 'Her grandfather and great great aunts' (Eliot 1972).

Both the papier mâché products and the shellac Union Cases presented manufacturers and consumers with a new option. Papier mâché and shellac both competed with materials such as wood and metal, but were unashamedly materials in their own right. As the chemical discoveries of the century continued, the new plastic materials looked to this personal fancy goods market rather than to heavy industry, although products such as vulcanised rubber and gutta percha were making headway in numerous trades. As mentioned earlier, gutta percha was used to insulate the telegraph cables across the Channel in 1850 and the Atlantic in 1866 (Figure 59). Personal plastics, although made of new materials, increasingly imitated traditional materials in order to establish themselves. They made no secret of this. Parkes's catalogue entry for the International Exhibition of 1862 described Parkesine as capable of being made as 'Hard as Ivory' and as the 'most perfect imitation of Tortoiseshell' (Suffolk Record Office no. 2). The Xylonite Company price list for October 1869 described Xylonite as 'an excellent substitute' for a wide range of materials (Hackney Archives no. 1). The imitation of horn combs and jet jewellery illustrates how the cheaper plastics built their markets.

Hand-cut horn combs for women's long hair styles were expensive, but Celluloid could be moulded and cut to replicate carved horn and tortoiseshell and sold at a far more competitive price. Once established in that market it prospered. This was in spite of attempts by the horn manufacturers to bring the new material into disrepute. In 1892 the Aberdeen Comb Company printed a circular entitled 'Beware of imitations', which claimed that Xylonite was liable to 'spontaneous combustion' and quoted the case of a woman whose clothing caught fire (Hackney Archives no. 2). The British Xylonite Company took them to court over the matter and won. This clearly shows that the new material was a real threat to the Aberdeen Comb Company, which had been one of the biggest manufacturers of horn and tortoiseshell combs in the 1850s. Celluloid goods continued to win sales and, despite the fashion for short hair in the 1920s, 90 per cent of toilet goods were made in Celluloid by 1944 (Katz 1984: 10).

Cost was clearly a factor in this success story. By 1929 Harrods sold not only silver and enamel toilet sets but a wide variety of 'Ebony, White Xylonite and Imitation Tortoiseshell Brushes and Mirrors' (Harrods 1985), most for under 20 shillings. Toothbrushes also provide a good illustration of how a cheaper material, linked to successful production techniques, could provide a mass-market product. Early toothbrushes were made with bone handles and were expensive. During the 1920s, high-speed machinery for the production of Celluloid handles meant they could be sold for as little as 3d (Kaufman 1963: 49).

It appears as though the plastics companies wanted to expand the fancy goods market and turn luxuries into commodities. Although seen as competitors by the luxury trade, the plastics manufacturers were moving towards the mass market. An example of this is the production of imitation jet jewellery.

The manufacture of hand-carved jet increased dramatically during the latter half of the nineteenth century to meet the demands of mourning fashions for women. So great was the demand that the main manufacturing town of Whitby could not meet it. Moulded imitations were produced in Vulcanite. As social conventions relaxed throughout the twentieth century, jet jewellery became no longer fashionable, and by the 1920s the Whitby industry was in irreversible decline. Meanwhile the plastics manufacturers had already moved on to other areas, especially the electrical industries.

It appears that such personal plastics were seen as good-quality products that were clearly not the top-quality, hand-made objects fashioned from precious or semi-precious materials. A great deal of research remains to be done in this field, but it does seem as though the Victorians and the Edwardians accepted these new materials without a great deal of thought. After all, why should they have done otherwise? The objects did their job and were available at an affordable price. This attitude was not shared by the Arts and Crafts Movement, which proposed the use of only traditional materials, and it was a long time before plastics became accepted by industrial designers, even from within the emerging Modern Movement. Walter Gropius proscribed the use of plastics at the Bauhaus. He felt they had no intrinsic qualities of their own and were by their nature imitative and derivative. Other designers, however, were quite happy to mix plastics with traditional materials (Bayley 1985: 206). Charles Rennie Mackintosh and Josef Olbrich both used the milk-based plastic casein as an inlay for some of their clock faces. Mackintosh also designed a candlestick in green Erinoid (a trade name for casein), which is now in the British Museum (accession no. MLA, 1983, 11-6.1; Collins, 1987, 46).

At least designers were becoming aware of the materials, whose growth is illustrated by the sales figures of the British Xylonite Company. Total yearly sales for combs grew from 34,613 in 1888 to 454,711 in 1918. It is also interesting to see the sales of their other key product, Celluloid collars. These, with cuffs for shirts, had first been produced in the USA as a substitute for starched linen (Figures 20–2). British production began in 1885. Sales were recorded in 1888 at 54,570 and peaked at 115,582 in 1916, falling to 99,192 in 1918 (Hackney

Archives no. 3) (Figure 17). Celluloid collars may well have been responsible for the public's suspicion of plastics. The collars were cold and stiff, and Robert Roberts remembered that 'All boys save the poorest wore Celluloid Eton collars that curled with age, turned yellow and exuded a peculiar smell' (Roberts 1980: 40). Wearing cheap suits and Celluloid collars, the poor of Roberts's Salford slum attempted to imitate the middle class, but as Roberts pointed out: 'the artisan in his best suit looked like the artisan in his best suit: no one could ever mistake him for a member of the middle classes' (Roberts 1980: 39). The Celluloid collar was a visible sign of class difference, a signal to be decoded in different ways across the class spectrum. It began to go out of fashion during the First World War. The 500 women who produced them at the British Xylonite Company moved to the production of a grimmer type of accessory: anti-gas eyeshields.

By the end of the First World War, there were newer synthetic plastics on the market. There were also great social changes as a result of the war. New industries were emerging away from the traditional centres, and new jobs were tempting many working people away from domestic service. Plastics were beginning to make inroads into this new world, especially phenolic and urea-formaldehyde. The only material that the rising numbers of office and clerical staff would ever associate with a telephone casing was a plastic, black phenolic.

People were becoming more used to plastics as familiar things began to be made from them. They also connected with new technologies which were entering the middle-class household. One of the most ubiquitous plastic products was the gramophone record. Millions of these shellac '78s' were produced. Following the gramophone was the radio; the British Broadcasting Company began in 1922. Meanwhile the electrical industry was expanding, especially after the passing of the Electricity Bill of 1926. The use of electricity was to bring the urban and suburban homes of the 1920s and 1930s closer to increasingly sophisticated and self-confident plastic products. The electrical-component manufacturers took to phenolic as a casing because of its excellent insulating properties, and produced millions of light-bulb fittings, switch cases and junction boxes.

Some of the most successful ranges of plastics produced at this time were for tableware. Trading under the names 'Beetle', 'Bandalasta' and 'Linga-Longa', these urea products were made in attractive marbled shades or bright colours (Figure 57). They were launched at the British

Empire Exhibition in 1924 and received a boost when successfully promoted at Harrods in 1926. Other stores soon began to stock them (Katz 1984: 11). The Harrods catalogue of 1929 had a whole page devoted to 'Beatl' ware, the new name given to Beetle to appease buyers who disliked the name of an insect being associated with tableware (Newport 1976: 4). It was described as:

> a delightful tableware delicately shaded, which gives a pretty touch of colour to any table. The fact that it is tasteless and odourless and does not warp or crack if placed in hot water, gives it a decided advantage over all other forms of tableware, but although it is considerably stronger than Glass or China, it is not offered as unbreakable. [Harrods 1985]

This illustrates an increasing confidence in the product. Unlike those for Parkesine and Xylonite, the advert promotes it as being superior to traditional materials, not just their equal. Here was an attractive plastic product which could withstand the rough-and-tumble of daily life. A Halifax woman recalled that these pieces were good for picnics, but: 'You couldn't drop them, they cracked, and the problem was that there was no glue around good enough to stick them back together' (Oral testimony 1991). Although marketed as tableware, most seem to have been used for picnics, replacing the glass, ceramic and enamelled containers which filled the wicker hampers that travelled down country lanes in the 1920s and 1930s. Urban people were becoming more mobile, as bicycles, motor cycles, coaches and cars carried parties out into the country on precious sunny weekends. An American observer remarked:

> In England, as in the USA, the urea materials find a large market in the chain stores, but perhaps the English love of picknicking, as we term lunching in the open, adds to the variety and extent of production in urea dishes and related items in England. [Anon. 1936: 364–5]

As the 1920s drew to a close, plastics would soon be associated with one of the most influential products of the twentieth century, the radio. Bakelite encased some of the most famous pre-war radio sets, now regarded as design classics. The Southend firm of Ekco were pioneers in this field. Their 1930–31 models 312 and 313 were housed in rectangular phenolic cases, made by AEG in Germany (Going 1990a: 12). Due to tightening import controls Ekco went into production themselves and

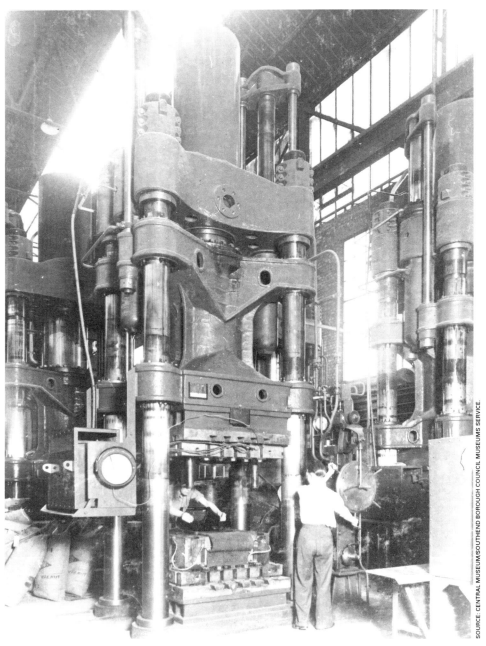

Figure 79   Large-scale moulding press at the E.K. Cole Factory, *c.*1935.

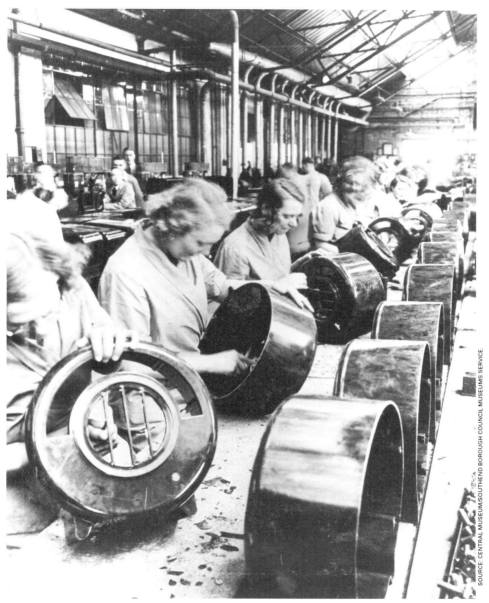

SOURCE: CENTRAL MUSEUM/SOUTHEND BOROUGH COUNCIL MUSEUMS SERVICE.

Figure 80   Production line of women trimming flash off AD65 Ekco radio cabinets, E.K. Cole Factory, 1934.

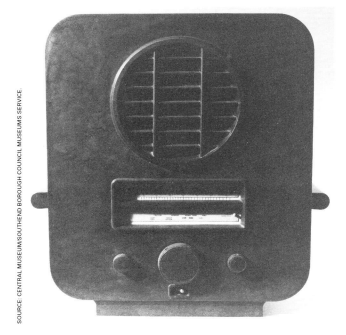

Figure 81   Ekco Radio Model AC74, by E.K. Cole Ltd, with phenolic cabinet, 1933.

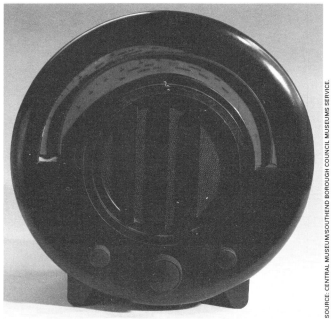

Figure 82   Ekco AD65 radio, designed by Wells Coates, manufactured by E.K. Cole, with phenolic cabinet, 1934.

developed a large plastics division within the company (Figures 79 and 80). During the 1930s they engaged leading architects and designers to design the cases (Figures 62, 63, 81 and 82). Other companies such as GEC, Philco and Ferranti also began to use moulded cases. The plastic case was a logical step from the earlier plastic speakers, such as the Philips of 1927 and the British Thomson-Houston of 1928. The designers took advantage of the moulding qualities of phenolics to produce dramatic new features within the landscape of the living room. The modernist Anthony Bertram noted that plastics had almost conquered certain fields of design, and commented that 'to make plastic materials imitate woodwork is a definate dishonesty of design that cannot be too strongly condemned' (Bertram 1938: 96).

The plastics companies were at the leading edge of industrial design, but had to respond to customers' tastes to stay in business, and the evidence suggests that those tastes were rather more conservative than Bertram's. As one woman remembered: 'They had a novelty value in them but people preferred the traditional materials' (Oral testimony 1991).

This view is supported by the documentary evidence. Ekco produced their cabinets in 'Walnut' or 'Ebony' with chrome trim (at a cost of 5 per cent extra). Recent research has revealed that Ekco also produced cabinets in 'Onyx Green' and 'Pearl Ivory'. These were produced in small numbers and did not sell well. One reason was that they stood out too much – they were too much of a novelty – and the other is that they were two guineas extra (Going 1990a: 12). The latter was an important consideration, as radios were not cheap; a 1939 model could cost £10 17s 6d, well over a month's pay for many people. Hire-purchase terms were available at twelve monthly payments of 18s 9d (Ekco 1939/40). It seems that the public would accept the plastic cases if they attempted to blend with the existing furnishings, which for many people would still be Victorian or Edwardian. Ekco catalogues showed their models in stylish modernist settings, but few people could afford this total look (Figure 83). Even before the Second World War, Ekco were beginning to return to wooden cabinets. The 1936 catalogue had more plastic cabinets than wooden ones, 'new and superb creations by Britain's leading architects and artists'; but by 1939 wood had overtaken plastic. Post-war models by all companies continued to use both wood and plastic. It was clear that plastic had become accepted as a material for cabinets and would eventually triumph as the favoured envelope for most household technologies.

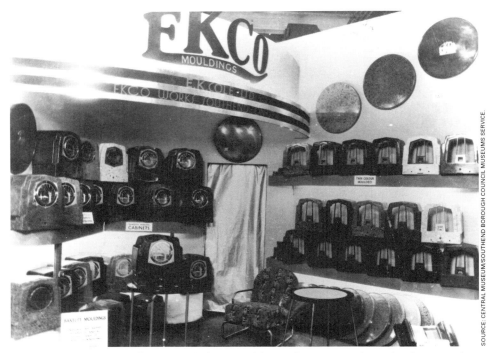

SOURCE: CENTRAL MUSEUM/SOUTHEND BOROUGH COUNCIL MUSEUMS SERVICE.

Figure 83   Display of Ekco Bakelite mouldings, by E.K. Cole Ltd, Ekco Works, Southend-on-Sea, 1930s.

Nevertheless, the plastics industry of the time knew that their products had an identity crisis. Morris Kaufman summed up the situation very neatly: 'People within the industry kept telling each other how important it was, but the world outside was not so sure ... The public, it appears, did not recognise the stuff' (Kaufman 1980: 4).

Such was the concern that the journal *British Plastics* ran a competition to find 'a suitable generic term to cover all plastics materials'. Entries received included 'Pucca Products' (an acronym of phenol, urea, cresol, casein and acetate), Adanond, Fictiloid, Synolics and Mouldin. The judges could not find a winner and carried on with the word 'plastics', while the majority of the public thought most plastic was Bakelite – or was it that Bakelite was different from plastic? Whatever it was, it was being used more and more. By 1939 moulded materials were being used in homes, offices, trains, works and shops. Celluloid film transmitted the screen dreams of Hollywood in packed British cinemas. Celluloid roll film was also becoming the medium of modern memory, as more and more people recorded holidays and outings using cheap Kodak cameras. The Second World War slowed down this development but simultaneously stimulated innovation and led to a whole range of new plastics: the world of nylon, PVC and Polythene.

The discovery of nylon was announced by the American company Du Pont in 1938. This new 'wonder fabric' was the result of $27 million-worth of research. Nylon stockings went on sale in October of that year, and the first complete outfit made of nylon appeared at the New York World's Fair in 1940 (Ewing 1978: 152). Its uses for women's underwear and stockings were widely acclaimed, as nylon was a cheaper substitute for silk. Silk stockings did wear well but were not cheap; in 1937 a good pair cost 2s 11d, which was a sizeable proportion of a young woman's wage, as clerical staff were paid between £3 and £4 a week. By 1940 Britain was already at war and so had to wait for the benefits of this new material, for:

> by a strange coincidence nylon, which was to have a profound effect upon the future of all clothing, was introduced into Britain on 1 January 1940, the day when wartime restrictions first hit the country in the way which traditionally hurts most – by the introduction of food rationing. [Ewing 1978: 153]

British nylon production went into wartime needs such as tents, parachutes and tarpaulins. 'Luxuries' such as stockings were in short supply, whatever material they were made of. Nylons were highly prized because they were the next best thing to silk and could be bought, at a price, on the black market. Only rayon stockings were allowed to be made under the Utility Scheme and each pair cost one-and-a-half clothes' coupons. A Nottingham woman recalled that she wore her first pair of nylons on her wedding day in 1942. They had travelled from the USA and came to her via a friend of a friend who had bought them while on duty in Egypt (Suggitt, 1991) (Figure 84).

The development of plastics continued throughout the war in Britain, the USA and Germany. Existing plastics technology was also widely exploited. The Ekco factory in Southend worked round the clock seven days a week, producing millions of mouldings for all the armed services. One of these was a practice bomb for the RAF; another was a 'gun flash simulator' designed to outwit enemy artillery. Plastics were clearly

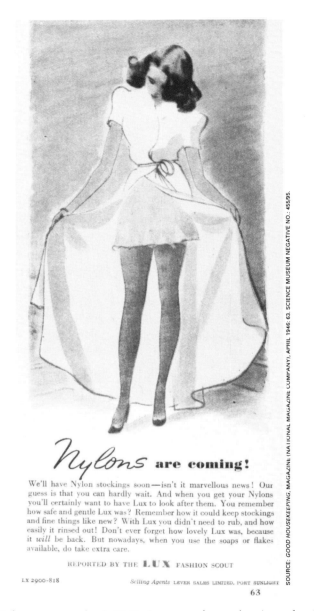

Figure 84   'Nylons are coming', 1946. Large-scale production of nylon hosiery began in 1939, but availability was greatly reduced by the war effort. After V-J Day it took two years and 700 million pairs of stockings to satisfy the intensified demand.

playing a vital part in wartime production. It was at this time that V.E. Yarsley and E.G. Couzens wrote their Pelican book on plastics. In this excellent study they concluded on an optimistic note. Looking to a future plastics age, they wrote of

> a world free from moth and rust and full of colour, a world largely built up of synthetic materials made from the most universally distributed substances ... When the dust and smoke of the present conflict have blown away and rebuilding has well begun, science will return with new powers and resources to its proper creative task. Then we shall see growing up a new, brighter, cleaner and more beautiful world ... the Plastics Age. [Yarsley and Couzens 1941: 152]

The war did give science new powers and resources and, once it was over, peacetime production had new materials ready to go onto the market. PVC, melamine, polyethylene, polystyrene and nylon took great strides in post-war America. Britain still had rationing and shortages to contend with, but the 'Britain Can Make It' exhibition of 1946 promoted plastics and rubber products, including a working press which produced 3000 egg cups a day. The Mass Observation scheme conducted a major survey of visitors to the exhibition and found that: 'antipathy to plastics goods was common, for they bore the stigma of "cheapness" and "commonness". China (then still in short supply) was a much more sought-after material' (Bullivant 1986: 150). 'Britain Can Make It' presented an optimistic view of British industry in its effort to stimulate exports and the home market. Many of the goods displayed were hard to find in the shops.

Things slowly got better, despite rationing continuing into the next decade. Clothes came off rationing in 1949 but demand for nylons exceeded supply. When the Mayor of York visited the USA in 1950, the *Yorkshire Post* gave headline coverage to a gift for his daughter: 'Lord Mayor of York brings home nylons' (*Yorkshire Post* 1950). For much of the 1940s and 1950s many British manufacturers continued to produce goods designed in the 1930s (Littlewoods 1986). New plastic designs followed familiar paths, and both the Bush TV12 television of 1949 (still too expensive for most people) and the DAC 90 radio of 1946 had a 1930s-style design. Both sold mainly in 'walnut'-finish phenolic.

As Britain reached the mid-1950s plastics were becoming more and more visible, both at home and in the high street. A 1955 Ekco brochure spoke of:

> The modern kitchen, to which Plastics make a valuable contribution, is playing a great part in easing the tasks of the present day housewife – The range includes jugs, sink bowls and tidies, colanders, hotplates, baths and accessories for the nursery, toilet seats and toilet brush holders, polythene bottles for powders and lotions. All these, and many more, flow from the Ekco factories to add to the comfort and convenience of life in modern homes throughout the world. [Ekco 1955]

On the high street women could buy nylon stockings and underwear. Both were inexpensive, hard wearing and quick to dry, and did not need ironing. Nylon clothes were becoming available for both sexes, with shirts and blouses also being produced in Terylene.

Formica surfaces were beginning to be seen in shops, cafés, and milk and coffee bars. Plastics were helping to change the shape and feel of everyday things. For those who held views like Orwell's, Hoggart's, Priestley's and Waugh's it must have seemed as though the 'Spectre of Americanisation' had arrived (Hebdige 1988: 45–76), and it was going to get far worse. Rock 'n' Roll was just around the corner; the white version of black American Blues and Rhythm 'n' Blues would blast out of juke boxes and record players from millions of LPs and 45s made of PVC.

We have returned to those cultural critics of 1957, but before concluding we must examine people's responses to those new products, which the manufacturers claimed were making everyone's lives easier in the post-war 'dream world'.

Polyethylene, commonly known by its Du Pont trade name 'Polythene', is certainly worthy of far more study. One of the most common plastics, it was promoted as part of the labour-saving arsenal in the housewife's battle against dirt and germs. The *Xylonite Magazine* of March 1955 stated that 'Next to electric light and stainless steel, polythene seems to us the answer to the housewife's prayer' (*Xylonite Magazine* 1955a: 6). The Industrial Revolution in the home is one that is still going on. Recent research (Bereano *et al.* 1985; Myers 1986) suggests that although labour-saving products do save time and effort, housework expands to fill the time allocated to it and contracts when time is set aside to do other things, such as paid work. Increased technology could also lead to increased standards, fuelled by advertisement-induced guilt about the conveniently invisible germs that lurked on your floors and work surfaces, waiting to attack your children and your social standing. In an environment such as this, Polythene products could be marketed very effectively. They had much to commend them: they were light and durable, they would not chip or rust. Like papier mâché before them they were up to the jobs they had to do, and they were also available in a variety of 'gay colours' (Plate 20). Women, who had to do the majority of the housework, found them to be a great improvement on the older materials of zinc, enamel ware and tin plate. Women in Halifax, when recalling what plastic object affected them most, tended to choose Polythene objects: 'a long-handled cleaning brush, I had it for years, it was so light', 'a plastic bucket', 'food containers for the fridge, they were light and had a sealable lid' (Oral testimony 1991).

Lightness and practicality were the things that impressed most – the food container that could be sealed was also praised. For Polythene the timing was perfect. More and more families were beginning to buy 'white goods' such as refrigerators, often available on 'the never-never'. Only 114,700 fridges were sold in 1948, but by 1959 sales had risen to 750,000. Polythene and polystyrene containers did not taint the food, and their lightness and strength allowed them to be stacked in the fridge. The product most associated with this use was Tupperware.

First marketed in 1948 by the American Earl S. Tupper, it arrived in Britain in 1960, and the Tupperware party became one of the social clichés of British suburbia throughout the 1960s and 1970s. Although just out of our period, it is worth discussing because of the reactions to it. The American method of holding selling parties was decried by the British press. The *Daily Mail* described it as 'Soft sell steals into suburbia', and a *Which?* consumer report condemned the new-fangled technique of turning British housewives into saleswomen in their own homes (Clarke 1990b: 65). In reality, women who attended these parties knew very well that the whole technique relied on them supporting their friends, and most of those in the group from Halifax admitted that one of the major reasons for the first purchase was a mixture of friendly support and avoiding the embarrassment or guilt of not buying. But they were impressed by the product; they felt the design was of a superior quality to that of cheaper high street versions, the seal was good, and it lasted. The sales technique may have been gimmicky for Britain, but the product delivered. People appreciated quality, and could also be wary of other, poor-quality plastic products, which often led to the public perception that they were all 'cheap and nasty'.

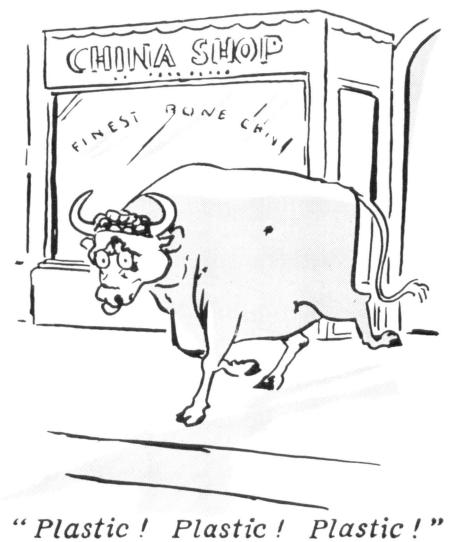

" Plastic ! Plastic ! Plastic ! "

Reproduced by kind permission of the " Evening Standard "

Figure 85   Bull in a china shop. From the *Xylonite Magazine*, 1955.

Percy Reboul, who joined the press office of the Bakelite Company in 1958, recalled a number of reasons why plastics tended to get a bad press. He felt that among the chief culprits were the 'ghastly PVC macs that were sold in millions after the war, which seemed to be such a good idea but which gave way at the seams and did great, great damage to the image of plastics' (Reboul 1991). He felt that this gave rise to an unfair journalistic way of looking at plastics. It also appeared that if the press needed less sensationalism then the public needed a little more education (Figure 85). It was not until 1957 that *Good Housekeeping* produced a feature on 'Home Plastics'. The Good Housekeeping Institute had tested a wide range of plastics and noted that:

> After the war, the market was flooded with somewhat indifferent plastic goods, which left many people with a poor impression of the capabilities of this material. In many cases the wrong type of plastic was used for the wrong articles and often they were badly manufactured. [*Good Housekeeping* 1957: 65]

Percy Reboul felt that the public were learning by experience:

> They didn't really understand the properties of the material [Polythene]. I remember one classic case where a very irate customer had bought a plastic colander which was meant to replace the old metal colander for draining vegetables and things and she had done what she had always done in the days of her enamelled metal colander. She had stuck this over a pan of boiling water and proceeded to chop the cabbage in the colander, at which point the bottom fell out and she was very disgruntled indeed. One got scores of examples where people really abused the material, in spite of warning labelling. There were still a lot of disgruntled customers and I think [this] possibly partly gave rise to the bad image that plastics were to enjoy for a time. It was a question of settling down. [Reboul 1991]

He also recalled a plumber who could not come to terms with the fact that plastic piping required just a push fit – he felt that a good seal could only be produced with a blow torch.

Perhaps the public expected too much of these products. Nevertheless it does seem that, once understood and experienced, their value was appreciated, provided they remained in defined areas. Although their usefulness and practicality moved opinion in a positive direction, cultural pressures moved that opinion in another. As we have seen, the design and cultural establishment did not approve of many plastic products. They felt that at the very least they should reveal themselves as truly plastic and not imitate (Catterall 1990). Paradoxically public taste, both here and in the USA, was going in the opposite direction (Meikle 1990). Pure plastic was fine for the kitchen, but when it came to the drawing room or the back parlour, pure plastic did not fit the bill. Tables should be of wood, tableware should be of earthenware or porcelain, and soft furnishings should be cottons and chintzes. If you had to have a plastic finish then at least let it look like something else. Here we re-enter the difficult areas of class and taste.

Appreciation of pure plastic is often for those of informed tastes. Peter Dormer has plunged into this dark pool and emerged to state that:

> if what you know in your daily world are plastic veneers, mock wood, chintz curtains, industrially printed textiles, and hotel foyer mock baronial, how can you miss or worry about what others call good taste – the natural order of Bauhaus modernism, the decorative grace of Biedermeier, the human rationalism of English Georgian classicism. If you are not aware of these things, you do not miss them, and it is, after all, perfectly possible to be happy with what you have got. [Dormer 1986: 13]

Dormer then went on to state that it is also a case of what you are offered, both materially and culturally. Riches lie in having choice, ignorance gives you no freedom of choice. What Britain had to offer in the way of plastics was simply not as good as in the USA and parts of Europe. The American companies may have produced some conservative products, but they continued to spend on research and development as well as quality control. Post-war Italy also took the material more seriously. Vico Magistretti produced his 'Selene' chair in plastic in 1962. In Germany, Dieter Ram's restrained, sculptural style of domestic appliances for Braun perfectly illustrated the aesthetic potential of plastics.

In Britain, the limited influence of the Modern Movement had yet to realise Anthony Bertram's wish 'to kill by ridicule the absurd "ye olde worlde" cult that has infected English design with dishonesty' (Bertram 1938: 19). Plastics and a cut-price version of modernism were to rise and rise in the 1960s. Thanks to the discredited tower block, modernism is currently out of favour, but plastics go on, and they are still surrounded by debate. Writing in 1986, Daniel Weil asserted that:

Plastic has not yet taken its place in our culture for what it is and really can do; it is still required to pretend to be something it is not. The next stage will be to use the material in its own right, and will require a re-assessment of the design of most familiar objects whose logic derives from out-dated technology and craft or materials of the Industrial Revolution. [Weil 1986: 31]

Weil was not looking at plastics simply in design terms; he wanted society to wake up to the fact that by the 1980s plastics were to be seen no longer as substitute materials but as improved replacements.

Although they do move the debate forward, such arguments have a familiar ring, and indicate the relationship between design, technology and culture. We have come full circle, back to the pioneering efforts of Celluloid. It has been noted that there was no technical reason why Celluloid products could not have been made in bright, shiny colours (Friedel 1990: 29). A few were, but, as we have seen, cultural and economic motives prompted the early manufacturers to imitate. Those motives still operate and inform contemporary perceptions of plastics. Ubiquitous to the point of invisibility, plastics still arouse suspicion when we are asked to think about them. Culturally, the hegemony of aristocratic taste suppresses innovation; economically, the vast production runs that make them affordable can become synonymous with 'cheap' and 'disposable'.

Peter Dormer felt the term 'plastic' was now far too limited, but: 'for the lay-person the word "plastic" conveys a set of values which may be out of date scientifically but which continues to dog the designer and manufacturer' (Dormer 1991: 63). Contemporary responses from people who grew up in the 1950s and 1960s confirm this, although following generations may well hold a more positive view:

'It's not something you're proud of though, is it, plastics? You'd rather forget that we do that, really.'

'We tend to degrade it nowadays, we don't give it the credit it deserves.'

'Rather have wood.' [Oral testimony 1990]

That such attitudes still prevail after more than a hundred years of production reveals more about British culture than about the products themselves. During this century, plastics have expanded enormously and the public has gradually accepted them, becoming aware of both their performance and their status in prescribed domestic and working environments. Writing in 1963, Morris Kaufman stated:

> There are people now, with more enthusiasm than knowledge, who speak of the 'plastics age', impending or already with us. They have in mind a situation in which everything or nearly everything will be made of plastics. A fanciful notion, but excusable perhaps in view of the quite astonishing growth of plastics since the war. [Kaufman 1963: 88]

At this time good-quality products, exemplified by Robin Day's polypropylene chair of 1962, were becoming commonplace. Cheaper plastic goods were coming in via imports from Hong Kong (Turner 1990: 10–15). Technology was advancing and the older iron- and steel-based industries were in decline. If we can accept the crude shorthand of naming periods after the predominant materials of the day, then Britain was moving into the plastics age. This was a technological and economic fact, but culturally many people had difficulty in admitting it.

5 Working with Plastics

Mark Suggitt

Sometimes, for weeks at a time, we did not know where the money
was coming from to pay our next Saturday's wages.

[C.P. Merriam n.d.]

Ten hours a day and five-and-a-half on Saturday.

[Harry Greenstock 1981: 11]

The plastics industry is still a comparatively new area and much of its
history has yet to be written. Earlier work concentrated on its 'great
men', the pioneering inventors and manufacturers who often staked both
reputation and capital to launch new materials. More recent writing has
looked at the design and style of plastic products. With a few notable
exceptions (Greenstock 1981), the lives and experiences of the workforce
have been neglected. The plastics industry is not alone in this; indeed, it
is the case for much of industrial history. Nevertheless, new approaches
to 'everyday history' have developed, especially in the use of oral
testimony. It is now understood that the experience of the shop floor is
an essential component in the history of any industry.

This is certainly the case with plastics. It was a pioneering industry,
taking new chemical processes and attempting to turn laboratory successes
into commercially viable production runs, an operation that could be
fraught with physical and financial danger. The first manufacturing places
were little more than workshops, but by the 1930s many had grown into
large, well-organised factories which continued to operate into the 1950s.
To serve as an illustration of this change, I intend to take a brief look at the
early years of the British Xylonite Company (BXL) (Figure 56). BXL is of
interest as it is the direct descendant of the Parkesine Company, which
pioneered the production of Celluloid in the UK.

The history of the company has been published (Merriam 1976) and
there is also an excellent unpublished thesis on the subject (Ashlee 1982).
Nevertheless, a brief outline is required in order to provide a context for
this examination of the working lives of the company's workforce.

The British Xylonite Company's roots lay with the inventor of
Celluloid, Alexander Parkes (who called his invention Parkesine) (Figure

15). He launched the Parkesine Company in 1866, basing it at Wallis Road in Hackney Wick. The venture was short-lived and the company closed in 1868. A fresh start was made with the setting up of the Xylonite Company, an undertaking which involved Daniel Spill, formerly Parkes's works manager. This was also unsuccessful and was wound up in 1874. Undeterred, Spill set up the Ivoride Company in Homerton, East London, in 1875.

In 1876 Spill leased part of the premises to an American, Levi Parsons Merriam, who intended to make articles such as imitation coral jewellery from the Celluloid produced next door (under the trade name 'Xylonite'). Merriam had a friend who was working for the Hyatt Brothers, the American Celluloid pioneers, who were attempting to negotiate setting up production in Britain. They had progressed further than Parkes, had developed better production techniques, and enjoyed higher sales as a result. Merriam became aware of Spill's works and was tempted to go into the production of the imitation coral jewellery that had sold well in America.

The two separate companies grew closer and closer, eventually sharing the same backers. Neither was prospering, Spill was not a good businessman and the fashion for coral jewellery was declining. In 1877 they were both refloated as the British Xylonite Company and the Homerton Manufacturing Company, and finally, in 1879, it was decided to amalgamate them as the British Xylonite Company. It became one of the major plastics companies in Britain, producing a huge range of products in a variety of materials. The company grew slowly, the turning point coming when it began to produce Celluloid collars in 1885. Profits began to rise and the company was able to open a new works on a greenfield site at Brantham, Suffolk, in 1887. This was a production centre for Celluloid; a new fabrication centre was established at Hale End, London, in 1897. As profitability increased, the numbers of employees grew. From a tiny workforce in 1877, the company employed over 2000 people at the outbreak of the First World War. It was already set to make a significant contribution to one of the key industries of the twentieth century.

Now we must look at the experiences of some of those who contributed to it. The workforce of the Parkesine Company was very small, comprising twelve men and some boys. Daniel Spill and Company employed between twenty and thirty. When BXL began in 1877 it employed 28 men who had previously worked for Spill, including a foreman and two assist-ants, two engineers, a carpenter, a blacksmith, a stoker, three acid room workers, four 'roller men', two hydraulic press men, a polisher, a watchman and a gate boy (Suffolk Record Office no. 1).

The job titles give some indication of the processes carried out in the factory. Celluloid was produced by mixing camphor and nitro-cellulose, along with colouring pigments. The resulting material could then be sawn or drilled into shape, shaped in hot moulds, rolled into sheets or extruded into rods and then cut up and worked. Much of the finishing was done by hand. The work was a potentially dangerous process involving the use of highly flammable and acidic materials. The bulk of this was carried out in a small, cramped factory lit by open gas jets. The majority of the workforce were people who lived locally in Hackney.

As the company became more profitable, more workers were taken on. By 1882, 102 people were employed, including women in the production process. Mrs Polly Lane, interviewed for the *Xylonite Magazine*, recalled how she started in 1879:

> I was fifteen, living in Homerton and a friend of mine said I could get a job with the Xylonite factory, and to mention her name. Mr Charlie Merriam looked at me and said 'Yes, you can start: I'll give you 1¾ d an hour.' I was on comb cutting. When I first began I was working one machine, and cut twelve dozen combs a day, and they thought that was good. [Suffolk Record Office no. 2: 948]

Women continued to be employed, and they formed the majority of the workforce at Hale End. Like many other companies of the day, it stipulated that only single women could work. This rule was relaxed during the First World War but reintroduced in 1918 (Merriam 1976: 113) (Figures 86 and 87).

H. M. Greenstock, whose children later worked in the industry, was also a local man. He joined the company in 1878 and:

> went to live at 22 Sedgwick Street, Homerton, the short back garden of which adjoined Macintosh Lane, right opposite to which were the entrance gates to the factory. His morning constitutional to get to work was therefore not more than twenty paces from the back kitchen. [Greenstock 1981: 5]

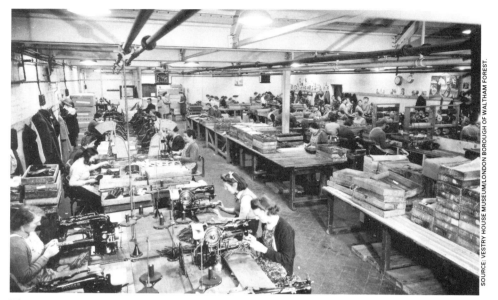

SOURCE: VESTRY HOUSE MUSEUM/LONDON BOROUGH OF WALTHAM FOREST.

Figure 86   Women in the eye shield workshop, Halex factory, *c.*1940.

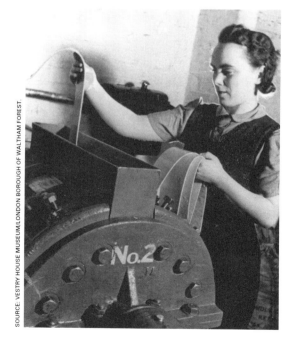

SOURCE: VESTRY HOUSE MUSEUM/LONDON BOROUGH OF WALTHAM FOREST.

Figure 87   Cutting up plastic strip at Brantham works, Suffolk, December 1944.

This was just as well, for the working hours for all employees were long, even by the standards of the day. It was a small operation with no trade union representation. The wage book of the Homerton factory shows that 60-hour weeks were common. The foreman and the watchman were paid weekly, the rest by the hour. The engineers received 8d per hour, the blacksmith 7d, the carpenter 6d and the production workers an average of 4d per hour. As we have seen, women production workers received considerably less. In the early days of the company the men had to work up to 60 hours to take home slightly more than £1 a week. Women and boys earned around 10s. There was no higher rate paid for overtime and no holiday pay (this was introduced in 1917). A system of fines to deduct pay for lateness, etc. was in operation from the beginning, however. A discretionary sickness fund was established in 1881. In the early days there was often a danger that the workforce would receive no pay at all, as Charles P. Merriam (the son of L.P. Merriam) recalled in the first of the quotations at the start of this chapter. Often, he or the foreman were sent out on desperate missions to collect outstanding debts in order to pay the workforce.

Despite the long hours and low pay, there was a sense of partnership between the workers and the management, which partly explains why, when the company moved to Brantham in Suffolk, a large number of the East End workforce moved with it. The move to Brantham did not lead to a reduction in the hours worked; often, being busy meant even longer hours. Harry Greenstock began work there at the age of 14 and recalled the breakdown of a working day in 1895:

> The hours were 7am to 8.30am, Breakfast 8.30am to 9am. Then 9am to 1pm. Dinner time 1pm to 2pm. Then 2pm to 6.30pm. Ten hours a day and five and a half on Saturday, making a total of fifty five and a half hours a week, for which I was paid one penny an hour. At the end of the week I received 4s 8d, the odd half penny being thrown in. [Greenstock 1981: 11]

Excessive hours of up to 78 a week continued to be worked when the pressure was on. The company relied on patriarchalism and the loyalty of the workers. Nevertheless, complaints did arise. Thirty-four workers signed a petition to Mr Merriam in September of 1894, requesting a reduction in the hours worked: 'We would respectfully call his attention to the fact that the bodily and mental strains of continuous labour from 7 to 6 is very wearing' (Suffolk Record Office no. 2). The management did not grant this request to reduce the 10-hour day, and, as Harry Greenstock's testimony suggests, the 55½-hour week was seen as a baseline. The wages books back this up, showing that 14-hour days were still worked (Suffolk Record Office no. 2). Hours did eventually reduce, however. In 1918 Brantham worked a 50-hour week, and the hours at Hale End were reduced to eight a day and five on Saturday (Hackney Archives no. 4).

In addition to the strain of long hours was the nature of the work itself. The production of Celluloid was dangerous, as the risk of fire and explosion was always present, from both the materials used in production and the combustible nature of the finished product (Figure 88). Such risks could become grim realities. The Homerton factory was the oldest and the most unsuitable. Harry Greenstock remembered the fire there in June 1885:

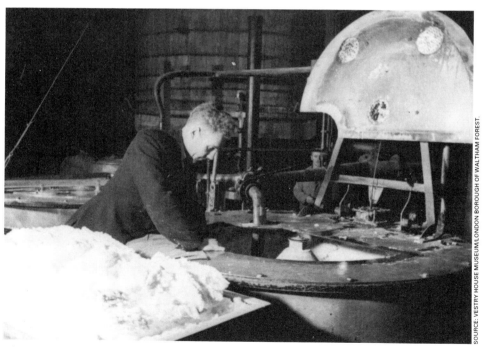

SOURCE: VESTRY HOUSE MUSEUM/LONDON BOROUGH OF WALTHAM FOREST.

Figure 88   Partly-dried nitrocellulose being removed from the centrifugal machine at Brantham works, Suffolk, December 1944.

in bed with measles, looking out at the bedroom window and seeing a huge sheet of flame. That was the acid shop on fire. The bedroom I was in was not more than 50/60 yards from it. We were wrapped in blankets and taken to the top of Sedgwick Street for safety. [Greenstock 1981: 5]

This fire caused so much damage that production stopped for three weeks. It spurred the company on to find new premises. Meanwhile, there were further fires at Homerton in 1893 and 1894, one caused by the ignition of spirit vapour by the naked gas lights and the other by sparks arising from the sawing of Celluloid sheets. A woman was killed in the fire of 1894. Another small fire in 1895 finally convinced the company to move to Hale End. The Homerton works closed in 1900.

Fire and explosion were still hazards for the workforce after the move from the East End. The Brantham works suffered from fires, the most serious being in 1905, and Hale End also experienced a fire in 1906. Safety precautions had to be observed rigorously. Harry Greenstock remembered that: 'Smoking of course was a crime. It was instant dismissal for anyone found with a pipe in his possession, or a match. Periodical searches were made and all coats gone through. Even the linings were searched' (Greenstock 1981: 12). Others remembered differently. Oliver Tarbard, manager of the Nitration Department, recalled unloading acid at Brantham in the 1920s:

This was a full time job for one man. The job was accident free for many years until one day the operator, a small bearded man, had trouble with the discharge of a drum of sulphuric acid. Smoking was allowed in those days, both in and around the acid shop. Leaning down over the drum with a lighted cigarette in his mouth he peered into the bung hole to see what was wrong – a flash – a bang and Turkey Oram (the foreman) had lost half his beard, one eyebrow and the hair from one side of his head. Fortunately he was not hurt but it took him a long time to live it down. [Suffolk Record Office no. 2]

Many of the men wore beards, and those of the men in the acid shop turned yellow from the fumes (Greenstock 1981: 8). It was an unhealthy place; most of the acid workers lost their teeth as a result of the poisonous atmosphere. For protection they wore scarlet army surplus tunics, thigh-high leggings and clogs.

Hale End was built on a large site and laid out on the lines of an explosives plant, with buildings strategically placed apart (Hackney Archives no. 7: 109). Harry Greenstock's son, Ron, worked at Hale End in the 1920s and 1930s. Things had improved by then:

> By the nature of the product, each building had to be isolated and in some cases a fire wall built between them, but the working conditions were good and possibly we had something there that the other factories wouldn't have had in those days and that was a safety inspector. His job was to go around and make absolutely sure that things were right. [Oral testimony 1988]

Other injuries could occur from fingers being caught in unguarded machinery such as rollers, or from the cements used to construct Celluloid boxes and casings. By the 1930s wire guards were installed to cover dangerous moving parts. All women employees had to wear caps to protect their hair, and those working with cements had to wear rubber aprons. Such protection was necessary on the production line. The workers were on piece work. The company made a wide variety of boxes, from table sets to casings for dry batteries. These were assembled by hand from sheets of Celluloid cemented with a mixture of one third amyl nitrate, one third acetone and one third methylated spirit. To ensure that piece work did not reduce quality, all 'wasters' had to be paid for in relation to the value of the scrap material. Waste material was recycled.

As the company grew, the size of the plant increased, as did the variety of plastics produced. Ron Greenstock recalled that Hale End had 50 presses in operation. These were a combination of 35-, 70- and 200-ton presses, moulding Celluloid, phenolics and ureas. The moulding workshop operated a two-shift system, 6 a.m. to 2 p.m. and 2 p.m. to 10 p.m. Ron Greenstock began work in the mould workshop in the 1920s. He felt that moulding was a matter of common sense:

> You knew damn well you didn't just bring the press down with a wallop, you brought it down gently and you gradually squeezed the material down to compression level, and then of course you would watch out for your setting times. [Oral testimony 1988]

The company also employed its own designers, engineers, and office and sales staff. Ron Greenstock remembered the chief designer at Hale End,

George Pierson, a Frenchman who worked there from the late 1920s until 1938. He designed the art-deco-inspired 'Halex' products, such as brushes, mirrors, combs and dressing-table sets. He was also responsible for the 'Mayfair', 'Pearlex' and 'Deauville' ranges. The designs were sent through to be approved by the sales director. If they passed the test, the design then went to the engineers, who produced the moulds. The engineering department was split between the mechanical engineers, who were responsible for all the moulds and mould-making machinery, and the works engineers, who kept the production and service plant in order.

Once made, the products had to be sold. In May 1892 a shop was opened at 117 Oxford Street, London. It only sold Xylonite products and was a short-lived venture, closing in June 1894 (Hackney Archives no. 5). Sales were not good, and it competed with local shops to which the company also wished to sell. After this the company relied on taking stands at trade fairs and on travelling representatives to promote the range personally. Both Harry and Ron Greenstock moved into sales. They set up in hotels, taking two rooms – one for sleeping, the other for a stockroom. A week before the visit the representative would send a postcard to all his present and prospective customers. Ron Greenstock described the content of the card sent out by his father before visiting the Royal Hotel, Cardiff in 1906:

> Our representative, Mr H. G. Greenstock will be showing the latest range of Xylonite products at his stockroom in the Royal Hotel, Cardiff from Monday to Friday (date/time). He will be pleased to welcome you during this time. [Greenstock 1981: 28]

The representatives were backed up by regional sales offices and warehouses in Sheffield, Birmingham and Manchester. Sheffield was the earliest, opening in 1884 to supply the cutlery trade with knife handles (Ashlee 1982: 65). Distribution from the factories was by rail.

The example of the British Xylonite Company gives an insight into the early days of the industry. Working with plastics did not offer an easy life. As we have seen, the conditions were often bad and the hours were very long. Despite this, the workforce remained largely un-unionised and loyal, according to the available documentary and oral evidence. Harry Greenstock never heard of discontent at Brantham: 'None that I ever heard. The job had to be done and that was that. You see, we all felt ourselves to be part of a "family"' (Greenstock 1981: 13). Edith Thomason, who started work at Hale End in 1903, said: 'There was little feeling of them and us but more a feeling of teamwork' (Ashlee 1982: 97). This is partly due to the fact that the company started in the poor East End, which had a pattern of irregular work. BXL offered stable work, even if it was poorly paid. The move to out-of-town sites created company 'villages' where there were few other opportunities, so it is no wonder that generations of families worked for the company. Nevertheless, the management must take much of the credit for ensuring that the workforce remained happy. It operated a brand of open patriarchalism which managed to keep one step ahead of the demands that would have been made by a trade union. In some cases it went beyond those expectations. Trade unions were not forbidden, but most workers felt that their conditions did not warrant one. Only the skilled engineers became unionised. During his time as managing director (1887–1927), C.P. Merriam maintained a policy that any employee could come and talk to him on any matter.

Despite the company's shaky financial beginnings it did not delay in providing facilities for the workforce. A company savings bank was established in 1882, in addition to the existing sick fund. Sports fields, allotments and club houses were provided from 1887. The company also built houses for those who moved to Brantham. It had little option in such a rural setting, and life proved to be hard for the early settlers – initially the cottages had no gas, sanitation or water supply. The minutes of the directors' meetings give numerous examples of the management's concern for the workforce. Jobs were kept open for men serving in the armed forces during the Boer War and the First World War, and payments were made to families of workers when problems arose. A sum of £25 a year was voted 'for the alleviation of genuine and unexpected misfortune amongst the company's workpeople' in 1895 (Hackney Archives no. 6). This practice continued; the sum was paid at the discretion of the managing director.

The company also organised special events for the workforce. Annual staff dinners were held from 1891, along with Christmas parties for children. A big party was held when the new factory opened at Hale End in 1897, with a special train laid on so that the Brantham workers could attend. When the company celebrated its silver jubilee, a 'Grand Sports Contest' was held between the two factories. Sports were encouraged:

Hale End had a tennis club, and teams for football, cricket and bowls. Works dances also took place once a month (Oral testimony 1988).

Overall, the documentary and oral evidence suggests that the British Xylonite Company was a well-meaning, patriarchal employer. Its management must have realised that much was expected of its workforce, who, as we have seen, had to work in unpleasant and potentially dangerous conditions. Future research into other plastics companies will reveal whether it was exceptional.

6 Other Technologies and Plastics

Morris Kaufman

The study of plastics touches on various aspects of the human condition. It is worth considering a number of other technologies which came on the scene as plastics and the plastics industry were being born and developing, namely automobiles, wireless telegraphy, the gas and electricity industries, and film. A number of these have used plastics materials from the earliest days, and plastics have been used increasingly as these technologies have developed into the late twentieth century.

By the end of the first decade of the twentieth century, Leo Baekeland had established a firm base for the manufacture and application of phenol-formaldehyde resins. He set out to exploit his discoveries in the USA and in other countries such as Germany and the UK. But the creation of a sound technical product and a process for making it is not the only requirement for its successful exploitation. Many examples from the history of technology could be cited to show that technical considerations are not necessarily critical in determining the fate of a good idea. An interesting illustration could be drawn from the history of related rubber technology.

The invention of the pneumatic tyre in 1888 (BP 10,607, 23 July 1888) is generally ascribed to J.B. Dunlop (Dunlop 1924). Today the blessings of millions of travellers are (or should be) bestowed on that pioneer for their relative comfort in the course of their road and air travel. But in fact, unbeknown to him as it turns out, Dunlop was anticipated by R. W. Thomson in his idea of the pneumatic tyre. In 1845 Mr Thomson patented the concept and a process for making it (BP 10,990, enrolled 10 June 1846). Such a tyre was even fixed to a brougham in 1846 with great success, as reported in the contemporary *Mechanics Magazine* (1849). But the idea of the pneumatic tyre did not catch on. Solid tyres continued to rule the day (DuCros 1938).

The causes of this failure have not been carefully investigated. It may have been attributable in part to the fact that traffic at that time was very slow moving and this obscured the advantages of the inflated tyre. It may have been because rubber was scarce at the time and consequently rather

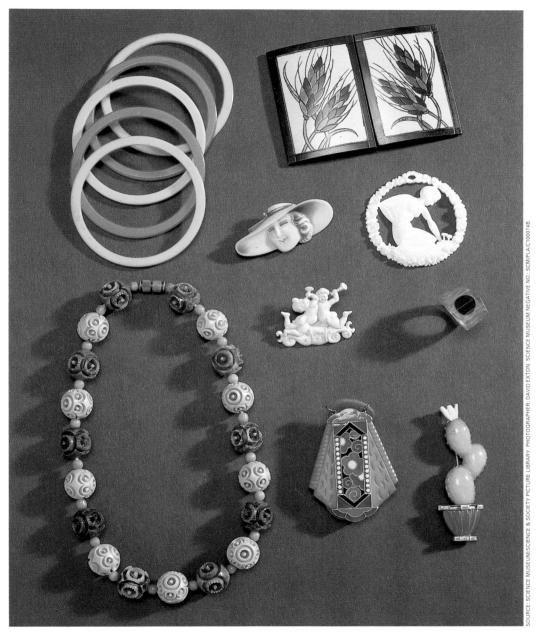

Plate 1   Jewellery from the Jesse Collection, including casein bangles (cat. no. 621), buckle (cat. no. 623), Chinese-style necklace (cat. no. 607), brooch (cat. no. 622) and pendants (cat. nos. 606, 610), in addition to an art deco cast phenolic ring (cat. no. 838), a Digby Morton brooch (cat. no. 837), and a cellulose nitrate brooch (cat. no. 512), c.1910–50.

Top to bottom, left to right: first row: cat. nos. 621, 623; second row: cat. nos. 622, 610; third row: cat. nos. 607, 512, 838; fourth row: cat. nos. 606, 837.

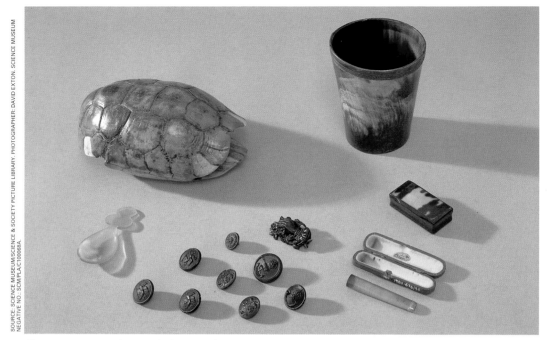

Plate 2 Group of natural plastics, showing a tortoiseshell (cat. no. 13), horn cup (cat. no. 7), spoon (cat. no. 3), brooch (cat. no. 12) and snuff box (cat. no. 2), amber cigarette holder (cat. no. 1) and eight pressed horn buttons (cat. nos. 4–6, 8–11).

Top to bottom, left to right: first row: cat. nos. 13, 7; second row: cat. nos. 3, 11, 12, 2; third row: cat. nos. 10, 4; fourth row: cat. no. 6 pt. 6; fifth row: cat. nos. 8, 9, 6 pt. 5.

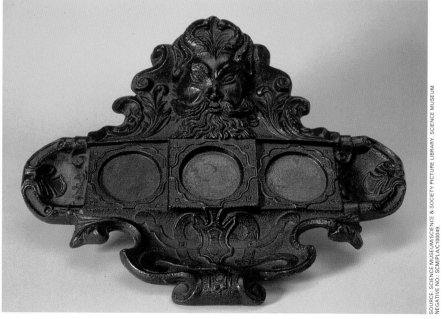

Plate 3 Gutta percha inkstand, *c.*1851; with head of Neptune. Made to commemorate the laying of the first transatlantic cable (cat. no. 24).

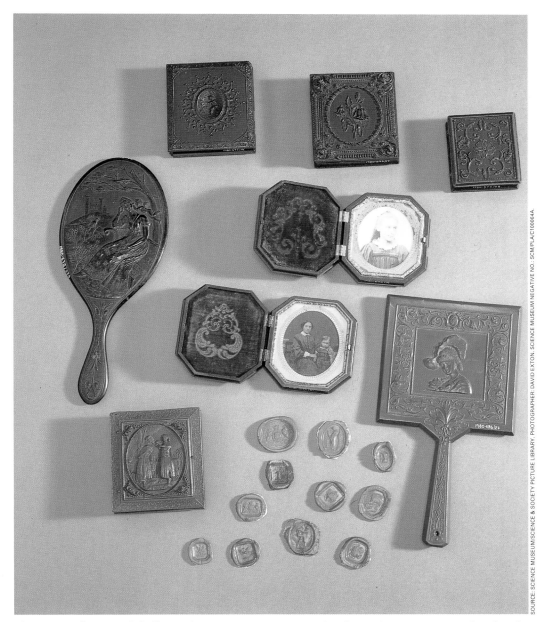

Plate 4   Collection of shellac Union Cases (cat. nos. 40–45), mirrors (cat. nos. 117–118) and seals (cat. nos. 48–49, 51, 54, 58, 61, 71, 81, 86, 110–111), *c.*1860–80.

Top to bottom, left to right: first row: cat. nos. 41, 40, 45; second row: cat. nos. 118, 42; third row: cat. nos. 44, 117; fourth row: cat. nos. 43, 51, 49, 61; fifth row: cat. nos. 71, 54, 48; sixth row: cat. nos. 58, 86, 111; seventh row: cat. nos. 81, 110.

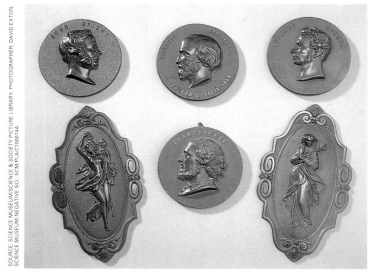

Plate 5 Group of Bois Durci objects, including two furniture plaques (cat. nos. 126 and 125) and four wall plaques representing famous men: John Bright (cat. no. 128), Giuseppe Garibaldi (cat. no. 124), Richard Cobden (cat. no. 129) and William Shakespeare (cat. no. 127), c.1850–70.

Top to bottom, left to right: first row: cat. nos. 128, 124, 129; second row: cat. nos. 126, 127, 125.

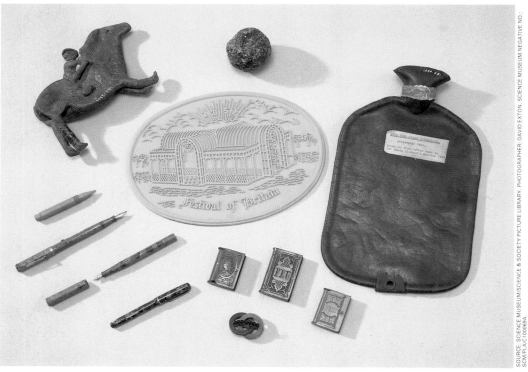

Plate 6 Group of rubber objects, both natural and vulcanised, dark and coloured, c.1600–1951. Group includes a Brazilian rubber toy (cat. no. 139) and a sixteenth-century Peruvian rubber ball (cat. no. 131), four Vulcanite pens (cat. nos. 213, 214, 211, 221), a pink Festival of Britain 1951 mat (cat. no. 142), a hot-water bottle (cat. no. 136), three Vesta Vulcanite rubber match boxes (cat. nos. 216, 215, 220), and a Vulcanite brooch (cat. no. 229).

Top to bottom, left to right: first row: cat. nos. 139, 131; second row: cat. nos. 213, 142, 136; third row: cat. no. 214; fourth row: cat. no. 211; fifth row: cat. nos. 221, 216, 215; sixth row: cat. nos. 229, 220.

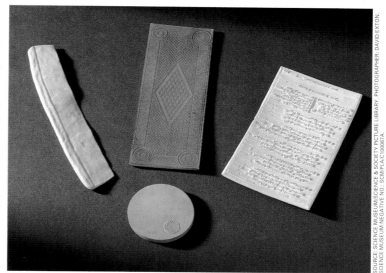

Plate 7 Parkesine (cellulose nitrate) objects made by Alexander Parkes, *c.*1862. Objects include a comb blank (cat. no. 240), a printing plate (cat. no. 246), a letter press mould for the poem 'The Morning Dream' (cat. no. 270), and a disc stamped with the circular trade mark of the Parkesine Company Limited (cat. no. 245).

Top to bottom, left to right: first row: cat. nos. 240, 246, 270; second row: cat. no. 245.

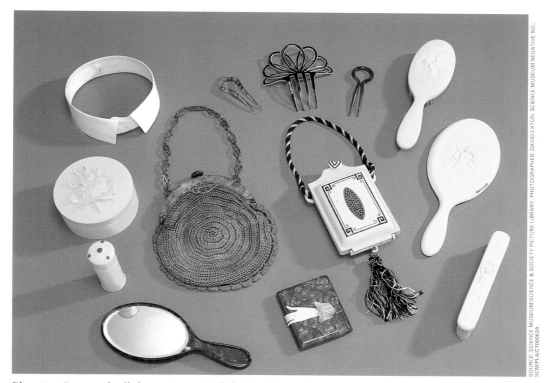

Plate 8 Group of cellulose nitrate (Celluloid) objects, showing combs (cat. nos. 425, 422, 380) and one of the collars (cat. no. 412) which made this material so commercially successful. Also handbags (cat. nos. 421, 366), imitation ivory cosmetic containers (cat. nos. 361, 387), a clothes brush (cat. no. 389) and matching mirror (cat. no. 391), and a classic hand-clasp-fastening cigarette box (cat. no. 341).

Top to bottom, left to right: first row: cat. nos. 412, 425, 422, 380, 390; second row: cat. nos. 361, 421, 366, 391; third row: cat. no. 387; fourth row: cat. nos. 509, 341, 389.

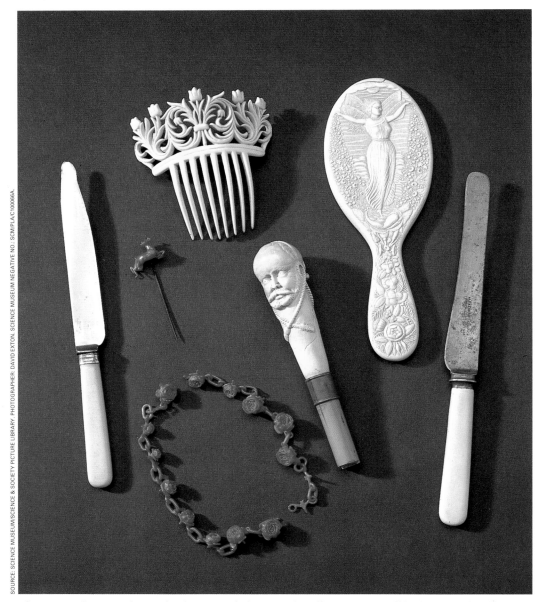

Plate 9 Xylonite and Ivoride objects made by Daniel Spill company. Spill had managed to buy out Parkes's patents by *c*.1873. Objects include Spill's own death's-head walking stick (cat. no. 322), an elaborate comb (cat. no. 321) and mirror (cat. no. 320), and knives (cat. nos. 323–324), all made of Ivoride, also an imitation coral (Xylonite) necklace (cat. no. 326) and cravat pin (cat. no. 325).

Top to bottom, left to right: first row: cat. nos. 321, 320; second row: cat. nos. 323, 325, 322, 324; third row: cat. no. 326.

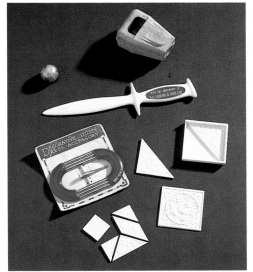

Plate 10 Group of cellulose acetate objects, a material developed to overcome the flammability problems of cellulose nitrate (Celluloid) *c.*1928–1948. Items include a 'Muguet' scent bottle (cat. no. 537), a toy film viewer (cat. no. 535), a paper-knife (cat. no. 538), a Second World War Utility buckle (cat. no. 534) and an elaborate puzzle (cat. no. 536).

Top to bottom, left to right: first row: cat. nos. 537, 535; second row: cat. no. 538; third row: cat. nos. 534, 536; fourth row: cat. no. 536.

Plate 11 Casein button books with the trade names 'Erinoid' (cat. nos. 641 and 642) and 'Lactoid' (cat. no. 660), mid-twentieth century. Casein is a plastic based on milk and was used largely for buttons but also for decorative rods, laminates and utensils such as napkin rings.

Top to bottom, left to right: first row: cat. no. 641 pt. 2; second row: cat. no. 641 pt. 3; third row: cat. no. 642 pt. 1; fourth row: cat. nos. 660, 641 pt. 1.

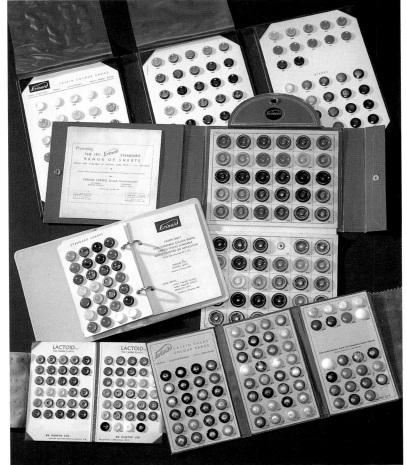

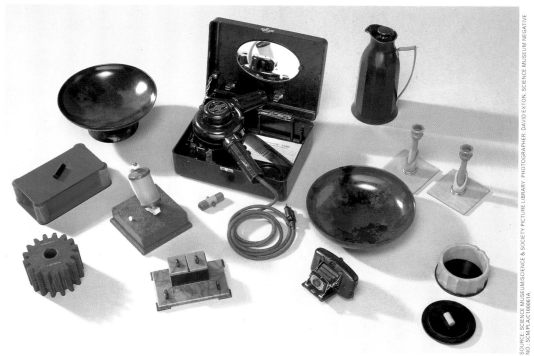

Plate 12 A group of phenolic (dark) and cast phenolic (brightly coloured) objects, showing the variety of objects that could be made, ranging from domestic items such as a hair-dryer (cat. no. 784), classic thermos flask (cat. no. 715), mottled bowls (cat. nos. 747, 746) and a cast phenolic container (cat. no. 793), candlesticks (cat. no. 787), cigarette box (cat. no. 698) and inkwell (cat. no. 833) to an electrical switch (cat. no. 826) and lamp (cat. no. 723), Coronet 'Vogue' camera (cat. no. 781) and TUFNOL gear wheel (cat. no. 682), c.1910–59.

Top to bottom, left to right: first row: cat. nos. 747, 784, 715; second row: cat. nos. 698, 826, 746, 787; third row: cat. nos. 723, 781; fourth row: cat. nos. 682, 833, 793.

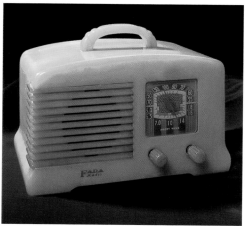

Plate 13 Fada radio with outer casing made of catalin (cast phenolic), USA, 1940s, (cat. no. 835).

Plate 14 (opposite) A range of domestic ware including a Bandalasta bowl (cat. no. 857) and sugar caster (cat. no. 856) (made of thiourea-urea-formaldehyde), and urea-formaldehyde objects including an art deco clock (cat. no. 908), a 'Kelvinator' jug (cat. no. 887), a thermos flask (cat. no. 913), cups and saucers (cat. no. 885), beakers (cat. no. 911), 'Quickmix' blender (cat. no. 870), condiment set (cat. no. 906), napkin ring (cat. no. 920), globular ashtray (cat. no. 873), art deco cigarette box (cat. no. 895) and table dustpan and brush (cat. no. 881), showing the domestic applications of this temperature-resistant material, 1920s–50s.

Top to bottom, left to right: first row: cat. nos. 887, 913, 857, 870, 895; second row: cat. nos. 911, 3 pts, 908, 885 6 pts; third row: cat. nos. 873, 856, 906, 920, 881.

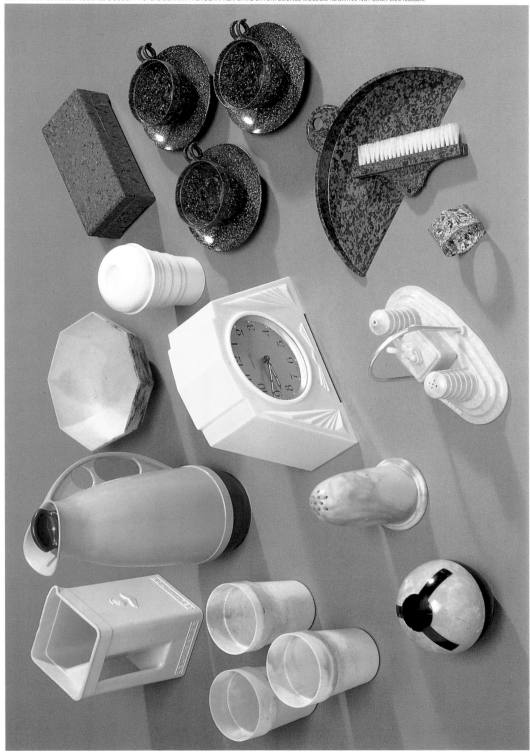

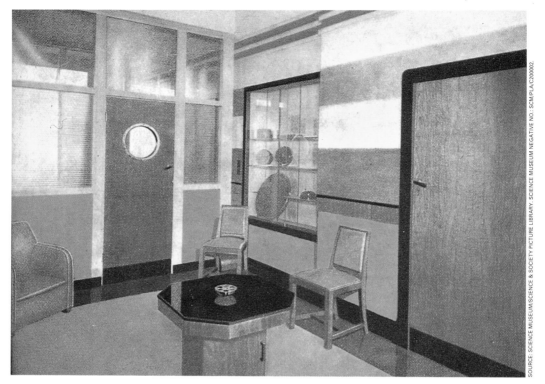

Plate 15   Warerite doors and laminated office surfaces from the Bakelite Limited Factory, Tyseley, 1936.

Plate 16   Polyethylene objects showing samples of the first pound (cat. no. 964) and first ton of polyethylene (cat. no. 963), dated to 1936 and 1938 respectively, and a third sample dated to 22 December 1938 (cat. no. 938). Used during the Second World War for military purposes such as submarine telegraph cable

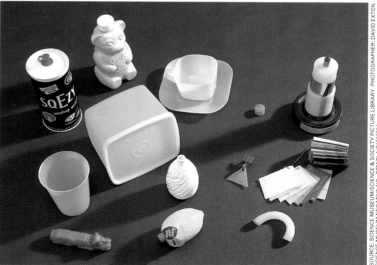

(cat. no. 940), polyethylene found a number of uses after the war, notably for blow-moulded bottles such as the Vinolia teddy bear (cat. no. 961), 'Jif' lemon (cat. no. 957) and 'Chocolate Whirl' (cat. no. 958) as well as the first 'Sqezy' bottle (cat. no. 960). Polyethylene was also used after the war to make domestic ware such as washing-up bowls, beakers (cat. no. 952), torches (dog shaped!) (cat. no. 953), picnic ware (cat. no. 950) and classic Tupperware (cat. no. 955).

Top to bottom, left to right: first row: cat. nos. 960, 961, 950; second row: cat. nos. 952, 955 pt. 1, 964, 940; third row: cat. nos. 958, 963, 945 pt.1; fourth row: cat. nos. 953, 957, 938.

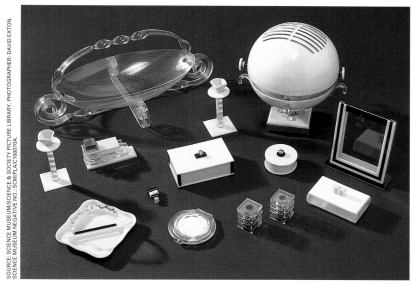

Plate 17 Acrylics came into wide use after the Second World War and led to some extravagant flights of fancy, such as the Champion 'Venus' globe radio (cat. no. 980), inspired by dreams of space-flight, and the curlicue fruit basket of the late 1940s (cat. no. 982). The realms of 'taste' are stretched with a pink and green table set with its candy-striped candlesticks (cat. nos. 989 and 991) and box (cat. no. 993), the green bon-bon tray with twisted clear acrylic handle (cat. no. 1000) and the pink table lighter (cat. no. 997). Other items include a powder compact (cat. no. 984), condiment set (cat. no. 981), dress clip (cat. no. 979), matching cigarette (cat. no. 975) and cosmetic (cat. no. 973) boxes, and picture frame (cat. no. 988).

Top to bottom, left to right: first row: cat. nos. 982, 991, 980; second row: cat. nos. 989, 997, 979, 975, 973, 988; third row: cat. nos. 1000, 984, 981 2 pts, 993.

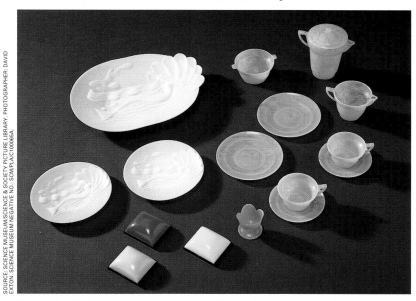

Plate 18 Polystyrene and urea-formaldehyde were practical materials used for a variety of domestic ware ranging from polystyrene samples (cat. no. 1038/1/2/5) and tea sets (cat. nos. 1024, 1026, 1028, 1030, 1032, 1034–1037), via egg cups (cat. no. 1022) to the urea-formaldehyde mermaid dishes shown here (cat. nos. 890, 889 2 pts), *c*.1950.

Top to bottom, left to right: first row: cat. nos. 890, 1036, 1037; second row: cat. nos. 1034, 1035; third row: cat. nos. 889 2 pts, 1032, 1024, 1030; fourth row: cat. nos. 1038/1, 1022, 1028, 1026; fifth row: cat. nos. 1038/2, 1038/5.

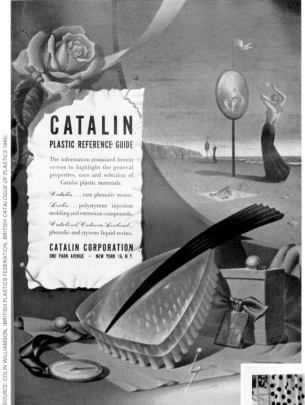

SOURCE: COLIN WILLIAMSON, (BRITISH PLASTICS FEDERATION, *BRITISH CATALOGUE OF PLASTICS* 1945).

Plate 19   Catalin plastics reference guide, 1945.

Cooking's more fun in a gay kitchen

See how 'Alkathene' Houseware brightens things up !

BRIGHT COLOURS make a lot of difference to your home, to your mood, and to *you!* Gay, lovely kitchen things made from 'Alkathene' make cooking more attractive, less like hard work. 'Alkathene' is long-lasting, hygienic, virtually unbreakable. It will not chip or dent or scratch. It can be washed clean in a jiffy with soap and water. It is as light as a feather. 'Alkathene' household goods come in a wide range of cheerful colours, made by many manufacturers. Whichever brand you choose, look for the label that says Made From 'Alkathene'.

LOOK FOR THIS LABEL

MADE FROM 'ALKATHENE'

Articles bearing this label are made from 'Alkathene', the sign of the highest quality.

It's light! It's bright!
IT'S MADE FROM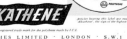

* 'Alkathene' is the registered trade mark for the polythene made by I.C.I.

IMPERIAL CHEMICAL INDUSTRIES LIMITED · LONDON · S.W.1

GH—44   171

SOURCE: *GOOD HOUSEKEEPING MAGAZINE* (NATIONAL MAGAZINE COMPANY), SEPTEMBER 1956, 171. SCIENCE MUSEUM NEGATIVE NO.: SCM/PLA/C200023A.

Plate 20   'See how Alkathene houseware brightens things up', 1956. Alkathene was an ICI trade name for polyethylene.

expensive. The quality of rubber might not have been up to the demands of the new product; it was, after all, just four years after the discovery of vulcanisation.

Whatever the reason(s), the lack of interest in pneumatic tyres in 1845 suggests that the idea came before the conditions for it were ripe. Forty years later Dunlop's proposal, so much more in tune with the then developing world, was taken up, improved and adapted, so that it is very difficult today to conceive of life without inflatable tyres.

How then was the world moving in the early part of the twentieth century when Baekeland stood ready to satisfy some of its emergent needs? Very big changes were already under way in the basic pattern of life, at least in the advanced industrialised countries. As well as the technological transformation that was heralding a new way of life, the shattering impact of the First World War and the subsequent economic breakdown at the end of the 1920s and in the 1930s ensured the complete rupture of the old mould and an end to the assumptions and moves that shaped the Victorian era.

At the turn of the century a number of the phenomena which now dominate our way of life were in gestation or had actually been born. The internal combustion engine, as part of the revolution in transport, made its debut in Germany in 1886 with the horseless carriage as designed by Daimler and Benz. In 1896 Marconi took out the first patent for wireless telegraphy (BP 12,039, 1896) and his first transatlantic signals were received on the far side of the Atlantic on Thursday 12 December 1901 (Jolly 1972; Baker 1970).

Edison in the USA and Swan in the UK produced an electric lamp (National Electrical Manufacturers Association 1946) at the beginning of the 1880s. The consequent demand for electric light unleashed the potential locked in the dynamo, when the first steam-powered generating Edison station giving a supply to the public formally opened at Holborn Viaduct in London on 12 April 1882, although it had already been running by 12 January of the same year. Edison built a similar station at Pearl Street, New York, which opened on 4 September 1882 (Bowers 1982). Berlin soon followed with a station in 1886. The era of mains electricity had arrived and with it all the possibilities of electrically-powered industrial and domestic machines.

Organic chemistry, which had flowered in the nineteenth century, was beginning to influence everyday life at the beginning of the twentieth. It was making a particular impact in the fields of dye stuffs, pharmaceuticals, semi-synthetic textiles such as rayon, and, most importantly for the future plastics industry, petroleum. Its first and major contribution was as the fuel for the new internal combustion engine, but a little later it began to be used as a source of chemicals. Isopropyl alcohol from propylene, in turn derived from oil, in 1920 is generally regarded as the first petrochemical.

These were some aspects of profound changes in society, which demanded, among other things, materials with new properties or combinations of properties for their fulfilment. Known substances no longer met these new requirements.

In some respects the first part of the twentieth century resembled its closing years. The major basic industries of the UK, such as steel, coal and shipbuilding, were in a state of acute crisis. There was high unemployment, and standards of living were desperately low for the unemployed and low-income groups but were simultaneously climbing for many other people. Most significantly, new industries were appearing and with them new patterns of living as the new technologies established themselves.

Just consider the insistent and inexorably probing demands of the automobile. In 1896 British law made its first concession by repealing the statute which limited horseless carriages to 4 m.p.h. on the open road and 2 m.p.h. in built-up areas. It went further – it dispensed with the person walking in front of the vehicle giving warning of its approach. But this did not unleash an uncontrollable rush to the new form of transport. Interestingly, the British Army in France felt no need, twenty years later at the height of the war, to establish petrol-base depots, and even then all petrol went forward in two-gallon cans. In the traffic census taken at that time, in the 24 hours of 21 July 1916 at Fricourt, there passed 564 motor cars, 95 motor buses, 617 motor cycles and 813 lorries. At the same time 3800 horse-drawn wagons and 5400 riding horses went through the town.

The powerful surge of motor vehicle traffic in the 1920s and its replacement of the until then ubiquitous horse-drawn transport is clearly illustrated in the contemporary statistics for road vehicle licences, shown in Table 2. There was a more than three-fold growth in cars during the period, which far exceeded that of the other forms of vehicle, and while the motor cycle appeared to be popular in the early part of the decade, it

Quarter ending 31/8	Cars	Motor cycles	Commercial vehicles	Buses	Total motors	Horse-drawn
1922	378	378	157	78	991	233
1923	383	430	173	86	1072	207
1924	473	495	203	94	1263	179
1925	579	571	224	99	1473	157
1926	676	629	248	99	1652	126
1927	778	672	276	96	1822	103
1928	877	691	294	93	1955	83
1929	970	705	318	96	2089	66
1930	1042	699	334	99	2174	52

Table 2 Number of road vehicle licences, 1922–30 (in thousands)

was soon overtaken by the car. The horse all this while was rapidly being pensioned off.

The 'petrol-driven light cars' were given a massive stimulus by Henry Ford's 'tin lizzie' (Model T Ford) and soon after by the small and cheap products of the British firms Morris and Austin. The 'Baby' Austin was so small that a contemporary joke had it that the designers were trying to cut its length by a couple of inches to allow it to be washed in the kitchen sink.

But there was no joke about the technical advances that had to be made to maintain the impetus for advance. Cars had to be made safer, more reliable, less spartan and cheaper. In this situation the properties of the new phenol-formaldehyde products offered interesting possibilities. But these possibilities resulted not only from their properties. The variety of forms in which they could be presented added to their range of applications. Furthermore, the new processing techniques by which they were fabricated made it simpler and therefore cheaper to produce articles of a complex shape as compared with the traditional crafts used to shape metals, wood and so on.

If the internal combustion engine was beginning to change the pattern and quality of life in society through revolutions in the means of transport, then radio, or 'wireless' as it was then known, was effecting a parallel revolution inside the home. Radio, as it impinged on the life of ordinary people, was the technological consequence of a theoretical concept relating to electro-magnetic waves, which was first set out by the English physicist Clark Maxwell in a paper he read to the Royal Society on 8 December 1864 (Maxwell 1864). The theory was confirmed in laboratory practice in 1888 by Heinrich Hertz, a German (Hertz 1888: 155). In 1896 the Italian Guglielmo Marconi applied for the first wireless patent (BP 12,039), which converted the theoretical concepts, in a very halting and crude way, into a process for sending radio signals from one place to another. At first these sites were separated by a few yards, but by 1901 a signal sent from Cornwall, England, was received in Newfoundland, two thousand miles away across the Atlantic.

At that time the signal was generated by switching a current on and off, giving the characteristic dots and dashes of the Morse code, but in 1906 R. Fessenden, an American, broadcast the sounds of music and speech. This was another seminal moment. Up to then people were thinking of 'wireless telegraphy' as an instrument for point-to-point communication, from ship to shore or between two individuals, for example. It was seen essentially as an instrument for private communication. 'Wireless telephone', on the other hand, opened up thoughts of a transmitter broadcasting to many receivers; a station providing a public service which could entertain and educate.

The British government, as did others, quickly appreciated the importance of radio, especially for military use, and took control of its development in 1904 by assuming powers to issue licences permitting the transmission and reception of wireless signals. Many were taken up by equipment manufacturers and others, and technical developments followed on apace. Marconi's company in England assumed a dominant role in this period. There was a sudden and complete hiatus for amateurs when the British government banned all their radio activities during the First World War, but the war generally acted as a forcing house for technical and economic progress in this field. With the return of peace, popular interest resumed, and the first radio station to come on the air was in 1920: KDKA Pittsburgh in the USA. Regular concerts were broadcast from the Hague in the Netherlands in the same year, and the Marconi Company began a broadcasting service from Chelmsford. The Post Office had second thoughts about these transmissions and withdrew its licence soon after. That did not prevent the first regular Marconi service starting up from Writtle on 14 February 1922 (Baker 1970), to be followed some three months later by the historic station in London, 2LO.

But all this amounted to a rather scrappy, disorganised and uncontrolled birth of this new and potentially powerful force. At least that was the feeling of the British government of the time, which was alarmed by what it saw of American developments. The chaos produced by the uninhibited competition of private enterprise might be tolerable there but could not, in its view, be sustained in Britain. As a consequence, with some stimulus from the Post Office, the major radio equipment manufacturers, 'the Big 6', came together to negotiate with the government to establish a national broadcasting organisation.

The British Broadcasting Company, a syndicate of the six companies, was the outcome, and it was to be financed by the sale of receiving licences at 10 shillings per year. It acquired its own transmitting licence from the Post Office in January 1923, but anticipated its arrival with the first BBC broadcast a couple of months earlier. The Company was transformed into the British Broadcasting Corporation, an independent publicly appointed body, some five years later. But that is another story. Those interested in the early days of radio can do no better than read *The History of Broadcasting in the United Kingdom* by Asa Briggs (1961–95). What is more immediately interesting is the speed with which these technical and administrative developments made their impact on society.

Within two or three months of the establishment of the BBC, 125,000 people had acquired receiving licences. It was easy enough to ascertain the number of people who had paid to operate their equipment; it was less easy to estimate the number who were not so meticulous about their legal obligations, particularly since these were 'home constructors' (amateurs who assembled their own sets). Nevertheless, estimates put their number at about 200,000. The continued growth in the number of radio receivers is given as reaching 595,496 in 1923. By 1930 the numbers had risen to 3,647,000. There was a captive market for radios made in the dazzling new array of plastics becoming available, such as the cast phenolic radio by Fada, an American company. The growing British market was capitalised on by the Ekco radio factory, which issued a classic range of phenolic radio cabinets in the 1930s (Going 1990b: 12ff).

Early radio enthusiasts came from all sections of society. The *Morning Post* in August 1922 reported that 'people of all classes were asking for advice about wireless sets', and a little later, in 1924, Sir John Reith, General Manager of the BBC, observed that continuous lines of aerials could be seen in the great towns.

This popular universal interest was possible because it was technically feasible to receive radio programmes on equipment costing relatively little or quite a lot. Most people listened through earphones, and their set with two valves cost about £25 in 1923. A very superior and more powerful assembly including a quality loudspeaker and rather more valves might cost £100. Variations in quality would place the price correspondingly somewhere between these extremes. An average skilled industrial worker was earning about £3 12s per week in the early 1920s.

Prices fell quite quickly, and this obviously helped in the spread of radio in overall numbers and in its ubiquity among the population. In 1925 it was possible to buy a two-valve set for just over £5. In the same year wireless sets could be acquired in cabinets 'designed in the style of any period'.

Another indicator of the wide interest in wireless was provided by the circulation figures for a number of magazines catering for that interest. In 1923–34 there were at least five such journals. The most popular, *Wireless Constructor*, had 250,000 readers, while the other four journals had a total of 475,000 readers. In short, by the 1930s radio was part of ordinary life. The sound issuing from the loudspeaker formed the background of family life in most homes, and to provide that sound plastics were essential, ranging from the humble phenolic plug and circuit board to the luxury of an Ekco radio cabinet.

Interestingly enough, plastics were also the foundation of another form of communication which was climbing towards its peak in the same period. The cinema was dominating the world of entertainment.

Without Celluloid, whether 'non-flam' (cellulose acetate) or its predecessor, cellulose nitrate film, there could be no movies. But plastics gave much more to the movies. In the difficult, drab and threatening inter-war years the cinema offered some moments of escape. The films themselves generally offered a world of make-believe, and the cinemas in which they were shown reinforced this by their opulent design and exotic furnishing and decor. In this the new plastics, particularly in the form of decorative thermo-setting laminates, helped to create the illusion of a non-threatening world, far removed from the realities of the clients.

A much more powerful change than we have considered so far was under way towards the end of the eighteenth and early part of the nineteenth century. It was to bring about a truly fundamental revolution and change the lives of every individual in society massively. The coming of electricity altered almost every aspect of the worlds of work, of the home and of leisure, and almost every other form of human activity.

To do this, many technical problems had to be overcome, and the new plastics were necessary to resolve some of them. The President of the Institute of Electrical Engineers commented in 1907 about the inadequacy of the insulation necessary for the transmission of electricity. Plastics were turning out to be almost ideal in this respect.

But how did matters stand in the developing story of the electrical industry at the time of the birth of plastics? The first theoretical appreciation of electricity was signalled by Michael Faraday's discovery of electro-magnetic induction in 1831 at the Royal Society, when he demonstrated the flow of electricity in wire which moved across the field of a magnet (Faraday 1832). That was the beginning of the generation of electricity and it marked a seminal moment in human history, advancing the conquest of darkness. Living as we do today, when on-coming night merely activates a reflex switching on of the electric light, it is difficult to envisage the millennia of human experience wherein dusk signalled the hours of all-pervasive darkness. Even in more recent centuries darkness was relieved only by pale candle or oil light.

Some fifty years after Faraday, the Gaiety Theatre in London was illuminated by electric arc lighting in August 1878 (Electricity Council 1982). Most football enthusiasts, who tend to regard evening matches as a relatively recent phenomenon, will be surprised to learn that in the same year the Sheffield Football Club at their Bramall Lane stadium staged an evening match before 30,000 spectators under arc lights. (It ought to be recorded that the brilliance of the light was said to be the cause of some strange blunders by the players, but the result of the game ought to be known before the light can be accepted as the real cause!)

In spite of those and other spectacular examples of the use of electricity, the future of this new phenomenon was the subject of con-flicting speculation. For example, the Parliamentary Select Committee on Lighting by Electricity reported in 1879:

while many practical witnesses see serious difficulty in the speedy adaptation of the electric light to useful purposes of illumination, the scientific witnesses see in this economy of force the means of great industrial development ... Scientific witnesses also considered that in the future the electric current might be extensively used to transmit power as well as light. [Houses of Parliament 1879]

Another committee reporting at about the same time confidently asserted that 'we are quite satisfied that the electric light can never be applied indoors without the production of an offensive smell which undoubtedly causes headaches and in its naked state it can never be used in rooms of even large size without damage to sight'. But then that committee might have been expected to make some such comment, as it was set up by the main London gas company, which, as the major provider of illumination, was speaking of a threatening competitor.

Towards the end of the century it was by no means clear whether gas or electricity would provide the light. The first electricity generating station came on stream at Godalming in Surrey in 1881 (Bowers 1982). This was a hydro-electric installation, with the generator driven by a water wheel to light the streets and houses, but it had to close three years later for lack of demand. The people of Godalming were not impressed, and indicated their wish to stay with gas. So did the citizens of Holborn, London, when their station gave them the chance from 1882 (Bowers 1982), and it too closed in 1886 (Parsons 1939).

There were various reasons for the preference for gas at that time. The most important was probably its relative cheapness, but there were technical reasons too. The early form of gas light was naked flame, which, though better than what was then available, could hardly be called bright. The advent of the commercial 'Welsbach incandescent mantle' in 1887 changed that and gave a steadier white light, using the same source (Chandler 1936). Electricity, on the other hand, was having to surmount its initial serious teething troubles. On the supply side there were frequent interruptions due to breakdowns in either generation or transmission. In the home there were problems arising from undeveloped incandescent electric lamps. In 1878 Swan in England and Edison in the USA first produced their carbon filament lamps, and in the following years these crude pioneering products suffered from a number of inadequacies, not least their short filament life and the tendency for the bulb to blacken. The development of artificial silk was the result of some of Swan's experiments to find a suitable material (BP 5978 1883). Another expensive exercise was in laying the mains.

But the inherent superiority of electricity as a source of illumination inevitably became evident as experience, technical know-how and theoretical and practical understanding grew. Its price fell, its reliability improved, electric light bulbs became immeasurably better, and there was a tenfold increase in electrical lighting consumption in the years between 1895 and 1905 (Byatt 1979; Hannah 1979: 17).

The battle between gas and electricity had been lost and won. Of course this did not lead to any overnight change. Non-electrical forms of illumination continued to be used for some decades, but the pressure for change was inexorable. The rate was accelerated after 1926 when the Central Electricity Board was set up with monopoly powers over the production of electricity. It replaced the large numbers of small, inefficient power stations with a new generation of 'super' stations connected by a national transmission grid.

The effect of all this was dramatic. Whereas in 1920 only one house in seventeen was wired for electricity, that proportion rose to one in three in 1930 and two in three in 1939. If one bears in mind the fact that three and a half million houses were built from 1925 to 1939 – that is, there was a simultaneous increase in housing stock alongside the increasing proportion of electricity-supplied housing – then the demand for the new plastics 'electricals' will be understood. Such demands took the form of phenolic and urea-formaldehyde plugs and sockets as well as an increasing market for plastics with good insulating properties like polyethylene and PVC, although the use of these materials in British domestic cabling did not happen until after the Second World War.

So far we have been considering only the use of electricity in lighting. Readers may recall the prediction made by the Parliamentary Select Committee on Lighting, which reported in 1879 that 'scientific witnesses also considered that in the future the electric current might be extensively used to transmit power as well as light' (Houses of Parliament 1879). Events soon proved them right. Trams and trains, electrically powered, replaced age-old horse-drawn transport to a considerable degree in three or four decades. Industrial machinery driven by electricity began to change the image of our factories from the turn of the century, and had overtaken lighting as the major consumer by 1909 in Britain (Hannah 1979: 19).

Hannah (1979) has explained how electrical traction was for many people the first encounter with electricity. The urban horse-drawn tramway network soon gave way to electricity. In the United States, 90 per cent of tramway mileage had been converted by 1897 (Byatt 1979). A similar figure was reached in 1905 in Britain. Electrification of suburban railways proceeded apace (Byatt 1979). London's Underground system was liberated from the traumas of travel on the smoky Metropolitan and Metropolitan District Railways, and the 'tube' made relatively comfortable travel to and from work more than a possibility. The results were evident almost overnight. In 1892 the London Underground network carried 8 million passengers; by 1906 the extended electrified system catered for 95 million.

The civic and social consequences of these and analogous changes in London and other industrial cities and conurbations were very considerable. They led to a big shift in population by allowing large numbers of workers to move out of the worst of inner-city slums to suburban areas. Cheap fares and an efficient system made it possible to commute to work from considerable distances. The lifestyle of whole sectors of the population was transformed, and that transformation in turn brought with it new demands.

The same point was made in a somewhat different way about the use of electricity in industry. It was not just potentially cheaper than steam; it was more flexible and could be used in quite new ways. Hannah, the author of *Electricity before Nationalisation,* quotes a Tyneside ship-building engineer on the transition to electricity in the shipyards:

> There were some prejudices to be overcome. They all wanted to know how much it would cost them compared with the numberless small steam engines they used, though actually it turned out that this was not by any means the most important point for them. The really important point about adopting electricity was that it made available for their operations a much more easily adaptable form of power. So much did this prove to be the case that within a very few years the different firms we connected up with the system were spending two or three times as much on electrical power as they had ever spent on steam power. This was not because electric power was more expensive but because they had applied it to so many uses for which before they had not used power at all. [Hannah 1979: 18]

What was true in the shipyards was equally valid in the rest of industry and society in general. Energy in a massive, convenient and flexible form was becoming available at the touch of a switch – shortly to become a plastic switch.

The demands of the market dictated the processes which were employed to make the products required. They also directed research and development to produce the optimum combination of properties to serve particular applications. The applications were legion, even in the early days, but they fell into a few major groups. In some, mechanical strength of the material was the dominant requirement; in others, it was good electrical insulating performance; in yet others, appearance was what mattered. In almost all cases, cost and factors influencing costs loomed large in the mind of the prospective customer and hence of the manufacturer.

Moulding articles from phenolic moulding powders was the most important process, as Leo Baekeland had shrewdly foreseen in his paper given in 1909 to the New York Section of the American Chemical Society (Baekeland 1909). He had gained two years of experience through his collaboration with the Boonton Rubber Company by the time he came to write this paper. Mr Richard W. Seabury, the owner, was probably the first man to make phenolic mouldings successfully. That was in the USA.

In the UK the Mouldensite Manufacturing Company was the first to make phenolic mouldings from resins of its own manufacture. It came on the scene rather later, in 1921, in Darley Dale in Derbyshire, and developed the new skills involved in the formulation and production of moulding powders, as well as the knowledge of moulding and of the design of moulds.

Plastics played a role in all these technologies. In some their part was incidental, in others essential. As we approach the end of the twentieth century, it is evident that all activities of civilised Western life depend to some extent on the family of materials known collectively as plastics. The plastics age is upon us.

Postscript

Susan Mossman

A wide range of views has been expressed in this book, from authors with differing backgrounds: social historical, design, museological, and plastics historical. The approach has been a varied one, helping to indicate the many perspectives which exist with regard to plastics.

Although plastics were of great importance during the period covered by this book (1850–1950) for developing technologies within the automobile and electrical industries, they also percolated into people's cultural perceptions. After a beginning where plastics were made into ornate objects (witness Parkesine and gutta percha mouldings) as well as more utilitarian tubing and the like, plastics became adapted for practical purposes and reached mass markets with applications such as Celluloid collars and cuffs, the vulcanised rubber tyre and, perhaps most significantly, Celluloid film. Plastics are materials which have made possible the visible recording of moving pictures: 'the canning of history'. The use which designers have made of these materials has greatly changed the way that we live in the Western world, where plastics are now all-pervading.

At the time of the birth of semi-synthetic plastics in the mid-nineteenth century, these new materials impinged on the public consciousness through cartoons in the newspapers or advertising leaflets. This did not, however, prevent the outrageous claims that some entrepreneurs made for their products, which apparently could be used for almost anything. The Great Exhibitions of 1851 and 1862 played their part in awakening the public to the variety of different moulding materials which were being developed. Before the advent of Celluloid, few mass-communication media existed apart from the printed word and the emerging telegraph service.

The majority of these early plastics materials quickly died a death. Bois Durci, a very beautiful natural plastics material with excellent moulding properties, flourished for just over twenty years from *c*.1850 to *c*.1870.

Was it the thought of using blood as one of the constituents that prevented its continuation? This is a question for further debate.

In the realm of synthetic fibres, Chardonnet artificial silk was a material which caused a sensation when it was first displayed in Paris in 1891. Unfortunately it came to grief due to its flammability. This was a tremendous material let down by the predilection of the day for lighting by candle light. However, its successor, viscose rayon, succeeded and became a world-wide success story.

'Plastics' as such was not a concept fully defined until the 1950s. Before then it was a matter of individual materials being developed and being found to be useful in different ways.

It has been shown that the plastics pioneers, such as Alexander Parkes, Leo Baekeland and Wallace Carothers, from small beginnings provided the basis for today's multibillion pound plastics industry. After a slow but promising start, growth was rapid in the 1930s, and gradually plastics became an accepted part of everyday life. However, in the 1950s, plastics reached their nadir with regard to popularity and became synonymous with 'cheap and nasty', due partly to the use of certain plastics such as polystyrene for inappropriate purposes, resulting in breakages. An additional reason was the misconception about how best to use these new plastics materials with regard to their advantages (such as lightness) while being aware of their disadvantages (such as their low melting point).

Post-1950s, plastics are gradually climbing back into good favour. In the 1960s they became fashionable with couturier designers such as Courrèges. This was the decade designated as the 'plastics age'. In the 1990s plastics have become almost invisible in many of their modern applications, such as the personal computer and the mobile phone. Developments of plastics reinforcements such as carbon fibre have led to production of very strong plastics composite materials, which are now regularly used in aircraft, vehicle bodies, and civil engineering structures such as bridges.

We are now in an age of 'designer plastics', when plastics materials can be custom-made for specific applications, such as the Concorde nose-cone. The realm of 'smart plastics' – for example, plastics materials which return back to shape after bending – is rapidly developing. Synthetic fibres play an important part in protective clothing, for example in fire-retardant applications, as well as in high fashion – a far cry from the

Chardonnet 'flammable' artificial silk dress. The synthetic fibre Lycra has become the vital ingredient of many high-fashion and sports garments.

The plastics of 1850–1950 have now turned full circle and become sought-after items. They are collectible and possess their own specialist societies. The relatively recent discovery that the earliest plastics based on cellulose, such as cellulose nitrate (Celluloid), are prone to rapid and, for the moment, unstoppable degradation has increased their scarcity. Plastics, certainly the earliest examples, do not last for ever and so must be valued and studied fully in the interim. Only time will tell whether the plastics products of today and tomorrow will be fully appreciated for the major changes they have brought to all our lives.

Catalogue of the Science Museum's Plastics Collection: *c.1850–c.1950*

Susan Mossman

The catalogue is arranged in roughly chronological order. The entries are arranged by plastics material, with plastics objects followed by related plastics machinery in each category. The catalogue categories are as follows:

* Object parts are indicated by stroke numbers ('/') or part numbers interchangeably, as found on the Science Museum Database. This system is currently being clarified.

AMBER

1. 1980-676/44: Amber cigarette holder in chamois-lined leather box. Early twentieth century. Inscription printed inside lid on red oval fabric sticker: 'MADE/FROM/PURE AMBER'; inscription printed in gold with gold border.

Length 76 mm, width 20 mm, thickness 17 mm.

Pt. 1: Amber tube, flattened at one end with raised lip. Holder end signed. Snap fastening.
Length 62 mm, width 12 mm, thickness 12 mm.

Pt. 2: Oval case, two-part, hinged. Made of leather.
Length 76 mm, width 20 mm, thickness 17 mm.
Source: Newport, R.
Plate 2

HORN

2. 1980-676/1: Rectangular horn snuff box, with hinged lid inlaid with tortoiseshell over ivory, early nineteenth century.

Length 56 mm, width 30 mm, height 20 mm.
Reference: Newport 1976: A1.
Source: Newport, R.
Plate 2

3. 1980-676/2: Tea-caddy spoon of pressed horn with a thistle-shaped handle, made in Scotland. Inscription on back of handle: 'MADE/IN/SCOTLAN', second half of the twentieth century. Last part of inscription worn away, 'D' missing from 'SCOTLAND'.

Length 85 mm, width 35 mm, height 9 mm.
Reference: Newport 1976: A2.
Source: Newport, R.
Plate 2

4. 1980-676/3: Button in black pressed horn with an anchor and crown on face; metal shank. Late nineteenth/early twentieth century.

Diameter 28 mm, height 13.5 mm.
Reference: Newport 1976: A7.
Source: Newport, R.
Plate 2

5. 1980-676/4: Postman's button in black pressed horn with a crown and a posthorn on face. Inscribed 'GROVE & SONS, HALESOWEN' on reverse (worn). Late nineteenth/early twentieth century.

Diameter 23 mm, height 13 mm.
Reference: Newport 1976: A8.
Source: Newport, R.
Plate 2

6. 1980-676/5 and 6: Pair of floral buttons made of black pressed horn, with finely detailed flowers on the face. c.1880. 1980-676/6 is chipped.

Diameter 21.5 mm, height 19.5 mm.
Reference: Newport 1976: A9.
Source: Newport, R.
Plate 2

7. 1980-676/7: Horn beaker with a nickel rim (ridged). Nickel monogrammed shield engraved 'JB' in ornate curled script, made c.1750.

Diameter 90 mm, height 120 mm, thickness 3 mm.
Reference: Newport 1976: A10.
Source: Newport, R.
Plate 2

8. 1980-676/12: Transport button, made of black horn with a winged griffin moulded on upper face. Metal shank. Late nineteenth/early twentieth century.

Diameter 24 mm, height 13 mm.
Source: Newport, R.
Plate 2

9. 1980-676/13: Transport button, made of black horn with a winged griffin moulded on upper face. Metal shank. Back inscribed 'JA⁵ GROVE & SONS./HALESOWEN'. Late nineteenth/early twentieth century.

Diameter 23 mm, height 12 mm.
Source: Newport, R.
Plate 2

10. 1980-676/14: Transport button, made of black horn with a winged griffin moulded on upper face. Moulded eye on back. Late nineteenth/early twentieth century.

Diameter 23 mm, height 10 mm.
Source: Newport, R.
Plate 2

11. 1980-676/15: Transport button, made of black horn with crown surrounded by wreath moulded on upper face. Late nineteenth/early twentieth century.

Diameter 17 mm, height 11.5 mm.
Source: Newport, R.
Plate 2

12. 1995-635: Black pressed horn brooch in form of a hand holding a spray of flowers, with metal clip. Late nineteenth century.

Length 46 mm, width 25 mm, height 12 mm.
Source: Plastic Fantastic.
Plate 2

TORTOISESHELL

13. 1980-676/8: Complete tortoiseshell pierced at rear of upper shell for hanging, twentieth century. Incomplete: three scales missing from tortoiseshell. Late nineteenth/early twentieth century.

Length 180 mm, width 112 mm, height 80 mm.
Source: Newport, R.
Plate 2

BITUMEN/CARTON PIERRE

14. 1980-676/42: Electrical terminal made of bitumen with two metal terminals, marked Lissen on base, between the terminals, *c.*1920. Trade mark moulded on upper surface: 'LISSEN'. 'L' has curved tail running under rest of word, which also curves up along top edge. Second inscription moulded under left-hand terminal: 'LS/*../+' contained in circle '-' appears directly under 'LS' to indicate negative terminal. Third inscription moulded under right-hand terminal contained in circle; '+' directly under indistinguishable upper letters to indicate positive terminal.

Length 47 mm, width 24 mm, height 31 mm.
Source: Newport, R.

15. 1980-676/43: Rectangular ornate 'scripture/parables' book covers, made of carton pierre, mid-nineteenth century.

Inscription moulded on centre of both covers: 'scripture/parables'. Gothic script in diagonal parallel scrolls. Second inscription moulded on spine: 'OF OUR THE PARABLES LORD'. 'OF OUR' and 'LORD' separated from 'THE PARABLES' by box; gothic script.

Length 168 mm, width 117 mm, thickness 17 mm.
Source: Newport, R.

GUTTA PERCHA

(*Note*: Certain gutta percha items may have been made in the twentieth century using nineteenth-century moulds. Where this is a possibility it is indicated by 'as produced' in the catalogue description.)

16. 1973-217: 5 'Ocobo' gutta percha golf balls, one of which is sectioned into two halves, made by James B. Halley, 15 Finsbury Circus, London, in original box. Inscription moulded on either side: 'THE OCOBO/27' arranged in circular, narrow band, two stamped on each golf ball. Trade mark printed on box lid: 'THIS GOLF BALL is made/specially from the best/selected Gutta-Percha./Registered No.210,248./THE-/'Ocobo'/James B. Halley, 15, Finsbury Circus, London, E.C.'.

Diameter 42 mm.
Source: Hansell, H.B.

17. 1974-428: Gutta percha bottle used for containing hydrofluoric acid, with stopper, 10 ½" high, used by Imperial College of Science and Technology. Surface cracked, *c.* 1950.

Height 267 mm, diameter 97 mm.
Source: Imperial College of Science and Technology.

18. 1974-436: Gutta percha bottle used for containing hydrofluoric acid, with stopper, 10 ½" high, used by the V & A Conservation Department. Crack running lengthwise: 92 mm long, *c.*1950.

Height 267 mm, diameter 98 mm.
Source: Victoria & Albert Museum.

19. 1984-1096: Square biscuit tray with raised edges with moulded foliage border. Centre of tray decorated with moulding of house and gardens with a couple in front holding hands, as illustrated on p. 57 of the 1851 Gutta Percha Company catalogue, made by the Gutta Percha Company, England, as produced in 1851. Three pieces of rim broken off. Base stamped: 'GUTTA PERCHA COMPANY/ WHARF/ ROAD/ CITY ROAD/ LONDON/ LONDON PATENTEES'; first and last lines arranged in circle around middle four lines. Colour is streaked brown so may be balata.

Length 270 mm, width 195 mm, height 45 mm.
Source: Wilson, H.F.

20. 1984-1097: Pen tray of gutta percha, made by the Gutta Percha Company, England, as produced in the second half of the nineteenth century. Inscribed on base: 'THE GUTTA PERCHA COMPANY PATENTEES/18 WHARF ROAD CITY ROAD LONDON'. Brittle and cracked.

Length 310 mm, width 105 mm, height 23 mm.
Source: Wilson, H.F.

21. 1984-1098/1: Unicorn made of gutta percha, made by the Gutta Percha Company, England, as produced in the second half of the nineteenth century. Cracked (slightly chipped).

Length 185 mm, width 162 mm, thickness 36 mm.
Source: Wilson, H.F.

22. 1984-1098/2: Gutta percha armorial moulding showing bishop's mitre, crossed crozier and sword, standing on Bible and cushion, made by the Gutta Percha Company, England, as produced in the second half of nineteenth century.

Length 174 mm, width 35 mm, height 110 mm.
Source: Wilson, H.F.

23. 1984-1099: Gutta percha armorial moulding in form of royal coat of arms showing the lion and the unicorn, made by the Gutta Percha Company, London, England, as produced in the second half

of the nineteenth century. Inscribed on the back: 'GUTTA PERCHA COMPANY/ WHARF/ ROAD/ CITY ROAD/ LONDON/ .PATENTEES'. Front of shield inscribed with: '[H]ONI SOIT QUI MAL Y PENSE' encircling upper part of shield and with: 'DIEU ET MON DROIT' on the ribbon running under the coat of arms. Cracked, fragile.

Length 233 mm, width 181 mm, thickness 29 mm.
Source: Wilson, H.F.

24. 1984-1102: Inkstand made from gutta percha with head of Neptune. Lower surface has three raised circular supports and tow legs. Base marked: '3614' in paint. Described as 'Inkstand No. 1' in the Gutta Percha Company 1851 catalogue made by the Gutta Percha Company, England, c.1851.

Length 472 mm, width 370 mm, thickness 150 mm.
Source: Wilson, H.F.
Plate 3

25. 1984-1103/1: Metal mould for gutta percha plaque showing family in rural setting, used by the Gutta Percha Company, second half of nineteenth century.

Length 141 mm, width 118 mm, thickness 13 mm.
Source: Wilson, H.F.

26. 1984-1103/2: Metal mould for gutta percha plaque showing two males, one female and one child, one male seated on barrel, gutta-percha holder, England, mid-nineteenth century.

Length 156 mm, width 139 mm, thickness 26 mm.
Source: Wilson, H.F.

27. 1984-1104: Rectangular brass mould for gutta percha embossed plaque of 1851 exhibition. Inscription in French and English, and depicting the Crystal Palace, c.1851. The French inscription is engraved on the left-hand side of the mould and reads: 'DESIGNE PAR/M PAXTON/LEDIFICE A HYDE PARK/FOUR LA GRANDE EXHIBITION DE 1851/LONGEUR 1848 FTS LARGEUR 403 FTS HAUTEUR 66 FTS/COUTE L150000

ENTREPRENEURS MESS FOX &
HENDERSON' in negative, i.e.: it runs
back to front; lines 1 and 2 around the
edge of the illustration. The English
inscription is engraved on the right-hand
side of the mould and reads:
'DESIGNED BY/MR PAXTON/THE
BUILDING IN HYDE PARK/FOR
THE GREAT EXHIBITION 1851/
LENGTH 1848 FT WIDTH 403 FT
HEIGHT 66 FT/COST L150000
CONTRACTORS MESS FOX &
HENDERSON'.

Length 125 mm, width 67 mm, thickness 12 mm.
Source: Wilson, H.F.

28. 1984-1105/1: Gutta percha rose
flower, moulded by the Gutta Percha
Company, England, as produced in the
second half of the nineteenth century.
Cracked, brittle.

Diameter 41 mm, height 27 mm.
Source: Wilson, H.F.

29. 1984-1105/2: Seated dog (spaniel)
moulded from gutta percha, made by the
Gutta Percha Company, England, as
produced in the mid-nineteenth century.

Length 70 mm, width 32 mm, thickness 34 mm.
Source: Wilson, H.F.

30. 1984-1105/3: Ivy leaf made of
moulded gutta percha, made by the Gutta
Percha Company, England, as produced
in the mid-nineteenth century.

Length 100 mm, width 66 mm, thickness 2 mm.
Source: Wilson, H.F.

31. 1984-1106: Plaster of Paris lion made
by Charles Hancock, pioneer of gutta
percha, 1830. Initialled and dated on base.
Cast in a gelatine mould the model
illustrates Hancock's early interest in
moulding techniques. Handwritten
inscription on edge of base reads: 'Cast in
a Gel.^{tin}/mould'. Second handwritten
inscription in centre of base reads: 'CH/
1830'. Chips missing from mane and left
foot.

Length 102 mm, width 57 mm, height 38 mm.
Source: Wilson, H.F.

32. 1984-1107: Oval mirror frame of
moulded gutta percha, with ornate foliate
border, made by the Gutta Percha
Company, England, as produced in the
second half of the nineteenth century.
Chipped and brittle.

Length 200 mm, width 125 mm, thickness 54 mm
(base), thickness 54 mm (frame).
Source: Wilson, H.F.

33. 1984-1108/1: Brown disc in form of
reversible chess piece (bishop) and
draughtsman made of gutta percha, made
by the Gutta Percha Company, England,
as produced in the second half of the
nineteenth century.

Diameter 40.5 mm, thickness 20 mm.
Source: Wilson, H.F.

34. 1984-1108/2: Dark brown disc in
form of reversible chess piece (pawn) and
draughtsman made of gutta percha, made
by the Gutta Percha Company, England,
as produced in the second half of the
nineteenth century. Slighty chipped
round edges.

Diameter 40.5 mm, thickness 19 mm.
Source: Wilson, H.F.

35. 1984-1108/3: Brown disc in form of
reversible chess piece (castle) and
draughtsman made of gutta percha, made
by the Gutta Percha Company, England,
as produced in the second half of the
nineteenth century. Edges slightly
chipped.

Diameter 41 mm, thickness 18 mm.
Source: Wilson, H.F.

36. 1984-1108/4: Red disc in form of
reversible chess piece (castle) and
draughtsman made of Vulcanite, made by
the Gutta Percha Company, England, as
produced in the second half of the
nineteenth century. Edges slightly
chipped.

Diameter 41 mm, thickness 17 mm.
Source: Wilson, H.F.

37. 1984-1109: Mottled brown
rectangular block of Raw Leaf gutta
percha, manufactured on Telcon Plastics

Ltd's plantation in Malaya during the Japanese occupation, 1942–45. Inscribed with Japanese inscription. Cracked.

Length 220 mm, width 146 mm, height 92 mm.
Source: Wilson, H.F.

SHELLAC

38. 1979-624/275: Rectangular Union Case of dark brown shellac, with elaborately moulded cover, with central lozenge on both sides showing a woman with the White House in the background. Lozenges are surrounded by ornate tendrilled design. Inside, the left-hand side is lined with maroon velvet; on the right-hand side the oval daguerreotype is missing, although the golden frame is still in place. American, *c*.1855. The inscription moulded on the lower edge of both covers on a banner reads: 'LIBERTY'.

Length 98 mm, width 88 mm, thickness 19 mm.
Source: Jesse, J.

39. 1980-676/16: Oval Union Case of black shellac, for an ambrotype or daguerreotype, with ornate moulding showing vase containing fruits and crops. Maroon velvet lining. American, mid-1850s. Inscribed: 'GENUINE UNION CASE/ IMPROVED/ FINE GILT AND BURNISHED HINGES/ S. PECK & CO./ MANUFACTURERS.' Case broken at hinge.

Length 54 mm, width 48 mm, thickness 19 mm.
Reference: Newport 1976: E3
Source: Newport, R.
Figure 2

40. 1980-676/17: Rectangular Union Case of dark brown shellac, moulded with flowers and a border. Maroon velvet lining. American, mid-1860s. Backing to missing photo enclosed within ornate golden oval frame and inscribed: 'Littlefield Parsons & Co./ MANUFACTURERS OF dageurreotype cases/L., P. & Co. are the sole proprietors and only legal Manufacturers of UNION

CASES, with the Embracing Riveted Hinge/ Patented October 14 1856 and April 21 1857'. The relevant patents are Alfred P. Critchlow's USP 15,915 of 1856 and USP 457 of 1857.

Length 95 mm, width 84 mm, thickness 27 mm.
Reference: Newport 1976: E4
Source: Newport, R.
Plate 4

41. 1980-676/18: Rectangular Union Case of dark brown shellac, elaborately moulded with a decorative border and with a central oval miniature of a boy bird-nesting. Velvet lining. Both covers inscribed: 'SEILER' on outer side, for the die engraver, Frederick Seiler. Ambrotype shows seated man. American, *c*.1860. Case base chipped.

Length 97 mm, width 87 mm, thickness 22 mm.
Reference: Newport 1976: E5
Source: Newport, R.
Plate 4

42. 1980-676/19: Octagonal Union Case of brown shellac, elaborate gothic motif; contains ambrotype showing young girl, surrounded by oval golden frame. Left half of case lined in maroon velvet. Made by S. Peck & Co., USA, *c*.1860. Edges of case chipped.

Length 96 mm, width 86 mm, height 25 mm.
Source: Newport, R.
Plate 4

43. 1980-676/20: Square Union Case of brown shellac, with biblical scene showing two figures and palm trees, enclosed within oval surrounded by decorative border, with ambrotype of small girl. American, *c*.1860.

Length 95 mm, width 85 mm, height 27 mm.
Source: Newport, R.
Plate 4

44. 1980-676/21: Octagonal Union Case of brown shellac, elaborately moulded; right-hand side contains hand-coloured ambrotype showing seated woman, with small child, golden frame; left-hand side of case lined in maroon velvet with elaborate motif. Made by S. Peck & Co.,

USA, *c*.1851. Photographed by H. Halverson. Edges slightly chipped.

Length 96 mm, width 85 mm, depth 26 mm.
Source: Newport, R.
Plate 4

45. 1980-676/22: Rectangular Union Case of dark brown shellac, elaborately moulded; contains hand-coloured ambrotype showing young man, in oval golden frame. Left side of case lined with maroon velvet. Made by S. Peck & Co., USA, *c*.1851. Photographed by H. Halverson.

Length 77 mm, width 66 mm, height 22 mm.
Source: Newport, R.
Plate 4

46. 1980-676/23: Box containing 67 shellac seals, of various kinds, religious and secular, dated between 1850 and 1940 (cat. nos. 47–113). Sharkskin box with silk lining. Inscription printed on rectangular, sticky label, gold on black, inside long edge: 'REGD NO/764295'.

Length 263 mm, width 110 mm, height 78 mm.
Source: Newport, R.

47. 1980-676/23 Pt. 1: Square seal of red shellac with square stamp showing forearm holding aloft an olive branch. "ROSS" stamped under stamp.

Length 45 mm, width 41 mm, height 2 mm.

48. 1980-676/23 Pt. 2: Octagonal seal of red shellac showing bearded man in left profile. Inscription printed on the backing: 'LAT../WOOLLE.../SSan ...'. Part of original document, black print.

Length 33 mm, width 28 mm, thickness 3 mm.
Plate 4

49. 1980-676/23 Pt. 3: Red shellac oval seal with oval stamp showing draped female figure. Coat of arms on column behind her.

Length 37 mm, width 31 mm, thickness 3 mm.
Plate 4

50. 1980-676/23 Pt. 4: Circular seal with red stamp showing coat of arms surmounted by double-headed eagle.

Arms show hatches, balls, plus worn central inscription: 'HILLIERS DEACON & MANCHESTER & SALFORD' inside border.

Diameter 36 mm, thickness 1.5 mm.

51. 1980-676/23 Pt. 5: Red shellac circular seal with circular stamp with royal coat of arms and marked: 'MASTER OF THE HORSE' around top of coat of arms. Cracked.

Length 39 mm, width 35 mm, thickness 4 mm.
Plate 4

52. 1980-676/23 Pt. 6: Circular seal with octagonal stamp showing Leda and the swan. Inscription printed on backing: 'J...(127 ..../..ranomet...'. Ornate gothic script, part missing, black on white, from document.

Length 26 mm, width 24 mm, thickness 3 mm.

53. 1980-676/23 Pt. 7: Red shellac seal with oval stamp showing anchor surrounded by inscription. Admiralty seal. Cracked. Inscription around border of stamp: 'SIGIL.OFFI.MAG.ADMIR. MAG. BR. &C'.

Length 30 mm, width 28 mm, thickness 2 mm.

54. 1980-676/23 Pt. 8: Roughly circular seal with square stamp showing coat of arms on cushion. Arms contain hatches, bars, chevrons and possibly birds.

Diameter 31 mm, thickness 4 mm.
Plate 4

55. 1980-676/23 Pt. 9: Oval seal with oval stamp showing seated figure of Christ with two attendants, females, after crucifixion. 'CHURCH INV' stamped under image. Inscription in scroll: 'CONSUMMATUIT EST' under seated figure.

Length 43 mm, width 37 mm, thickness 2 mm.

56. 1980-676/23 Pt. 10: Oval seal with red stamp showing head of Shakespeare in left profile. Inscription printed on backing: '..../AND/..ONDON.' Printed black on white, from original document.

Diameter 24 mm, thickness 2 mm.

57. 1980-676/23 Pt. 11: Roughly circular seal with square stamp, made of brown shellac, with Greek inscription, backing paper printed in English. As no. 78. Greek inscription inside stamp: '*Ζωη μοῦ / σαζ / ἀγαπῶ*'.

Length 26 mm, width 22 mm, thickness 2 mm.

58. 1980-676/23 Pt. 12: Roughly circular seal of red shellac with square stamp showing royal coat of arms. Inscription above and below coat of arms: 'T..Y COUNCIL.DIEU ET MON DROIT'. Last line on scroll below coat of arms.

Length 29 mm, thickness 3 mm.
Plate 4

59. 1980-676/23 Pt. 13: Irregular seal of red shellac with oval stamp showing coat of arms, left side with boar, right side chevrons and fleur-de-lys. Crown above shield.

Length 23 mm, thickness 3 mm.

60. 1980-676/23 Pt. 14: Circular seal of red shellac with coat of arms on cushion, inside square stamp. Arms show lion, three pelicans and chevron.

Diameter 28 mm, thickness 3 mm.

61. 1980-676/23 Pt. 15: Oval seal of red shellac showing egg timer. Warped. Inscription around edge: 'TEMPS PASS'; very faint, rest unreadable.

Length 30 mm, width 21 mm, thickness 5 mm.
Plate 4

62. 1980-676/23 Pt. 16: Seal of red shellac with oval stamp of the master of the horse, with royal coat of arms. Inscription around edge: 'MASTER OF THE HORSE' curved under royal coat of arms.

Diameter 22 mm, thickness 3 mm.

63. 1980-676/23 Pt. 17: Irregular seal with rectangular stamp with cross and inscription around edge. Backing printed

with red floral pattern. Inscription around edge of stamp: 'UNITED ...'. Rest of inscription unreadable.

Length 18 mm, width 18 mm, thickness 3 mm.

64. 1980-676/23 Pt. 18: Tiny circular seal of red shellac with round stamp showing running horse on turf.

Diameter 11 mm, thickness 2 mm.

65. 1980-676/23 Pt. 19: Seal of black shellac with oval stamp showing female head in left profile; classical Greek influence. Same design as seal nos. 67 and 73.

Diameter 23 mm, thickness 1 mm.

66. 1980-676/23 Pt. 20: Circular seal of red shellac showing face, possibly Dionysus.

Diameter 21 mm, thickness 3 mm.

67. 1980-676/23 Pt. 21: Seal of black shellac with oval stamp showing female head in left profile; classical Greek influence. Same design as seal nos. 65 and 73.

Diameter 25 mm, thickness 2 mm.

68. 1980-676/23 Pt. 22: Roughly circular seal of red shellac with oblong stamp showing male figure, bowing, doffing his bonnet and wearing a kilt and sword. Inscribed above figure: 'HOO'S A WI YE' curved around upper edge of seal.

Diameter 21 mm, thickness 2 mm.

69. 1980-676/23 Pt. 23: Circular seal of red shellac with round stamp showing lion, with star above it.

Diameter 23 mm, thickness 2 mm.

70. 1980-676/23 Pt. 24: Circular seal of red shellac with round stamp showing bird of prey with outspread wings, surmounted by name: 'CHADACRE'.

Diameter 22 mm, thickness 2 mm.

71. 1980-676/23 Pt. 25: Red shellac seal with square stamp showing clenched fist holding branch.

Length 28 mm, width 26 mm, thickness 2 mm.
Plate 4

72. 1980-676/23 Pt. 26: Roughly circular seal with square stamp showing large-winged insect and surrounded by inscription: 'IT LIKE MY LOVE EXISTS FOR EVER'.

Length 29 mm, width 29 mm, thickness 2 mm.

73. 1980-676/23 Pt. 27: Seal of red shellac with oval stamp showing female head in left profile; classical Greek influence. Same design as seal nos. 65 and 67.

Diameter 24 mm, thickness 2 mm.

74. 1980-676/23 Pt. 28: Roughly circular seal of red shellac with circular stamp showing arm holding small handbag, as no. 75, from envelope.

Diameter 26 mm, thickness 3 mm.

75. 1980-676/23 Pt. 29: Red shellac; regular seal with oval stamp showing arm holding small handbag, as no. 74, from envelope.

Diameter 20 mm, thickness 2 mm.

76. 1980-676/23 Pt. 30: Circular seal of black shellac with round stamp showing palm tree and mosque. Inscription printed on backing: 'SERVICE'.

Diameter 20 mm, thickness 2 mm.

77. 1980-676/23 Pt. 31: Square seal of red shellac with circular stamp, showing palm tree and mosque.

Length 25 mm, thickness 4 mm.
Seal: length 25 mm, width 16 mm, thickness 4 mm.

78. 1980-676/23 Pt. 32: Irregular seal of red shellac with square stamp, with Greek inscription. Document backing seal printed in English. As no. 57. Inscription inside stamp: 'Ζωη μοῦ/ σαζ / ἀγαπῶ'.

Diameter 20 mm, thickness 3 mm.

79. 1980-676/23 Pt. 33: Irregular seal of red shellac with round stamp showing female head in profile, with flowing tresses and bust visible. Classical influence (right profile).

Diameter 27 mm, thickness 3 mm.

80. 1980-676/23 Pt. 34: Irregular seal of red shellac with round stamp showing St George killing the dragon, with inscribed border: 'THATCHED HOUSE CLUB' curved around edge of stamp.

Diameter 28 mm, thickness 25 mm.

81. 1980-676/23 Pt. 35: Roughly circular seal of red shellac with square stamp showing eagle with wings spread standing on crown. Cracked. Inscription printed on backing: '...10,/..t../ ..Glassho...', probably a nineteenth-century printed advertisement.

Length 24 mm, width 22 mm, thickness 2 mm.
Plate 4

82. 1980-676/23 Pt. 36: Roughly circular seal of red shellac with oblong stamp showing purse and inscribed: 'FRAE YE KEN WHA' above purse and curved around top of seal.

Diameter 18 mm, thickness 2 mm.

83. 1980-676/23 Pt. 37: Irregular seal with round stamp, of red shellac. Stamp shows shield with three birds and three spheres, surmounted by bird about to fly, and circled with wreath.

Diameter 29 mm, thickness 3 mm.

84. 1980-676/23 Pt. 38: Circular seal of red shellac with rectangular stamp showing house with inscription around roof of house. Inscription around top of house: 'IS IT YOU GOODBYE' curved around top of house.

Diameter 22 mm, thickness 3 mm.

85. 1980-676/23 Pt. 39: Roughly circular seal of red shellac with oblong stamp showing thistle, and inscribed above thistle: 'DINNA FORGET' curved round top of stamp.

Diameter 21 mm, thickness 2 mm.

86. 1980-676/23 Pt. 40: Irregular seal of red shellac with oval stamp showing two figures, male and female, entwined. Greek inscription on right-hand side of seal: 'ΠΙΧΛΕΡ'.

Length 35 mm, width 32 mm, thickness 2 mm.
Plate 4

87. 1980-676/23 Pt. 41: Circular seal of shellac with oblong stamp showing column and inscribed around edge: 'SECURE WHILE UPRIGHT' around three sides of stamp, sides and top of column.

Diameter 17 mm, thickness 2 mm.

88. 1980-676/23 Pt. 42: Roughly circular seal showing hand holding a wine glass. Inscribed around stamp edge: 'HERE'S A HEALTH TO ANE I LO' DEAR'.

Diameter 20 mm, thickness 3 mm.

89. 1980-676/23 Pt. 43: Red shellac irregular seal with square stamp with coat of arms of Lord Lurgan's Office, with greyhound and Scottish soldier on either side of shield. Scroll unreadable. Inscription on arms above and below shield: 'LORD LURGAN'S OFFICE/LURGAN'.

Length 31 mm, width 28 mm, thickness 2 mm.

90. 1980-676/23 Pt. 44: Roughly circular seal of brown/red shellac with round stamp showing coat of arms held by tiger and rhinoceros and surmounted by crown.

Length 29 mm, width 27 mm, thickness 2 mm.

91. 1980-676/23 Pt. 45: Roughly circular seal of black shellac with octagonal seal showing bird with outspread wings, and carrying branch in beak.

Diameter 21 mm, thickness 2 mm.

92. 1980-676/23 Pt. 46: Irregular seal of red shellac with oval stamp showing dove standing on upper branches of tree.

Length 20 mm, width 18 mm, thickness 3 mm.

93. 1980-676/23 Pt. 47: Irregular seal of red shellac with oblong stamp showing pair of wolves in forest.

Length 18 mm, width 14 mm, thickness 2 mm.

94. 1980-676/23 Pt. 48: Roughly circular seal of red shellac with round stamp. Latin inscription: 'Finem/respice' in centre of stamp.

Diameter 20 mm, thickness 2 mm.

95. 1980-676/23 Pt. 49: Rectangular seal of black shellac showing coat of arms: shield with three keys, surmounted by swan, and above an inscribed scroll (unreadable).

Length 23 mm, width 20 mm, thickness 2 mm.

96. 1980-676/23 Pt. 50: Irregular-shaped seal stamped with ovoid stamp with inscribed border, with: 'P' crossed at base in centre, ecclesiastical monogram, from envelope. Seal monogram reads: 'Sig.Austin Buchanan Prole Rector of Bathealton'.

Length 26 mm, width 24 mm, thickness 2 mm.

97. 1980-676/23 Pt. 51: Circular seal of red shellac with circular stamp showing winged Pegasus. Very worn. Inscription printed on backing: '...,CONW.../....NGLISH & FOREIG...'. Only part remains, from document.

Diameter 19 mm, thickness 2 mm.

98. 1980-676/23 Pt. 52: Irregular seal of black shellac with oval stamp showing coat of arms, surmounted by crown, with stag and horse on either side.

Diameter 26 mm, thickness 2 mm.

99. 1980-676/23 Pt. 53: Irregular seal of oblong stamp showing cupid, surrounded by French inscription: 'LA..... EST

L AMOUR SANS AILLES'. Very worn. Second word unreadable.

Length 25 mm, width 22 mm, thickness 2 mm.

100. 1980-676/23 Pt. 54: Irregular seal of red shellac with round stamp with Latin inscription: 'credete mi' around edge in gothic script.

Length 15 mm, width 13 mm, thickness 2 mm.

101. 1980-676/23 Pt. 55: Roughly circular seal of red shellac with oval stamp showing the sphinx.

Diameter 19 mm, thickness 2 mm.

102. 1980-676/23 Pt. 56: Roughly circular seal of red shellac with square stamp (small) showing owl standing on branch.

Diameter 18 mm, thickness 3 mm.

103. 1980-676/23 Pt. 57: Oval seal of red shellac with oval stamp showing female head in left profile. Classical Greek influence.

Diameter 23 mm, thickness 2 mm.

104. 1980-676/23 Pt. 58: Circular seal of brown shellac with circular stamp with coat of arms topped by arm smiting with a scimitar, and over prone male figure. Arms show pair of leopards, triangles, heads possibly of hounds. Latin inscription on either side of arms: 'Veritas usque/ad einem' in gothic script.

Diameter 23 mm, thickness 2 mm.

105. 1980-676/23 Pt. 59: Roughly circular seal of red shellac with oblong stamp showing cushion adorned with three stags.

Diameter 18 mm, thickness 3 mm.

106. 1980-676/23 Pt. 60: Circular seal of black shellac with round stamp of lion holding a cross, from envelope.

Length 22 mm, width 21 mm, thickness 1 mm.

107. 1980-676/23 Pt. 61: Irregular seal of brown shellac with round stamp showing eagle with outstretched wings.

Length 17 mm, width 16 mm, thickness 2 mm.

108. 1980-676/23 Pt. 62: Irregular seal of red shellac with square stamp showing head of man in left profile.

Length 21 mm, width 21 mm, thickness 3 mm.

109. 1980-676/23 Pt. 63: Roughly circular seal of red shellac showing coat of arms with merman on left and mermaid on right side of shield containing three fish, crossed knives, and three pairs of crossed keys. Inscription on scroll under arms: 'ALL WORSHIP BE TO GOD'.

Diameter 26 mm, thickness 2 mm.

110. 1980-676/23 Pt. 64: Round seal of red shellac, square stamp showing crane.

Length 28 mm, width 27 mm, thickness 8 mm.
Plate 4

111. 1980-676/23 Pt. 65: Irregular seal with square stamp made of red shellac, showing coat of arms surmounted by scroll.

Length 29 mm, width 29 mm, thickness 3 mm.
Plate 4

112. 1980-676/23 Pt. 66: Irregular seal of red shellac with oval stamp showing head of Athena in left profile. From envelope.

Length 20 mm, width 17 mm, thickness 1 mm.

113. 1980-676/23 Pt. 67: Irregular seal of red shellac with round stamp with motif of starfish above sea anemone on rock. Latin inscription on scroll above motif: 'SINE MACULA'.

Length 22 mm, width 22 mm, thickness 2 mm.

114–116. 1980-676/24–26: Three circular buttons of shellac coloured to imitate horn, surface decorated with incised oval metal eyelet affixed to base, nineteenth century.

Diameter 25 mm, height 11 mm.
Source: Newport, R.

117. 1980-676/27: Hand mirror of moulded red shellac, square body with circular mirror, handle decorated with tendril and flower design, frame of mirror decorated with fleur-de-lys, back decorated with head of a lady, early twentieth century. Inscription moulded on front at top of handle: 'PAT.JUNE.19.1866./Florence/12'. 'Florence' written in backward-sloping, flowing script. Second inscription printed on back of mirror: 'FEB 1925'. Stamped in blue ink with hand-held stamp. Third inscription printed on backing paper made of newspaper which includes line: 'YEAR OF OUR LORD 1885'. Handle cracked where joins body.

Length 241 mm, width 130 mm, depth 10 mm.
Source: Newport, R.
Plate 4

118. 1980-676/274: Oval mirror of black shellac, back decorated with seated woman and cherub, in front of castle, second half of nineteenth century. Mirror in very poor condition, shellac slightly chipped.

Length 259 mm, width 17 mm, thickness 7 mm.
Source: Newport, R.
Plate 4

119–123. 1993-164: Five medallions of brown shellac, with metal border and velvet backing. Decorated with moulded representations of mythological figures in profile, *c.*1880.

Source: Bright, I.

119. 1993-164/1: Oval medallion showing right profile of bearded Ancient Greek warrior wearing elaborate helmet decorated with winged animal (griffin). 'BARNETIIN' inscribed behind head.

Length 39 mm, width 32 mm, thickness 3 mm.

120. 1993-164/2: Oval medallion showing left profile of bearded Ancient Greek warrior wearing elaborate helmet decorated with dragon. 'BARNETIIN' inscribed behind head. Possible inscription in front of the head is indecipherable.

Length 39 mm, width 33.5 mm, thickness 3 mm.

121. 1993-164/3: Oval medallion showing right profile of bearded Ancient Greek

philosopher wearing headband. Unmarked.

Length 39 mm, width 33.5 mm, thickness 3 mm.

122. 1993-164/4: Oval medallion showing left profile of bearded Ancient Greek philosopher. Surface pockmarked. Possible inscription behind the head is indecipherable.

Length 40 mm, width 32.5 mm, thickness 3 mm.

123. 1993-164/5: Oval medallion showing right profile of horned boy, possibly Pan. 'BROWN' inscribed under head.

Length 37 mm, width 33 mm, thickness 3 mm.

BOIS DURCI

124. 1980-676/28: Black circular plaque of Bois Durci, depicting profile of Garibaldi. Moulded inscription on upper face: 'GIUSEPPE GARIBALDI/ GUERRA D'ITALIA 1859' and on reverse 'Bois Durci'. Patented in Paris, France, by François Charles Lepage and sold by M. Latry, early 1860s. Chipped along lower edge and at suspension point; ring missing.

Diameter 113 mm, thickness 14 mm.
Reference: Newport 1977: F2.
Source: Newport, R.
Plate 5

125. 1980-676/29: Furniture plaque of dark brown Bois Durci, decorated with ornate border and oval showing hooded female figure, with handful of crops, *c.*1860. Patented in Paris, France, by François Charles Lepage and sold by M. Latry, early 1860s.

Length 221 mm, width 123 mm, thickness 15 mm.
Source: Newport, R.
Plate 5

126. 1980-676/30: Furniture plaque of dark brown Bois Durci, decorated with ornate border and oval showing female figure, draped, bearing staff and bunch of grapes, *c.*1860. Patented in Paris, France, by François Charles Lepage. Two small chips.

Length 220 mm, width 121 mm, thickness 14 mm.
Source: Newport, R.
Plate 5

127. 1980-676/31: Dark brown circular plaque of Bois Durci, depicting Shakespeare. Inscription moulded on face: 'SHAKESPEARE' and on reverse: 'BOIS DURCI/2', letters uneven, '2' upside down and crossed with vertical stroke; metal suspension ring, *c.*1860. Patented in Paris, France, by François Charles Lepage. Edges chipped in three places.

Diameter 113 mm, thickness 13 mm.
Source: Newport, R.
Plate 5

128. 1994-1253: Dark brown circular plaque of Bois Durci, depicting right profile of John Bright. Marked: 'JOHN BRIGHT' and on reverse: 'BOIS DURCI'. Pierced at top for hanging. Patented by François Charles Lepage and sold by M. Latry, French, early 1860s.

Diameter 114 mm, thickness 16 mm.
Source: Fielder. J.
Plate 5

129. 1994-1254: Dark brown circular plaque of Bois Durci, depicting left profile of Richard Cobden. Marked: 'RICHARD COBDEN' and on reverse: 'BOIS DURCI'. Pierced at top for hanging (where slightly chipped). Patented by François Charles Lepage and sold by M. Latry, French, early 1860s.

Diameter 114 mm, thickness 16.5 mm.
Source: Fielder. J.
Plate 5

RUBBER

130. 1884-227: Grey vulcanised rubber medallion portrait of Thomas Hancock, 1786–1865, in gold frame, *c.*1843.

Diameter 255 mm, thickness 50 mm.
Science Museum Negative No.: 2/43.
Source: Patent Office Museum.
Figure 12

131. 1934-675: Rubber ball from Peruvian child's grave (reputed to be over three hundred years old), *c.*1600. Sticky on lower surface.

Diameter 60 mm.
Science Museum Negative No.: 3/43.
Source: Jones, F.
Plate 6

132. 1934-676: Plaster cast of original clay sketch of Sir Henry Wickham, by Mrs Alan Wyon. Late nineteenth/early twentieth century.

Length 220 mm, width 152 mm, height 365 mm.
Science Museum Negative No.: 4/43.
Source: Jones, F.

133. 1934-678: Two original rubber seeds brought by Sir Henry Wickham from Brazil in 1876.

Length 20 mm, width 17 mm, thickness 15 mm.
Science Museum Negative No.: 6/43.
Source: Jones, F.

134. 1934-679: Three modern rubber seeds from Ceylon, *c.*1934.

Length 28 mm, width 24 mm, thickness 18 mm.
Science Museum Negative No.: 6/43.
Source: Jones, F.

135. 1934-680: Frame containing three early rubber cartoons. Titled: 'THE AGE OF INDIA RUBBER', *c.*1830.

Pt. 1: The first cartoon shows farmers in smocks talking and being eyed askance by two gentlemen. The caption reads: 'For they Indian Rubber Smock Frocks wear/ And call them Macintoshes'.
Pt. 2: The second cartoon shows a man wearing rubber boots and standing in a pail of water. The caption reads: 'Boots made of Indian Rubber you/ See are every where I'm told.'
Pt. 3: The third cartoon shows a woman holding a squalling baby. A man is telling her: 'If they Indian Rubber Aprons wear,/ They'll never spoil their dresses.'
Length 310 mm, width 280 mm, thickness 12 mm.
Science Museum Negative No.: 1015/75 B,
   1016/75 B, 1017/75 B.
Source: Jones, F.
Figure 10, Figure 11

136. 1934-681: Hot-water bottle made from Wickham's heavily smoked hard-cure Para rubber. Attachment flap broken off. Label stuck on bottle is typed and reads: '*PURE VULCANISED RUBBERWARE.* / Antiseptic cure/ produced from rubber made on/ Sir Henry Wickham's machine 1924'.

Length 325 mm, width 198 mm, thickness 43 mm.
Source: Jones, F.
Plate 6

137. 1935-57: Five early vulcanised rubber mouldings in frames (two in one frame), made by Thomas Hancock, *c.*1840.

Pt. 1: Rectangular black plaque with moulded floral design.
Length 195 mm, width 110 mm, height 12.5 mm.

Pt. 2: Two rectangular black plaques in glass-fronted wooden frame, covered with brown passe-partout. Both plaques decorated with moulded gothic design. Left-hand plaque is a floral design; right-hand plaque shows the Virgin Mary and Child, attended by an angel on either side and a cherub below, the whole contained within a gothic screen. White plaque on front reads: 'EARLY MOULDING AND VULCANISING BY THOMAS HANCOCK'.
Length 232 mm, width 190 mm, thickness 14 mm.

Pt. 3: Rectangular black plaque in glass-fronted wooden frame. Decorated with raised moulding showing a military camp of a cavalry regiment, enclosed in a border of trees and military flags and a cherub below. White plaque on front reads: 'EARLY MOULDING AND VULCANISING BY THOMAS HANCOCK'.
Length 175 mm, width 125 mm, thickness 22 mm.

Pt. 4: Rectangular buff plaque in glass-fronted wooden frame. Decorated with raised moulding showing four horses with a man and dog in attendance, enclosed in a border of flowers and foliage.
Length 179 mm, width 124 mm, thickness 22 mm.
Science Museum Negative No.: 7/43, 8/43, 9/43, 10/43.
Source: James Lyne Hancock Ltd.
Figure 13 (pt. 2)

138. 1935-58: Three early moulded rubber mats, made by Thomas Hancock, all octagonal, buff in colour, with flowered border and central floral design, on fabric backing, *c.*1830.

Pt. 1: Length 230 mm, width 155 mm, thickness 3.5 mm.

Pt. 2: Length 233 mm, width 155 mm, thickness 4 mm.

Pt. 3: Length 290 mm, width 222 mm, thickness 10 mm.
Science Museum Negative No.: 11/43, 12/43.
Source: BTR plc.

139. 1935-59: Native Brazilian rubber toy in form of a boy in a hat, on horseback. Horse's body decorated with various designs including zig-zags and spots. Now flattened, and neck of boy repaired; probably latter half of nineteenth century.

Length 195 mm, width 134 mm, thickness 30 mm.
Science Museum Negative No.: 13/43.
Source: BTR plc.
Plate 6

140. 1975-166: Two rubber air cushions, dating from *c.*1903–13.

Pt. 1: Cushion no. 1 is cream with a criss-cross pattern, with an inscription: '18:10' and a second inscription: '3:4'.
Length 440 mm, width 440 mm, thickness 20 mm.

Pt. 2: Cushion no. 2 is folded in half (now rigid) and is cream with a criss-cross pattern with a blue trim; stamped: '18×15'.
Length 377 mm, width 230 mm, thickness 11 mm.
Source: Blount, B.K.

141. 1977-429: Half block of rubber built up by repeated dipping of a wooden pole in rubber latex, followed by drying out over a smoky wood fire, and final slicing in half after removal of the pole. Probably *Hevea brasiliensis* ex-Malaya, date unknown, provenance known back to *c.*1950.

Length 215 mm, width 180 mm, height 114 mm.
Source: ICI (Organics Division).

142. 1980-676/35: Flat oval mat made of pink rubber, moulded with raised picture of the Crystal Palace, made to commemorate the Festival of Britain, 1951, by Suba-Maid, England, 1951. Inscription moulded on Crystal Palace: '1851/51/51' in two places. Second inscription moulded above Crystal Palace: '1951' in gothic numbers. Third inscription moulded below Crystal Palace: 'Festival of Britain' in gothic letters. Fourth trade mark under above inscription: 'REGD/SUBA-

MAID/MADE IN ENGLAND'
contained within oval.

Length 279 mm, width 204 mm, thickness 6 mm.
Reference: Newport 1976: G10.
Source: Newport, R.
Plate 6

143. 1981-134/28: Three-pin electrical
plug made of dark brown rubber,
moulded in two parts, *c.*1940. Front
inscribed with a trade mark:
'DURAPLUG' and sticker: 'ALL
RUBBER/BRITISH MADE'. Back
inscribed: 'MADE IN ENGLAND',
'B.S.546/A', '5 AMP/250V'.

Length 50 mm, width 41 mm, thickness 40 mm.
Source: Greenaway, F.

144. 1987-659: Black rubber mat
embossed 'Charles Macintosh & Co …
May 1st 1851' with moulding of medal
marked: 'Council medal of the
Exhibition'. Moulded with the profiles of
Queen Victoria and Prince Albert.
Inscription: 'CHA. MACINTOSH &
CO. CLASS XXVIII/ VICTORIA D.G.
BRIT: REG. P.D. ALBERTIS
PRINCEPS CONJUX'. Also shown are
three mythological figurines, possibly
including Demeter, with inscription:
'COUNCIL MEDAL OF THE
EXHIBITION/ EST ETIAM IN
MAGNO QUAEDAM RESPUBLICA
MUNDO/ MDCCC/1'. Third
inscription bordered on three sides by
floral border and surmounted by royal
coat of arms: 'CHARLES
MACINTOSH & CO/ PATENTEES/
and manufacturers of the/
VULCANISED INDIA RUBBER/
UNDER THE PATENTS OF
THOMAS HANCOCK/21ST Nov 1843
and 18 March 1846/
MANUFACTURERS AND DEALERS/
IN/ INDIA RUBBER/ AND/ INDIA
RUBBER GOODS/ GENERALLY/
LONDON and MANCHESTER/ 1851'.

Length 252 mm, width 202 mm, thickness 3 mm.
Source: Birley, B.

145. 1988-624: Flying Anti-G suit,
MK4A, made by the Dunlop Rubber Co.
Ltd., Aviation Division, 1950. Grey/blue
fabric with rubber tubing and lacing.
Label sewn to suit: 'SUITS FLYING
ANTI-G MK 5A/ SIZE EX LARGE
REF. NO./ SERIAL NO. D1381 YEAR
5-6-61/ CONTRACT / MADE BY /
DUNLOP RUBBER CO. LTD./
AVIATION DIVISION' with: 'UNFIT
FOR SERVICE' stamped across
diagonally. Paper label attached; one side
reads: 'ANTI-G SUIT/ Suit No. D1381
Type MK5A Size/ Contract No./ Suit
made by 6600 checked 7171/ Bladder
6584/ Suit assembled 6565/ Suit tested/
Approved by A.I.D./ Despatched to
Endurance'; back of label reads: '5-6-61/
Repair Mon/ 1381'.

Length 1700 mm, width 900 mm, thickness 10 mm.
Source: BTR Industries Ltd.

146. 1988-625: Flying Anti-G suit,
MK4A, made by the Dunlop Rubber Co.
Ltd., Aviation Division, 1950. Grey/blue
fabric with rubber tubing. Label sewn to
suit: 'SUITS FLYING ANTI-G MK 4A/
SIZE SMALL REF. NO. 220/1059/
SERIAL NO. C739 YEAR 6-50/
CONTRACT 033/ MADE BY /
DUNLOP RUBBER CO. LTD./
AVIATION DIVISION' with: 'UNFIT
FOR SERVICE' stamped across
diagonally. Paper label attached; one side
reads: 'ANTI-G SUIT/ Suit No. C739
Type MK4A Size Small/ Contract No./
Suit made by 6602/ Suit tested/ Approved
by A.I.D./ Despatched' with 'UNFIT
FOR SERVICE' stamped across
diagonally; on label in biro: 'Tested at
/10000 cycles (9000 @ 5 PSI/ 1000 @ 7.5
PSI)/ for Endurance test'.

Length 1150 mm, width 940 mm, thickness 10 mm.
Source: BTR Industries Ltd.

147. 1988-627: Pair of shiny black rubber
galoshes, size 7, made by Dunlop in
Korea, *c.*1950. Sole marked: 'DUNLOP/

MADE IN KOREA/ 7/ MADE IN KOREA'; last line repeated three times.

Length 307 mm, width 105 mm, thickness 92 mm.
Source: BTR Industries Ltd.

148. 1988-628: Pair of olive-green rubber women's galoshes, size 8, high heel. Mid-twentieth century. Sole marked: '8'.

Length 257 mm, width 80 mm, thickness 180 mm.
Source: BTR Industries Ltd.

149. 1988-629: Two children's black 'Seaspray' plimsolls, made in England.

Pt. 1: Has a black sole and is marked: inside heel: '8/ Seaspray/ MADE IN ENGLAND'. Also 'BRITISH BOOT SHOES & ALLIED TRADES/ RESEARCH ASSN/ *SATRA*/ APPROVED/ LAST'; first two lines forming circle around last two lines. Toe painted '66'.
Length 170 mm, width 64 mm, thickness 46 mm.

Pt. 2: Has a brown sole and is marked: inside heel: 'BRITISH BOOT SHOES & ALLIED TRADES/ RESEARCH ASSN/ *SATRA*/ APPROVED/ LAST'; first two lines forming circle around last two lines. Toe marked: '38' (painted). Mid-twentieth century.
Length 170 mm, width 65 mm, thickness 47 mm.
Source: BTR Industries Ltd.

150. 1988-630: Sectioned white plimsoll, size 8, right foot, cushioned insole, made by Dunlop, marked: 'Dun.../Green/ cushion.../ insole.../8'. Sole marked: '8/ Dunlop/ 42/ MADE IN ENGLAND'. Mid-twentieth century.

Length 290 mm, width 75 mm, thickness 72 mm.
Source: BTR Industries Ltd.

151. 1988-631: Pair of flat mules, large, speckled brown rubber sole, white PVC upper sewn onto sole. Mid-twentieth century.

Length 278 mm, width 108 mm, thickness 53 mm.
Source: BTR Industries Ltd.

152. 1988-635: Two pieces of synthetic rubber (Butadiene-styrene copolymer).

Pt. 1: Shapeless translucent grey piece of rubber in envelope marked: 'this is a piece of the first/ Synthetic Rubber (G.R.S.) / to be made by Dunlop/ in England. January 1951/ RG'. 'G.R.S.' stands for Government-Rubber-Styrene, the American name for this material.
Length 70 mm, width 33 mm, thickness 9.5 mm.

Pt. 2: Black flat rectangular sample marked: 'R. GEDDES' with explanatory note stating that it is thought to be from the first production of I.S.R. Made by Dunlop in England, January 1951. 'I.S.R.' stands for International-Synthetic-Rubber, the British name for this material.
Length 92 mm, width 47 mm, thickness 3.5 mm.
Source: BTR Industries Ltd.

153. 1988-636: Section of black rubber ball, marked: 'BRU...', '2873' and 'MIN...'. Cream and red part of spot on either side. Mid-twentieth century.

Length 114 mm, width 61 mm, thickness 59 mm.
Source: BTR Industries Ltd.

154. 1988-637: Miniature black rubber Dunlop tyre, marked: '5.00-16' and 'DUNLOP FORT', the latter surmounted by a trade mark showing a tyre tread within a circle. Mid-twentieth century.

Diameter 135 mm, height 28 mm.
Source: BTR Industries Ltd.

155. 1988-638: Small black rubber tyre with valve, marked: 'DUNLOP/ UNDER DUNLOP PATENTS SEE/ ...ATIONS OF LIMITED/ LICENCE/ MADE IN GREAT BRITAIN', 'ESG', '...8×2, 10×2 INDUSTRIAL' and 'B', made by Dunlop, Great Britain. Mid-twentieth century.

Diameter 220 mm, height 47 mm.
Source: BTR Industries Ltd.

156. 1988-639: Two rectangular samples of black sueded fabrics, made by the Dunlop Rubber Co. Ltd, General Rubber Goods Division, Cambridge St, Manchester. Marked: 'SUEDED FABRICS/ MADE BY/ DUNLOP/ DUNLOP RUBBER Co., Ltd./ General Rubber Goods Division/ Cambridge Street – Manchester,/ Italian Distributors S.A.I.F. Via Barberini 3 Rome'. Mid-twentieth century.

Length 158 mm, width 110 mm, thickness 2 mm.
Source: BTR Industries Ltd.

157. 1988-640: Sample colour chart of Dunlop Rubber colours, seven strips of different colours: black, olive, dark brown, brown, ochre, peach, pale peach;

back of chart marked: 'EMERGE'. Mid-twentieth century.

Length 69 mm, width 16 mm, thickness 5 mm.
Source: BTR Industries Ltd.

158. 1988-641: 'Unistud' cat's eye, made of cream rubber, marked: 'UNISTUD' twice. Mid-twentieth century.

Length 100 mm, width 100 mm, thickness 20 mm.
Source: BTR Industries Ltd.

159. 1988-646: Three rubber samples on green card, contained in green box, made by the Dunlop Rubber Co. Ltd, London. Mid-twentieth century. Box decorated with picture of person cutting a rubber tree and marked: 'RUBBER SAMPLES' and 'with the compliments of the Information Office. Dunlop Rubber Co. Ltd. • St James's House • St James's Street • London, S.W.1.'. Inside the box lid is a map entitled: 'The chief/RUBBER GROWING AREA'. The card is marked: 'LATEX FOAM RUBBER (DUNLOPILLO)/ SMOKED SHEET RUBBER/ LIQUID LATEX/ Issued by the Dunlop Rubber Company Limited, St. James's House, St. James's Street, London, S.W.1.'

Box: length 177 mm, width 160 mm, thickness 37 mm.
Card: length 161 mm, width 149 mm, thickness 1.5 mm.
Pt. 1: Glass tube of liquid latex; light brown. Mid-twentieth century.
Length 80 mm, diameter 100 mm.
Pt. 2: Latex foam rubber (Dunlopillo); pale grey. Mid-twentieth century.
Length 69 mm, width 66 mm, thickness 27 mm.
Pt. 3: Smoked sheet rubber; light brown. Mid-twentieth century.
Length 51 mm, width 50 mm, thickness 3 mm.
Source: BTR Industries Ltd.

160. 1988-652: Baby's gas mask made of khaki-green rubber with metal frame, made by the L. and B.R. Co., November 1939. Marked: 'L & B.R. CO. NOV. 1939'. Inscription on brass-coloured label: 'THIS APPLIANCE IS/ GOVERNMENT PROPERTY/ ANY PERSON WHO HAS IT/ IN HIS POSSESSION IS/ RESPONSIBLE IN

LAW FOR / USING CARE TO KEEP IT IN / GOOD CONDITION. IT IS / TO BE RETURNED TO THE / LOCAL AUTHORITY IN/ WHOSE AREA THE / POSSESSOR MAY BE AT ANY/ TIME EITHER ON REQUEST/ OR WHEN NO LONGER/ REQUIRED'. Printed on rubber: 'LOT 993 985/ C 612'.

Length 500 mm, width 380 mm, thickness 310 mm.
Source: BTR Industries Ltd.

161. 1988-655: Set of twelve black rubber 'Gripstuds' and nails in original box. Each stud has six holes for attachment. Stud marked: 'MADE IN ENGLAND' on lower side. Upper side marked: 'PAT APP/ GRIP STUD REG./ DES.'. Envelope containing nails marked: 'NAILS FOR ONE SET OF/ GRIPSTUDS/ These nails are of a special size and/ are designed for fixing GRIPSTUDS only'. Card box is pea-green and marked on top: 'GRIPSTUDS/ PAT. APP. FOR REG. DESIGN', '3/- PER SET' , 'A special tough rubber stud for Football, Rugby and Hockey/ boots supplied with special nails and holes ready moulded/ for easy fixing' and 'JUST PRESS THE NAIL THROUGH – THEN HAMMER HOME'. Side marked: 'EXTRACT FROM THE LAWS OF THE GAME…/…/…/… shall be worn'. Base marked: 'ONLY GRIP STUDS HAVE ALL THESE FEATURES/…/…/…all weathers. Second side marked: 'DIRECTIONS FOR USE:…/…/… heel'. Either end marked: 'GRIPSTUDS'. Mid-twentieth century.

Stud: diameter 31 mm, height 17.5 mm.
Source: BTR Industries Ltd.

162. 1988-656: Black rubber wallet. Mid-twentieth century.

Length 337 mm, width 160 mm, thickness 2 mm.
Source: BTR Industries Ltd.

163. 1988-657: Black rubber bicycle saddle, made by Dunlop. Mid-twentieth century. Two holes for attchment. Top marked: 'MADE IN/ DUNLOP/ ENGLAND' on both sides of saddle. Underside marked: '8', 'JO', 'V' and '17'.

Length 260 mm, width 224 mm, thickness 64 mm.
Source: BTR Industries Ltd.

164. 1988-658: Woman's black rubber toe protector, sole marked: 'Work-Bud' and 'S', heel strap for attachment. Mid-twentieth century.

Length 235 mm, width 80 mm, thickness 67 mm.
Source: BTR Industries Ltd.

165. 1988-659: Protective buff-coloured rubber glove, for left hand, palm moulded with non-slip criss-cross pattern. Mid-twentieth century.

Length 460 mm, width 185 mm, thickness 69 mm.
Source: BTR Industries Ltd.

166. 1988-660: Protective grey rubber glove, for left hand, marked: 'Rated voltage 3,300 tested to 15,000 volts, RETESTED by Dunlop, Jan 1946' and: 'F.WT O' on other side.

Length 335 mm, width 175 mm, thickness 75 mm.
Source: BTR Industries Ltd.

167. 1988-665: Hospital bed, metal frame, with three Dunlopillo rubber mattresses, two blankets and three pillows. Said to be the first 'Dunlopillo' bed, *c.*1935.

Length 967 mm, width 900 mm, height 987 mm.
Source: BTR Industries Ltd.

168–173. 1988-667: Collection of six rubber bladders. Mid-twentieth century.

Source: BTR Industries Ltd.

168. 1988-667/1: Red, u-shaped.

Length 515 mm, width 460 mm, thickness 22 mm.

169. 1988-667/2: Grey, small, ovoid, attached to red tube.

Length 225 mm, width 28.5 mm, thickness 6 mm.

170. 1988-667/3: Red, circular, marked: 'Mandelle/3^66'.

Length 365 mm, width 315 mm, thickness 15 mm.

171. 1988-667/4: Red, elliptical with metal valve marked: 'SCHRADER

GLR'. Two grey reinforcement patches at joins.

Length 335 mm, width 102 mm, thickness 17.5 mm.

172. 1988-667/5: Red, ovoid, marked: 'No/3/DUNLOP NW', tube in centre, and three grey reinforcing patches.

Length 235 mm, width 150 mm, thickness 15 mm.

173. 1988-667/6: Red, ovoid, marked: 'No.5 DUNLOP WW', tube at one end, with two grey reinforcing patches at joins.

Length 310 mm, width 106 mm, thickness 12 mm.

174. 1988-668/3: Diving mask with buff canvas straps. Inside marked: 'BIM57/26D/ TESTED'. Mid-twentieth century.

Length 430 mm, width 320 mm, thickness 230 mm.
Source: BTR Industries Ltd.

175. 1988-668/5: Diving mask, brass air valve, marked: 'D.R. Co. 16 Jan 1950'. Marked: 'D.G.R./20' contained within circle. Inside stamped in ink unreadable apart from: 'MANCHESTER'.

Length 230 mm, width 120 mm, thickness 230 mm.
Source: BTR Industries Ltd.

176. 1988-669: Large rubber water tank. Mid-twentieth century. Marked: 'DUNLOP 100/ WATER TANK' twice. Marked: 'D>' twice; trade mark, with 'D' enclosed within a large crescent and '>' representing a large arrow. Also marked: 'MAX HEIGHT OF TANK WHEN FULL/ 1FT 6INS', 'AIR VENT' and 'THREADED ASPPT'. All writing in yellow.

Length 2094 mm, width 1345 mm, height 92 mm.
Source: BTR Industries Ltd.

RUBBER MACHINERY AND EQUIPMENT

177. 1933-576: Model, scale 1:12 of a single-geared rubber mixing machine, in glazed case. Inscription on cream plaque: 'HEAVY SINGLE GEARED RUBBER

MIXING MACHINE/ ROLLS 22" & 26" DIA. × 84" WIDE/ SCALE 1" = ONE FOOT/ MADE BY T. R. HAMPSON/ FROM DRAWINGS SUPPLIED BY MESSERS JOSEPH ROBINSON & Cᴼ· Lᵀᴰ/ SPRINGFIELD LANE IRON WORKS/ SALFORD, MANCHESTER'. Early twentieth century.

Length 510 mm, width 305 mm, height 230 mm.
Science Museum Negative No.: 1014/75 B
Source: Hampson, T.R.

178. 1935-53: Experimental rubber-mixing mill used and or made by Thomas Hancock, *c.*1820. Cogs marked: '1', '2', '3' and '4' respectively.

Length 850 mm, width 340 mm, height 240 mm.
Science Museum Negative No.: 1018/75 B.
Source: James Lyne Hancock Ltd.

179. 1935-54: Experimental calender (for rubber) (used or made by Thomas Hancock), with two smooth rollers and a change of two rough rollers, *c.*1820.

Pt. 1: Calender: length 210 mm, width 370 mm, height 202 mm.

Pt. 2: Rough roller: length 204 mm, diameter 60 mm.

Pt. 3: Rough roller: length 162 mm, diameter 60 mm.
Science Museum Negative No.: 1019/75 B.
Source: BTR plc.

180. 1935-55: Experimental masticator for rubber. Used and made (?) by Thomas Hancock, *c.*1820. Together with three parts, including handle and two masticator parts: one toothed, the other grooved.

Pt. 1: Main piece: length 200 mm, width 120 mm, height 100 mm.

Pt. 2: Handle: length 250 mm, width 25 mm, height 95 mm.

Pt. 3: Toothed piece: length 100 mm, width 35 mm, height 40 mm.

Pt. 4: Grooved piece: length 170 mm, width 45 mm, height 45 mm.
Science Museum Negative No.: 750/57.
Source: BTR plc.

181. 1973-274: Schwartz rubber hysteresis testing machine (believed *c.*1900). Wooden frame with metal fittings. Metal plate on front inscribed: 'Prof. Schwartz/ Rubber Testing Machine/ Manufactured by/ G. Cussons Lᵀᴰ/MANCHESTER'.

Length 637 mm, width 503 mm, height 1850 mm.
Source: Stevens, A.D.

182. 1988-626: Men's yellow plastic shoe mould, size 7, with metal base, jointed, marked: 'M7934 MM', probably for rubber shoes. Mid-twentieth century.

Length 284 mm, width 95 mm, thickness 90 mm.
Source: BTR Industries Ltd.

183. 1988-632: Tension gauge in wooden box, gauge marked: 'SP.I.31014' and 'DESIGNED AND MADE/ BY/ INSTRUMENT DEPT: FORT DUNLOP/ BIRMINGHAM'. Box marked: 'MPJ' within circle. Mid-twentieth century.

Gauge: length 267 mm, width 132 mm, thickness 40 mm.
Box: length 295 mm, width 180 mm, thickness 55 mm.
Source: BTR Industries Ltd.

184. 1988-633: White, hollow and glazed ceramic rubber glove mould, right hand, on rectangular base, marked: '8 1/2 /50434'. Mid-twentieth century.

Length 118 mm, width 98 mm, height 375 mm.
Source: BTR Industries Ltd.

185. 1988-634: White, hollow and glazed ceramic rubber glove mould, right hand, on rectangular base, marked: '10/ '4'8837'. Mid-twentieth century.

Length 158 mm, width 108 mm, height 415 mm.
Source: BTR Industries Ltd.

186. 1988-643: Three miniature steel boot moulds with attachment rings on top; for rubber. Mid-twentieth century.

Pt. 1: Length 91 mm, width 40.5 mm, thickness 19 mm.

Pt. 2: Length 81 mm, width 34 mm, thickness 17 mm.

Pt. 3: Length 147 mm, width 102 mm, thickness 40 mm.
Source: BTR Industries Ltd.

187. 1988-645: 'Star' rubber scraper, wooden handle with curved metal blade. Blade marked: 'STAR'. Mid-twentieth century.

Length 344 mm, width 70 mm, thickness 28 mm.
Source: BTR Industries Ltd.

188. 1988-647: Glass vessel marked with Dunlop trade mark. Mid-twentieth century.

Length 111 mm, width 111 mm, height 84 mm.
Source: BTR Industries Ltd.

189–191. 1988-648: Three metal photographic plates illustrating boots. Mid-twentieth century.

Source: BTR Industries Ltd.

189. 1988-648 Pt. 1: Dunlop 'Safetymaster Boot'. Mid-twentieth century.

Length 216 mm, width 111 mm, thickness 1.5 mm.
Source: BTR Industries Ltd.

190. 1988-648 Pt. 2: Dunlop 'Oil King' boot. Mid-twentieth century.

Length 216 mm, width 114 mm, thickness 1.5 mm.
Source: BTR Industries Ltd.

191. 1988-648 Pt. 3: Dunlop safety boot, unidentified type. Plate broken. Mid-twentieth century.

Length 152 mm, width 114 mm, thickness 1.5 mm.
Source: BTR Industries Ltd.

192. 1988-649: 'Gestefilm' exposure press. Wooden box containing cardboard, foam and rubber sheets. Stamped: '1405'; remains of inscription illegible. Instructions for use are printed on sheet attached under a glass lid to the underside of the lid. Mid-twentieth century.

Length 537 mm, width 317 mm, thickness 72 mm.
Source: BTR Industries Ltd.

193. 1988-651: Cream rubber-pouring jug, surface coated with rubber. Mid-twentieth century.

Height 180 mm, width 270 mm, thickness 150 mm.
Source: BTR Industries Ltd.

194. 1988-653: Steel rubber press with mould of a royal crown, with two crossed spears, and scrolls, with the negative of: 'JUNE 2ND, 1953' and 'CORONATION ELIZABETH R', the latter on a scroll.

Height 373 mm, width 247 mm, thickness 177 mm.
Source: BTR Industries Ltd.

195–199. 1988-654: Selection of white ceramic hollow moulds of various shapes and sizes from ICI; for rubber. Mid-twentieth century.

Source: BTR Industries Ltd.

195. 1988-654/1: Small stemmed segmented bulb shape, fourteen complete and one broken example, of two shapes, contained in box marked: 'IMPERIAL CHEMICAL INDUSTRIES LTD/(DYESTUFFS DIVISION)/ Oliver Wilkins Works,/ Siddals Road, Derby.' and 'ICI': trade mark above two wavy lines and contained within circle (on sides of box).

Pt. 1: Eight of small stemmed segmented circular bulb shape, seven complete and one broken examples, contained in box marked as above.
Length 116 mm, diameter 14 mm.

Pt. 2: Seven of small stemmed segmented oval bulb shape, marked: 'CHOP'?; contained in box marked as above (with 1988-654/1/1).
Length 122 mm, diameter 14 mm.
Source: BTR Industries Ltd.

196. 1988-654/2: Medium-sized stemmed bulb shape, screw-base, twelve examples, two slightly bigger in size. Two of each size in cork base.

Big: length 178 mm, diameter 41.5 mm.
Big with base: length 192 mm, diameter 54 mm.
Smaller: length 172 mm, diameter 33 mm.
Smaller with base: length 162 mm, diameter 52 mm.
Source: BTR Industries Ltd.

197. 1988-654/3: 'Mickey Mouse' head-shaped mould, screw base, one example.

Length 233 mm, width 70 mm, thickness 14.5 mm.
Source: BTR Industries Ltd.

198. 1988-654/4: Glazed mould, with waved edge, protruding trunk, screwed into cork base, one example.

Length 282 mm, width 58 mm, thickness 18.5 mm.
Source: BTR Industries Ltd.

199. 1988-654/6: Glazed, stemmed bulb, with rippled body, base has screw fitting into wax base, one example.

Length 264 mm, diameter 25 mm.
Source: BTR Industries Ltd.

200. 1988-661: Civil Defence Kit for the Dunlop Rubber Company, from the Second World War, *c*.1940, containing 19 items: 1. Four Ever Ready 'Flag' batteries bound together with black tape; 2. Three chalks, pink, mauve, blue; 3. Blackboard rubber; 4. Thirty-two film strips and accompanying instructional booklets; 5. Two tins; 6. Rag; 7. Glass jar of Detector powder; 8. Yellow can of No. 1 Detector powder; 9. Bottle of nerve gas stimulant; 10. Glass jar of charcoal granules; 11. Circular filter; 12. 'Aldis' film holder; 13. 'Crabtree' electric switch, square; 14. Three Bakelite plugs; 15. Glass lens; 16. Wire, wrapped around card; 17. Air pump in khaki canvas pouch; 18. Buff canvas harness; 19. Selection of Civil Defence stationery.

Length 439 mm, width 435 mm, thickness 132 mm.
Source: BTR Industries Ltd.

201. 1988-662: Steel plaque mould and rubber positive, made by Charles Macintosh and Co. for the Great Exhibition, dated 1 May, 1851. Mould engraved with negative image and positive with the profiles of Queen Victoria and Prince Albert. Inscription (in negative on mould) transcribes as: 'CHA. MACINTOSH & CO. CLASS XXVIII/ VICTORIA D.G. BRIT: REG. P.D. ALBERTIS PRINCEPS CONJUX.' Also shown are three mythological figurines, possibly including Demeter, with inscription: 'COUNCIL MEDAL OF THE EXHIBITION/ EST ETIAM IN MAGNO QUAEDAM RESPUBLICA MUNDO/ MDCCC/1'. Third inscription bordered on three sides by floral border and surmounted by royal coat of arms: 'CHARLES MACINTOSH & C<u>O</u>/ PATENTEES/ and manufacturers of the/ VULCANISED INDIA RUBBER/

UNDER THE PATENTS OF THOMAS HANCOCK/21ST Nov 1843 and 18 March 1846/ MANUFACTURERS AND DEALERS/ IN/ INDIA RUBBER/ AND/ INDIA RUBBER GOODS/ GENERALLY/ LONDON and MANCHESTER/ 1851'.

Plaque: length 355 mm, width 305 mm, height 15 mm.
Mould: length 255 mm, width 202 mm, height 10 mm.
Positive: length 250 mm, width 200 mm, height 5 mm.
Source: BTR Industries Ltd.

202–209. 1988-663: Eight Dunlop Factory warning signs. Mid-twentieth century.

Source: BTR Industries Ltd.

202. 1988-663/1: 'It is imperative that…'
Length 757 mm, width 502 mm, thickness 17 mm.

203. 1988-663/2: 'When ladder…'
Length 306 mm, width 205 mm, thickness 2.3 mm.

204. 1988-663/3: 'Dunlop Engineers Speke…'
Length 416 mm, width 127 mm, thickness 3 mm.

205. 1988-663/4: 'Warning under no circumstances…'
Length 382 mm, width 255 mm, thickness 6.5 mm.

206. 1988-663/5: 'Notice 1) Goods only to be…'
Length 329 mm, width 295 mm, thickness 1 mm.

207. 1988-663/6: 'Notice no unauthorised person…'
Length 355 mm, width 280 mm, thickness 1 mm.

208. 1988-663/7: 'Notice to Pan Operators…'
Length 610 mm, width 508 mm, thickness 2 mm.

209. 1988-663/8: 'NOTICE/ NO UNAUTHORISED PERSON MAY OPERATE/ THIS HOIST'.
Length 355 mm, width 280 mm, thickness 1 mm.

210. 1988-666: Metal punch for stamping 'Light Industrial' onto rubber, wooden handle; arrow on handle. Mid-twentieth century.

Length 110 mm, width 34 mm, thickness 35 mm.
Source: BTR Industries Ltd.

VULCANITE

211. 1979-624/144: Vulcanite fountain pen in variegated black with brass nib. Marked: 'Onoto the Pen De la Rue Co Ltd London'. *c.*1900. Clip and trimming missing. Inscription on body: 'ONOTO THE PEN/DE LA RUE & Cᵒ Lᵀᴰ LONDON'.

Length 134 mm, diameter 12 mm.
Source: Jesse, J.
Plate 6

212. 1980-676/32: Black Vulcanite fountain pen with brass clip, nib and trim. Late nineteenth/early twentieth century. Inscription engraved on body: '"ANCIENT ORDER OF FORESTERS"' and: 'WARRENTED/40t' in gold lettering.

Length 138 mm, diameter 13 mm.
Reference: Newport 1976: G1.
Source: Newport, R.

213. 1980-676/33: Red Vulcanite stylograph with hollow metal nib and wire flow control, *c.*1905. Cap missing.

Length 92 mm, diameter 12 mm.
Reference: Newport 1976: G3.
Source: Newport, R.
Plate 6

214. 1980-676/34: Vulcanite fountain pen in variegated brown and black. Marked: '64' on base. Brass clip, filler, trim and nib: brass. 1928/29. Hallmark on cap trim: 'F.D.W/.375 n.'. Trade mark on clip: 'WATERMAN'S IDEAL'. 'IDEAL' enclosed in globe. Same inscription on filler originally. Now only 'AL' of 'IDEAL'. Inscription on nib: 'WATERMAN'S/IDEAL/CANADA'.

Length 134 mm, diameter 13 mm.
Reference: Newport 1976: G2.
Source: Newport, R.
Plate 6

215. 1980-676/36: Rectangular Vesta match box of dark brown Vulcanite with metal studs, decorated ornately with Moorish design, spine marked: 'HANNOV./G.K.C./HANNOVER' (topped and tailed by elaborate tendril pattern), top marked: 'FEU', side flaps hinged for opening, 1900s.

Length 65 mm, width 42 mm.
Reference: Newport 1976: G12.
Source: Newport, R.
Plate 6, Figure 2

216. 1980-676/37: Rectangular Vesta match box of black Vulcanite, with metal studs and hinged side flaps for opening, upper surface decorated with Jubilee portrait of Queen Victoria, reverse marked: 'VR', encircled by leaf and flower decoration, 1897. Top chipped at corners: incomplete (chipped).

Length 51 mm, width 36 mm, height 12 mm.
Reference: Newport 1976: G13.
Source: Newport, R.
Plate 6

217. 1980-676/38: Rectangular Vesta match box of black Vulcanite, with metal studs and hinged side flaps for opening, upper surface decorated with a portrait of Edward VII in left profile contained within oval and surmounted by a crown surrounded by tendrils. Other side marked: 'HONI SOIT QUI MAL Y PENSE' encircling: 'EVII', all contained within a circle surrounded by foliage. After 1901.

Length 38 mm, width 51 mm, height 12 mm.
Reference: Newport 1976: G14.
Source: Newport, R.

218. 1980-676/39: Long tubular cigarette holder, with flattened mouthpiece, and expanded end to hold cigatette, made of dark brown Vulcanite. Late nineteenth/early twentieth century. Small chips.

Length 176 mm, diameter 13 mm.
Source: Newport, R.

219. 1980-676/40: Rectangular Vesta match box of black Vulcanite with metal studs, ornate moulded surface decoration including the word: 'FEU'; side flaps hinged for opening, 1900s.

Length 40 mm, width 28 mm, depth 12 mm.
Source: Newport, R.

220. 1980-676/41: Rectangular Vesta match box of red Vulcanite with metal studs and brown hinged side flaps and striking surface, top and base decorated with leaf design, 1900s. Top marked: 'FEU/MADE ABROAD'. Second inscription moulded on spine: 'NEW-YORK/HAMBURG./G.W.Co.' Top chipped at corner.

Length 50 mm, width 38 mm, height 12 mm.
Source: Newport, R.
Plate 6

221. 1980-676/279: Fountain pen in variegated blue and grey, Vulcanite? or possibly casein, with brass fittings and nib, marked: 'Burnham' on clip, and: 'Burnham medium S20' on knob, *c*.1900s. Trade mark moulded on clip: 'BURNHAM'. Letters arranged vertically, running down clip. Inscription on nib: 'BURNHAM/MEDIUM/S20'.

Length 113 mm, width 13 mm.
Source: Newport, R.
Plate 6

222. 1981-134/26: Three-pin electrical plug made of dark brown Vulcanite, ovoid, moulded in two parts, *c*.1920. Back inscribed with a trade mark: 'DURA PLUG/ PAT PEND/15 AMP'.

Length 80 mm, width 50 mm, thickness 48 mm.
Source: Greenaway, F.

223. 1988-642: Rectangular red box containing three samples of dental rubber in original wrapping (cat. nos. 224–226). Mid-twentieth century.

Box: length 155 mm, width 80 mm, thickness 27 mm.
Source: BTR Industries Ltd.

224. 1988-642 Pt. 1: De Trey's Rubber Golden Base marked: 'DE TREY'S RUBBER/ GOLDEN BASE, No. 8./ Manufactured by/ THE NORTH

BRITISH RUBBER CO. LTD/ EDINBURGH/ Sole World Agents:/ DE TREY & CO. LTD./ LONDON'. Mid-twentieth century.

Length 147 mm, width 76 mm, thickness 2 mm.
Source: BTR Industries Ltd.

225. 1988-642 Pt. 2: Quick vulcanising pink, made by the Amalgamated Dental Co. Ltd, England. Marked: 'Manufactured…in England', '…' marks place of circular trade mark: 'THE AMALGAMATED/ DENTAL CO. LTD' encircling motif using letters 'dTe' above eight-pointed star. Below '…QUICK VULCANISING PINK', '…' marks motif made of letters 'QV' crossed by a zig-zag line. Mid-twentieth century.

Length 140 mm, width 70 mm, thickness 2 mm.
Source: BTR Industries Ltd.

226. 1988-642 Pt. 3: Alston Brand Brown, made by the Dental Manufacturing Company Ltd, London, England. Packaging marked in pink lettering: 'BCM/DMC/ Alston … Brand/ BROWN/ MADE BY THE DENTAL MFG. Co. LD. LONDON ENGLAND'; '…' represents circular trade mark: 'TRADE MARK/ REG. NO. 3818657/ M/D C/ Ld'; first two lines encircle last four which are arranged in the form of a cross. Mid-twentieth century.

Length 144 mm, width 76 mm, thickness 1.5 mm.
Source: BTR Industries Ltd.

227. 1988-644/1: Red Vulcanite denture plate, marked: 'No 1/60 MIN/AT/60'. Early twentieth century.

Length 60 mm, width 55 mm, thickness 14 mm.
Source: BTR Industries Ltd.

228. 1988-644/2: Vulcanite denture plate with pink rim, red ridge, black centre. Early twentieth century.

Length 57 mm, width 51 mm, thickness 20 mm.
Source: BTR Industries Ltd.

229. 1995-636: Dark brown Vulcanite brooch in form of two interlinked rings crossed by a semi-circular band decorated with seven beads of French jet, with metal clip, *c.*1880.

Length 45 mm, width 30 mm, height 20 mm.
Source: Plastic Fantastic.
Plate 6

VULCANISING EQUIPMENT

230. 1935-56: Vulcanising lamp. Used and made (?) by Thomas Hancock, *c.*1840.

Length 140 mm, width 112 mm, height 252 mm.
Science Museum Negative No.: 1020/75 B.
Source: BTR plc.
Figure 14

231. 1935-208: Equipment used by Thomas Hancock, *c.*1840, for the vulcanising process.

Pts 1 and 2: Pair of vulcanising lamps made of tin.
Diameter 108 mm, height 182 mm.

Pt. 3: Steel mould, showing a negative image of a knight in armour, on horseback with raised sword, with decorative border including a coat of arms showing three stars in one half and a crescent in the other.
Length 145 mm, width 115 mm, height 18 mm.

Pt. 4: Rectangular steel mould base.
Length 259 mm, width 152 mm, thickness 25 mm.

Pt. 5: Steel lamp stand used by Thomas Hancock, *c.*1840.
Length 420 mm, width 125 mm, height 192 mm.
Science Museum Negative No.: 1020/75 B.
Source: Research Association of British Rubber Manufacturers.

232. 1938-516: Thermometer used by Thomas Hancock in his experiments on the vulcanisation of rubber (used with 1935-208), *c.*1840. Scale marked: from -30° to 570° Fahrenheit.

Length 425 mm, width 37 mm, thickness 23 mm.
Science Museum Negative No.: 1021/75 B.
Source: Research Association of British Rubber Manufacturers

233. 1988-650: Walker's Patent Phoenix Vulcaniser, Dental, made by Thos Walker and Son Ltd, 56 Oxford Street, Birmingham. Plate at front marked: 'WALKER'S PATENT / PHOENIX VULCANIZER/ THOS. WALKER & SON L^TD/ 56 OXFORD STREET/ BIRMINGHAM'. Pressure gauge

marked: 'ESSGEE'. Mid-twentieth century.

Height 620 mm, width 280 mm, thickness 295 mm.
Source: BTR Industries Ltd.

CELLULOSE NITRATE (CN, PARKESINE, XYLONITE, IVORIDE, CELLULOID)

234–317. 1937-30: Collection of 84 original specimens of Parkesine (cellulose nitrate). Invented and made by Alexander Parkes between 1855 and 1881 in England. BP 2675/1864, BP 1313/1865.

Science Museum Negative No.: 203/55, 204/55, 205/55, 206/55, 207/55, 208/55.
Source: Parkes, A.

234. 1937-30/ 1 Pt. 1: Roughly circular crude sample of Parkesine (cellulose nitrate), buff-coloured, *c.*1860.

Length 62 mm, width 58 mm, height 42 mm.

235. 1937-30/1 Pt. 2: Flat irregular piece of Parkesine (cellulose nitrate), sample. Buff-coloured, *c.*1860. Part missing.

Length 67 mm, width 56 mm, thickness 3 mm.

236. 1937-30/1 Pt. 3: Roughly circular disc of pale grey Parkesine (cellulose nitrate), *c.*1860.

Diameter 45 mm, thickness 6 mm.

237. 1937-30/1 Pt. 4: Thin, roughly circular, flat disc of yellow-brown Parkesine (cellulose nitrate), transparent spots in places, *c.*1860.

Diameter 50 mm, thickness 1 mm.

238. 1937-30/1 Pt. 5: Curved sample of dark brown Parkesine (cellulose nitrate), crude, roughly triangular, *c.*1860.

Length 83 mm, width 27 mm, thickness 10 mm.

239. 1937-30/1 Pt. 6: Rectangular flat piece of dark brown Parkesine (cellulose nitrate), uneven surface, *c.*1860.

Length 110 mm, width 58 mm, thickness 2 mm.

240. 1937-30/2: Unfinished comb of ivory Parkesine (cellulose nitrate), *c.*1860.
Length 188 mm, width 31 mm, thickness 6 mm.
Plate 7

241. 1937-30/3 Pt. 1: Flat triangular sample of variegated blue/pink/cream Parkesine (cellulose nitrate) sheet, *c.*1860.
Length 67 mm, width 26 mm, thickness 1.5 mm.

242. 1937-30/3 Pt. 2: Flat disc of bottle-green Parkesine (cellulose nitrate), sample, stamped: 'Patent Parkesine', *c.*1865. Trade mark die-stamped on top: '.PATENT PARKESINE.' in circular border; small flower separates.
Diameter 60 mm, thickness 10 mm.

243. 1937-30/3 Pt. 3: Flat disc of variegated coloured Parkesine (cellulose nitrate), *c.*1865.
Diameter 59 mm, thickness 19 mm.

244. 1937-30/3 Pt. 4: Flat sample of variegated blue/pink/cream Parkesine (cellulose nitrate) sheet, *c.*1860.
Length 77 mm, width 45 mm, thickness 1.5 mm.

245. 1937-30/3 Pt. 5: Flat disc of pea-green Parkesine (cellulose nitrate), sample, *c.*1865. Trade mark die-stamped on top: '•PATENT PARKESINE•' in circular border, small flower separates the two '•'.
Diameter 60 mm, thickness 5 mm.
Plate 7

246. 1937-30/4 Pt. 1: Rectangular experimental lithographic block of cream Parkesine (cellulose nitrate), stained green from ink on one surface, 1879.
Length 178 mm, width 66 mm, thickness 3 mm.
Plate 7

247. 1937-30/4 Pt. 2: Roughly rectangular experimental lithographic block of dirty brown and cream Parkesine (cellulose nitrate), inscribed in ink on upper surface with: 'Septr. 18th/79.' in mirror image, 1879.
Length 97 mm, width 76.5 mm, thickness 21 mm.

248. 1937-30/5: Transparent thin film, two rolls originally now broken into many pieces, now yellow, *c.*1860.
Length 55 mm, width 5 mm, thickness 4 mm.

249. 1937-30/6: Pen nib, now broken into many pieces, made of orange Parkesine (cellulose nitrate), *c.*1860.
(unmeasurable)

250. 1937-30/7 Pt. 1: Salmon-pink billiard ball of Parkesine (cellulose nitrate), *c.*1860.
Diameter 52 mm.

251. 1937-30/7 Pt. 2: Parkesine (cellulose nitrate) billiard ball, yellow cream in colour with brown patches, *c.*1860.
Diameter 30 mm.

252. 1937-30/7 Pt. 3: Salmon-pink billiard ball of Parkesine (cellulose nitrate), *c.*1860.
Diameter 56 mm.

253. 1937-30/7 Pt. 4: Ivory billiard ball of Parkesine (cellulose nitrate), *c.*1860.
Diameter 48 mm.

254. 1937-30/8 Pt. 1: Circular handle of green marble-effect Parkesine (cellulose nitrate), *c.*1860.
Diameter 56 mm, height 48 mm.

255. 1937-30/8 Pt. 2: Circular handle of green and white marble-effect Parkesine (cellulose nitrate), *c.*1860. Handle chipped in two places.
Height 22 mm, diameter 23 mm.

256. 1937-30/9: Toothed gear wheel of black Parkesine (cellulose nitrate), *c.*1860.
Diameter 64 mm, height 39 mm.

257. 1937-30/10 Pt. 1: Two spherical buttons of green Parkesine (cellulose nitrate), *c.* 1860.
Pt. 1/1: Button made of green Parkesine (cellulose nitrate), with a metal core and attachment.
Diameter 6 mm, height 15mm.

Pt. 1/2: Button made of variegated green and white Parkesine (cellulose nitrate), with metal core and loop for attachment.
Diameter 12 mm, height 15 mm.

258. 1937-30/10 Pt. 2: Button of black and white mottled Parkesine (cellulose nitrate), two holes for attachment, *c.*1860.
Diameter 27 mm, thickness 5 mm.

259. 1937-30/11 Pt. 1: Section of Prussian blue fluted tubing, handle? grooved at either end; narrows down length, made of Parkesine (cellulose nitrate), *c.*1860.
Length 199 mm, diameter 14–16 mm.

260. 1937-30/11 Pt. 2: Section of black Parkesine (cellulose nitrate) tubing with wooden core, *c.*1860.
Length 191 mm, width 17 mm, thickness 11 mm.

261. 1937-30/12: Rectangular piece of flat variegated green Parkesine (cellulose nitrate), *c.*1860.
Length 128 mm, width 112 mm, thickness 2 mm.

262. 1937-30/13: Flat roughly oval purse with brass fittings and green marble-effect Parkesine (cellulose nitrate). Lid and base, red silk lining, *c.*1860. Lining torn.
Length 71 mm, width 52 mm, height 18 mm.

263. 1937-30/14 Pt. 1: Hand-carved medallion of brown Parkesine (cellulose nitrate), decorated with handled basket of flowers, *c.*1860. Base has small chip at edge.
Length 27 mm, width 19 mm, thickness 8 mm.

264. 1937-30/14 Pt. 2: Hand-carved plaque of black Parkesine (cellulose nitrate), showing five cherubs at play, *c.*1860. One hole.
Length 123 mm, width 58 mm, thickness 2 mm.

265. 1937-30/14 Pt. 3: Hand-carved circular plaque of ivory Parkesine (cellulose nitrate), decorated with three cherubs and a billy goat, *c.*1860.
Diameter 85 mm, height 9 mm.

266. 1937-30/15 Pt. 1: Medallion in metal holder, of buff Parkesine (cellulose nitrate), showing cupid on back of swan, *c.*1860.
Length 23 mm, width 17 mm, thickness 6 mm.

267. 1937-30/15 Pt. 2: Female head showing right profile, made of red Parkesine (cellulose nitrate), *c.*1860.
Length 31 mm, width 25 mm, height 5 mm.

268. 1937-30/15 Pt. 3: Female head showing left profile, made of bottle-green Parkesine (cellulose nitrate), *c.*1860.
Length 42 mm, width 35 mm, height 5 mm.

269. 1937-30/16: Circular moulded plaque of green Parkesine (cellulose nitrate), showing eight gods and goddesses, *c.*1860.
Diameter 158 mm, thickness 4 mm.
Reference: Kaufman 1963: 26 (illustrated).

270. 1937-30/17: Letter-press mould of ivory-coloured Parkesine (cellulose nitrate), rectangular, for printing 'The Morning Dream' number 188, *c.*1860. Raised inscription on the upper surface in mirror image for 'The Morning Dream'.
Length 150 mm, width 87 mm, thickness 2 mm.
Reference: Kaufman, 1963: 27 (illustrated).
Plate 7

271. 1937-30/18: Flat, blue square plaque, saw-pierced and carved with a tendril design with circle in middle, made of Parkesine (cellulose nitrate), *c.*1855.
Length 49 mm, width 49 mm, thickness 2 mm.

272. 1937-30/19 Pt. 1: Crescentic hair slide of ochre-coloured Parkesine (cellulose nitrate), inlaid with elaborate design in brass, silver and mother-of-pearl, *c.*1860. Some of inlay missing and silver inlay missing.
Length 101 mm, width 26 mm, thickness 7 mm.

273. 1937-30/19 Pt. 2: Pointed oval hair slide of ochre-coloured Parkesine (cellulose nitrate), inlaid with silver border, and raised silver shield in centre surmounted by crown, *c.*1860. Pin from clip missing.

Length 82 mm, width 27 mm, thickness 5 mm.

274. 1937-30/19 Pt. 3: Rectangular box of horn Parkesine (cellulose nitrate) inlaid with brass, silver and mother-of-pearl, *c.*1860. One edge chipped.

Length 60 mm, width 31 mm, thickness 15 mm.

275. 1937-30/19 Pt. 4: Convex circular sample of yellow Parkesine (cellulose nitrate), inlaid with brass and mother-of-pearl, *c.*1860.

Diameter 38 mm, height 11 mm.

276. 1937-30/19 Pt. 5: Hand-carved, guitar-shaped sample of red Parkesine (cellulose nitrate), inlaid with brass and mother-of-pearl, *c.*1860. Some of the metal inlay missing.

Length 41 mm, width 22 mm, thickness 8 mm.

277. 1937-30/20: Rectangular piece of flat, cream-coloured Parkesine (cellulose nitrate), *c.*1881. Handwritten inscription in black ink on upper surface reading: 'No.2 Nov 12/81', in Alexander Parkes's handwriting. Handwritten pencil inscription on lower surface reading: 'No 2 /Nov 12/81 5-0' in Parkes's handwriting.

Length 117 mm, width 103 mm, thickness 4 mm.

278. 1937-30/21: Rectangular piece of cotton-cloth-backed Parkesine (cellulose nitrate) with stamping residue from same; brown, *c.*1860.

Length 82 mm, width 64 mm, thickness 2.5 mm.

279. 1937-30/21 Pt. 1: Brown flat sheet of Parkesine (cellulose nitrate).

Length 82 mm, width 64 mm, thickness 2.5 mm.

280. 1937-30/21 Pt. 2: Parkesine (cellulose nitrate) sheet from which discs have been stamped out, *c.*1860.

Length 46 mm, width 36 mm, thickness 2 mm.

281. 1937-30/21 Pt. 3: Brown Parkesine (cellulose nitrate) sheet from which discs have been stamped out, *c.*1860.

Length 18 mm, width 23 mm, thickness 2 mm.

282. 1937-30/22 Pt. 1: Roughly square, flat piece of variegated green Parkesine (cellulose nitrate) sheet, *c.*1860.

Length 83 mm, width 72 mm, thickness 3 mm.

283. 1937-30/22 Pt. 2: Specimen variegated sheet, example of the first experiments in colour of Alexander Parkes with Parkesine (cellulose nitrate), 1851, England. Inscription handwritten on back: 'Specimen of the first "experiments" in color/of Alexander Parkes' invention "Parkesine" 1851/ Mrs Gordon Scott (Grandaughter)' written in ink pen on sticky label. Second inscription handwritten on back: 'The property of Mrs Gordon Scott/ Grandaughter of Alexander Parkes of Birmingham – the "father" of plastics 1851/& inventor of "Parkesine"/ Specimens were exhibited in the Great Exhibitions of 1851/(Specimen in Colour)' written in ink pen on sticky label.

Length 197 mm, width 107 mm, thickness 3 mm.

284. 1937-30/22 Pt. 3: Flat strip of petrol blue Parkesine (cellulose nitrate), *c.*1865.

Length 152 mm, width 22 mm, thickness 1.5 mm.

285. 1937-30/23: Transparent orange film, possibly originally circular, *c.*1860. Cracked.

Length 69 mm, width 56 mm, thickness 0.5 mm.

286. 1937-30/24: Fragments of red-yellow marble-effect Parkesine (cellulose nitrate) block, with artificial cracks. Now broken into many pieces, *c.*1860.

(unmeasurable).

287. 1937-30/25 Pt. 1: Small transparent roll of green thin film of Parkesine (cellulose nitrate), *c.*1860.

Length 111 mm, width 5 mm, thickness 3 mm.

288. 1937-30/25 Pt. 2: Small roll of transparent brown film of Parkesine (cellulose nitrate), *c.*1860.

Length 53 mm, width 10 mm, thickness 3 mm.

289. 1937-30/25 Pt. 3: Small roll of transparent brown film of Parkesine (cellulose nitrate), *c.*1860.

Length 50 mm, width 8 mm, thickness 3 mm.

290. 1937-30/26 Pt. 1: Flat Parkesine (cellulose nitrate) dark brown circular button, double piercing centrally, moulded, upper surface striated, border, *c.*1860.

Diameter 22 mm, thickness 3 mm.

291. 1937-30/26 Pt. 2: Brown, circular button of Parkesine (cellulose nitrate), central double piercing, moulded, concavo-convex in cross-section, border, *c.*1860. Chipped.

Diameter 16 mm, thickness 3 mm.

292. 1937-30/26 Pt. 3: Moulded, brown, circular button, central double piercing, concavo-convex in cross-section, *c.*1860.

Diameter 15 mm, thickness 2.5 mm.

293. 1937-30/26 Pt. 4: Small, moulded, brown, circular button, central double piercing concavo-convex in cross-section, *c.*1860, border.

Diameter 9 mm, thickness 2 mm.

294. 1937-30/27 Pt. 1: Flat, circular seal of brown Parkesine (cellulose nitrate), elaborately carved with ecclesiastical motif of Madonna and child with two female attendants, with cotton backing, *c.*1861. Inscription on upper surface: 'Sedes Sapientia/Ora Pro nobis' around edges of seal; 'Sedes..' at top, 'Ora..' at bottom, gothic script (no dots on 'i' in 'nobis' and 'Sapientia').

Diameter 54 mm, thickness 2 mm.

295. 1937-30/27 Pt. 2: Flat, circular seal of dark brown Parkesine (cellulose nitrate), elaborately carved with ecclesiastical motif of Madonna and child within a shield border, with cotton backing, *c.*1861. Inscription on upper surface: 'Aoll S Maria Oseot/Literi Moribus Prastanti' in border around edge of seal, 'Aoll...' at top, 'Literi...' at bottom. Gothic script (no dots on 'i's).

Diameter 53 mm, thickness 2 mm.

296. 1937-30/28: White curtain ring of ivory Parkesine (cellulose nitrate), ring is circular in cross-section, *c.*1860.

Diameter 45 mm, thickness 9 mm.

297. 1937-30/29: White rod of Parkesine (cellulose nitrate) circular in cross-section, *c.*1860.

Length 502 mm, diameter 12.5 mm.

298. 1937-30/30: Paper-knife of red (ochre) Parkesine (cellulose nitrate), flat handle, blade oval in cross-section, *c.*1860.

Length 393 mm, width 36 mm, thickness 6.5 mm.

299. 1937-30/31 Pt. 1: Circular brooch of blue Parkesine (cellulose nitrate), with bar crossing centre and split by variegated red and green bead, with brass, *c.*1860. Incomplete (pin and hinge missing).

Length 50 mm, diameter 47 mm, height 15 mm.

300. 1937-30/31 Pt. 2: Circular brooch of Parkesine (cellulose nitrate), decorated with green, blue and red concentric circles, individually raised; blue knob in centre, with brass clip, *c.*1860. Clip attachment missing.

Diameter 54 mm, thickness 12 mm.

301. 1937-30/32: Fishing-rod-spool of yellow Parkesine (cellulose nitrate) with brass fittings, *c.*1860. Incomplete (one screw missing).

Length 70 mm, width 66 mm, height 62 mm.

302. 1937-30/33 Pt. 1: Circular moulded dish of Prussian blue Parkesine (cellulose nitrate), with ornate border, and cotton backing, *c.*1860. Parkesine cracked.

Diameter 119 mm, thickness 3 mm.

303. 1937-30/33 Pt. 3: Circular moulded dish of maroon Parkesine (cellulose nitrate), with ornate border, with cotton fabric backing, *c.*1860. Broken into two pieces with part of one edge missing.

Diameter 215 mm, height 16.5 mm, thickness 2 mm.

304. 1937-30/34: Rectangular hair slide of mahogany brown Parkesine (cellulose nitrate), inlaid brass and mother-of-pearl, with silver border, in square key design, *c.*1860. Incomplete (some brass inlay missing).

Length 86 mm, width 27 mm, thickness 1 mm.

305. 1937-30/35 Pt. 1: Rectangular hair slide of Parkesine (cellulose nitrate) coloured to simulate a pale wood, inlaid with brass and mother-of-pearl in design of stars and grapes, *c.*1860. Some of inlay missing.

Length 117 mm, width 39 mm, thickness 2 mm.
Reference: Kaufman 1963: 27 (illustrated).

306. 1937-30/35 Pt. 2: Manufacturer's sample of brown Parkesine (cellulose nitrate) inlaid with two decorative circular designs in silver, brass and mother-of-pearl, *c.*1860.

Length 94 mm, width 60 mm, height 6 mm.

307. 1937-30/36 Pt. 1: Medallion of green Parkesine (cellulose nitrate), showing right profile of female head, adorned with wreath, *c.*1860.

Length 20 mm, width 12 mm, thickness 3 mm.

308. 1937-30/36 Pt. 2: Medallion of black Parkesine (cellulose nitrate), showing left profile of male head adorned with ivy wreath, *c.*1860. Base chipped.

Length 19 mm, width 16 mm, thickness 3 mm.

309. 1937-30/37 Pt. 1: Tiny carved head of Jesus on plinth, made of amber-coloured Parkesine (cellulose nitrate), *c.*1860.

Length 10 mm, width 10 mm, height 27 mm.

310. 1937-30/37 Pt. 2: Carved head of brown Parkesine (cellulose nitrate), now collapsed, *c.*1860.

(unmeasurable).

311. 1937-30/38: Flat, thin square piece of fabric coated with gold-coloured Parkesine (cellulose nitrate), *c.*1860. One side chipped; corners discoloured.

Length 88 mm, width 92 mm, thickness 0.5 mm.

312. 1937-30/39: Rectangular strip of buff transparent Parkesine (cellulose nitrate) film, sample, made by the Parkesine Company Ltd, London, 16 January 1867, in envelope dated and stamped with the company name. Two corners missing. Trade mark punched on front of envelope: 'THE PARKESINE COMPANY LIMITED/WORKS/ HACKNEY WICK/LONDON/NE' in oval, first line inside border; next lines contained within oval centre. Second inscription on front top left-hand corner of envelope: 'Sample of Transparent/Parkesine Janry 16th 1867' handwritten in pencil in flowing script.

Length 97 mm, width 55 mm, thickness 0.5 mm.

313. 1937-30/40: Decorated, inlaid square plaque of Parkesine (cellulose nitrate), inlaid with wreathed design, consists of two sheets of brown and ochre Parkesine (cellulose nitrate), riveted together, *c.*1860. Some inlay missing; one rivet missing.

Length 77 mm, width 70 mm, thickness 5 mm.

314. 1937-30/41: Flat disc of cream-coloured Parkesine (cellulose nitrate), probably a sample, *c.*1860.

Diameter 63 mm, thickness 4 mm.

315. 1937-30/42: Flat, moulded, rectangular plaque of brown Parkesine (cellulose nitrate), decorated with cross in centre and corners filled with leaf design, *c.*1860s. Broken into two pieces.

Length 128 mm, width 72 mm, thickness 2 mm.

316. 1937-30/43: Rectangle of yellowy-cream Parkesine (cellulose nitrate), stone finish, sample, c.1860.

Length 108 mm, width 75 mm, thickness 13 mm.

317. 1937-30/44: Knife handle, part only, of green marble-effect Parkesine (cellulose nitrate), with iron core, c.1860.

Length 70 mm, width 16 mm, thickness 1 mm.

318. 1985-864: Parkesine (cellulose nitrate) denture containing two teeth, late nineteenth century, now degraded into pieces.

(unmeasurable).
Source: Plastics and Rubber Institute.

319. 1937-30/33 Pt. 2: Circular moulded and decorated dish of Prussian blue moulded Parksine (cellulose nitrate), made by Samuel Robotham's, Warwicks, Birmingham, England, c.1865. Used as base of budgie's cage, BP 1394, 25 April 1868 (Suggitt 1991). Trade mark die-stamped on centre of base: '•SAM^L ROBOTHAM'S•/ BIRMINGHAM/ PATENT PARKSINE/CAGE' – lines circular; first two lines outer border; last two lines in centre. Appears to be fake Parkesine.

Diameter 285 mm, height 18 mm.
Source: Parkes, A.

320–326. 1963-157/1–7: Collection of seven objects of cellulose nitrate (Xylonite and Ivoride) manufactured by D. Spill, as follows. Hair comb (Ivoride), part of hair comb (Xylonite), part of necklace (Xylonite), cravat pin with head (Xylonite), small hand mirror (Ivoride), two knives with cellulose nitrate (Ivoride) handles, walking stick handle (Ivoride), c.1870.

Science Museum Negative No.: 83/76 A.
Source: Frith, G.K.L.

320. 1963-157/1: Cellulose nitrate (Ivoride) mirror. The back is decorated with a moulded design showing a winged female fairy amid a flowery garden, with moon above her head. The mirror is bordered with red braid, and the frame of the mirror is decorated with moulded flowers.

Length 226 mm, width 80 mm, thickness 19 mm.
Reference: Kaufman 1963: 32 (illustrated).
Plate 9

321. 1963-157/2: Cellulose nitrate (Ivoride) hair comb of elaborate design with top decorated with leaves surmounted by four tulips.

Length 115 mm, height 32 mm, thickness 3.5 mm.
Plate 9

322. 1963-157/3: Cellulose nitrate (Ivoride) death's-head walking stick handle, with bearded man on one side and skull on other. Top of wooden walking stick attached. Said to have belonged to Daniel Spill.

Length 170 mm, diameter 38.5 mm.
Reference: Kaufman 1963: 32 (illustrated).
Plate 9

323. 1963-157/4: Knife with cellulose nitrate (Ivoride) handle. Steel blade tapered at end.

Length 249 mm, width 22 mm, thickness 13 mm.
Plate 9

324. 1963-157/5: Knife with cellulose nitrate (Ivoride) handle. Steel blade marked: 'ALEXANDER PATERSON/ FORTH WORKS SHEFFIELD'.

Length 264 mm, width 24 mm, thickness 15 mm.
Plate 9

325. 1963-157/6: Steel cravat pin with head of coral-coloured cellulose nitrate (Xylonite) in form of a running deer.

Length 84 mm, width 31 mm, thickness 11 mm.
Plate 9

326. 1963-157/7: Necklace of coral-coloured cellulose nitrate (Xylonite) in form of roses with chain links. In poor condition and broken into two lengths, with four roses and two links broken off.

Length 330 mm, width 14 mm, thickness 10 mm.
Plate 9

327. 1975-527/8: Black hearing aid with metal back and cellulose nitrate front, rectangular with rounded corners, with speaker on front with three ridges running vertically below it, with metal clip on back for attachment. Back marked: '"EMITOME"/ REG. TRADE MARK/ BRITISH MADE/ 318'. Black woven covered cable for earpiece. Large earpiece of black phenolic. Original box made of imitation black leather paper. Side marked: 'E1-1401'. Original cellophane wrapping. 1920s (see also cat. nos. 521–527).

Device: length 157 mm, width 83 mm, thickness 33 mm.
Earpiece: diameter 50 mm, height 20 mm.
Box: length 157 mm, width 83 mm, thickness 33 mm.
Source: Gregory, R.H.

328. 1979-624/1: Ivory cellulose nitrate umbrella handle moulded in the form of a mythical fish with teeth and fangs biting a circular imitation piece of wood, details highlighted in brown paint, red eyes also painted, 1910s. Two cracks in handle.

Length 151 mm, width 97 mm, thickness 30 mm.
Source: Jesse, J.

329. 1979-624/2: Bread knife in black leather presentation case. The knife has a cream cellulose nitrate handle moulded in the form of sweet corn. Made by Geo. Wostenholm, Sheffield, 1900s. The knife's steel blade is engraved: 'I*XL/ SAWEDGED BREAD KNIFE FIRTH STAINLESS/ GEO. WOSTENHOLM & SONS. SHEFFIELD, ENGLAND'. The blade has a silver attachment inscribed: 'STERLING'. Case lid lined with white silk, printed in gold: 'Wostenholm's/ I*XL/Gallery'. Case base lined in blue velvet, now faded to green where exposed to light. Brass fastenings; one broken.

Knife: length 360 mm, width 30 mm, thickness 23 mm.
Case: length 392 mm, width 70 mm, thickness 33 mm.
Source: Jesse, J.

330. 1979-624/3: Paper-knife of ivory cellulose nitrate, handle in the form of

moulded holly and mistletoe, 1900s. Slightly chipped.

Length 250 mm, width 25 mm, thickness 12 mm.
Source: Jesse, J.

331. 1979-624/4: Vase of horn cellulose nitrate, rectangular in cross-section, wider at base than at top, stands on rectangular plinth, front moulded with figure of a maiden in Ancient Greek dress reaching up to blossoms, 1900s. Rim cracked with two small pieces broken off.

Height 139 mm, width 49 mm, breadth 35mm
Source: Jesse, J.

332. 1979-624/8: Decorative ornate candelabrum of various multicoloured plastics, possibly cellulose nitrate, with three imitation candles and wicks and cast phenolic stem, early twentieth century. Probably French.

Height 456 mm, width 155 mm, thickness 126 mm.
Source: Jesse, J.
Figure 26

333. 1979-624/16: Cream and amber cellulose nitrate lamp modelled after the beacon on the Empire State Building, with fluorescent tube, made in USA by the All-Lite Manufacturing Company, Chicago (Illinois), 1938. Upper casing cracked. Inscription moulded on base: 'AL-LITE/FLUORESCENT LAMP/ PAT.NO.132645, 2293924/110V.50 CYCLE A.C./ ALL-LITE MFG.CO./ CHICAGO'; whole contained within outline, indented at top into V-shape. Second inscription printed on bulb: 'GENERAL GE ELECTRIC/FI5 T8:W...15-WATT/WHITE...U.S.A' in gold letters, 'GE' in handwriting contained within circle. Third inscription printed on base: 'A MAXILUME FIXTU/MAXILUME COMPAN"'; 'FIXTU' in first line is half missing, probably 'FIXTURE' originally, 'COMPAN"' must have been 'COMPANY'.

Height 525 mm, diameter 170 mm.
Fluorescent tube: length 420mm.
Source: Jesse, J.
Figure 27

334. 1979-624/20: Lamp of pearlised cellulose nitrate, in shades of cream, pink and maroon arranged in geometric design, designed by Auguste Bonaz, *c.*1930, made in France. Inscription engraved on base of lamp: 'AB....' rest of signature in cursive script. Second inscription between plug prongs: '6A 250V/REF 501'.

Overall: length 340 mm, width 116 mm, height 278 mm.
Pt. 1: Roughly rectangular shade with two cream sides, top and ends pink, silk braid stitching faded from salmon-pink.
Length 340 mm, width 116 mm, height 128 mm.
Pt. 2: Rectangular base with geometric block topped by two bulb holders, base pink and cream, top maroon, pink and cream.
Length 202 mm, width 88 mm, height 180 mm.
Reference: Exhibited at the World of Art Deco Exhibition, Minneapolis, 1971.
Source: Jesse, J.

335. 1979-624/47: Rectangular box, hinged, of cellulose nitrate, mother-of-pearl inlay effect, 1930s.

Length 160 mm, width 110 mm, height 30 mm.
Source: Jesse, J.

336. 1979-624/48: Semi-circular container with lid, of cellulose nitrate, with semi-circular handle on lid and cross-shaped feet on base, pearlised orange, made by Halex, late 1930s. Inscription on foot: 'MADE IN/HALEX/ENGLAND'.

Diameter 110 mm, height 78 mm.
Source: Jesse, J.

337. 1979-624/49: Circular powder box of pearlised green cellulose nitrate (Xylonite), conical lid which overlaps edge of base, base decorated with two incised parallel lines running around rim, made in England by the Xylonite Company, 1930s. Trade mark on base: 'XYLONITE/TRADE MARK/MADE IN ENGLAND'.

Diameter 110 mm, height 70 mm.
Source: Jesse, J.

338. 1979-624/50: Cigarette box in the form of a die, made of pearlised pale brown cellulose nitrate; markings painted in black; made in France, late 1930s.

Inscription on base: 'MADE IN FRANCE/INIXFLAMMABLE'.

Length 80 mm, width 80 mm, height 80 mm.
Source: Jesse, J.

339. 1979-624/79: Rectangular, yellow, mother-of-pearl cellulose nitrate cigarette case, clasp in form of a white hand with pearlised dark green sleeve, bracelet of gold set with diamanté and finger ring, art deco design, 1930s. Incomplete (bracelet stud missing).

Length 94 mm, width 80 mm, height 15 mm.
Reference: Hillier 1971: 176, 212 (no.1392).
Source: Jesse, J.

340. 1979-624/80: Rectangular ivory cellulose nitrate cigarette case, clasp in form of a hand with green sleeve and gold and diamanté bracelet, lid rimmed with blue-and-white-striped strip, art deco design, 1930s. Inscription on side of partition: 'FOREIGN' stamped in gold letters.

Length 88 mm, width 74 mm, depth 16 mm.
Source: Jesse, J.

341. 1979-624/81: Rectangular, blue, mother-of-pearl cellulose nitrate cigarette case, clasp in form of a white hand with marked green sleeve and bracelet of gold set with diamanté, box lined with ivory cellulose nitrate, art deco design, 1930s. Incomplete (ring missing).

Length 90 mm, width 75 mm, height 15 mm.
Reference: Hillier 1971: 176, 212 (no. 1392).
Source: Jesse, J.
Plate 8

342. 1979-624/82: Rectangular, pink, mother-of-pearl cellulose nitrate cigarette case, clasp in form of a hand with sleeve and bracelet, lid rimmed with blue-and-white-striped strip, art deco design, 1930s. Incomplete (ring missing). Inscription inside lid: 'FOREIGN'.

Length 86 mm, width 79 mm, depth 16 mm.
Reference: Hillier 1971: 176, 212 (no. 1392).
Source: Jesse, J.

343. 1979-624/83: Rectangular, yellow, mother-of-pearl cellulose nitrate cigarette case, clasp in form of a white hand holding a gem, lid edged with blue-and-white-striped border, art deco design, 1930s. Incomplete (ring missing). Inscription inside base: 'FOREIGN'.

Length 95 mm, width 80 mm, height 14 mm.
Source: Jesse, J.

344. 1979-624/119: Black cellulose nitrate vanity case in form of a pair of opera glasses with silk tassle, containing powder compact, lipstick, rouge and scent compartments, large black tassel, *c.*1920. Rouge missing.

Length 106 mm, width 65 mm, height 37 mm.
Pt. 1: Cylindrical glass scent bottle with lid attached to dipper.
Length 42 mm, diameter 9 mm.
Pt. 2: Cylindrical lipstick with metal casing containing crimson lipstick, attached to cellulose nitrate casing.
Length 58 mm, diameter 11 mm.
Pt. 3: Circular compact containing pale pink powder and white cotton puff.
Diameter 34 mm.
Source: Jesse, J.

345. 1979-624/122: Cylindrical cellulose nitrate cigarette case in form of female clown (Pierrette); painted brown and orange on cream base, with cylindrical cigarette holder in pale pea-green cast phenolic, which widens out where holds cigarette, *c.*1930, French. Inscription painted on base: 'DEPOSE'. Second inscription in form of signature painted on bottom edge: 'Adm'. 'd' could be small 'a'. Cursive script.

Length 87 mm, diameter 16 mm.
Case: length 87 mm, diameter 16 mm.
Holder: length 51 mm, diameter 10 mm.
Source: Jesse, J.

346. 1979-624/123: Cylindrical painted cellulose nitrate needle case, in form of hatted and blazered female, with cropped hair; purple base with brass eagle crest; made in France, *c.*1920. Inscription printed on base: 'MADE IN FRANCE'. Black on white, oval sticker with black border. Eagle surmounts shield showing circle of nine stars split by torch.

Length 73 mm, diameter 16 mm.
Source: Jesse, J.

347. 1979-624/124: Manicure set inside red cellulose nitrate tube, containing three steel manicure tools, *c.*1920.

Length 78 mm, diameter 18 mm.
Pt. 1: Cylindrical red tube, screw fitting.
Length 78 mm, diameter 18 mm.
Pt. 2: Steel nail file with cylindrical red cellulose nitrate handle.
Length 71 mm, diameter 6 mm.
Pt. 3: Steel cuticle pusher with cylindrical red cellulose nitrate handle.
Length 70 mm, diameter 6 mm.
Pt. 4: Steel cuticle trimmer with cylindrical red cellulose nitrate handle.
Length 70 mm, diameter 6 mm.
Source: Jesse, J.

348. 1979-624/127: Pair of painted dancing figures on clip, of cellulose nitrate, male figure in evening dress with tails, female figure in long blue dress with gold decoration and orange shoes, 1914. Figures broken off clip.

Figures: height 44 mm, width 15 mm, breadth 10 mm.
Clip: height 28 mm, width 12 mm, breadth 9 mm.
Source: Jesse, J.

349. 1979-624/128: Pair of painted dancing figures on clip, of cellulose nitrate, male figure in evening dress with tails, female figure in blue jacket with gold decoration, long orange skirt, black hat, blue shoes, 1914.

Height 67 mm, width 16 mm, breadth 16 mm.
Source: Jesse, J.

350. 1979-624/143: Pin tray made of cellulose nitrate, in Japanese style; black lacquer base of phenolic, with rectangular tray of cream marble effect, *c.*1930s.

Length 69 mm, width 53 mm, height 11 mm.
Source: Jesse, J.

351. 1979-624/160: Brooch of white cellulose nitrate in form of hat, gloves and cane, cane has black handle, 1940s.

Length 92 mm, width 42 mm, height 18 mm.
Source: Jesse, J.

352. 1979-624/161: Brooch of horn cellulose nitrate, moulded in form of a large bird in flight, 1920s. Incomplete (tail broken off).

Length 102 mm, width 65 mm, height 8 mm.
Source: Jesse, J.

353. 1979-624/166: Bracelet of ivory cellulose nitrate, moulded with decoration of flowers, 1920s. Inscription printed on inner surface: 'IRENN'; blurred blueprint, penultimate letter not certain.

Diameter 73 mm, height 17 mm.
Source: Jesse, J.

354. 1979-624/178: Mother-of-pearl cellulose nitrate portable speaker decorated with a stylised, art deco woman's head. The base in tortoiseshell effect, with brass feet and fittings. Made by Minilux Herror, 1930. Base impressed: 'Minilux Herror No 495. Brevete et Depose'.

Diameter 87 mm, height 133 mm.
Source: Jesse, J.

355. 1979-624/185: Cellulose nitrate paper-knife and pencil holder in the form of an alligator with open jaws encasing pencil topped by a head (black), 1900s.

Length 202 mm, width 45 mm, thickness 16 mm.
Source: Jesse, J.

356. 1979-624/203: Amber cellulose nitrate vase, with geometric shape, sprayed with stencilled art deco design of triangles in pink, black, white and blue. Black base flat. Made in the USA, *c.*1930.

Height 149 mm, width 82 mm, depth 42 mm.
Source: Jesse, J.

357. 1979-624/208: Seven-sided, jade-coloured box, probably cellulose nitrate, with lid decorated in Sino-Deco style, *c.*1920s. Trade mark in centre of base: 'LAVERNE/../AMER-LITE'. Middle line contains arch motif round which 'LAVERNE' and 'AMER-LITE' curve.

Length 120 mm, width 120 mm, height 46 mm.
Source: Jesse, J.

358. 1979-624/212: Octagonal cellulose nitrate box, black lid and base, sides are black alternating with orange and brown, 1920s.

Length 79 mm, width 79 mm, height 53 mm.
Source: Jesse, J.

359. 1979-624/220: Fry's chocolate box, cardboard covered with light blue velvet. Lid decorated with pinned sheet of cellulose nitrate moulded with classical scene showing musicians and dancing maidens; made in England, by J.S. Fry & Sons, Bristol, *c.*1910. Trade mark printed inside lid: 'PURE CONCENTRATED COCOA/BY SPECIAL APPOINTMENT/J.S. FRY & SONS,/ LIMITED/BRISTOL AND LONDON' in gold on white oval sticker; in centre of lid inside, royal coat of arms after line two.

Length 304 mm, width 156 mm, height 41 mm.
Source: Jesse, J.

360. 1979-624/221: Circular container with lid, of cellulose nitrate, in black and yellowed-ivory checkerboard pattern, *c.*1930s

Height 33 mm.
Lid: diameter 75 mm, height 13 mm.
Box: diameter 67 mm, height 25 mm.
Reference: Bennett 1979: 16 (centre row left).
Source: Jesse, J.

361. 1979-624/226: Circular box of ivory cellulose nitrate, slip-on lid decorated with applied bouquet of flowers, incised line runs around rim of base, 1900s.

Diameter 110 mm, height 50 mm.
Source: Jesse, J.
Plate 8

362. 1979-624/228: Rectangular spectacles case of cellulose nitrate, black base, mother-of-pearl lid, snap fastening, hinged, early twentieth century, probably French. Inscription inside edge of base: 'DEPOSE'. Second inscription inside edge of base: 'Hermann Julliard' in cursive script; difficult to read as appears to have been overstamped.

Length 130 mm, width 60 mm, thickness 15 mm.
Source: Jesse, J.

363. 1979-624/231: Square cellulose nitrate plaque of the head of Queen Victoria, head is white on blue ground surrounded by flowered lattice work picked out with gold paint, black frame with gold edging, 1900, possibly French. Inscription moulded on base of veil: 'Deponirl 1056' in cursive script, underlined backwards from 'L'.

Length 182 mm, width 182 mm, thickness 13 mm.
Source: Jesse, J.

364. 1979-624/232: Vase of ivory cellulose nitrate decorated with a moulded figure of a girl in classical drapery seated on the shoulder of the vase and with a cupid at the base, vase stands on circular black plinth, 1900s.

Height 105 mm, diameter 35 mm.
Source: Jesse, J.

365. 1979-624/233: Handle of walking stick or umbrella, of cellulose nitrate, cylindrical narrowing towards base, yellowy-green in colour, decorated at top with raised moulded pattern of leaves and flowers, leaves painted green, flowers white, 1900s. One leaf broken off.

Length 203 mm, diameter 42 mm.
Source: Jesse, J.

366. 1979-624/234: Evening handbag of ivory cellulose nitrate, lid decorated with linear black decoration and metal studs, centre of lid decorated with oval pattern of black paste brilliants and peach brocade, with mirror, black and white silk string handle and tassel, 1925.

Length 151 mm, width 100 mm, height 38 mm.
Source: Jesse, J.
Plate 8

367. 1979-624/235: Ornate hair comb of ivory cellulose nitrate, four teeth, body trapezoidal in shape and decorated with linear design of painted black edge; right-angled line of black brilliants alternating with brass studs, cut across by cut-out design of black paste stones, 1925.

Length 187 mm, width 78 mm, thickness 7 mm, height 14 mm.
Source: Jesse, J.

368. 1979-624/236: Paper-knife of ivory cellulose nitrate, handle in form of moulded woman's head, with long hair and coned head dress in the form of a whirl, 1900s.

Length 196 mm, width 24 mm, thickness 18 mm.
Source: Jesse, J.

369. 1979-624/237: Tape measure in form of three-masted galleon; made of ivory cellulose nitrate with red cross on each of the three flags; two green stripes run around the hull of the ship; measures in centimetres and inches; made in England, 1920s. Scale printed on tape: '0(1)100cm'. Second scale printed on tape: '0(1)40 inches'.

Length 60 mm, height 56 mm, width 23 mm.
Reference: Pascale and Cernia 1983: 47, Fig. 8 (parallel).
Source: Jesse, J.

370. 1979-624/238: Mirror pendant of ivory cellulose nitrate, lid decorated with moulded head of a woman in the art nouveau style, 1900s.

Diameter 55 mm, thickness 15 mm.
Source: Jesse, J.

371. 1979-624/260: Table lamp of pearlised cellulose nitrate with grey and blue base and grey shade. French.

Diameter 240 mm, height 321 mm.
Source: Jesse, J.

372. 1979-624/265: Square clock overlaid with brown pearlised cellulose nitrate sheet, the numerals applied on tortoiseshell-effect discs, with tortoiseshell-effect discs running vertically down sides. 1930s.

Length 159 mm, width 64 mm, height 132 mm.
Source: Jesse, J.

373. 1979-624/267: Art-deco style clock, with semi-ovoid cellulose nitrate casing, pearlised yellow in colour, front decorated with three curved green parallel bands on either side of square turquoise framed face, two wooden feet, 1930s. Inscription on back plate:

'Foreign'. Scale painted on face: '1(1)12 hours'.

Length 187 mm, width 60 mm, height 75 mm.
Source: Jesse, J.

374. 1979-624/279: Belt of cellulose nitrate, green and black links, black links are circular and cylindrical, ovoid pendant of green plastic at hook fastening, 1920s.

Length 1060 mm, width 20 mm, thickness 6 mm.
Source: Jesse, J.

375. 1979-624/282: Circular box of moulded cellulose nitrate; light, mid- and dark brown in colour, lid decorated with a chamoix standing on a rock and backed by a dark brown disc, 1920s.

Diameter 44 mm, height 15 mm.
Source: Jesse, J.

376. 1979-624/286: Circular powder box of ivory cellulose nitrate with slip-on lid, contains powder puff of pale blue pleated silk with white down and ivory knob-shaped handle, made in Britain, 1920s. Inscription on box: 'BRITISH/MAKE'.

Diameter 70 mm, height 60 mm.
Source: Jesse, J.

377. 1980-676/9: Napkin ring of tortoiseshell-effect cellulose nitrate, 1900s.

Diameter 48 mm, height 23 mm.
Source: Newport, R.

378. 1980-676/10: Napkin ring of blond horn cellulose nitrate, 1900s.

Diameter 46 mm, height 25 mm.
Source: Newport, R.

379. 1980-676/11: Napkin ring of transparent green cellulose nitrate, decorated with Japanese-style moulded bird, flower and leaves which are glued on, 1900s.

Diameter 47 mm, height 25 mm.
Source: Newport, R.

380. 1980-676/45: Hair grip of tortoiseshell-effect cellulose nitrate rod,

which is circular in cross-section, grip is bulbous at bent end, c.1900.

Length 97 mm, width 35 mm, diameter 5mm
(of rod).
Reference: Newport 1976: M1.
Source: Newport, R.
Plate 8

381. 1980-676/46: Hair grip of tortoiseshell-effect cellulose nitrate rod, which is circular in cross-section, grip is indented twice along its length, c.1900.

Length 74 mm, width 14 mm, diameter 2mm (of rod).
Reference: Newport 1976: M2.
Source: Newport, R.

382. 1980-676/47: Hair grip of tortoiseshell-effect cellulose nitrate rod, which is circular in cross-section, grip is indented twice along its length, c.1900.

Length 74 mm, width 18 mm, diameter 2mm
(of rod).
Reference: Newport 1976: M2.
Source: Newport, R.

383. 1980-676/48: Hair grip of tortoiseshell-effect cellulose nitrate rod, which is circular in cross-section, grip is indented twice along its length, c.1900.

Length 74 mm, width 20 mm, diameter 2mm
(of rod).
Reference: Newport 1976: M2.
Source: Newport, R.

384. 1980-676/49: Hair grip of tortoiseshell-effect cellulose nitrate rod, which is circular in cross-section, grip is indented twice along its length and appears gently waved, c.1900.

Length 57 mm, width 14 mm, diameter 3mm
(of rod).
Reference: Newport 1976: M3.
Source: Newport, R.

385. 1980-676/50-52: Three circular black and cream marble-effect cellulose-nitrate-covered steel buttons, backing painted black. Front decorated with brass pressings in form of flowering branch encircled by gold band, 1920s.

Diameter 40 mm, thickness 8 mm.
Reference: Newport 1976: M6.
Source: Newport, R.

386. 1980-676/53: Circular black and cream marble-effect cellulose-nitrate-covered steel button, backing painted black. Front decorated with brass pressings in the form of a flowering branch, encircled by gold band, 1920s.

Diameter 40 mm, thickness 9 mm.
Reference: Newport 1976: M6.
Source: Newport, R.

387. 1980-676/54: Cylindrical hair-pin box of ivory cellulose nitrate, with separate lid embossed with an art nouveau pattern of flowers completed by four imitation rubies, *c.*1900. Lid shows hair-line cracks.

Diameter 35 mm, height 95 mm.
Reference: Newport 1976: M17.
Source: Newport, R.

388. 1980-676/55: Heart-shaped box of ivory cellulose nitrate, with separate lid embossed with an art nouveau pattern of flowers completed by four imitation gems which are orange, *c.*1900.

Length 50 mm, width 50 mm, height 36 mm.
Reference: Newport 1976: M18.
Source: Newport, R.

389. 1980-676/56: Rectangular clothes brush of ivory cellulose nitrate with an embossed scene showing a water nymph holding a conch shell, standing amid water lilies, probably French, *c.*1900.

Length 154 mm, width 25 mm, height 40 mm.
Reference: Newport 1976: M19.
Source: Newport, R.
Plate 8

390. 1980-676/57: Oval hair brush of ivory cellulose nitrate with an embossed scene showing a water nymph gesturing to dragonflies, standing amid waterlilies and bullrushes, probably French, *c.*1900.

Length 208 mm, width 65 mm, height 27 mm.
Reference: Newport 1976: M20.
Source: Newport, R.
Plate 8

391. 1980-676/58: Oval hand mirror of ivory cellulose nitrate with an embossed scene showing a water nymph standing amid waterlilies and river bank

vegetation, dragonflies and a fish's tail also visible, probably French, *c.*1900.

Length 245 mm, width 100 mm, depth 13 mm.
Reference: Newport 1976: M21.
Source: Newport, R.
Plate 8

392. 1980-676/59: Circular powder box with lid, of ivory cellulose nitrate, onion-dome-shaped handle, shouldered, made in England, 1900s. Tip of handle chipped. Inscription on base: 'MADE IN/ ENGLAND'.

Height 74 mm, diameter 132 mm.
Reference: Newport 1976: M23.
Source: Newport, R.

393. 1980-676/60: Circular box of ivory cellulose nitrate, lid is pierced at top, 1900s.

Diameter 80 mm, height 85 mm.
Reference: Newport 1976: M24.
Source: Newport, R.

394. 1980-676/61: Circular dressing table box of ivory cellulose nitrate, lid is shouldered, made in Britain, 1900s. Inscription on base: 'BRITISH MAKE'.

Diameter 80 mm, height 80 mm.
Reference: Newport 1976: M25.
Source: Newport, R.

395. 1980-676/62: Circular hand mirror with handle in the shape of a ring, made of ivory cellulose nitrate, made in England, 1900s. Inscription on front of handle: 'MADE IN ENGLAND' within rectangle.

Length 250 mm, width 182 mm, depth 12 mm.
Reference: Newport 1976: M27.
Source: Newport, R.

396. 1980-676/63: Dressing table tray with waved sides and lipped edge, of ivory cellulose nitrate, made in England, 1900s. Inscription on base: 'MADE IN/ ENGLAND'.

Length 256 mm, width 191 mm, height 26 mm.
Reference: Newport 1976: M28.
Source: Newport, R.

397. 1980-676/64: Napkin ring of ivory cellulose nitrate, applied silver initial 'P' in ornate style, British Xylonite

Catalogue No. 471, late nineteenth/early twentieth century.

Diameter 46 mm, height 32 mm.
Reference: Newport 1976: M29.
Source: Newport, R.

398. 1980-676/65: Napkin ring of ivory cellulose nitrate, applied silver initial 'P' in ornate style, British Xylonite Catalogue No. 471, *c.* 1900.

Diameter 48 mm, thickness 33 mm.
Reference: Newport 1976: M29.
Source: Newport, R.

399–400. 1980-676/66–7: Two napkin rings of ivory cellulose nitrate, applied silver initial 'P' in ornate style, British Xylonite Catalogue 1899 No. 471, *c.*1900.

Diameter 46 mm, height 32 mm.
Reference: Newport 1976: M29.
Source: Newport, R.

401. 1980-676/68: Dressing-table tray with waved sides and round corners, of tortoiseshell-effect cellulose nitrate, *c.*1900. Made in England. Inscription on base: 'MADE IN/ENGLAND'.

Length 254 mm, width 192 mm, height 2 mm.
Reference: Newport 1976: M32.
Source: Newport, R.

402. 1980-676/69: Egg-shaped powder box of tortoiseshell-effect cellulose nitrate, weighted base contains pink powder container, separate lid contains mirror, *c.*1920.

Diameter 42 mm, height 63 mm.
Reference: Newport 1976: M35.
Source: Newport, R.

403. 1980-676/70: Oval hair brush moulded of tortoiseshell-effect cellulose nitrate, *c.*1920.

Length 233 mm, width 63 mm, height 47 mm.
Reference: Newport 1976: M36.
Source: Newport, R.

404. 1980-676/71: Dressing-table tray with waved sides and round corners, of tortoiseshell-effect cellulose nitrate, *c.*1900, made in England. Inscription on base: 'MADE IN/ENGLAND'.

Length 167 mm, width 67 mm, height 11 mm.

Reference: Newport 1976: M37.
Source: Newport, R.

405. 1980-676/72: Rectangular photograph frame of tortoiseshell-effect cellulose nitrate, blow-moulded into an art nouveau style, contains picture backing supported by two bands running across back, made in England, *c.*1900. Inscription on lower support band: 'MADE IN/ENGLAND'.

Length 171 mm, width 145 mm, thickness 11 mm.
Reference: Newport 1976: M40.
Source: Newport, R.

406. 1980-676/73: Rectangular photograph frame of tortoiseshell-effect cellulose nitrate blow-moulded into an art nouveau style, contains picture backing supported by two bands running across back, made in England, *c.*1900. Inscription on lower support band: 'MADE IN/ENGLAND'.

Length 171 mm, width 145 mm, thickness 11 mm.
Reference: Newport 1976: M40.
Source: Newport, R.

407. 1980-676/74: Circular dressing-table cellulose nitrate box in Loetz irridescent glass-effect with octagonal faceting, amber coloured, lid has waved edges and sharp corners, art nouveau style, *c.*1900, made in England. Inscription on base: 'MADE IN/ENGLAND'.

Diameter 94 mm, height 58 mm.
Reference: Newport 1976: M43.
Source: Newport, R.

408. 1980-676/76: Circular powder box of pearlised green cellulose nitrate, knob on lid and three circular feet made of transparent amber cellulose nitrate (Xylonite) which also edges the lid and appears in two stripes around body, made by Halex in England, 1920s. Hair-line cracks on lid and round body. Trade mark stamped on base: 'MADE IN/HALEX/ENGLAND', 'HALEX' contained within oval encircled by first and third lines.

Diameter 122 mm, height 80 mm.
Reference: Newport 1976: M48.
Source: Newport, R.

409. 1980-676/77: White billiard ball moulded in Bonzoline or other similar cellulose nitrate material; heavily filled, *c.*1900.

Diameter 45 mm.
Reference: Newport 1976: M54.
Source: Newport, R.

410. 1980-676/78: Ornate handbag pressed from ivory cellulose nitrate sheet, decorated with a pastoral scene on both surfaces and hand coloured, with brass catch, leather plaited thong strap and tassels, contains mirror, powder puff, and kohl tube, 1920s.

Case: length 116 mm, width 95 mm, thickness 21 mm.

Pt. 1: Deep red lipstick contained within cylindrical metal container, rounded ends, lid slots onto stud on base, whole slots into clips on handbag lid.
Length 51 mm, width 10 mm, thickness 9 mm.

Pt. 2: Kohl pencil contained within cylindrical metal container, round ends, lid slots onto stud on base, whole slots into clips on handbag lid.
Length 51 mm, width 10 mm, thickness 9 mm.

Pt. 3: Circular blue silk powder puff with fluffy cotton? base, oversewn by machine at edges, lower surface marked with original powder, whole fits into circular enclosure inside handbag lid.
Diameter 37 mm, thickness 4 mm.

Pt. 4: Circular bevelled mirror clipped into raised ridge in lower half of the handbag.
Diameter 59 mm.
Reference: Newport 1976: M55.
Source: Newport, R.
Figure 1

411. 1980-676/79: White cellulose-nitrate-treated cloth collar marked: 'H/ CLIMAX/ SEMI-STIFF/ STARCH SLIGHTLY C9/16', 'X700', '692?0?X'.

Diameter 139 mm, height 61 mm, thickness 6 mm.
Reference: Newport 1976: M59.
Source: Newport, R.

412. 1980-676/80: White cellulose-nitrate-treated cloth collar marked: 'GENUINE QUALITY/MORLEY', 'THE PRINCE', 'X700' and '16×14'.

Diameter 132 mm, height 48 mm, thickness 4 mm.
Reference: Newport 1976: M59.
Source: Newport, R.
Plate 8

413. 1980-676/81: Napkin ring of yellow cellulose nitrate trimmed with tortoiseshell-effect; in form of tube, first half of twentieth century.

Diameter 45 mm, height 30 mm.
Reference: Newport 1976: M60.
Source: Newport, R.

414–416. 1980-676/82–4: Three napkin rings of yellow cellulose nitrate trimmed with tortoiseshell-effect in form of tube, first half of twentieth century.

Diameter 45 mm, height 30 mm.
Reference: Newport 1976: M60.
Source: Newport, R.

417. 1980-676/85: Napkin ring of pink cellulose nitrate trimmed with tortoiseshell-effect in form of tube, first half of twentieth century.

Diameter 45 mm, height 30 mm.
Reference: Newport 1976: M60.
Source: Newport, R.

418. 1980-676/86: Heart-shaped box of horn-effect cellulose nitrate, separate lid has a bulldog-shaped handle also of horn, 1900s. Rim of base and lid cracked.

Length 52 mm, width 50 mm, height 50 mm.
Reference: Newport 1976: M62.
Source: Newport, R.

419–420. 1980-676/87–8: Pair of dice made of ivory cellulose nitrate with black markings, first half of twentieth century.

Height 22 mm, width 22 mm, breadth 22mm
Reference: Newport 1976: M63.
Source: Newport, R.

421. 1980-676/89: Handbag with marble-effect multicoloured mount and 27-link chain of cellulose nitrate with metal catch; bag crocheted from dull gold silk, with multicoloured lining of cotton attached by strip to a circular mirror framed with passe-partout. Probably French, 1920–30.

Length 192 mm, width 170 mm, thickness 18 mm.
Reference: Newport 1976: M70.
Source: Newport, R.
Plate 8

422. 1980-676/90: Hair comb of cellulose nitrate, cream base and black upper surface, body consists of petal-shaped loops arranged in a fan design, art deco style, 1930s.

Length 125 mm, width 110 mm, height 20 mm, thickness 2 mm.
Source: Newport, R.
Plate 8

423. 1980-676/91: U-shaped hair comb of amber cellulose nitrate, two teeth, formed from rod which is plano-convex in cross-section and widens round to form body which is decorated with 21 brilliants, 1900s. Incomplete (metal studs missing).

Length 115 mm, width 47 mm, height 23 mm.
Source: Newport, R.

424. 1980-676/92: Ornate hair comb of tortoiseshell-effect cellulose nitrate, three teeth, body decorated with cut-out tendril design, brilliants and metal studs, art nouveau style, 1900s.

Length 120 mm, width 60 mm, height 15 mm, thickness 2 mm.
Source: Newport, R.

425. 1980-676/93: Hair comb of tortoiseshell-effect cellulose nitrate, two teeth, body V-shaped and decorated with brilliants, incised oval decoration, edged with white-painted spots, art nouveau style, 1900s.

Length 92 mm, width 35 mm, height 12 mm, thickness 4 mm.
Source: Newport, R.
Plate 8

426. 1980-676/94: Rectangular box with lid, one side of box decorated with a raised figure of cupid which has been glued onto the surface, 1900s. Lid cracked down one side.

Length 114 mm, width 22 mm, height 22 mm.
Source: Newport, R.

427. 1980-676/95: Plain tortoiseshell-effect cellulose nitrate hair comb, with two teeth, square form, late nineteenth/early twentieth century.

Length 103 mm, width 42 mm, thickness 2 mm.
Source: Newport, R.

428. 1980-676/96 Pt. 1: Blue Amberol phonograph cylinder, of black cellulose nitrate, with recording of the Flying Squadron N.M. Band, made by Thomas A. Edison, Inc., Orange, New Jersey, USA, *c.*1917. Moulded inscription on end of cylinder reads: 'THE FLYING SQUADRON. N.M. BAND. Thomas A. Edison PAT'D 9 23345' in white letters, 'Thomas A. Edison' in cursive script.

Length 105 mm, diameter 55 mm.

Pt. 2: Cylindrical cardboard container, lid missing, printed in blue and black, on orange, includes details of manufacture and patentee. Printed inscription on front of cover reads: 'EDISON/BLUE AMBEROL/RECORD/PRICE IN THE U.S. – 35 CENTS'. 'RECORD' surrounded on either side by the trade mark of Thomas A. Edison saying: 'A PRODUCT OF THE EDISON LABORATORIES'. Second inscription printed on back of cover reads: '.../Patented in the U.S. July/12,1910, Sept.29,1914/DEC.4,1917. Patented in/ foreign countries./ NOTICE/No license whatever .../ .../ .../ .../ .../.../.../Phonograph/Thomas A. EDISON, INC./ORANGE, N.J., USA./.../.../...countries'.
Length 120 mm.
Source: Newport, R.

429. 1980-676/97: Cut-throat razor in case, *c.*1911.

Pt. 1: Cut-throat razor with plain handle of black cellulose nitrate, slightly curved, steel blade made by Kramm. Inscription engraved near end of blade reads: 'KRAMM'.
Length 160 mm, width 23 mm, thickness 8 mm.

Pt. 2: Case, of pressed paper, made by Puma, *c.*1900s. Incomplete (lid missing). Trade mark printed on long side of case reads: 'PUMA THE/WARRANTED TRADE MARK'.
Length 156 mm, width 32 mm, thickness 16 mm.
Source: Newport, R.

430. 1980-676/98: Cut-throat razor in case, with instruction leaflet. Made by the Durham-Duplex Razor Company Ltd. (Sheffield: 72 Arundel Street), No. 100, made in England, 1911.

Pt. 1: Cut-throat razor with plain handle of black cellulose nitrate, slightly curved, blade guard of chrome-plated metal contains replacement steel blade. Inscription engraved near the end of the blade reads: 'MADE IN/SHEFFIELD, ENG.'. Second inscription engraved on the flat surface of the blade reads: 'DURHAM DUPLEX RAZOR CO. LTD/JULY 4 1911/SHEFFIELD ENGLAND'.
Length 145 mm, width 24 mm, thickness 12 mm.

Pt. 2: Rectangular flat box, black base, red lid, made of cardboard, red of lid is mottled. Inscription printed on lid reads: 'DURHAM DUPLEX RAZ.../NO.100'. 'RA..' is short for 'RAZOR', last letters covered by price sticker. Second inscription printed on lid reads: 'Price/2/6/including Tax'.

Pt. 3: Instruction leaflet for the Durham-Duplex Razor, full instructions with black-and-white photographs. Inscription printed on both sides of leaflet reads: 'NOTICE WHEN SHAVING ... SHEFFIELD, 1, ENGLAND'. Leaflet gives detailed instructions for assembly, and uses are illustrated.
Length 210 mm, width 140 mm.
Source: Newport, R.

431. 1980-676/99: Milkmaid statuette of ivory cellulose nitrate, carrying yoke across shoulders, with metal chain, one chain and bucket missing, standing on circular flat black base, remains of red and black paint, made in Japan, *c.*1950s. Inscription on base: 'MADE IN JAPAN'.
Height 105 mm, diameter 52 mm.
Source: Newport, R.

432. 1980-676/100: Milkboy statuette of ivory cellulose nitrate, carrying yoke across shoulders, with metal chains, bucket missing, standing on circular flat black base, figure originally coloured, made in Japan, *c.*1950. Statuette broken off base, and broken at feet. Inscription on base reads: 'TN003504/MADE IN JAPAN'.
Height 112 mm, diameter 52 mm.
Source: Newport, R.

433. 1980-676/101: Rectangular cigarette box, surfaces gently curved, made of tortoiseshell-effect cellulose nitrate with brass trim and hinges, contains two cigarette holders, inside of yellow elastic, *c.*1900. Incomplete (fastening has part missing).
Length 84 mm, width 50 mm, thickness 17 mm.
Source: Newport, R.

434. 1980-676/102: Hair comb of tortoiseshell-effect cellulose nitrate, body decorated with tendril pattern which has been cut out, *c.*1900.
Length 163 mm, width 61 mm, thickness 2 mm.
Source: Newport, R.

435. 1980-676/103: U-shaped hair comb of black cellulose nitrate, two teeth, which are wavy in shape, body decorated with 11 brilliants, 9 in the form of a diamond, *c.*1900.
Length 110 mm, width 45 mm, height 15 mm, thickness 2 mm.
Source: Newport, R.

436. 1980-676/104: Handbag mount of ivory cellulose nitrate, button fastening attached to metal bar for catch, mount roughly semi-circular, with two links remaining, holes drilled along edges for attachment to bag, *c.*1920.
Length 142 mm, width 85 mm, thickness 14 mm.
Source: Newport, R.

437. 1980-676/105: U-shaped walking-stick handle of horn cellulose nitrate, end decorated with incised zig-zag and wavy line design, *c.*1900.
Length 112 mm, width 95 mm, diameter 20 mm.
Source: Newport, R.

438. 1980-676/106: Flat rectangular Vesta match box of metal with hinged lid, covered with cellulose nitrate, which is printed with decoration to make it a souvenir of Carlisle, *c.*1900. Inscription printed on one side of cover reads: 'CARLISLE COURT HOUSES' surmounted by engraved picture of these with figures and carriages in foreground, black on ivory. Second inscription printed on other side of cover reads: 'BE JUST AND FEAR NOT/CARLISLE' surmounted by two coats of arms of Carlisle, one a red cross on gold ground, the other showing a gold lion and castle and water. Third inscription printed on edge of cover reads: 'Q.E.B. & Cº./REGD. Nº.430409/ PRINTED IN RHINELAND'.
Length 59 mm, width 36 mm, height 11 mm.
Source: Newport, R.

439. 1980-676/107: Ornate hair comb of black cellulose nitrate, two teeth, body decorated with cut-out and incised tendril pattern, black stones and incised spots, art nouveau design, *c.*1900.

Length 112 mm, width 52 mm, thickness 3 mm, height 15 mm.
Source: Newport, R.

440. 1980-676/108: Rectangular clock of wood covered with cellulose nitrate which is pearlised light brown trimmed with tortoiseshell-effect face, figures moulded out of white cellulose nitrate; 1930s. Backplate and inner mechanism made of brass; inner casing wood. Incomplete (hour hand broken off). Face has moulded scale reading: '1(1) 12 hours'.

Length 160 mm, width 52 mm, height 133 mm.
Source: Newport, R.

441. 1980-676/109: Cut-throat razor in box. Lid of pressed paper case is not original, *c.*1900. Incomplete (original case lid missing).

Pt. 1: Cut-throat steel razor has a black cellulose nitrate handle ornately impressed with decoration of woman's head and tendrils, blade made in Germany by Crown and Castle. Trade mark engraved on main part of blade reads: 'CROWN...AND...CASTLE/EXTRA HOLLOW GROUND RAZOR'. 'CROWN' and 'CASTLE' are either side of trade mark within an oval showing a crown and a castle. Inscription in form of a trade mark engraved near end of blade: 'CROWN AND CASTLE/MADE A.....IN GERMANY'.
Razor: length 156 mm, width 23 mm, thickness 6 mm.

Pt. 2: Coffin-shaped paper box with slip-on lid, body decorated on one side with impressed diamond pattern, on other with impressed flower and line decoration, lid decorated with impressed pattern of large diamonds on one side and lines on other. Inscription impressed on top of lid reads: 'EFFIELD', short for 'SHEFFIELD'.
Length 164 mm, width 33 mm, thickness 13 mm.
Reference: Newport 1976: M16.
Source: Newport, R.

442. 1980-676/110: Circular button of cellulose-nitrate-covered steel, black ground decorated with yellow and light brown tartan, gold fluted border, 1920s.

Diameter 50 mm, thickness 10 mm.
Source: Newport, R.

443. 1980-676/111: Circular button of cellulose-nitrate-covered steel, black ground decorated with yellow and light brown tartan, gold fluted border, 1920s.

Diameter 50 mm, thickness 9 mm.
Source: Newport, R.

444. 1980-676/112: Button of cellulose-nitrate-covered steel, black ground decorated with yellow and light brown tartan, gold fluted border, 1920s.

Diameter 50 mm, height 12 mm.
Source: Newport, R.

445–446. 1980-676/113-14: Two circular buttons of cellulose-nitrate-covered steel, black ground decorated with yellow and light brown tartan, gold fluted border, 1920s.

Diameter 50 mm, thickness 9 mm.
Source: Newport, R.

447. 1980-676/115: Circular button of cellulose-nitrate-covered steel, black ground decorated with yellow and light brown tartan, gold fluted border, 1920s.

Diameter 51 mm, thickness 9 mm.
Source: Newport, R.

448. 1980-676/116: Circular button of cellulose-nitrate-covered steel, black ground decorated with yellow and light brown tartan, gold fluted border, 1920s

Diameter 50 mm, thickness 10 mm.
Source: Newport, R.

449–450. 1980-676/117–18: Two circular buttons of cellulose-nitrate-covered steel, black ground decorated with yellow and light brown tartan, gold fluted border, 1920s.

Diameter 50 mm, thickness 9 mm.
Source: Newport, R.

451. 1980-676/119: Circular button of cellulose-nitrate-covered steel, black ground decorated with yellow and light brown tartan, gold fluted border, 1920s.

Diameter 50 mm, thickness 10 mm.
Source: Newport, R.

452. 1980-676/120: Circular button of cellulose-nitrate-covered steel, black ground decorated with yellow and light brown tartan, gold fluted border, 1920s. Edge chipped.

Diameter 51 mm, thickness 9 mm.
Source: Newport, R.

453. 1980-676/121: Circular button of cellulose-nitrate-covered steel, black ground decorated with red and yellow tartan, gold fluted border, 1920s.

Diameter 50 mm, thickness 10 mm.
Source: Newport, R.

454. 1980-676/122: Circular button of cellulose-nitrate-covered steel, black ground decorated with red and yellow tartan, gold fluted border, 1920s.

Diameter 51 mm, thickness 10 mm.
Source: Newport, R.

455. 1980-676/123: Circular button of cellulose-nitrate-covered steel, black ground decorated with red and yellow tartan, gold fluted border, 1920s.

Diameter 50 mm, thickness 10 mm.
Source: Newport, R.

456–462. 1980-676/124–6, 128–31: Seven circular buttons of cellulose-nitrate-covered steel, black ground decorated with red and yellow tartan, gold fluted border, *c.*1920s.

Diameter 50 mm, thickness 10 mm.
Source: Newport, R.

463. 1980-676/127: Button of cellulose-nitrate-covered steel, black ground decorated with red and yellow tartan, gold fluted border, 1920s.

Diameter 50 mm, thickness 12 mm.
Source: Newport, R.

464–466. 1980-676/132–4: Three circular buttons of cellulose-nitrate-covered steel, olive-green ground decorated with brown swirls and octagonal edging, 1920s.

Diameter 39 mm, thickness 10 mm.
Source: Newport, R.

467. 1980-676/135: Circular button of cellulose-nitrate-covered steel, olive-

green ground decorated with brown swirls and octagonal edging, 1920s.

Diameter 39 mm, thickness 9 mm.
Source: Newport, R.

468–469. 1980-676/136–7: Two circular buttons of cellulose-nitrate-covered steel, olive-green ground decorated with brown swirls and octagonal edging, 1920s.

Diameter 39 mm, thickness 10 mm.
Source: Newport, R.

470. 1980-676/138: Circular button of cellulose-nitrate-covered steel, olive-green ground decorated with brown swirls and octagonal edging, 1920s.

Diameter 39 mm, thickness 7 mm.
Source: Newport, R.

471. 1980-676/139: Circular button of cellulose-nitrate-covered steel, olive-green ground decorated with brown swirls and octagonal edging, 1920s.

Diameter 39 mm, thickness 10 mm.
Source: Newport, R.

472. 1980-676/140: Circular button of cellulose-nitrate-covered steel, olive-green ground decorated with brown swirls and octagonal edging, 1920s. Steel fastening bent.

Diameter 39 mm, thickness 10 mm.
Source: Newport, R.

473. 1980-676/141: Circular button of cellulose-nitrate-covered steel, olive-green ground decorated with brown swirls and edging, *c.*1920.

Diameter 39 mm, height 9 mm.
Source: Newport, R.

474. 1980-676/142: Circular button of cellulose-nitrate-covered steel, bottle-green ground decorated with red green and yellow tartan, gold fluted border, *c.*1920.

Diameter 39 mm, height 8 mm.
Source: Newport, R.

475. 1980-676/143: Circular button of cellulose-nitrate-covered steel, bottle-green ground decorated with red green and yellow tartan, gold fluted border, *c.*1920.

Diameter 39 mm, thickness 9 mm.
Source: Newport, R.

476–477. 1980-676/144–5: Two circular buttons of cellulose-nitrate-covered metal, painted with a lily-of-the-valley design on black ground and lacquered, metal backing painted black, *c.*1920.

Diameter 40 mm, height 8 mm.
Source: Newport, R.

478–479. 1980-676/146–7: Two circular buttons of horn cellulose nitrate with metal inlay in art nouveau style around edge, *c.*1900.

Diameter 32 mm, height 10 mm.
Source: Newport, R.

480. 1980-676/148: Circular box of ivory cellulose nitrate with slip-on lid which is decorated with metal floral band which is nailed to it, 1900s.

Diameter 57 mm, height 62 mm.
Source: Newport, R.

481. 1980-676/149: Christmas greetings card of white paper, front embossed with border of ivy and horse shoes, framing white pressed and coloured cellulose nitrate plaque saying: 'Remembrance' in letters covered with glitter, 1920s. Published by Tuck, Raphael & Sons Ltd, London, early twentieth century. Second inscription printed inside left-hand side of insert saying: 'CHRISTMAS/GREETINGS/FROM With my/Love To/Harry XX' – first two lines and 'FROM' printed in gold, rest handwritten in black ink. Third inscription printed inside right-hand side of card insert says: 'Fair as dawn of flowerful spring/Be life's Way,/.../.../.../.../.../As you are' printed in gold in script imitating handwriting. Fourth inscription is a trade mark printed in gold on the back of the insert: '.../Raphael Tuck & Sons Ltd./Publishers to the King and Queen./PRODUCED IN THE UNITED KINGDOM/COPYRIGHT.

LONDON.' The last two lines are at the of bottom of the page, the top two lines in middle surmounted by trade mark.

Length 125 mm, width 98 mm.
Source: Newport, R.

482. 1980-676/150: Christmas greetings card of white paper embossed with a gold-painted design of tendrils and horse shoes on front, which is also cut out to show an insert of clear cellulose nitrate coloured with a vase of purple and yellow pansies, *c.*1920. First inscription embossed on the front of the card reads: 'With/HEARTY/GREETINGS' in gold-painted, elaborate script. Second inscription is printed inside left-hand side of card inset: 'WITH MY LOVE/AND CHRISTMAS/GREETINGS/To Harry/from Laura xxx'. Last two lines handwritten. Printed inscription surmounts two bluebells. The third inscription is printed inside the right-hand side of card inset: 'DEAREST LOVE AND /... /... /... /... /... /... /LIFE ENDURES'; blue print in depressed circle, above spray of bluebells. The fourth inscription is the sale price handwritten in pencil on the back left-hand corner: '853/£1'.

Length 164 mm, width 115 mm.
Source: Newport, R.

483. 1980-676/151: Christmas greetings card of white paper embossed with flower design on front of card also decorated with pressed and coloured plaque of cellulose nitrate saying: 'with fondest love' and surrounded by pink roses, 1920s. Inscription on the front of card reads: 'With/Fondest Love', letters on gold scroll, raised, capitals decorated with glitter, probably red, which is now almost gone. Second inscription printed inside left-hand side of card insert says: 'Merry/Christmas/Greetings/From Laura/To Dear Harry x'. 'Laura' and 'Harry x' are handwritten in black ink, rest printed in green. Third inscription is printed inside the right-hand side of card insert and says: 'Christmas! When warm wish /.../.../.../.../.../.../full share of life's best/things' in green gothic script above a flower motif. Fourth inscription is the sale price handwritten on the back in the top left-hand corner and reads: '1-50/853'. '50' crossed out.

Length 156 mm, width 118 mm.
Source: Newport, R.

484. 1980-676/152: Birthday greetings card of white paper, front embossed with flower design and decorated with pressed and coloured square cellulose nitrate panel, which says 'good luck', 1920s. Inscription on fan on decorative panel reads: 'GOOD LUCK' in white letters curved round edge of gold fan. Second inscription is printed on the inside left-hand side of card insert: 'With/Sincere Good Wishes/for a/Happy Birthday/From Laura/To Harry/xxx/xx/x'. 'Laura' and 'Harry' handwritten in blue ink, rest printed in green gothic script. Third inscription printed inside right-hand side of card insert: 'A Birthday Wish I Send You,/.../.../.../Her Sunshine to the last' in green print surmounted and above semi-circle of pearls. Fourth inscription is a trade mark printed in the centre of the back: 'THE SUMMIT SERIES/BRITISH [...] PRODUCTION'. First line in curve above scroll which shows superimposed 'T' and 'H' within shield with 'BRITISH' and 'PRODUCTION' on either side, in blue. Fifth inscription is the sale price handwritten in the top left-hand corner of the back: '853 £1'.

Length 132 mm, width 113 mm.
Source: Newport, R.

485. 1980-676/153: New Year greetings card of white paper, front embossed with ivy design framing rectangular cellulose nitrate pressed and coloured plaque saying: 'Ever True in thought and Wish', decorated with pastoral scene, flowers and bells, 1920s. Second inscription on gold scroll on decorative panel: 'EVER/ TRUE/ IN/ THOUGHT/ AND/ WISH'. Third inscription is printed and

handwritten inside left-hand side of card insert: 'With all/Good Wishes/and/Kind Thoughts/for/a Happy/New Year/From Laura with Love/To Harry xx'. Fourth inscription printed inside right-hand side of card insert: 'Best Wishes/ .../ ... / .../ .../ .../ of love and joy of heart'. Fifth inscription is handwritten on back top left-hand corner: '853 £1'.

Length 133 mm, width 91 mm.
Source: Newport, R.

486. 1980-676/154: Christmas greetings card of white paper, front embossed with border of rectangles and circles and a wavy line, framing clear cellulose nitrate plaque pressed and coloured saying: 'BEST LOVE', c.1920. Second inscription printed inside left-hand side of card insert: 'FROM Father & Mother/TO Issie'. 'FROM' and 'TO' printed in blue, rest handwritten in black ink. Third inscription printed on right-hand side of card insert: 'Health, wealth, good luck your Christmas fill,/.../.../A Merry Christmas/and Prosperity in the New Year'. Fourth inscription embossed inside right-hand side of card: 'BRITISH MANUFACTURE'.

Length 107 mm, width 87 mm.
Source: Newport, R.

487. 1980-676/155: Christmas greetings card of white paper, front edged with lace border, framing cut-out cellulose nitrate plaque saying: 'To My Love', c.1920. Incomplete (border broken off). Second inscription is a love poem printed inside left-hand side of card insert: 'With Most Hearty/ Wishes for a/ Happy Christmas./ .../ .../ .../ .../ .../ .../ .../ .../ .../ .../Nothing true heart e're can sever' printed in green. The third inscription printed inside right-hand side of card insert says: '"There seems a magic/in the very name of Christmas". /DICKENS./ To Beaty/from Jos Salisbury'. Names handwritten, 'Salisbury' unreadable, rest printed in green.

Length 150 mm, width 93 mm.
Source: Newport, R.

488–496. 1980-676/156-7, 159–60, 162–3, 166–8: Nine circular cellulose-nitrate-covered steel buttons, coloured to imitate horn. Early twentieth century.

Diameter 19 mm, thickness 4 mm.
Reference: Newport 1976: M7.
Source: Newport, R.

497–500. 1980-676/158, 161, 164–5: Four cellulose-nitrate-covered steel buttons, coloured to imitate horn, early twentieth century.

Diameter 18 mm, thickness 3 mm.
Reference: Newport 1976: M7.
Source: Newport, R.

501. 1980-676/169: Circular cellulose-nitrate-covered steel button, coloured to imitate horn, early twentieth century.

Diameter 29 mm, thickness 6 mm.
Reference: Newport 1976: M8.
Source: Newport, R.

502–507. 1980-676/170–5: Six circular cellulose-nitrate-covered steel buttons, painted black apart from two half-moon shapes lying opposite each other, *c.*1930.

Diameter 18 mm, thickness 8 mm.
Reference: Newport 1976: M9.
Source: Newport, R.

508. 1980-676/176: Hexagonal dressing-table box in ivory and tortoiseshell-effect cellulose nitrate sheet, lid and sides are tortoiseshell, base and lid trim are ivory, *c.*1900. Two corners of base are cracked.

Length 105 mm, width 94 mm, height 45 mm.
Reference: Newport 1976: M42.
Source: Newport, R.

509. 1980-676/276: Hand mirror with oval frame and handle with curved end, frame and handle made of thin cellulose nitrate tortoiseshell-effect sheet, *c.*1920.

Length 204 mm, width 81 mm, thickness 9 mm.
Source: Newport, R.
Plate 8

510. 1980-676/277: Circular tortoiseshell-effect cellulose nitrate box with hole in lid, early twentieth century.

Diameter 76 mm, height 66 mm.
Source: Newport, R.

511. 1980-676/282: Button hook with steel hook and handle of pearlised blue and clear cellulose nitrate, painted with thin white and black strip, late nineteenth/early twentieth century.

Length 182 mm, width 20 mm, thickness 11 mm.
Source: Newport, R.

512. 1980-676/284: Brooch showing pair of cherubs with trumpets and cavorting on cloud. Made of ivory cellulose nitrate with chrome clip, *c.*1920. Inscription moulded on cloud under cherubs: 'GEMINI'.

Length 43 mm, width 33 mm, thickness 8 mm.
Source: Newport, R.
Plate 1

CELLULOSE NITRATE MACHINERY

513. 1976-48: Pilot plant for cellulose nitrate manufacture. Baker-Perkins 2-batch 16"×16" trough mixer, machine no. 40230, 1937. Inscription on raised oval plate: 'BX PLASTICS LTD/ PLANT NO 00384/ BRANTHAM'. Second larger rectangular plate unreadable.

Length 1230 mm, width 860 mm, height 1570 mm.
Source: British Industrial Plastics Ltd.

514. 1976-49: Pilot plant for cellulose nitrate manufacture. Mixing mill, size 4, made by Baker-Perkins Ltd Engineers, London and Peterborough, in 1944, serial no. 7/389422, ref. no. 45585 BP A50. Fitted with 0.5-HP Crompton Parkinson electric motor, serial no. SM-824 G F4780, driving through Crofts reducing gear, reduction 1435 to 150, serial no. ME. 1. 293545.

Length 1250 mm, width 650 mm, height 740 mm.
Science Museum Negative No.: 1983/76, 1984/76, 350/78.

Pt. 1: Pilot plant for cellulose nitrate manufacture; mixing mill. Inscription on plaque: 'BAKER PERKINS LTD/ ENGINEERS/ LONDON & PETERBOROUGH/ REFERENCES NO. 45585 BP650'. Second inscription on plate: 'B.X. PLASTICS LTD/ PLAN NO 2003/BRANTHAM'.
Length 590 mm, width 335 mm, height 565 mm.

Pt. 2: 0.5-HP Crompton-Parkinson electric motor, serial no. SM-824 G F4780.
Length 950 mm, width 650 mm, height 390 mm.
Source: British Industrial Plastics Ltd.

515. 1976-50: Pilot plant for cellulose nitrate manufacture. Mill, two roll, 5" diameter, 1940, fitted with Crompton Parkinson 3-HP electric motor, no. 618698, and FLP starter. Inscribed: 'THE ELECTRICAL/ APPARATUS CO LTD/ ST ALBANS' ENGLAND'. Second inscription stamped in circle: 'MADE IN ENGLAND Nᴼ 4'. Third stamped inscription: 'B.S.A. ACME / SNAP-LOCK/ SWITCH/ No 16 D - 1200 - 1/ MKII/ 220 V.A.C. 10 AMPS 125 V.D.C. 5 AMPS/ 440 V.A.C. 7.5 AMPS 125 V.D.C. 1/3 HP/ B.S.A. TOOLS LTD/ BIRMINGHAM 33/ MADE IN ENGLAND/ UNDER LICENCE/ PATENT NO 1989277/2270951 2294559'. Fourth inscription on plate: 'B.X. PLASTICS LTD/ PLANT Nᵒ 00099/BRANTHAM'. Fifth inscription on power switch in raised letters: 'DO NOT REMOVE COVER/ UNTIL CURRENT HAS BEEN/ ISOLATED ELSEWHERE/ ELECTRICAL APPARATUS CO LTD/ TYPE 2PBF SERIAL Nᵒ 374368/ CERT Nᵒ /.../ GROUP/ FLP 192... 11.' '...' denotes FLP contained within 8-sided shape (trade mark). Sixth inscription: 'Nᵒ 974367 H.P.3/VOLTS 400 3 PHASE 502/TYPE M2 CRL/S/REV.A/...'.

Length 1710 mm, width 1180 mm, height 1660 mm.
Science Museum Negative No.: 1985/76, 1986/76, 351/78, 1373/78, 1374/78.
Source: British Industrial Plastics Ltd.

516. 1976-51: Pilot plant for cellulose nitrate manufacture. Robinson mill, two roll 9"×24", with Doctor Knife, 30 FPM, made by Joseph Robinson and Co. Ltd, Salford, Manchester, in 1932. Inscription in raised letters on side of machine: 'JOSEPH ROBINSON/ SALFORD MANCHESTER'.

Length 1370 mm, width 1670 mm, height 1450 mm.
Source: British Industrial Plastics Ltd.

517. 1976-52: Pilot plant for cellulose nitrate manufacture. Block press size 8, 12" square platen, 7" ram no. 5643, working load 38 tons, made in 1948 by Tangyes Ltd Birmingham. Metal plate with inscription showing Tangyes trade mark: triangle with wavy border, within border with one word on each side: 'TANGYES TESTED TACKLE' and three Ts contained within triangle, one in each corner. Adjacent to inscription: 'WORKING LOAD/ 38 tons/ FOR SERVICE AND/ SPARES QUOTE NO./ 5643/ TANGYES LTD. BIRMINGHAM'. Second inscription is a stamped: '5643'. Third inscription is raised: 'TANGYES/ BIRMINGHAM'.

Length 760 mm, width 600 mm, height 1650 mm.
Science Museum Negative No.: 353/78, 354/78.
Source: British Industrial Plastics Ltd.
Figure 16

518. 1976-53: Pilot plant for cellulose nitrate manufacture. Single ram press, hard rubber class G. serial no. 7077, 1933, with block. Number painted on side: '00578'.

Length 1580 mm, width 1140 mm, height 1800 mm.
Source: British Industrial Plastics Ltd.

519. 1976-54: Pilot plant for cellulose nitrate manufacture. Polishing press, 15 daylights 24"×20", steam-heated platform, 1948.

Length 2390 mm, width 1070 mm, height 900 mm.
Source: British Industrial Plastics Ltd.

520. 1976-55: Pilot plant for cellulose nitrate manufacture. Burroughs slicing machine, serial no. SR 6686 42576, job no. 11854, made by the Burroughs Co., Builders, Newark, NJ, USA, in 1931. Oval plate inscribed: 'B.X. PLASTICS LTD/ PLANT NO 00716/ BRANTHAM'.

Length 3480 mm, width 1500 mm, height 1700 mm.
Source: British Industrial Plastics Ltd.

CELLULOSE ACETATE (CA)

521–527. 1975-527/1–7: Seven 'Emitome' hearing aids; components of some of these being produced on NV-10-H injection moulding machine (also see cat. no. 1054).

Source: Gregory, R.H.

521–522. 1975-527/1–2: Two black hearing aids each with japanned metal front and cellulose acetate back, rectangular with rounded corners, with silver clip for attachment. Front marked: 'EMITOME/ REGISTERED TRADE MARK'. Pink cable for earpiece. Earpiece missing. Original box made of light brown imitation leather with white silk upper lining marked: 'EMITOME/ REGISTERED TRADE MARK' in gold letters, and faded red lining for device, with two divisions. Mid-twentieth century.

Device: length 102 mm, width 44 mm, thickness 27 mm.
Box: length 119 mm, width 78 mm, thickness 34 mm.

523. 1975-527/3: Black hearing aid with cellulose acetate back, rectangular with rounded corners, with pink backing to speaker and two silver clips for attachment. Front marked: 'EMITOME/ REGISTERED TRADE MARK'. Pink cable for earpiece. Earpiece missing. Original box made of light brown imitation leather with white silk upper lining marked: 'EMITOME/ REGISTERED TRADE MARK' in gold letters, and faded red lining for device, with two divisions. Mid-twentieth century.

Device: length 102 mm, width 42 mm, thickness 23 mm.
Box: length 119 mm, width 78 mm, thickness 34 mm.

524. 1975-527/4: Hearing aid with gold metal front and white cellulose acetate back, rectangular with rounded corners, with silver clip for attachment. Front marked: 'EMITOME/REG. TRADE MARK'. Gold cable for earpiece. Earpiece missing. Original box made of imitation crocodile skin with white silk upper lining marked: 'EMITOME/ REGISTERED TRADE MARK' in gold letters, and faded red lining for device, with three divisions. Top and side of box lid marked: with stick-on labels: 'STANDARD/ TEST/ CRESCENT' handwritten. Mid-twentieth century.

Device: length 100 mm, width 60 mm, thickness 30 mm.
Box: length 138 mm, width 95 mm, thickness 41 mm.

525. 1975-527/5: Hearing aid of white cellulose acetate, rectangular with rounded corners, with metal clip for attachment. Front marked in white: 'EMITOME/ REG. TRADE MARK/ BRITISH MADE'. Pink cable for earpiece. Earplug missing. Original box made of imitation black leather paper with blue lining; marked: 'SM 299' on side and: '507' handwritten on base. Mid-twentieth century.

Device: length 125 mm, width 65 mm, thickness 26 mm.
Earpiece: diameter 22 mm, height 13 mm.
Box: length 222 mm, width 84 mm, thickness 34 mm.

526. 1975-527/6: Black hearing aid with japanned metal front and cellulose acetate back, rectangular with rounded corners, with metal clip for attachment. Front marked in white: 'EMITOME/ REG. TRADE MARK/ BRITISH MADE'. Gold cable for earpiece made of pink cellulose acetate?, marked: 'PAT'D'. Original box made of imitation black leather paper with blue lining. Mid-twentieth century.

Device: length 139 mm, width 65 mm, thickness 27 mm.
Earpiece: diameter 22 mm, height 30 mm.
Box: length 222 mm, width 84 mm, thickness 34 mm.

527. 1975-527/7: Black hearing aid with metal front and cellulose acetate back, rectangular with rounded corners, with metal clip for attachment, with rubber cover. Front marked in white: 'EMITOME/ REG. TRADE MARK/ BRITISH MADE'. Black with red flecked woven covered cable for earpiece. Earpiece marked: 'MADE IN ENGLAND'. Original box made of imitation black leather paper with blue lining. Lid labelled: 'BRITISH MADE/ EMITOME/ Registered Trade Mark'. Mid-twentieth century.

Device: length 139 mm, width 65 mm, thickness 27 mm.
Earpiece: diameter 20 mm, height 15 mm.
Box: length 222 mm, width 84 mm, thickness 34 mm.

528. 1979-624/18: Electric lamp and shade, in geometric form, made of blue and cream cellulose acetate, with matching blue flex and plug, French, 1928. Top of lamp chipped.

Diameter 114 mm, height 250 mm.

Pt. 1: Octagonal-shaped base, with alternating blue and cream panels and cream slide switch, attached to flex and plug.
Diameter 112 mm, height 138 mm.

Pt. 2: Octagonal-shaped lampshade, with alternating blue and cream panels, coming to a point at top, where blue panels are pierced.
Diameter 114 mm, height 160 mm.
Source: Jesse, J.

529. 1979-624/54: Ten-sided box in tortoiseshell-effect cellulose acetate, lid moulded and painted with stylised foliage. Made by E. Fornells, Paris, France, c.1930s. Trade mark moulded inside: '.EDITIONS./-/ PARIS/- /E.FORNELLS' contained in circle; first and last line curve round top and bottom of 'Paris'. Second inscription inside base at edge: 'FRANCE'. Third inscription moulded on lid: 'FORNELLS PARIS' runs in decreasing size along top of one leaf edge.

Length 98 mm, width 98 mm, height 39 mm.
Source: Jesse, J.

530. 1979-624/96: Clothes brush with dark brown back and duck's head with orange beak, both made of cellulose acetate, brush concealed in duck's body of grey, brown and cream marble-effect

polyethylene, standing over wooden egg (not original), English, 1955. Inscription moulded on back of brush: 'MADE IN ENGLAND/BRISTLE'; second line inverted. Second inscription moulded on base of duck: 'MADE IN ENGLAND/1'; '1' is inverted.

Duck: height 30 mm, width 90 mm, breadth 135 mm.
Egg: diameter 66 mm.
Source: Jesse, J.

531. 1979-624/117: Pair of sunglasses with orange frames and dark green lenses, probably cellulose acetate, mid-twentieth century.

Length 133 mm, width 125 mm, height 46 mm.
Lens: diameter 41 mm.
Source: Jesse, J.

532. 1979-624/216: Red cellulose acetate box intricately designed with cherries by Eduard Fornells for René Lalique. Moulded on lid: 'LALIQUE'.

Length 75 mm, width 75 mm, height 29 mm.
Source: Jesse, J.

533. 1979-624/262: Hexagonal green pearlised cellulose acetate lamp with shade, two bulb holders, electric. Made by Crayonne Ltd, England. Early twentieth century.

Length 125 mm, width 112 mm, height 280 mm.
Source: Jesse, J.

534. 1980-676/177: Transparent red cellulose-acetate- and chrome-plated metal buckle, ovoid in shape, mounted on yellow sales card decorated with brown, marked: 'Decorative Utility Dress Accessory', made in England, 1940s.

Buckle: length 87 mm, width 50 mm, height 8 mm.
Card: length 87 mm, width 84 mm.
Reference: Newport 1976: N12.
Source: Newport, R.
Plate 10

535. 1980-676/178 Toy film-strip viewer of cellulose acetate, pink marble-effect casing with view lens and light diffusing screen, injection moulded in two halves, late 1940s.

Length 62 mm, width 45 mm, height 34 mm.

Reference: Newport 1976: N13.
Source: Newport, R.
Plate 10

536. 1980-676/179: Elaborately decorated piece puzzle and box with sliding lid, made of ivory cellulose acetate, late 1940s? Small chip on edge of lid.

Length 50 mm, width 50 mm, thickness 9 mm.
Reference: Newport 1976: N18.
Source: Newport, R.
Plate 10

537. 1980-676/180: Pink hand-decorated 'Muguet' scent box, spherical with flat, circular base, containing original cream scent, box made of cellulose acetate by J. Molinard, Paris, France, 1920s? Inscription printed on base: 'CONCRETA/MADE/IN FRANCE/MUGUET/GRASSE/PARIS/ Molinard Jne'.

Diameter 21 mm, height 20 mm.
Source: Newport, R.
Plate 10

538. 1980-676/181: 'Larkins' paper-knife of ivory cellulose acetate, handle decorated with inset red leather ovoid on both sides, stamped with gold letters, made in England, 1930s? Inscription on both sides of handle: 'WITH THE COMPLIMENTS OF/S.C. LARKINS & SONS LTD'. Second inscription moulded into the end of the handle reads: 'MADE IN ENGLAND'.

Length 181 mm, width 44 mm, thickness 6 mm.
Source: Newport, R.
Plate 10

ETHYL CELLULOSE (EC)

539. 1980-676/182: Snuff box of ethyl cellulose, marble effect browns/cream. Hinged lid decorated with moulded starfish design. Inscription moulded and trade-marked: 'BEX/ MADE IN ENGLAND' contained in framed box, *c.*1940.

Length 57 mm, width 36 mm, height 16 mm.
Reference: Newport 1976: P1.
Source: Newport, R.

540. 1980-676/183: Rectangular snuff box of red marble-effect ethyl cellulose, with ringed lid. 1940s? Trade mark moulded inside lid: 'BEX/MADE IN/ENGLAND' enclosed in bordered square.

Length 58 mm, width 37 mm, height 17 mm.
Reference: Newport 1976: P2.
Source: Newport, R.

CELLOPHANE

541. 1985-657: Sample of wood pulp as it arrives at British Cellophane Ltd's factory to make Cellophane, 1985, in form of 22 square sheets, creamy white with textured surface.

Length 200 mm, width 200 mm, thickness 1 mm.
Source: British Cellophane Ltd.

542. 1985-658: Sample of alkaline cellulose in jar, the first stage in production of Cellophane, at British Cellophane Ltd, 1985. Inscription on bottle: 'Alkaline Cellulose'.

Height 150 mm, diameter 58 mm.
Source: British Cellophane Ltd.

543. 1985-659: Sample of cellulose xanthate from the reaction of aged alkali cellulose crumbs with carbon disulphide in jar, at British Cellophane Ltd, 1985, golden yellow.

Height 150 mm, diameter 58 mm.
Source: British Cellophane Ltd.

544. 1985-660: Sample of viscose liquid in jar, the final stage before casting to make Cellophane, at British Cellophane Ltd, 1985.

Height 150 mm, diameter 58 mm.
Source: British Cellophane Ltd.

ARTIFICIAL SILK

545. 1977-178: Framed advertisement for Chardonnet artificial silk, including mounted dyed and undyed samples, 1896. Advert reads: 'ARTIFICIAL SILK./ Count Hilaire de Chardonnet's Patent./

The Artificial <u>Silk Company</u> Limited/ A New British Industry./ Superior Brilliant Silk produced mechanically and cheaply without the Silk Worm./ [sample] ARTIFICIAL SILK/ SILK UNDYED [sample] SAMPLE OF GOODS/ Manufactured with /Artificial Silk [sample] ARTIFICIAL/ SILK/ DYED./ ARTIFICIAL SILK/ TAPESTRIES & DRESS GOODS, (GRAND PRIZE Lyons Exhibition)/ ARTIFICIAL SILK/ COSTUME PATTERNS, (Manufactured in Lancashire.)/ ARTIFICIAL SILK/ RIBBONS (Plain, Fancy, and Watered, Grand Prize.)/ ARTIFICIAL SILK/ BRAIDS AND CORDS (for Dress trimming.)/ ARTIFICIAL SILK/ EMBROIDERY & TWIST, for Fancy Work./ ARTIFICIAL SILK/ For NECKTIES, SCARVES, BELTS & HATBANDS./ ARTIFICIAL SILK/ For SILK-STRAW BONNET & HAT SHAPES./ ARTIFICIAL SILK/ FOR EVERY PURPOSE./ Samples of Dress-pieces, Tapestries, Ribbons, Braids, Cords, Embroidery, Passmenterie etc. etc., can be seen at the Offices of the Company./ Temporary Offices:/ May 1896/ LONDON'. The advert is labelled in typescript: 'CHARDONNET NITRO-CELLULOSE SILK, 1896'.

Length 412 mm, width 308 mm, thickness 13 mm.
Source: Science Museum.
Figure 31

546. 1915-574/5: Four skeins of artificial ivory silk 1908, in glass jar, labelled: '1908'.

Diameter 91 mm, height 208 mm.
Source: Swan, J.

547. 1915-574/6: Wooden reel of Lehner's Seide. End of reel marked: 'LEHNER'S SEIDE'.

Diameter 135 mm, height 135 mm.
Source: Swan, J.

VISCOSE RAYON

548. 1914-42: Crude thread spun from viscose solution (1908); four skeins, cream coloured.

Pt. 1: Length 250 mm, width 65 mm, thickness 10 mm.
Pt. 2: Length 246 mm, width 60 mm, thickness 13 mm.
Pt. 3: Length 230 mm, width 60 mm, thickness 19 mm.
Pt. 4: Length 245 mm, width 85 mm, thickness 19 mm.
Source: Roscoe, H.E.

549–556. 1914-43: Eight samples of dyed threads made of viscose.

Science Museum Negative No.: 124/67.
Source: Roscoe, H.E.

549. 1914-43/1 Black skein, labelled: 'Viscose Artificial Silk' and: 'Dyed Thread'.

Length 235 mm, width 30 mm, thickness 22 mm.

550. 1914-43/2 Magenta skein, labelled: 'Viscose Artificial Silk' and: 'Dyed Thread'.

Length 220 mm, width 32 mm, thickness 21 mm.

551. 1914-43/3 Ivory skein, labelled: 'Viscose Artificial Silk' and: 'Dyed Thread'.

Length 230 mm, width 28 mm, thickness 19 mm.

552. 1914-43/4 Blue skein, faded in places; labelled: 'Viscose Artificial Silk'.

Length 252 mm, width 50 mm, thickness 26 mm.

553. 1914-43/5 Ivory skein, labelled: 'Viscose Artificial Silk' and: 'Finished/ Thread/ Bleached'.

Length 227 mm, width 40 mm, thickness 26 mm.

554. 1914-43/6 Ivory skein, thicker thread. Labelled: 'Viscose Artificial Silk' and: 'Floss/Twist/Unbleached'; 'Floss' is uncertain as it is in very faint script.

Length 257 mm, width 35 mm, thickness 17 mm.

555. 1914-43/7 Cardboard reel of orange thread, faded in places, plus sample of thread.

Diameter 41 mm, height 120 mm.

556. 1914-43/8 Sample of gold thread in small skein. Green label reads: 'grind ~ 500/...no 100'; first word uncertain as it is difficult to read.

Length 252 mm, width 50 mm, thickness 26 mm.

557–563. 1914-44: Seven samples of various fabrics, prepared *c.*1908 by the 'viscose' artificial silk process.

Source: Roscoe, H.E.

557. 1914-44/1: Woven golden brocade viscose fabric with waz lily design, *c.*1908.

Length 835 mm, width 210 mm, thickness 0.2 mm.

558. 1914-44/2: Cream gauze viscose fabric with embroidered pale green buds, *c.*1908.

Length 1030 mm, width 210 mm, thickness *c.*0.1 mm.

559. 1914-44/3: Blue net viscose fabric with bands, *c.*1908.

Length 960 mm, width 175 mm, thickness *c.*0.1 mm.

560. 1914-44/4: Golden silk viscose fabric with woven shamrock design, *c.*1908.

Length 855 mm, width 145 mm, thickness *c.*0.1 mm.

561. 1914-44/5: White georgette viscose fabric with woven pink flowers and green leaves, and zig-zag design woven into the georgette, *c.*1908.

Length 960 mm, width 200 mm, thickness 0.1 mm.

562. 1914-44/6: Peach gauze viscose fabric with chequered pattern woven in, *c.*1908.

Length 950 mm, width 182 mm, thickness *c.*0.1 mm.

563. 1914-44/7: Ivory gauze viscose fabric with bands of flowering shrub design woven in, *c.*1908. Fabric possibly faded from blue original.

Length 952 mm, width 215 mm, thickness *c.*0.1 mm.

564. 1915-574/1: Two early specimens of lustra cellulose from wood pulp (red and white), in glass containers. White tube marked: 'MADDER'.

Length 155 mm, diameter 32 mm.
Source: Swan, J.

565. 1915-574/2: Specimens of viscose from cotton wool (1898); skein. Label with skein reads: 'VISCOSE SPINNING SYNDICATE L^TD/ 47, Victoria S^t/ LONDON, S.W./ STEARN • ARTIFICIAL SILK/ PATENT./ Den 135/...'. Last two lines handwritten so '1' uncertain.

Length 245 mm, width 120 mm, thickness 28 mm.
Source: Swan, J.

566. 1915-574/3: Two skeins of unbleached viscose in test tubes (Pts 3 and 4) and two wooden reels of Stearn artificial silk (Pts 1 and 2), 1903. Reel no. 1 is gold in colour; reel no. 2 is old gold in colour.

Pt. 1: Length 42 mm, diameter 38mm.
Pt. 2: Length 45 mm, diameter 36 mm.
Skeins:
Pt. 3: Length 135 mm, diameter 15.5 mm.
Pt. 4: Length 208 mm, diameter 29 mm.
Source: Swan, J.

567. 1915-574/4: Three woven fabrics partly of Stearn artificial silk 1903. No. 1 is a cream fabric with two green stripes. No. 2 is an elaborate cream fabric with thin stripes of gold, olive, cream and red; larger olive stripes contain a phoenix motif (in cream). No. 3 is a gold striped fabric with three stripes filled with floral design.

1. Length 250 mm, width 15 mm, thickness 0.2 mm.
2. and 3 in frame: Visible dimensions: length 124 mm, width 70 mm, thickness unmeasurable.
Source: Swan, J.
Figure 34

568. 1931-130: Earliest existing specimen of viscose artificial silk (dated 30 August 1898), in flask.

Length 122 mm, diameter 77 mm.
Source: Cross and Bevan Laboratories.
Figure 35

569. 1931-131: Early monofil of viscose artificial silk, golden colour.

Length 245 mm, width 50 mm, thickness 18 mm.
Source: Cross and Bevan Laboratories.

570. 1931-132: Two specimens of material partly woven with viscose, *c.*1900.

Pt. 1: Golden fabric with wide bands of darker gold.
Length 220 mm, width 130 mm, thickness 0.2 mm.

Pt. 2: Golden fabric woven with a rich floral design.
Length 170 mm, width 100 mm, thickness 0.2 mm.
Source: Cross and Bevan Laboratories.

571. 1952-102: Two skeins of viscose silk wound on wooden reels, 1903.

Pt. 1: Two labels tied to reel: first inscription reads: '297 Den/35 Fils/ .78gm/den/7.3% Wet/Dry'. Other side of label marked: 'TOPHAM'. Second label marked: 'Original Viscose/Artificial Silk/ Made about 1903/ C.F.Topham'; handwritten in ink with Topham's signature.
Diameter 56 mm, height 88 mm.

Pt. 2: Two labels tied to reel: first label reads: '54 Den/.80gm/den/2.8% Wet/Dry'. Second label marked: 'Original Viscose/Artificial Silk/ Made about 1903/ C.F.Topham'; handwritten in ink with Topham's signature. Reel marked at top: 'COURTAULD's LTD'.
Diameter 56 mm, height 88 mm.
Source: Topham, C.F.
Figure 36

572. 1952-103: Specimen of viscose in sealed glass tube, 1903, liquid brown in colour.

Length 255 mm, diameter 22.5 mm.
Source: Topham, C.F.

573. 1992-680: Umbrella handle in marble-effect brown solid viscose. Produced by a partner of Cross and Bevan, Clayton Beadle in Erith. 1895.

Length 75 mm, width 90 mm, diameter 19.5 mm.
Source: Cross and Bevan Laboratories.

574. 1992-681: Three walking-stick handles in solid viscose. Produced by a partner of Cross and Bevan, Clayton Beadle in Erith. 1895.

Pt. 1: Marble-effect pink walking-stick handle, notch at one end.
Height 88 mm, diameter 26.5 mm.

Pt. 2: Marble-effect brown walking-stick handle.
Height 108 mm, diameter 23.5 mm.

Pt. 3: Marble-effect blue walking-stick handle.
Height 94 mm, diameter 18 mm.
Source: Cross and Bevan Laboratories.

575. 1992-682: Bobbin (?) in light brown solid viscose. Produced by a partner of Cross and Bevan, Clayton Beadle in Erith. 1895.

Length 139 mm, diameter 34 mm, thickness 7 mm.
Source: Cross and Bevan Laboratories.

576. 1992-683: Viscose sponge. Forerunner of Spontex, *c.*1895.

Length 122 mm, width 80 mm, thickness 33 mm.
Source: Cross and Bevan Laboratories.

577. 1992-684: Two knitted viscose stockings that won a gold medal at the Paris Exhibition in 1900. Knitted by a Miss May for Cross & Bevan.

Pt. 1: Viscose stocking.
Length 880 mm, width 52 mm, thickness 2 mm.

Pt. 2: Viscose stocking.
Length 2040 mm, width 56 mm, thickness 2 mm.
Source: Cross and Bevan Laboratories.

578. 1992-685: Bag containing nine viscose-covered medicine bottle corks. 1895–99.

Pt. 1: 'Viscorks' bag. Black printed inscription: '"VISICORKS"/(Viscose-covered corks.)/*SAMPLES*/ Size Number'.
Length 157 mm, width 115 mm, thickness 0.5 mm.

Pt. 2: Viscose-covered cork.
Diameter 20.5 mm, height 27.5 mm.

Pt. 3: Viscose-covered cork.
Diameter 20.5 mm, height 27.5 mm.

Pt. 4: Viscose-covered cork.
Diameter 22.5 mm, height 27 mm.

Pt. 5: Viscose-covered cork. Inscribed: '10'. Singed on one side.
Diameter 24.5 mm, height 30 mm.

Pt. 6: Viscose-covered cork.
Diameter 22 mm, height 27.5 mm.

Pt. 7: Viscose-covered cork.
Diameter 21 mm, height 22.5 mm.

Pt. 8: Viscose-covered cork.
Diameter 19.5 mm, height 25 mm.

Pt. 9: Viscose-covered cork.
Diameter 20.5 mm, height 27 mm.

Pt. 10: Viscose-covered cork.
Diameter 22 mm, height 27 mm.
Source: Cross and Bevan Laboratories.

579. 1992-686: Early sample of spun viscose containing sulphur in large corked test tube. 1912. Labelled: 'VISCOSE SILK/ as spun/ containing sulphur'.

Length 265 mm, diameter 38 mm.
Source: Cross and Bevan Laboratories.

580. 1992-688: Envelope containing sample of viscose. 1904–05.

Pt. 1: Envelope with piece missing. In handwriting: 'Mr Topham 1904-5. Artificial Si...', 'from Mr Stea...'.
Length 118 mm, width 90 mm, thickness 12 mm.

Pt. 2: Sample of artificial silk.
Length 170 mm, width 90 mm, thickness 12 mm.
Source: Cross and Bevan Laboratories.

581. 1995-164: Five samples of viscose lace spun by the late Auguste Delubac of the Viscose Archedoise at his Vals-Les-Bains factory, 1904–05, and made up into 'Le Puy Laces', with explanatory letter, in wood and glass frame.

Length 815 mm, width 585 mm, thickness 18 mm.

Pt. 1: Sample 1 (cream): First viscose fibres made by Auguste Delubac using his own process without water, invented by him. Lace of Le Puy made by the nuns of the order of St Clare of Vals.
Length 394 mm, width 32 mm, thickness unmeasurable.

Pt. 2: Sample 2 (cream): First viscose fibres made by Auguste Delubac using his own process without water, invented by him. Lace of Le Puy made by the nuns of the order of St Clare of Vals.
Length 400 mm, width 62 mm, thickness unmeasurable.

Pt. 3: Sample 3 (red and gold): The very first rayon fibres to be worked on a lace-making pillow with a mixture of '1904' Archedoise viscose fibre spun by Auguste Delubac.
Length 360 mm, width 35 mm, thickness unmeasurable.

Pt. 4: Sample 4 (cream): Second trial in the making of pillow lace carried out at Le Puy with Archedoise Viscose 'silk' fibre spun by Auguste Delubac in 1905. Lace has a zig-zag edge with groups of four circles in each section.

Length 395 mm, width 87 mm, thickness unmeasurable.

Pt. 5: Sample 5 (cream): Second trial in the making of pillow lace carried out at Le Puy with Archedoise Viscose 'silk' fibre spun by Auguste Delubac in 1905. Lace design: flowers and granulated design.
Length 535 mm, width 74 mm, thickness unmeasurable.

Pt. 6: Letter (typed): 'These samples are the first threads of viscose yarn spun by the Late Auguste Delubac of the Viscose Archedoise at Val-Les Bains and made up into "Le Puy Laces". M. Delubac had close relations with the late Mr Samuel Courtauld and it is his daughter Madame Juliette Balas-Delubac who has presented them to me for our historic records/ W.R. Courtauld [signed]/ December 1955'.
Length 200 mm, width 170 mm, thickness unmeasurable.
Source: Courtaulds Focus Polymers.

VISCOSE MACHINERY AND EQUIPMENT

582. 1925-794: Specimens relating to the manufacture of acetate and viscose artificial silk.

Pt. 1: Alkali cellulose (white, fluffy) in test tube.
Length 121 mm, diameter 30 mm.

Pt. 2: Calcium bisulphite (white, powder) in test tube.
Length 114 mm, diameter 26 mm.

Pt. 3: Sodium hydroxide (clear, liquid) in glass ampoule.
Length 146 mm, diameter 31 mm.

Pt. 4: Viscose solution (dark brown, liquid) in glass ampoule.
Length 141 mm, diameter 31.5 mm.

Pt. 5: Viscose block (marble-effect green).
Length 97 mm, diameter 21 mm.

Pt. 6: Twenty-two sheets of ?Punford wood cellulose (white), tied together.
Length 93 mm, width 84 mm, thickness 20 mm.

Pt. 7: Two rectangular pieces of crude wood pulp, tied together.
Length 110 mm, width 75 mm, thickness 41 mm.

Pt. 8: Cellulose acetate solution (white) in glass ampoule.
Length 150 mm, diameter 31 mm.

Pt. 9: Acetic anhydride solution (clear) in glass ampoule.
Length 160 mm, diameter 30 mm.

Pt. 10: Acetic acid (clear) in glass ampoule.
Length 148 mm, diameter 30 mm.

Pt. 11: Cellulose acetate in tube.

Length 104 mm, diameter 25 mm.

Pt. 12: Alkali cellulose (white, powder) in flask.
Length 130 mm, diameter 86 mm.

Pt. 13: Skein of viscose (golden).
Length 142 mm, width 70 mm, thickness 17 mm.

Pt. 14: Wood chips in box.
Length 104 mm, width 104 mm, thickness 45 mm.

Pt. 15: Specimen of linters (fibres).
Length 95 mm, width 95 mm, thickness 40 mm.

Pt. 16: Specimen of sliver (fibres).
Length 145 mm, width 115 mm, thickness 50 mm.

Pt. 17: Specimen of cotton (fibres).
Length 145 mm, width 130 mm, thickness 100 mm.

Pt. 18: Twenty small skeins in various colours:
pink/purple, peach (two), bright blue, lilac/grey
(two), mauve, purple/white, pink/lilac (two), old
gold, yellow/lilac/orange, black, green/lilac,
black/white, ivory (two), lilac (two), magenta.
Average length 190 mm, diameter 8 mm.

Pt. 19: Four large skeins in various colours: ivory
('BLEACHED 500'), old rose ('100'), old gold ('DRAB
300'), gold ('500').
Average length 202 mm, width 25 mm, thickness 9
mm.

Source: Cross and Bevan Laboratories.

583. 1927-1096: Godet of early spinning
machine for viscose silk, designed by C.F.
Topham Esq. in 1901.

Length 355 mm, width 177 mm, height 215 mm.
Science Museum Negative No.: 3446.
Source: Cross and Bevan Laboratories.

584. 1928-669: First experimental
spinning box for producing continuous
viscose filaments, 1901.

Diameter 88 mm, height 145 mm.
Science Museum Negative No.: 3566, 641/51, 124/67.
Source: Topham, C.F.

585. 1928-670: Later form of
experimental spinning box (see cat. no.
584) embodying first flexible spindle,
1901, cogged top and blue base (a reused
enamelled saucepan). Base decorated with
a transfer of a lion leaning on a coffee pot.
Spindle now attached to label.

Box: diameter 195 mm, height 120 mm.
Spindle: height 460mm, width 175 mm, breadth 175
mm.
Science Museum Negative No.: 3566.
Source: Topham, C.F.
Figure 36

586. 1928-671: First platinum jet through
which viscose was drawn into filaments.

Diameter 13 mm, height 45 mm.
Science Museum Negative No.: 3566, 124/67.
Source: Topham, C.F.

587. 1928-672: First apparatus (pump) for
forcing viscose through filter and jet.

Length 162 mm, width 57 mm, height 95 mm.
Science Museum Negative No.: 3566, 124/67.
Source: Topham, C.F.

588. 1928-1088: Eight photographs of the
first machines for preparing viscose
artificial silk (invented by Topham in
1901). Photograph of piece of the fabric
in which viscose silk was employed.
Entitled: 'PHOTOGRAPHS OF/ FIRST
PLANT FOR VISCOSE ARTIFICIAL
SILK'. From original slides taken by C.F.
Topham.

Length 1120 mm, width 610 mm, thickness 23 mm.
Science Museum Negative No.: 3609-3620.
Source: Science Museum Workshops.

589. 1929-285: One Vulcanite filter case
with glass bend and spinning jet complete
(for 'viscose' artificial silk).

Length 300 mm, width 110 mm, thickness 435 mm.
Source: Topham, C.F.

590. 1952-104: Collection of stereoscopic
slides relating to early viscose apparatus
and personalities in two boxes. No. 1
marked: 'Transparencies of first <u>Viscose
Artificial Silk</u> apparatus/ Presented by
F.C. Topham/[Nos A - H incl]'. No. 2
marked: 'Transparencies of first <u>Viscose
Artificial Silk</u> apparatus/ & personalities.
Presented by F.C. Topham/[Nos I to M &
209 incl. 2 and /Nos 206-7-8-11-12-13]'.

Length 116 mm, width 52 mm, height 21 mm.
Science Museum Negative No.: 590/52, 591/52,
592/52, 593/52, 594/52, 595/52.
Source: Topham, C.F.

591. 1992-687: Sample of cellulose acetate
soluble in acetic acid with stick-on label
inscribed: 'Acetic Acid soluble/ Cellulose
ACETATE/ 1912'. Typewritten. 1912.

Length 118 mm, diameter 24 mm.
Source: Cross and Bevan Laboratories.

592. 1995-165: Twenty pieces of equipment used for spinning viscose fibres, plus one piece in outline drawing only; dating from pre-1914 to 1949. Used by Courtaulds plc, in wood and glass display cabinet. Each type identified by an outline drawing.

Length 565 mm, width 175 mm, height 240 mm.

Pt. 1: A: One glass jet of the multi-filament type, pre-1914.

Length 38 mm, diameter 22 mm.

Pts 2–3: B: Two glass jets of the ribbon filament type, pre-1914.

Length c.90 mm, diameter 17 mm.

Pt. 4: C: One glass jet of the single filament type, pre-1914.

Length c.27 mm, diameter 19 mm.

Pts 5–7: D: Three jets of the Monel Ribbon filament type, used from 1915 onwards.

1 × diameter 16 mm; 2 × diameter 22 mm; height unmeasurable.

Pts 8–10: E: Three jets with nickel, thin platinum or gold tips, used between 1915 and 1918, one piece sectioned.

Diameter 16 mm, height 12 mm.

Pts 11–12: F: Two platinum jets, used from 1915 to 1928.

Diameter 16 mm; height unmeasurable.

Pt. 13: G: One Periodicity Test jet.

Diameter 16 mm; height unmeasurable.

Pt. 14: H: One experimental jet, pointed.

Diameter 16 mm; height unmeasurable.

Pt. 15: I: One experimental jet; not in display although in text.

Pt. 16: J: One experimental jet.

Diameter 11 mm; height unmeasurable.

Pt. 17: K: One Fibrojet with 1000 holes, 1926.

Diameter 16 mm; height unmeasurable.

Pt. 18: L: One Fibrojet with 1200 holes, 1934.

Diameter 38.5 mm; height unmeasurable.

Pt. 19: M: One Fibrojet with 1400 holes, 1946.

Diameter 68 mm; height unmeasurable.

Pt. 20: N: One Fibrojet with 7500 holes, 1946.

Diameter 68 mm; height unmeasurable.

Pt. 21: O: One Fibrojet with 10000 holes, 1949.

Diameter 68 mm; height unmeasurable.

Source: Courtaulds Focus Polymers.

CASEIN (CS, CASEIN-FORMALDEHYDE)

593. 1979-624/7: Pair of casein candlesticks, marble-effect green and black striped with stepped green base, c.1930.

Height 163 mm, diameter 92 mm.

Reference: Hillier 1971: 176.

Source: Jesse, J.

594. 1979-624/13: Pair of green marble-effect casein candlesticks, with black striped decoration, square columnar stem and square holders and bases, 1930s.

Length 64 mm, width 64 mm, height 117 mm.

Source: Jesse, J.

595. 1979-624/39: Circular purple box of casein, with snap lid, lid engraved with picture of a flamenco dancer, made in France, c.1930. Signature scratched on lid to right of figure: 'LVC' in cursive script. Second inscription inside lid: 'MADE IN FRANCE'.

Diameter 112 mm, height 52 mm.

Source: Jesse, J.

596. 1979-624/56: Circular box of lapis lazuli casein?, lid moulded with stylised flowers, possibly French, 1930s. Surface has hairline cracks in a few places, lid chipped (see cat. no. 617).

Diameter 100 mm, height 60 mm.

Source: Jesse, J.

597. 1979-624/118: Casein red cigarette holder and case decorated with silver and black designs, 1930s. Probably German.

Length 97 mm, diameter 15 mm.

Pt. 1: Expanding holder, trumpet-shaped at cigarette holding end, tubular handle slides out of opposite end.

Length 132 mm, diameter 10 mm.

Pt. 2: Cylinder, with lid which screws onto base. Inscription on base: 'ERMAN', possibly remains of 'Y' after 'N', 'Germany' originally?

Length 97 mm, diameter 15 mm.

Source: Jesse, J.

598. 1979-624/125: Casein compact for lipstick and scent disguised as a blue book decorated with a girl in a short chemise, holding a mirror, with silk tassel. French, c.1920s.

Length 52 mm, width 39 mm, height 14 mm.

Pt. 1: Compact in form of blue book with gold page edging. Hinged lid opened with gold tassel. Two hollows inside for scent and lipstick.
Length 52 mm, width 39 mm, height 14 mm.

Pt. 2: Cylinder of clear glass with stopper and scent dipper.
Length 37 mm, diameter 7 mm.

Pt. 3: Metal cylinder containing deep red lipstick. Clip-in fastening. Cylinder oval in cross-section.
Length 42 mm, width 10 mm, thickness 8 mm.
Source: Jesse, J.

599. 1979-624/135: Letter rack of green watered-effect casein with rectangular base and four rectangular vertical partitions, with angled upper corner, one solid, rest cut out in middle, forming thin strips, base rests on four apsidally placed ball feet. Surface slightly cracked.
Length 150 mm, width 107 mm, height 125 mm.
Source: Jesse, J.

600. 1979-624/140: Paper-knife of yellow/orange marble-effect casein. Flat with pointed tip. First half of twentieth century. Tip and base slightly chipped.
Length 188 mm, width 23 mm, thickness 4 mm.
Source: Jesse, J.

601. 1979-624/141: Rod, square in cross-section of yellow/orange marble-effect casein. First half of twentieth century.
Length 294 mm, width 12 mm, thickness 12 mm.
Source: Jesse, J.

602. 1979-624/142: Pen holder of yellow/orange marble-effect casein. Rod, square in cross-section and pointed at one end. First half of twentieth century. Repaired (has been broken into two at one time).
Length 157 mm, width 12 mm, thickness 11 mm.
Source: Jesse, J.

603. 1979-624/146: Circular clock with ovoid base of lapis lazuli casein, face is cut out of chrome and has art deco style figures, 1930s. Surface slightly cracked in places, chrome missing in places; number 1 missing from face. Scale on face: '1 (1) 12' hours. Trade mark painted on face and back: two arrows crossed over each other, possibly representing points of the compass.
Height 140 mm, width 121 mm, breadth 54 mm.
Reference: Bennett 1979: 16 (top middle).
Source: Jesse, J.

604. 1979-624/148: Casein brooch in the form of the French liner *Normandie*. Inscribed: 'NORMANDIE'. Metal clip inscribed: 'DEPOSE'.
Length 80 mm, width 27 mm, thickness 9 mm.
Source: Jesse, J.

605. 1979-624/149: Necklace of blue casein, with cylindrical and round-tipped conical beads, four chrome beads, two of which separate cylindrical from conical plastic beads, two marking off three conical beads which form a pendant, art deco design, 1930s.
Length 240 mm, width 35 mm, diameter 15 mm.
Source: Jesse, J.

606. 1979-624/151: Pendant of orange-red casein with metal, horizontal mount enamelled with art deco floral design, with dark red string with screw fastening, 1920s–30s.
Length 60 mm, width 47 mm, depth 7 mm.
Source: Jesse, J.
Plate 1

607. 1979-624/152: Casein necklace with jade- and tortoiseshell-effect beads moulded in the Chinese style, interspersed with imitation coral beads, 1930s.
Length 180 mm, diameter 145 mm, bead diameter 17 mm.
Source: Jesse, J.
Plate 1

608. 1979-624/153: Necklace of buff marble-effect shield-shaped casein beads inset with green and black strips, 1930s.
Length 220 mm.
Bead: width 25 mm, thickness 4 mm.
Source: Jesse, J.
Figure 2

609. 1979-624/154: Necklace made of coral-coloured casein: beads are coral cylinders interspersed with blue/turquoise cylinders; flat oval coral pendant mounted with olive cast phenolic, *c.*1930.

Length 200 mm, width 135 mm, thickness 6mm (pendant and bead).
Source: Jesse, J.

610. 1979-624/155: Carved pendant of ivory casein, in form of woman kneeling down and picking roses, surrounded by wreath of roses, 1920s.

Diameter 56 mm, thickness 5 mm.
Source: Jesse, J.
Plate 1

611. 1979-624/157: Casein brooch, in form of black cylinder threaded with six white rings, with metal pin, mid-twentieth century.

Length 75 mm, width 24 mm.
Source: Jesse, J.

612. 1979-624/158: Casein brooch, in form of red cylinder threaded with six navy rings, with metal pin, mid-twentieth century.

Length 75 mm, width 24 mm.
Source: Jesse, J.

613. 1979-624/163: Buckle in the form of a woman's head, carved and moulded of white plastic, probably casein, glossy finish, Egyptianising style, 1920s–30s, French.

Length 95 mm, width 73 mm, thickness 13 mm.
Reference: Bennett 1979: 16 (bottom row left) (illustrated).
Source: Jesse, J.

614. 1979-624/165: Ring of orange casein inset with three black strips, 1930s. Inset surface cracked.

Diameter 27 mm, height 12 mm.
Source: Jesse, J.

615. 1979-624/186: Propelling-pencil case made of mottled black and brown casein, made for E.A. Chamberlain Ltd, Nailsworth, England, 1950s. Cracked and chipped at top. Inscription on side: 'E.A. CHAMBERLAIN LTD. NAILSWORTH' inlaid with gold.

Length 136 mm, diameter 11 mm.
Source: Jesse, J.

616. 1979-624/222: Cosmetic powder box, circular, in highly polished deep brown casein, with ornate finial, *c.*1920.

Diameter 119 mm, height 90 mm.
Source: Jesse, J.

617. 1979-624/223: Circular box, apple green, probably casein, the lid moulded with stylised flowers, French, 1920s–30s. (see cat. no. 596).

Diameter 102 mm, height 60 mm.
Source: Jesse, J.

618. 1979-624/224: Rectangular cigarette box and match box, with two compartments, made of green marble-effect casein with silver mounts and hinges, match box has shagreen lighter. Knob-shaped handles are decorated with circular sectioned silver and mounted on silver supports, the silver mounts are dated 1911 and were made by Child and Child, London. Hallmark punched on silver mounts: London hallmark dated to 1911, makers' mark consists of ornate 'N' and 'C' contained within shield topped by three fleur-de-lys, eight in total. Second inscription punched on silver hinges: 'CHILD & CHILD/LONDON SW'; two of these inscriptions appear, one on each hinge. Broken.

Length 130 mm, width 85 mm, height 45 mm.
Source: Jesse, J.

619. 1979-624/241: Casein photo frame with black rectangular base, photo supports are black at sides and back, waved at the edges, front painted with a pink and white art deco design showing a seated girl playing a wind instrument; she is surrounded by flowering shrubs and hanging plants, the moon and water; late 1920s, French. Inscription on base: 'MADE IN FRANCE'.

Height 120 mm, width 194 mm, breadth 39 mm.
Source: Jesse, J.

620. 1979-624/245: Pair of maroon casein candlesticks, each ringed with five transparent acrylic circles and cup, and

three flat circular feet, late 1940s.
Cracked in places.

Height 250 mm, diameter 124 mm.
Source: Jesse, J.

621. 1979-624/280: Five bracelets, two of
red and three of orange casein, 1930s.

Diameter 75 mm, height 3 mm.
Source: Jesse, J.
Plate 1

622. 1979-624/281: Brooch of moulded
buff casein in form of a woman's head
with a hat on, features and hat band
painted on in dark brown, traces of red
lips, 1930s or 1940s. French.

Length 58 mm, width 25 mm, height 10 mm.
Source: Jesse, J.
Plate 1

623. 1979-624/287: Buckle consisting of
two rectangular plaques of casein with
wheat design in green and black on cream
ground, framed with black rim, metal
hook fastening, French, 1930s or 1940s?
Two inscriptions: inscription on metal
straps reads: 'B<u>TÉ</u>/SGDG'; inscription
back of right hand plaque reads:
'FRANCE'.

Length 99 mm, width 68 mm, height 7 mm.
Source: Jesse, J.
Plate 1

624. 1979-624/289: Necklace of white
ivory casein and metal cup-shaped beads,
with walnut and metal flat discs and
rectangular walnut spacers, art nègre
style, 1930s, France.

Length 345 mm, diameter 20mm (disc).
Source: Jesse, J.

625. 1979-624/290: Pendant of carved and
moulded green casein in form of papyrus
flower, Egyptian style, 1920s to 1930s.
Inscription: 'Y B'; letters superimposed
on each other.

Length 78 mm, width 83 mm, depth 10 mm.
Source: Jesse, J.

626. 1980-676/184: Black circular casein
plaque with raised rim, shows moulded
head in profile of Napoleon engraved by
F. Muller, early twentieth century.

Inscription moulded around edge:
'NAPOLEON'. Second inscription
moulded around base of neck reads:
'Muller.f.' in cursive script.

Diameter 91 mm, height 10 mm.
Source: Newport, R.

627. 1980-676/185: Circular flat casein
plaque showing moulded three-masted
galleon, tortoiseshell-effect, early
twentieth century?

Diameter 94 mm, thickness 7 mm.
Source: Newport, R.

628. 1980-676/186: Circular flat casein
plaque showing moulded head of a
fisherman in foul-weather gear, marble-
effect green and black, early twentieth
century?

Diameter 95 mm, thickness 11 mm.
Source: Newport, R.

629. 1980-676/275: Fountain pen,
marble-effect orange and brown,
probably casein, with gold fittings and
nib, *c.*1920s. Cap missing and body
chipped where screws onto nib unit.
Trade mark on body: '"SWAN" SELF-
FILLER/MABIE. TODD & Co
LTD/MADE IN ENGLAND'. To left of
this is outline of swan with:
'TRADEMARK' written below it; runs
lengthwise along body. Second
inscription on nib: 'MABIE/-/TODD/&
Co/-N.Y'. 'MABIE' curved above rest of
inscription. Third inscription is a trade
mark on nib unit: '"SWAN" SF 1' runs
round edge. Fourth inscription on back
of nib: '"SWAN" S.F.1'.

Length 104 mm, diameter 10 mm.
Source: Newport, R.

630. 1980-676/280: Fountain pen in
variegated browns, probably casein, with
chrome fittings (clip missing) and brass
nib. Made in England, *c.*1900s.
Incomplete (clip missing and part of clip
support). Trade mark on body:
'"Stephens" LEVERFIL No 56/MADE
IN ENGLAND'. 'Stephens' is in cursive
script. Inscription runs along length of

body. Second inscription on nib: 'OSMIROID/35'.

Length 126 mm, diameter 14 mm.
Source: Newport, R.

631. 1981-25: Collection of casein plastic samples including: five casein rods (6 mm diam.) suitable for knitting needles – two green (Pts 1 and 2), one red (Pt. 3), one yellow (Pt. 4) and one blue (Pt. 5). Seven sheets of casein showing range of colours and surfaces, colours including watered red (Pt. 6), watered pink (Pt. 7), watered green, L-shaped (Pt. 8), horn (Pt. 9), antler (Pt. 10), tortoiseshell-effect (Pt. 11), marble-effect black (Pt. 12). Mid-twentieth century.

Pts 1–5: Length 725 mm, diameter 6 mm.

Pt. 6: Length 512 mm, width 205 mm, thickness 9 mm.

Pt. 7: Length 517 mm, width 290 mm, thickness 7 mm.

Pt. 8: Length 506 mm, width 418 mm, thickness 5 mm.

Pt. 9: Length 498 mm, width 421 mm, thickness 3 mm.

Pt. 10: Length 512 mm, width 425 mm, thickness 11 mm.

Pt. 11: Length 512 mm, width 424 mm, thickness 6 mm.

Pt. 12: Length 511 mm, width 415 mm, thickness 4 mm.

Source: BP Chemicals Ltd and Cassolith B.V. (Holland).

632. 1981-618: Framed Erinoid, advertisement from *British Plastics*, Vol. 1, No. 1, June 1929.

Length 361 mm, width 284 mm, thickness 20 mm.
Source: BP Chemicals Ltd (Stroud).

633. 1981-619: Book of dye recipes used in casein production *c.*1938.

Length 275 mm, width 261 mm, thickness 57 mm.
Source: BP Chemicals Ltd (Stroud).

634. 1981-620: Button Blank Calculator used by Erinoid Ltd to find the number of discs of given diameter and thickness to be manufactured from 1lb of casein,

*c.*1940. Marked: 'Erinoid/ BUTTON BLANK CALCULATOR'.

Diameter 150 mm, thickness 3 mm.
Source: BP Chemicals Ltd (Stroud).

635. 1981-621: Wooden case containing display of seven formalisation stages of 10-mm casein blanks, marked in weeks: 1 week to 7 weeks. Mid-twentieth century.

Length 218 mm, width 190 mm, thickness 45 mm.
Source: BP Chemicals Ltd (Stroud).

636. 1981-622: Sample of unpressed casein sheet showing formation from extruded rods (cured in formaldehyde). '19' handwritten on one side. Mid-twentieth century.

Length 257 mm, width 253 mm, thickness 18 mm.
Source: BP Chemicals Ltd (Stroud).

637. 1981-623: Sheet of unpolished casein coloured cream from which twenty-four experimental button blanks have been stamped. Mid-twentieth century.

Length 527 mm, width 525 mm, thickness 5 mm.
Source: BP Chemicals Ltd (Stroud).

638. 1981-624: Six large shade cards of coloured casein samples marked: with Erinoid Logo, *c.* late 1920s.

Pt. 1: Three cards bound together, originally with 369 buttons, 24 buttons now missing; marked with trade mark: 'Erinoid' in cursive script on each of its three cards. Fastening marked: 'Erinoid/ Limited'.
Length 512 mm, width 330 mm, thickness 23 mm; average button: diameter 29.5 mm, thickness 2.5 mm.

Pt. 2: As Pt. 1, with 405 buttons (135 on each card), 44 buttons now missing.
Length 512 mm, width 342 mm, thickness 29 mm; average button: diameter 29.5 mm, thickness 2.5 mm.

Pt. 3: Card covered on one side with imitation grey leather, other side originally had 100 square samples of variously coloured casein (four samples missing); each sample stamped in gold with sample number; card inscribed at top: ' ERINOID LIMITED •STROUD • GLOUCESTERSHIRE/ Telephone: STROUD 810* • Telegrams: ERINOID • STROUD'.
Length 345 mm, width 372 mm, thickness 7 mm; average sample: length 30 mm, width 30 mm, thickness 3 mm.

Pt. 4: Card covered on one side with imitation grey leather, other side originally had 100 square samples of variously coloured casein (three samples missing); card covered with PVC sheet for protection; card marked: '1288-4746'.
Length 345 mm, width 374 mm, thickness 10 mm; average sample: length 25 mm, width 25 mm, thickness 3 mm.

Pt. 5: Sample card as Pt. 4, with 100 buttons; card is inscribed at top as Pt. 3; each button has its sample number written in ink in the lower right-h and corner of each square on card.
Length 345 mm, width 372 mm, thickness 8.5 mm; button: diameter 24.5mm or 29 mm, thickness 4.5 mm.

Pt. 6: One sheet of a button book as Pts 1 and 2; it had 108 buttons originally, now 5 are missing; button sample numbers are printed in the lower left hand corner; fastening attached to cover marked: 'Erinoid/Limited'.
Length 442 mm, width 330 mm, thickness 6.5 mm; average button: diameter 29 mm, thickness 4.5 mm.

Source: BP Chemicals Ltd (Stroud).

639. 1981-625: Four shade cards of coloured casein samples, two marked with Erinoid logo, probably *c.*1930s.

Pt. 1: Cream card with red border, and red string tied through top. Eighteen buttons arranged in three curved rows in a semi-circle, each sample area is underlined below with a semi-circle of two red lines. Buttons have a fish-scale pattern in different colours, each marked with a number underneath. Top marked: '"POPEYE" (crossed through) ERINOID /LIMITED/ BLANKS'. Base of card marked: 'ERINOID LTD, STROUD, GLOS, TELEPHONE STROUD 810*'. *c.*1930.
Card: length 279 mm, width 202 mm, thickness 1 mm.
Buttons: diameter 11–22 mm, thickness 3 mm.

Pt. 2: Cream card with brown border with twelve samples, each stamped with sample number. In colours ranging from beige to green, *c.*1930.
Card: length 198 mm, width 146 mm, thickness 7 mm.
Blank: diameter 18.5–33.5 mm, thickness 4.5–6 mm.

Pt. 3: Sample card showing colour blanks in muted camouflage tones (probably military) of taupe, grey, blue, brown and olive. Each blank stamped with sample number–shade card of coloured casein samples, two marked with Erinoid logo, *c.*1930.
Card: length 301 mm, width 205 mm, thickness 2 mm.
Blank: diameter 28 mm, thickness 4 mm.

Pt. 4: Grey shade card with dark grey border showing sixteen variously coloured casein buttons. Card inscribed: 'BLANKS/ COLOUR RANGE', 'ERINOID /LIMITED' (trade mark), and 'LIGHTPILL MILLS, STROUD,/ GLOUCESTERSHIRE/ Telephone: Stroud 810/ Telegrams: ERINOID, STROUD.../ OFFICES AND SHOWROOMS/LONDON: EAST INDIA HOUSE/ 208A REGENT STREET, W.1./ TELEPHONE REGENT 4637 (3 lines)/ BIRMINGHAM, 3 COLESHILL ST./ BIRMINGHAM, 4/ Telephone: BIRMINGHAM CENTRAL 1886'. Sample number printed in lower right-hand corner of each button square.
Card: length 216 mm, width 155 mm, thickness 4 mm.
Button: diameter 22 mm, thickness 3 mm.
Source: BP Chemicals Ltd (Stroud).

640. 1981-626: One trade card of casein door handle samples marked with Erinoid logo, *c.*1930s. Comprises 12 samples arranged in a fan design around central Erinoid logo, with one sample at the base of the card. All the samples are rectangular with oblique corners and are stamped with the sample number. The colours include transparent cream ('2'), mottled orange ('4604'), pearlised green ('470'), mottled brown ('1180'), pearlised rose ('1220'), cream ('378'), pearlised beige ('214'), pearlised sea-green ('509'), pearlised brown ('509'), pearlised grey ('16'), tortoiseshell effect ('224'), black ('1'). Top marked: 'ERINOID for FURNITURE HANDLES'. In centre is trade mark: 'Erinoid/ LIMITED'. At bottom of card is: 'LIGHTPILL MILLS/ STROUD, GLOS./ Telephone: Stroud 810/ Telegrams: Erinoid, Stroud...[four lines blanked out]/ 3 COLESHILL STREET/ BIRMINGHAM 4/ Telephone: Birmingham Central 1886'. Label on bottom reads: 'OFFICES AND SHOWROOMS/ LONDON: 96 PICADILLY. LONDON W.1/ TEL: GROSVENOR 7111./ BIRMINGHAM, 4/ TEL: BIRMINGHAM CENTRAL 1886/ REGISTERED OFFICE/ KENT HOUSE, TELEGRAPH STREET, LONDON, E.C.2./ TEL MONARCH 7631'.

Length: 304 mm, width 227 mm, thickness 1 mm.
Sample: length 73 mm, width 18 mm, thickness 6 mm.
Source: BP Chemicals Ltd (Stroud).

641. 1981-627: Three sample books of coloured casein bound in green and marked with the Erinoid Logo, *c.*1950s.

Pt. 1: Green sample book, cover marked: with the Erinoid logo, in gold within a black circle with three encircling black rings. Contains three cards. Card 1 has 24 buttons. Card 2 has 32, and card three 33 buttons. Card 1 inscribed: 'Erinoid CASEIN SHEET/ COLOUR RANGE/ STROUD • GLOUCESTERSHIRE. Telephone: STROUD 810*'. Each button marked: with the sample number. Third card inscribed: 'COLOURS BELOW WITHDRAWN FROM RANGE/ (supply position on application)'.
Length 182mm, width 117 mm, thickness 16.5 mm; average button: diameter 18 mm, thickness 3 mm.

Pt. 2: Green sample book, cover marked with the 'Erinoid' trade mark. Spine marked: 'Erinoid CASEIN SHEETS', last two words written vertically. Contains three cards. Card 1 has 30 buttons. Card 2 has 35, and card three 32 buttons. Card 1 inscribed: 'Erinoid CASEIN SHEET/ COLOUR RANGE/Telephone: STROUD 810* STROUD •GLOUCESTERSHIRE Telegrams: ERINOID STROUD'. Each button marked with the sample number. Third card inscribed: 'BLANKS'.
Length 267 mm, width 209 mm, thickness 20 mm; average button: diameter 17.5 mm, thickness 4 mm.

Pt. 3: Green sample book, cover marked with the 'Erinoid' trade mark. Second logo on flap in gold within a black circle with three encircling black rings. Contains two cards. Card 1 has 30 buttons. Card 2 has 29 (one missing). Numbers written in lower right-hand corner. Inside front cover the flysheet reads: ' PRESENTING THE 1951 Erinoid STANDARD / RANGE OF SHEETS/ STOCKS ARE AVAILABLE IN NORMAL SIZES FROM 2mm UPWARDS/ All these colours have been tested and found to be fast to Dry Cleaning and Laundry Processes/ ERINOID limited, Stroud, Gloucestershire/ Telegrams/ ERINOID, STROUD/ TELEPHONE/ STROUD 810/4/ OFFICES AND SHOWROOMS'. 'LONDON:/ EAST INDIA HOUSE/ 208A REGENT STREET, W.1/ TELEPHONE:/ REGENT 4637 (3 lines)'. 'BIRMINGHAM: 3 COLESHILL STREET/ BIRMINGHAM 4/ TELEPHONE:/ BIRMINGHAM CENTRAL 1886'.
Length 255 mm, width 182 mm, thickness 23 mm; average button: diameter 25 mm, thickness 6 mm.
Source: BP Chemicals Ltd (Stroud).
Plate 11 (Pts 1 and 2)

642. 1981-628: Two sample books of coloured casein bound in grey and plastic and marked with the Erinoid logo, mid-twentieth century.

Pt. 1: Pale grey sample book with four sample sheets, three with 28 buttons, and one with 26 buttons. Cover inscribed with trade mark: 'Erinoid'; spine inscribed: 'ERINOID'.
Length 183 mm, width 142 mm, thickness 37 mm; average button: diameter 17.5 mm, thickness 3.5 mm.

Pt. 2: Grey covered book containing six sample sheets, each with 20 samples (21 buttons missing). Book front inscribed: 'ERINOID casein/ Shade Cards'; 'ERINOID' is a trade mark and also appears on spine.
Length 250 mm, width 200 mm, thickness 57 mm; average button: diameter 22 mm, thickness 5 mm.
Source: BP Chemicals Ltd (Stroud).
Plate 11 (Pt. 1)

643. 1981-640: Forty-six samples of casein pinched rod, formed by compression moulding of sheet material showing the range of colours and effects achieved. Mid-twentieth century.

Pt. 1: Marble-effect green.
Length 489 mm, diameter 12.5 mm.

Pt. 2: Marble-effect green.
Length 499 mm, diameter 12.5 mm.

Pt. 3: Black with green elongated spots. Inscribed '737'.
Length 159 mm, diameter 11 mm.

Pt. 4: Marble-effect brown, pierced at one end with white tag inscribed: 'MUST NOT BE POROUS'.
Length 140 mm, diameter 16 mm.

Pt. 5: Lilac/white striped marble effect pierced at one end. Inscribed: '138'.
Length 140 mm, diameter 16 mm.

Pt. 6: Blue-grey marble effect. Inscribed: 'M14' twice and '2057?'.
Length 159 mm, diameter 11 mm.

Pt. 7: Dark brown/bronze marble effect. Inscribed: '3066' and: 'M BROWN SILK THEATRE'.
Length 147 mm, diameter 12 mm.

Pt. 8: Blue/black marble effect. Inscribed: '663' twice.
Length 123 mm, diameter 13 mm.

Pt. 9: Green/black stripe; pierced at one end. Inscribed: '67'.
Length 142 mm, diameter 11.5 mm.

Pt. 10: Black with white speckled marble effect. Inscribed: '3040'.
Length 177 mm, diameter 9 mm.

Pt. 11: Blue/ochre/pale green dappled marble effect. Inscribed: '614' twice.
Length 170 mm, diameter 9 mm.

Pt. 12: 1981-640/12: Grey with black vein. Inscribed: 'BRUMLIK 2021'.
Length 195 mm, diameter 10 mm.

Pt. 13: 1981-640/13: Black veined cream. Inscribed: '2080'.
Length 148 mm, diameter 11.5 mm.

Pt. 14: Brown veined cream. Inscribed: '2061' and 'M2A'.
Length 165 mm, diameter 11.5 mm.

Pt. 15: Black/old gold marble effect. Inscribed: '2059' and: 'M16' twice.
Length 172 mm, diameter 12 mm.

Pt. 16: Marble-effect gold. Inscribed: '372' twice.
Length 160 mm, diameter 13.5 mm.

Pt. 17: Marble-effect maroon. Inscribed: '2040' and: 'BJ7' twice.
Length 188 mm, diameter 12.5 mm.

Pt. 18: Marble-effect black/grey. Inscribed: '687' twice.
Length 165 mm, diameter 9.5 mm.

Pt. 19: Grey marble effect with black. Inscribed: '287'.
Length 163 mm, diameter 10 mm.

Pt. 20: Striped grey/black. Inscribed: '2011'.
Length 149 mm, diameter 11.5 mm.

Pt. 21: Marble-effect brown. Inscribed: '3037'.
Length 114 mm, diameter 8.5 mm.

Pt. 22: Candy-striped grey. Inscribed: 'BRUMLIK 1016' and: '3104'.
Length 136 mm, diameter 10 mm.

Pt. 23: Mottled grey/black. Inscribed: 'M10' twice and: '2053'.
Length 176 mm, diameter 11.5 mm.

Pt. 24: Pink fluted stripes. Inscribed: '3161'.
Length 124 mm, diameter 10.5 mm.

Pt. 25: Pearlescent green. Inscribed: '3075' and: 'PLAIN GREEN WILSON'.
Length 150 mm, diameter 10 mm.

Pt. 26: Marble-effect blue/grey. Inscribed: '853' twice.
Length 130 mm, diameter 11.5 mm.

Pt. 27: Marble-effect turquoise. Inscribed: '3025' and: 'M GREEN M & C'.
Length 157 mm, diameter 10.5 mm.

Pt. 28: Marble-effect purple/brown. Inscribed: '850' twice.
Length 119 mm, diameter 12.5 mm.

Pt. 29: Mottled brown/black. Inscribed: '1100', 'WYVERN 1100' and: 'BROWN WYVERN 1100'.
Length 139 mm, diameter 10.5 mm.

Pt. 30: Marble-effect blue/old gold. Inscribed: '618' twice.
Length 163 mm, diameter 10 mm.

Pt. 31: Marble-effect black. Inscribed: '969' or '696'.
Length 139 mm, diameter 9 mm.

Pt. 32: Blue with fluted stripes. Inscribed: '3146'.

Length 78 mm, diameter 12.5 mm.

Pt. 33: Black and blue candy stripe. Inscribed: '3092' and blue and black twist.
Length 147 mm, diameter 11.5 mm.

Pt. 34: Mottled cream/black/silver. Inscribed: 'KL33' twice and: '2024'.
Length 210 mm, diameter 9.5 mm.

Pt. 35: Waved lines of green/black. Inscribed: '3145' and: 'SAX 11'.
Length 100 mm, diameter 9 mm.

Pt. 36: Pearlescent candy stripe. Inscribed: '2012' and: 'BRUMLIK 10160'.
Length 184 mm, diameter 8.5 mm.

Pt. 37: Marble-effect navy. Inscribed: '2031' and: 'VAL 10833'.
Length 184 mm, diameter 8.5 mm.

Pt. 38: Fluted striped pearlised rust. Inscribed: '3144' twice.
Length 86 mm, diameter 10 mm.

Pt. 39: Striped gold/black.
Length 173 mm, diameter 8 mm.

Pt. 40: Mottled maroon/silver/black. Inscribed: 'BJ5' and: '2038'.
Length 189 mm, diameter 10 mm.

Pt. 41: Elongated gold-spotted black, pierced at one end. Inscribed: '2116'.
Length 76 mm, diameter 10 mm.

Pt. 42: Marble-effect sepia with dark brown. Pierced at one end with white tag inscribed: '201' twice.
Length 51 mm, diameter 11 mm.

Pt. 43: Marble-effect green with dark brown. Pierced at one end.
Length 180 mm, diameter 5.5 mm.

Pt. 44: Marble-effect olive green with black.
Length 140 mm, diameter 4.5 mm.

Pt. 45: Marble-effect grey/black with blue veins.
Length 57 mm, diameter 12 mm.

Pt. 46: Brown within black stripe, pierced at one end. Inscribed: '99'.
Length 18 mm, diameter 12 mm.
Source: BP Chemicals Ltd (Stroud).

644. 1981-641: Fourteen samples of casein tubes and sections of tubes produced by machining pinched rod. Mid-twentieth century.

Pt. 1: Half tube cut longitudinally. Dark brown wood colour, marked: '389'.
Length 205 mm, diameter 32 mm.

Pt. 2: Half tube cut longitudinally. Pearlised brown/cream marble-effect, marked: 'BROWN PEARL RIFKIDD/3201'.
Length 150 mm, diameter 26 mm.

Pt. 3: Tube. Marble-effect red/brown, marked: '64'.
Length 138 mm, diameter 19 mm.

Pt. 4: Tube. Marble-effect blue/black, marked: '3180' and: 'BLUE PEARL ILLNER'.
Length 140 mm, diameter 19 mm.

Pt. 5: Tube. Fine blue marble effect, marked: '755'.
Length 171 mm, diameter 12 mm.

Pt. 6: Tube. Pink/black marble effect, marked: '732'.
Length 157 mm, diameter 11 mm.

Pt. 7: Tube. Blue/gold marble effect, marked: 'T4'.
Length 134 mm, diameter 12 mm.

Pt. 8: Tube. Fine pink/white marble effect, marked: '3239'.
Length 113 mm, diameter 12 mm.

Pt. 9: Tube. Cream/brown swirl, marked: '3060'.
Length 116 mm, diameter 12 mm.

Pt. 10: Tube. Brown/cream/gold swirl, with two notches at end.
Length 109 mm, diameter 11 mm.

Pt. 11: Tube. Brown/cream/gold swirl, very small bore, marked: '3151'.
Length 102 mm, diameter 10 mm.

Pt. 12: Tube. Pink/cream swirl, marked: '3152'.
Length 88 mm, diameter 12 mm.

Pt. 13: Tube. Black/cream marble effect, both ends broken off, with gouge mark.
Length 68 mm, diameter 18 mm.

Pt. 14: Tube. Red/black. Label stuck on marked: '3237'.
Length 92 mm, diameter 11 mm.
Source: BP Chemicals Ltd (Stroud).

645. 1981-642: Erinoid sample band of 52 coloured casein rod items, with white triangular tag inscribed in gold with the 'Erinoid' trade mark. Mid-twentieth century.

Length 555mm (overall), width 32 mm, thickness 8.5 mm.
Rods: length 32 mm, diameter 8.5 mm.
Source: BP Chemicals Ltd (Stroud).

646. 1981-643: Twelve samples of plain coloured casein rods of varying diameters. Mid-twentieth century.

Pt. 1: Purple rod stamped: '33'.
Length 298 mm, diameter 10 mm.

Pt. 2: Yellow rod, pierced at one end.
Length 227 mm, diameter 9 mm.

Pt. 3: White rod, stamped: '3007'.
Length 149 mm, diameter 11 mm.

Pt. 4: Black rod, stamped: '19'.
Length 200 mm, diameter 11 mm.

Pt. 5: Green rod, stamped: '10' and: '13-2-46'.
Length 172 mm, diameter 12 mm.

Pt. 6: Rust rod, stamped: '195'.
Length 185 mm, diameter 11 mm.

Pt. 7: Brown rod.

Length 110 mm, diameter 15 mm.

Pt. 8: Black tube, pierced at one end. White tag attached to one end, stamped: 'ELLWIN BROS/BLACK TUBES/BORE MUST BE TO SAMPLE'.
Length 119 mm, diameter 9 mm.

Pt. 9: Transparent rod, pierced at one end.
Length 116 mm, diameter 5 mm.

Pt. 10: Magenta rod stamped: '3133'.
Length 119 mm, diameter 6.5 mm.

Pt. 11: Black rod, pierced at one end. White tag attached to end stamped: 'SP/SAPPHIRE/AUSTRIA'.
Length 173 mm, diameter 5 mm.

Pt. 12: Pale blue rod.
Length 161 mm, diameter 5 mm.
Source: BP Chemicals Ltd (Stroud).

647. 1981-644: Three casein rods machined into the following cross-sections:

Pt. 1: Ellipse, marble-effect salmon pink; stamped: '799'.
Length 158 mm, width 13 mm, thickness 8 mm.

Pt. 2: Ellipse, marble-effect lilac stamped: '800'.
Length 160 mm, width 13 mm, thickness 8 mm.

Pt. 3: D-shaped, yellow, transparent stamped: '206 THURGAM' with stick-on label marked: '3156' in ink.
Mid-twentieth century.
Length 172 mm, width 9 mm, thickness 3 mm.
Source: BP Chemicals Ltd (Stroud).

648. 1981-645: Four drilled and shaped rods of casein fastened to a white tag inscribed: 'RED HORN/CS'. Other side marked: '3112'. Mid-twentieth century.

Overall length: 81 mm, width 22 mm, thickness 5 mm.
Source: BP Chemicals Ltd (Stroud).

649. 1981-646: Twelve samples of casein sheet (4"×4" approx.) polished on one side only, showing range of colours and mottled effects. Mid-twentieth century.

Sheet: length 105 mm, width 103 mm, thickness 6 mm.
Source: BP Chemicals Ltd (Stroud).

650. 1981-647: Eleven samples of casein sheet, showing range of thicknesses, colours and mottled effects. Mid-twentieth century.

Sheet: length 154 mm, width 154 mm, thickness 5 mm.
Source: BP Chemicals Ltd (Stroud).

651. 1981-648: Sixty samples of casein sheet (unpolished) (2 ½"×2 ½" approx.) showing a wide range of colours, each stamped with sample number. Mid-twentieth century.

Pt. 1: Black. Marked: 'T04038B'.

Pt. 2: Rose-red. Marked: 'T0374B'.

Pt. 3: Pale blue pearlised. Marked: 'T03539A'.

Pt. 4: Airforce blue. Marked: 'T03540A'.

Pt. 5: Midnight blue. Marked: 'T03705C'.

Pt. 6: Matt lilac. Marked: '4023B' (handwritten).

Pt. 7: Salmon-pink pearlised. Marked: 'T03537A'.

Pt. 8: Beige pearlised. Marked: 'T03535B'.

Pt. 9: Black. Marked: 'T0404B'.

Pt. 10: Rose-pink. Marked: 'T03772A'.

Pt. 11: Cream pearlised. Marked: 'T03930B'.

Pt. 12: Transparent, yellowed. Marked: 'T04067D'.

Pt. 13: Midnight blue. Marked: 'T030705A'.

Pt. 14: Rose pink. Marked: 'T03772B'.

Pt. 15: Transparent, yellowed. Marked: 'T04024B'.

Pt. 16: Pale pink, marble effect. Marked: 'T03539B'.

Pt. 17: Midnight blue. Marked: 'T03821B'.

Pt. 18: Cream pearlised. Marked: 'T03980C'.

Pt. 19: Pale pink, marble effect. Marked: 'T03539A'.

Pt. 20: Transparent, yellowed. Marked: 'T04067A'.

Pt. 21: Cream pearlised. Marked: 'T04016E'.

Pt. 22: Matt salmon-pink. Marked: 'T04043B' (handwritten).

Pt. 23: Lilac. Marked: 'T4023A'.

Pt. 24: Apple-green pearlised. Marked: 'T03535A'.

Pt. 25: Cream pearlised. Marked: 'T04016O'.

Pt. 26: Cream pearlised. Marked: 'T03980A'.

Pt. 27: Transparent, yellowed. Marked: 'T04024C'.

Pt. 28: Cream pearlised. Marked: 'T03980B'.

Pt. 29: Beige pearlised. Marked: 'T03980B'.

Pt. 30: Cerise. Marked: 'T03828B'.

Pt. 31: Black. Marked: 'T04038A'.

Pt. 32: Canary-yellow. Marked: 'T03847A'.

Pt. 33: Transparent, yellowed. Marked: 'T04067B'.

Pt. 34: Semi-opaque. Marked: 'T04024A'.

Pt. 35: Airforce blue, pearlised. Marked: 'T03540B'.

Pt. 36: Mud-brown. Marked: 'T03631A'.

Pt. 37: Sea-green, pearlised. Marked: 'T03642B' and: 'NOR/ANZ/ PREMIUM'.

Pt. 38: Electric blue. Marked: 'T03829B'.

Pt. 39: Cream pearlised. Marked: 'T03980E'.

Pt. 40: Canary-yellow. Marked: 'T03847B'.

Pt. 41: Cerise. Marked: 'T03828B'.

Pt. 42: Sea-green, pearlised. Marked: 'T03642A'.

Pt. 43: Electric blue. Marked: 'T03829A'.

Pt. 44: Midnight blue. Marked: 'T03821A'.

Pt. 45: Cream pearlised. Marked: 'T04016A'.

Pt. 46: Black. Marked: 'T04040A'.

Pt. 47: Cream pearlised. Marked: 'T04016C'.

Pt. 48: Brown. Marked: 'T03864B'.

Pt. 49: Black. Marked: 'T04038C'.

Pt. 50: Matt salmon-pink. Marked: 'T04043A' (handwritten).

Pt. 51: Black. Marked: 'T04038D'.

Pt. 52: Apple-green, pearlised. Marked: 'T03536B'.

Pt. 53: Mud-brown. Marked: 'T03631B'.

Pt. 54: Transparent. Marked: 'T040670'.

Pt. 55: Blue, light pearlised. Marked: 'T03534B'.

Pt. 56: Grey/blue, pearlised. Marked: 'T03534A'.

Pt. 57: Midnight blue. Marked: 'T03705B'.

Pt. 58: Cream pearlised. Marked: 'T04016C'.

Pt. 59: Brown. Marked: 'T03864A'.

Pt. 60: Aquamarine, pearlised. Marked: 'T03538B'.

All: length 75 mm, width 75 mm, thickness 3.5 mm.

Source: BP Chemicals Ltd (Stroud).

652. 1981-649: Polished sheet of green watered-effect casein 16"×10" (broken in two pieces). Mid-twentieth century.

Length 408 mm, width 252 mm, thickness 3.2 mm.

Source: BP Chemicals Ltd (Stroud).

653. 1981-651: Five laminated casein buttons coloured black and white, with feathered pattern, in two sizes, one large and two small. Mid-twentieth century.

Large: diameter 43.5 mm, thickness 7.5 mm. Small: diameter 31 mm, thickness 7 mm.

Source: BP Chemicals Ltd (Stroud).

654. 1981-652: Four samples of casein laminate (wood effect). Mid-twentieth century.

Pt. 1: Unpolished strip laminated on one side only, with cream base.

Length 198 mm, width 25 mm, thickness 8 mm.

Pt. 2: Polished button blank laminated on both sides.

Diameter 38 mm, thickness 6.5 mm.

Pt. 3: Black button with laminated elliptical inset.

Diameter 37 mm, thickness 8.5 mm.

Pt. 4: Laminated button with two holes drilled through.

Diameter 36 mm, thickness 6.5 mm.

Source: BP Chemicals Ltd (Stroud).

655. 1981-653: Buttons including: three maroon (Pt. 1), one brown (Pt. 2), one green (Pt. 3), one blue (Pt. 4), and unpolished casein button blanks, numerous cream (Pts 5 and 6). Mid-twentieth century.

Pt. 1: (× 3) Diameter 29 mm, thickness 8 mm.
Pt. 2: Diameter 25 mm, thickness 6 mm.
Pt. 3: Diameter 18 mm, thickness 4.5 mm.
Pt. 4: Diameter 18.5 mm, thickness 4 mm.
Pt. 5: (× 41) Diameter 37 mm, thickness 7 mm.
Pt. 6: (× 577) Diameter 6.5 mm, thickness 2.5 mm.
Source: BP Chemicals Ltd (Stroud).

656. 1981-654: Fifty-one unpolished casein button blanks diagonally cut from an extruded rod (bark finish artificial horn). Plastic bag marked: '5538/5×40/ BARK FINISH/ SLOPE'. Mid-twentieth century.

Length 37 mm, width 24 mm, thickness 5 mm.
Source: BP Chemicals Ltd (Stroud).

657. 1981-655: Polished casein buttons in a range of sizes and shapes (artificial horn effect); 30 types and/or sizes. Mid-twentieth century.

Pt. 1: Diameter 22 mm, thickness 6 mm (four-hole).
Pt. 2: Diameter 25 mm, thickness 7 mm (two-hole).
Pt. 3: Diameter 22.5 mm, thickness 4 mm.
Pt. 4: Diameter 23.5 mm, thickness 3.5 mm (four-hole).
Pt. 5: Diameter 19.5 mm, thickness 3.5 mm (four-hole).
Pt. 6: Diameter 22.5 mm, thickness 3.5 mm (four-hole).
Pt. 7: Diameter 25 mm, thickness 7 mm (two-hole).
Pt. 8: Diameter 22.5 mm, thickness 3.5 mm (four-hole).
Pt. 9: Diameter 22 mm, thickness 4 mm (four-hole).
Pt. 10: Diameter 16 mm, thickness 3 mm (four-hole).
Pt. 11: Diameter 17 mm, thickness 3 mm (four-hole).
Pt. 12: Diameter 28 mm, thickness 5.5 mm (two-hole).
Pt. 13: Diameter 19 mm, thickness 2.5 mm (four-hole).
Pt. 14: Diameter 20 mm, thickness 3.5 mm (four-hole).

Pt. 15: Diameter 25 mm, thickness 7.5 mm (four-hole).
Pt. 16: Diameter 18.5 mm, thickness 3.5 mm (four-hole).
Pt. 17: Diameter 16 mm, thickness 3.5 mm (two-hole).
Pt. 18: Diameter 22 mm, thickness 4 mm (four-hole).
Pt. 19: Diameter 19 mm, thickness 6 mm (four-hole).
Pt. 20: Diameter 27 mm, thickness 7.5 mm (four-hole).
Pt. 21: Diameter 28 mm, thickness 5.5 mm (two-hole).
Pt. 22: Diameter 22 mm, thickness 5 mm (four-hole).
Pt. 23: Diameter 22.5 mm, thickness 3.5 mm (four-hole).
Pt. 24: Diameter 18 mm, thickness 3.5 mm (four-hole).
Pt. 25: Diameter 16 mm, thickness 3.5 mm (four-hole).
Pt. 26: Diameter 18 mm, thickness 3.5 mm (four-hole).
Pt. 27: Diameter 14 mm, thickness 4 mm (two-hole).
Pt. 28: Diameter 13 mm, thickness 3.5 mm.
Pt. 29: Diameter 29 mm, thickness 3.5 mm (four-hole).
Pt. 30: Diameter 30 mm. thickness 4 mm (four-hole).
Source: BP Chemicals Ltd (Stroud).

658. 1981-657: Polished casein buttons coloured cream, in three styles: (a) round, four holes, four sizes; (b) round, two holes, one size; (c) hemispherical, four holes, one size. Mid-twentieth century.

(a) 1 × 15: diameter 24 mm, thickness 7 mm; (a) 2 × 19: diameter 31 mm, thickness 7.5 mm; (a) 3 × 19: diameter 28.5 mm, thickness 5.5 mm; (a) 4 × 19: diameter 22 mm, thickness 5.5mm.
(b) × 260: diameter 13.5 mm, thickness 3.5 mm.
(c) × 5: diameter 24 mm, thickness 8 mm.
Source: BP Chemicals Ltd (Stroud).

659. 1981-658: Twenty-two miscellaneous casein buttons in a variety of colours, shapes and sizes. Mid-twentieth century.

Pt. 1: Black, two-hole, with raised rim with incised cuts across it.
Diameter 43 mm, thickness 8 mm.

Pt. 2: Horn, two-hole, with raised rim.

Diameter 37 mm, thickness 6 mm.

Pt. 3: Grey, pearlised.
Diameter 36 mm, thickness 14mm (with attachment).

Pt. 4: Horn, four-hole.
Diameter 31 mm, thickness 7 mm.

Pt. 5: Horn
Diameter 38 mm, thickness 7 mm.

Pt. 6: Clear blank with with rods visible inside.
Diameter 30 mm, thickness 6 mm.

Pt. 7: Horn, with incised petal design.
Diameter 34 mm, thickness 8 mm.

Pt. 8: Aquamarine, two-hole, circular centre with moulded gouged design.
Diameter 28 mm, thickness 4.5 mm.

Pt. 9: Ivory, with irregular indented moulded design.
Diameter 30 mm, thickness 8 mm.

Pt. 10: Orange/brown marble effect, four-hole.
Diameter 28 mm, thickness 3.5 mm.

Pt. 11: Square, pearlised grey, with grooves running across.
Length 21.5 mm, width 21.5 mm, thickness 7 mm.

Pt. 12: Pearlised grey, with four-blade moulded design.
Diameter 22 mm, thickness 10 mm.

Pt. 13: Orange/brown marble effect, four-hole, raised rim.
Diameter 25 mm, thickness 8 mm.

Pt. 14: Square, green, four-hole.
Length 24 mm, width 24 mm, thickness 9 mm.

Pt. 15: Orange/brown marble effect, four-hole, raised rim.
Diameter 25 mm, thickness 8 mm.

Pt. 16: Pentagonal, white, with raised rim decorated with series of cuts, two-hole.
Diameter 31 mm, thickness 7 mm.

Pt. 17: Navy, with four-blade moulded design.
Diameter 22 mm, thickness 9 mm.

Pt. 18: Pearlised green, two-hole, circular centre with moulded gouged design.
Diameter 28 mm, thickness 6 mm.

Pt. 19: Dark green, with raised edge, square-shaped groove around centrally placed four holes.
Diameter 22 mm, thickness 6 mm.

Pt. 20: Red/blue/white stripe, two-hole.
Diameter 22 mm, thickness 5.5 mm.

Pt. 21: Red/blue/white swirl, two-hole.
Diameter 22 mm, thickness 6 mm.

Pt. 22: Orange/brown marble effect, four-hole, raised rim.
Diameter 19 mm, thickness 3 mm.
Source: BP Chemicals Ltd (Stroud).

660. 1981-671: Shade card of casein samples produced by BX Plastics Ltd under the trade name Lactoid, in red cover. Contains two cards, with 29 buttons on one card, and 34 on the other. The sample numbers are written in the lower right-hand corner under each button. Cover inscribed: 'Lactoid' (trade mark). Cards inscribed: 'LACTOID REGD. / THE CASEIN PLASTIC/...BX PLASTICS LTD/ HIGHAM STATION AVENUE, LONDON' and: 'LACTOID/REGD/ THE CASEIN PLASTIC/.../ BX PLASTICS LTD./ TELEPHONE LARKSWOOD 5511'.

Length 157 mm, width 18 mm, thickness 7.5 mm.
Source: BP Chemicals Ltd (Stroud).
Plate 11

661–672. 1981-675: Collection of casein articles originally the property of E.A. Peterson (grandfather of the donor) who was works manager of the Erinoid works 1913–28.

Source: Peterson, E.R.

661. 1981-675/1: Circular coaster, dark brown with light brown wood grain pattern. Flat base with slightly raised edge.

Diameter 87 mm, height 9 mm, thickness 2.5 mm.

662. 1981-675/2: Circular coaster, beige pearlised water effect. Flat base with slightly raised edge. Cigarette burns.

Diameter 85 mm, height 11.5 mm, thickness 3 mm.

663. 1981-675/3: Circular coaster, light brown marble effect. Flat base with slightly raised edge. Cigarette burns.

Diameter 92 mm, height 11 mm, thickness 2.5 mm.

664. 1981-675/4: Circular coaster, navy/gold swirled design. Flat base with slightly raised edge.

Diameter 92 mm, height 11 mm, thickness 2.5 mm.

665. 1981-675/5: Cylindrical napkin ring, transparent red.

Diameter 41 mm, height 31 mm, thickness 2.5 mm.

666. 1981-675/6: Cylindrical napkin ring, mottled blue.

Diameter 39 mm, height 31 mm, thickness 2.5 mm.

667. 1981-675/7: Cylindrical napkin ring, transparent ochre.

Diameter 41 mm, height 31 mm, thickness 3.5 mm.

668. 1981-675/8: Cylindrical napkin ring, green with white streaks.

Diameter 40 mm, height 31 mm, thickness 3 mm.

669. 1981-675/9: Cylindrical napkin ring, pale orange with white streaks.

Diameter 40 mm, height 31 mm, thickness 3 mm.

670. 1981-675/10: Square sharkskin box for two cigarette holders with brass closure. White lining with 'Erinoid' trade mark written in gold and compliments card: 'With every good wish/ from/ Erinoid LTD'.

Length 135 mm, width 57 mm, height 22 mm.

Pt. 1: Cigarette holder in black casein, cylindrical with flattened end, two-part with screw fitting and white band at join. Inscribed: 'PAT.Nº 359685/31'.
Length 100 mm, diameter 12 mm.

Pt. 2: Cigarette holder in black casein, cylindrical with hexagonal cigarette end and flattened mouth-end, two-part with screw fitting and white band at join. Inscribed: 'PAT.Nº 359685/31'.
Length 100 mm, diameter 10 mm.

671. 1981-675/11: Black leather case with cigar holder made of black casein. Upper part of case lined with red velvet, lower part with white silk. Case has rounded end.

Box: length 83 mm, width 29 mm, height 22 mm.
Cigar holder: length 72 mm, diameter 9 mm.

672. 1981-675/12: Propelling pencil of mottled green/black/ silver/orange casein with brass tip and black end; steel clip. Side inscribed: 'PAT. NO 35174/ MADE IN ENGLAND'.

Length 106 mm, diameter 13 mm.

CASEIN MACHINERY

673. 1981-612: Grinding machinery comprising grinder, bucket elevator and sieve used for casein production; manufactured by Bauermeister Ottensen *c.*1900, complete with three sacks of casein.

Length 6930 mm, width 2600 mm, height (est.) 8500 mm.
Source: BP Chemicals Ltd (Stroud).

674. 1981-613: Planetary mixer for Casein dough, mid-twentieth century.

Length 1150 mm; width 870 mm, height 980 mm.
Source: BP Chemicals Ltd (Stroud).

675. 1981-614: Extruder, take-off table and oil pump for casein production *c.*1930. Marked as follows: extruder – 'R.H.P. England', 'Hoffmann England'; oil pump – 'V.P. Albany Pump'; take-off table motor – 'The Cub Motor'.

Pt. 1: Length 2030 mm, width 1360 mm, height 1240 mm.

Pt. 2: Length 1560 mm, width 500 mm, height 800 mm.
Source: BP Chemicals Ltd (Stroud).

676. 1981-615: Masson chopper, used for casein production *c.*1940. Motor manufactured by Brooks Motors Ltd, Huddersfield. Inscription on plate: 'MADE IN ENGLAND/ B.S.S. 168 1936/ BROOKS/ MOTORS LTD/ HUDDERSFIELD/ AC MOTOR 3 PHASE/ R9 E60842/ LOAD SPEED VOLTS/ 1420 4001440/FULL/ H.P. (?) LOAD 43/ AMPS'. Rest of inscription unreadable.

Length 1080 mm, width 385 mm, height 980 mm.
Source: BP Chemicals Ltd (Stroud).

677. 1981-616: Button lathe manufactured by Sylbe & Pondorf, maschinenbaugesellschaft Schmölln S.A. *c.*1910. Inscription on raised plate: 'Sylbe & Pondorf/ maschinenbaugesellschaft/ SCHMöLLN S.A.'. Stamped underneath on body of machine: 'Serie 230 Nº 1586'. Round plate inscribed: 'SHOP/ 44/ machine/ 2'. Sticky label marked: 'BP PLASTICS/ Erinoid Works • Stroud • PLANT 007476/ REGISTER/ DEPT. NO.'.

Length 950 mm, width 510 mm, height 1160 mm.

Source: BP Chemicals Ltd (Stroud).

678. 1981-617: Button press used for experimental laboratory production of casein buttons.

Length 800 mm, width 320 mm, height 1060 mm.
Source: BP Chemicals Ltd (Stroud).

PHENOLICS (PF, PHENOL-FORMALDEHYDE, BAKELITE)

679. 1934-27: Blank from which gear wheels are cut, of dark brown fabric-based phenolic laminate. Top marked: 'TUFNOL' twice. Base marked: '46'.

Diameter 103 mm, height 75 mm.
Source: Ellison Insulations Ltd.

680–682. 1934-28 (1–3): Three gear wheels cut from fabric-based phenolic laminate (different types).

Source: Ellison Insulations Ltd.

680. 1934-28/1: Gear wheel, made of steel-faced and -backed, fabric-based, dark brown phenolic laminate. Top and bottom marked: 'TUFNOL' twice and four times respectively. Side marked: '46'.

Height 146 mm, diameter 180 mm.

681. 1934-28/2: Wheel with treaded edge made of dark brown fabric-based phenolic resin. Top marked: 'TUFNOL' twice and: '46'.

Height 30 mm, diameter 198 mm.

682. 1934-28/3: Cogged wheel made of brown fabric-based phenolic laminate. Top marked: 'TUFNOL' twice.

Height 76 mm, diameter 107 mm.
Plate 12

683. 1934-29: Machine castor with wheel cut from dark brown phenolic laminate; attachment steel. Wheel marked: '46'.

Length 125 mm, width 100 mm, height 135 mm.
Source: Ellison Insulations Ltd.

684–689. 1934-30: Three rods and three tubes of phenolic paper or fabric-based laminate.

Source: Ellison Insulations Ltd.

684. 1934-30/1: Brown tube of laminated phenolic resin, circular in cross-section.

Length 168 mm, diameter 30 mm.

685. 1934-30/2: Brown tube of laminated phenolic resin, square in cross-section.

Length 170 mm, diameter 20 mm.

686. 1934-30/3: Brown tube of laminated phenolic resin, circular in cross-section.

Length 167 mm, diameter 16 mm.

687. 1934-30/4: Black rod of laminated phenolic resin, circular in cross-section.

Length 188 mm, diameter 9 mm.

688. 1934-30/5: Brown rod of laminated phenolic resin, square in cross-section.

Length 156 mm, width 44 mm, breadth 44 mm.

689. 1934-30/6: Brown rod of laminated phenolic resin, square in cross-section.

Length 168 mm, width 16 mm, breadth 16 mm.

690. 1934-31: Railway chair wedge of laminated phenolic resin bonded sheet (fabric base). Marked: 'PATENT Nº/220622/G.K.N.'.

Length 254 mm, width 40 mm, thickness 23.5 mm.
Source: Ellison Insulations Ltd.

691. 1934-32: Bell-type insulator of dark brown laminated phenolic resin-bonded paper base, in wood effect, with brass screw fitting.

Height 94 mm, diameter 75 mm.
Source: Ellison Insulations Ltd.

692. 1934-33: Round strain insulator for cables, base made of laminated phenolic resin-bonded paper in dark brown wood effect, with two black cast-iron rings, top and bottom, for attachment.

Length 190 mm, diameter 69 mm.
Source: Ellison Insulations Ltd.

693–694. 1934-34: Two rods of metal with covering of phenolic resin-bonded paper mounted on.

Source: Ellison Insulations Ltd.

693. 1934-34/1: Rod of metal; circular in cross-section.

Length 204 mm, diameter 19 mm.

694. 1934-34/2: Rod of metal; square in cross-section.

Length and width 242 mm, thickness 21 mm.

695. 1974-82: Rajar camera with black phenolic body and metal clips, introduced in 1929. Front inscribed: 'RAJAR/ Nº 6'. Back marked: 'ONLY RAJAR Nº 6 SPOOL WILL FIT THIS CAMERA' and: 'PAT. APPLIED FOR'.

Length 165 mm, width 107 mm, height 35 mm.
Source: Hallam, J.C.

696. 1974-179: Dewald valve radio with radio case moulding made of dark brown phenolic, *c.*1935. Front inscribed: 'DEWALD'.

Length 201 mm, width 125 mm, height 122 mm.
Source: Science Museum.

697. 1979-624/5: Red, phenolic step-cut circular candlestick mounted with chrome, with green felt flat base. Art deco design. Late 1930s.

Diameter 102 mm, height 38 mm.
Source: Jesse, J.

698. 1979-624/31: Rectangular red cigarette box with lid, phenolic, with four columns cast from cast phenolic at each corner, orange/red marble effect, black cylindrical handle on lid, 1935. Six screw covers missing; one damaged.

Length 189 mm, width 112 mm, height 80 mm,
Columns: diameter 28 mm.
Handle: length 38 mm, diameter 13 mm.
Source: Jesse, J.
Plate 12

699. 1979-624/32: A phenolic 'Jaxonite' box. Lid has circular handle with a pointed top. Black with green and beige splotches. Base inscribed: 'JAXONITE'. Inside inscription reads: 'REG. Nº. 482780/ JAXONITE/ MADE IN ENGLAND'.

Diameter 89 mm, height 63 mm.
Source: Jesse, J.

700. 1979-624/36: Rectangular cigarette box of walnut-effect phenolic, hinged lid decorated with moulded horseman spearing a lion in the Assyrian style, made by Birkby's Ltd, Liversedge, Yorkshire, England, 1930s, under the trade name 'Elo Ware'. Inscription die-stamped on base: 'ELO/REGD/MADE IN ENGLAND/WARE'; inscription contained in circle.

Length 168 mm, width 85 mm, height 60 mm,
Feet: diameter 12 mm.
Source: Jesse, J.
Figure 4

701. 1979-624/37: Brown phenolic fluted box impressed: 'JiF/ MADE IN FRANCE' on the lid and: 'DEPOSE' on the base. Inside base marked: '53589/ M.I.O.M.'.

Diameter: 59 mm, height 80 mm.
Source: Jesse, J.

702. 1979-624/59: Rectangular cigarette box of red lacquer phenolic, lid inlaid with brass in art deco design, 1930s, French. '80A' scratched onto inside of lid.

Length 130 mm, width 85 mm, height 37 mm.
Source: Jesse, J.

703. 1979-624/63: Rectangular cigarette box with rounded edges, base has two compartments, lid hinged (hinge damaged), of walnut phenolic, 1930s. Inscription die-stamped on back: 'PAT.NO.447203 REG.NO.819699' enclosed within rectangle.

Length 210 mm, width 60 mm, height 100 mm.
Source: Jesse, J.

704. 1979-624/72: Black phenolic powder box moulded with the stylised head of a girl. The base marked: 'MADE IN ENGLAND'.

Diameter 99 mm, height 40 mm.
Source: Jesse, J.

705. 1979-624/73: Globular ashtray, unscrews in centre, of walnut-effect phenolic, a British Buttner Product, made in England, 1940s. Inscription inside base: 'ROXON./MADE IN

ENGLAND' arranged around edge of base.

Diameter 82 mm, height 80 mm.
Source: Jesse, J.

706. 1979-624/74: Globular phenolic ashtray, unscrews in middle. Upper half of walnut-effect phenolic, lower half of cream marble-effect urea-formaldehyde. A British Buttner Product, made in England, 1940s. Trade mark moulded on base: 'British Buttner Product' in cursive script which curls round central screw in base.

Diameter 87 mm, height 78 mm.
Source: Jesse, J.

707. 1979-624/76: Globular phenolic ashtray, unscrews in middle, three feet, top half of black phenolic, lower half of green urea-formaldehyde, made in France. Mid-twentieth century. Trade mark on base: 'MODELE/DÉPOSE' in circle around edge of base.

Diameter 67.5 mm, height 59 mm.
Source: Jesse, J.

708. 1979-624/77: Electric lighter of mottled electric-red phenolic, tubular, in three parts, one part with wick, second with two-pin plug, screw-on base, *c.*1930. Inscription on plug base: '110'. Trade mark on base: 'COUIC'.

Length 116 mm, width 60 mm.
Source: Jesse, J.

709. 1979-624/78: Circular ashtray of walnut-effect phenolic with Michelin man of ivory urea-formaldehyde seated on edge, made in England for Michelin Tyres, 1940s. Inscription moulded across chest of Michelin Man: 'MICHELIN' on sash running diagonally down across chest from right shoulder to under left arm. Second inscription die-stamped on base: 'MADE/IN/ENGLAND' contained within circle.

Height 120 mm, diameter 153 mm.
Reference: Pascale and Cernia 1983: 125, Fig.119.
Source: Jesse, J.
Figure 37

710. 1979-624/84: Chrome striker lighter fixed to a square block of phenolic resin in the form of a die, coloured yellow with black spots, 1930s? Striker broken.

Height 80 mm, width 62 mm, breadth 62 mm.
Source: Jesse, J.

711. 1979-624/85: Electrically powered table cigarette lighter of black phenolic resin in form of hemisphere surmounted by sphere, probably made for the British Astral Co. Ltd, Great Britain, 1930s. Inscription printed on base: 'THE/ BRITISH/ ASTRAL/ CO.LTD/....'; letters are printed red on gold background, within three larger circles, five-pointed star motif below.

Height 130 mm, diameter 100 mm.
Source: Jesse, J.

712. 1979-624/106: Pepper and salt pots of phenolic, spring loaded, pots in form of mushroom with bulbous stem, caramel coloured plunger and disc-shaped base coloured black, 1930s. Incomplete (tray and mustard pot missing).

Height 65 mm, diameter 35 mm.
Source: Jesse, J.

713. 1979-624/136: Pin box desk calendar of walnut-effect phenolic, comprises two rectangular boxes with lids on either side of calendar section, with three slots for calendar, and sloping plate marked with the name of the Bell Telephone Mfg. Co, USA, late 1930s. Small chip in edge of one container.

Length 130 mm, height 76 mm, width 48 mm.
Source: Jesse, J.

714. 1979-624/139: Desk pen holder of mottled red/brown phenolic, with flat round base, and cylindrical holder attached at an angle to base, *c.*1920.

Diameter 86 mm, height 76 mm.
Source: Jesse, J.

715. 1979-624/191: Thermos flask of dark brown phenolic with chrome handle, with glass inner vessel and metal base; phenolic stopper with wooden base. Made by Thermos Ltd, British. Base marked: 'THERMOS (1925) LIMITED LONDON/ PAT. Nº. 327838 Nº 24 JUG – THIS TAKES REFILL' in two lines circling circumference of base.

Diameter 110 mm, height 248 mm.
Source: Jesse, J.
Plate 12

716. 1979-624/199: Roanoid phenolic door knob, marble-effect beige with faceted knob and circular base, made by Roanoid Ltd, *c.*1930.

Diameter 61 mm, height 60 mm.
Source: Jesse, J.

717. 1979-624/218: Commemorative box of black phenolic made by Beetleware with white urea-formaldehyde head of King Edward VIII in left profile with shoulders, in uniform. May be an example of a two-colour moulding. Base inscribed: 'Beetleware/ MADE IN ENGLAND'.

Diameter 100 mm, height 41 mm.
Source: Jesse, J.

718. 1979-624/246: Pair of phenolic brown mottled candlesticks with circular base and cup.

Diameter 82 mm, height 126 mm.
Source: Jesse, J.

719. 1979-624/247: Pair of phenolic candlesticks, brown/black marble effect in colour, regency style, with circular base, Linsden Ware, made in England, *c.*1920. One badly chipped at top. Trade mark moulded on base: 'Linsden Ware/MADE IN ENGLAND','Linsden' in cursive script.

Diameter 148 mm, height 362 mm.
Source: Jesse, J.

720. 1979-624/248: Globular ashtray of black phenolic screwed to green marble-effect urea-formaldehyde base. A British Buttner Product, *c.*1940. Inscription moulded on base: '.British . Buttner . Product' in cursive script arranged in circle.

Diameter 148 mm, height 56 mm.
Source: Jesse, J.

721. 1979-624/253: Barrel-shaped ashtray of green phenolic, two parts which screw together in middle, made by Velos, England, Patent no. 414224, *c.*1934. Trade mark moulded on base: '"NONSMOKER"/NO.1350/PATENT NO.414224/REGD. DESIGN 784762/VELOS/TRADE MARK/MADE IN ENGLAND/THE VELOS ASH BARREL'. First and last lines in circle around inscription. 'VELO' within lozenge and large V.

Diameter 75.5 mm, height 81 mm.
Source: Jesse, J.

722. 1979-624/254: Pipe rack of pale walnut-effect phenolic for six pipes, large twelve-sided base with six moulded indentations for pipe bowls, smaller twelve-sided top with six holes for pipe handles, joined to base by central post which is hexagonal in cross-section, English, 1930s?

Height 110 mm, diameter 140mm (base), diameter 75mm (top).
Source: Jesse, J.

723. 1979-624/259: Bedside night lamp in the form of a microscope, with brown phenolic base and bulb trim; battery operated (battery concealed in base). Made in England, first half of twentieth century. Inscription inside base: 'MADE IN ENGLAND/1039/1'. Two lines '1039/1' as written.

Length 127 mm, width 127 mm, height 170 mm.
Source: Jesse, J.
Plate 12

724. 1979-624/264: Phenolic mantel clock, coloured mottled green with black base, in art deco design, with square face, stepped base, edges and hands, French, 1930s. Scale moulded on face: '1(1)12 hours'. Inscription painted on face: 'FRENCH JAZ MAKE'; 'FRENCH' and 'MAKE' are painted on, 'JAZ' is moulded, contained within a square frame, and in larger letters. Second inscription moulded on back: 'JAZ/MADE IN FRANCE.'; whole contained within square frame. Third inscription moulded on back: 'MODELE DEPOSE/BREVETE S.G.D.G.' contained within square frame with rounded corners.

Length 143 mm, width 107 mm, height 244 mm.
Source: Jesse, J.

725. 1979-624/269: Green, oval-faced clock made of phenolic paper laminate, with brass circular dial, supported by two half-cylindrical columns, which are marble-effect, orange in colour, on flat, rectangular stepped base, electric, made by Goblin, Great Britain, 1930s. Inscription on back: '200–250 VOLTS/50-A.C./SELF STARTING/GOBLIN/..../BRITISH MADE /PAT.NO.571849./ LICENSED UNDER LETTERS 0946/PAT.NO.366710'; Goblin trade mark between 'GOBLIN' and 'BRITISH MADE'. Second inscription on back dial: 'HAND SET'. Scale on face: '1(1)12 hours'.

Overall: height 180 mm, depth 115 mm.
Base: length 254 mm, width 72 mm, thickness 10 mm, diameter 217mm.
Dial: diameter 84 mm.
Column: width 28 mm, height 38mm,
Source: Jesse, J.

726. 1979-624/270: Brown phenolic electric digital clock with 'TELE-VISION' in black lettering on the face. Made by Pennwood Numerchron Co, USA, c.1930. Art deco design. Top fin broken. Second inscription moulded on inside base of workings: 'PENNWOOD NUMERCHRON CO./ PITTSBURGH. PA. U.S.A./ PAT. NO.1990645'. Scale painted on clock face, left-hand side: '1:(1)12' hours; black on white. Scale painted on clock face: '0(1)9' minutes; black on white (tens). Scale painted on clock face: '0(5)60' seconds; red on white.

Length 260 mm, width 114 mm, height 109 mm.
Source: Jesse, J.
Figure 5

727. 1979-624/271: Bush television set, with case made of dark brown wood phenolic. Made in 1949 by British Mouldings Ltd, front marked: 'Bush'.

Length 380 mm, width 320 mm, height 375 mm.
Source: Jesse, J.

728. 1979-624/272: Circular table of dark brown phenolic, art deco design, with four legs joined to upper and lower discs which are decorated with concentric circles, c.1930.

Diameter 550 mm, height 650 mm.
Source: Jesse, J.

729. 1979-624/273: Walnut-effect phenolic valve radio, with ivory urea-formaldehyde knobs, silver face with red, yellow and white lettering, Sonorette make, French, late 1940s. Inscription moulded on back: 'Sonorette' in gothic script. Second inscription painted on face: 'LUXEMBOURG DROITWICH ANKARA FRANCE /... /... /... /... /... /... /... /... /... /... /... /LONDRES 35M. MOSCOV 45M. 12 MIR PARIS 50M. ANDORRE'; top three lines red, middle yellow, apart from 'Sonorette' which is white, bottom two lines are white letters.

Length 220 mm, width 160 mm, height 140 mm.
Source: Jesse, J.

730. 1979-624/285: Ashtray, circular, stacking, made of mottled red phenolic, stepped, with three cigarette rests in rim, 1930s.

Diameter 108 mm, height 20 mm.
Source: Jesse, J.

731. 1980-676/75: Hearing aid with brown phenolic battery box and earpiece, black phenolic control unit, flat circular amplifier with tortoiseshell-effect cellulose nitrate case and metal clip pocket attachment, ear piece has tortoiseshell-effect cellulose nitrate ear plug and metal hook for hanging over the ear, brown cloth-covered flex, made in England, c.1929. Battery box chipped, case of amplifier cracked. Inscription moulded into base of battery box:

'BRITISH MADE/PAT.No. 14404/29'. Lines at top and bottom edges. Second inscription in back of ear piece: 'MADE IN/ENGLAND' arranged round rim of base. Third inscription moulded in front of control unit: 'LOUD/OFF/SOFT'.

Length 1106mm (max.).
Battery case: width 49 mm.
Amplifier: diameter 72 mm, height 29 mm.
Reference: Newport 1976: M44.
Source: Newport, R.

732. 1980-676/187: Murphy mains radio with black phenolic cabinet. Type AD94. Rectangular cabinet has seven vertical fins over the loudspeaker aperture and three controls, 1940. Various instructional and identifying marks. Front marked: 'MURPHY/ RADIO'.

Length 315 mm, width 173 mm, height 334 mm.
Reference: Newport 1976: R1.
Source: Newport, R.

733. 1980-676/188: Philco mains radio 'People's Set' Model 444, with a curvilinear black phenolic cabinet, three vertical fins extending over the loudspeaker aperture and three controls. Various identifying and instructional marks. Made by the Philco Radio & Television Corporation of Great Britain Ltd, 1936. Front marked: 'PHILCO'.

Length 330 mm, width 260 mm, height 403 mm.
Reference: Newport 1976: R2.
Source: Newport, R.

734. 1980-676/189: Circular 12-volt buzzer, moulded in dark brown phenolic. Inscribed: '-H-/DRP' and: '12V= ~'. Trade mark on back within circle.

Length 80 mm, width 68 mm, height 55 mm.
Reference: Newport 1976: R9.
Source: Newport, R.

735. 1980-676/190 & 191: Two electric black phenolic capacitors, marked: 'LISSEN' and: '0003' on back, with metal terminals, *c.*1920s. Trade mark moulded on upper surface: 'LISSEN' contained in oval. 'L' has curving tail under rest of word. Upper parts of letter curves round

so whole word is roughly oval. Inscription on lower surface: '0003'.

Length 64 mm, width 25 mm, thickness 18 mm.
Reference: Newport 1976: R10.
Source: Newport, R.

736. 1980-676/192: Dark brown phenolic rectangular wall plate for two electrical light switches, decorated with border of seven parallel lines. Back inscribed: 'CRABTREE PATENT/ M1792/ REGD. DESIGN/ MADE IN ENGLAND', 1940s.

Length 134 mm, width 82 mm, height 12 mm.
Reference: Newport 1976: R11.
Source: Newport, R.

737. 1980-676/193: Circular brown phenolic electric plug and socket (plugged together), plug base of urea-formaldehyde, metal plug attachments, made by Wylex, in England, *c.*1930. Patented by George H. Scholes, 1926. Inscription moulded on top: 'E M 25/2/WYLEX/N/250V./NON TRACK/L MADE/IN/ENGLAND'. 'WYLEX' is a trade mark contained in a circle with vertical stripes surrounding it, inscription arranged around. Second inscription is moulded into the base: 'BRITISH PATENT NO.281366/EARTH/NEUTRAL/ LIVE/250V/POLARISED/WYLEX/2K W.10AMP.', words arranged around area of base.

Diameter 57 mm, height 38 mm.
Reference: Newport 1976: R12.
Source: Newport, R.

738. 1980-676/194: Circular dark brown phenolic and pressed fibre 15-amp, three-pin plug, *c.*1930. Base inscribed: 'MARBO'.

Length 60 mm, diameter 55 mm.
Reference: Newport 1976: R13.
Source: Newport, R.

739. 1980-676/195: Circular phenolic 10-amp, three-pin electrical plug, moulded in three pieces with a withdrawing knob, *c.*1930. Inscribed: 'CRABTREE PATENT'.

Diameter 50 mm, width 64 mm.
Reference: Newport 1976: R14.
Source: Newport, R.

740. 1980-676/196: Dark brown phenolic 15-amp, three-pin electrical plug, moulded in three parts. Mid-twentieth century. Inscribed: 'PAT.No.371404/ 371418/ 403448/ 426943/ 457113/ B.S.546/15 AMP/MADE IN ENGLAND/REGD. DESIGN No. 778161/ MADE IN ENGLAND/CLIX/PLUG' (last two lines in square).

Length 72 mm, width 52 mm, height 65 mm.
Reference: Newport 1976: R15.
Source: Newport, R.

741. 1980-676/197 Pts 1–2: Rectangular box of walnut-effect phenolic with hinged lid, containing a Gillette steel safety razor and two blade containers, one containing two packets of razor blades, 1930s. A trade mark is moulded inside the box lid: 'TRADE Gillette MARK/ MADE IN ENGLAND'. The first line contained within lozenge, arrow runs horizontally through Gillette, second line contained within rectangular box. A second trade mark is moulded on the inner surface of the razor head: 'Gillette MADE IN ENGLAND'. 'Gillette' contained within lozenge, arrow runs horizontally through it.

Pt. 1: Box: length 90 mm, width 52 mm, height 33 mm.

Pt. 2: Razor: length 84 mm, width 41 mm, depth 25 mm.

Pt. 3: Two packets of razor blades, blue paper with picture of King C. Gillette. Inscription printed on front of packet reads:
'BLUE/Gillette/BLADE/REGD. TRADE MARK/.../King C Gillette/REGD.TRADE MARK'.
'...' represents picture, blue letters. Second inscription: 'REGISTERED TRADE MARK/Gillette/MADE IN ENGLAND'.
Length 45 mm, width 25 mm, thickness 1 mm.
Reference: Newport 1976: R31.
Source: Newport, R.

742. 1980-676/198: Bowl with lid, of mottled green and black phenolic, ornately decorated with milled bands, foliate bosses and rosette feet, *c.*1910.

Diameter 150 mm, height 90 mm.
Source: Newport, R.

743. 1980-676/199: Bowl of dark brown/green/beige/ochre mottled phenolic, with faceted edge. Made in Britain, *c.*1930. Inscription moulded on base: 'BRITISH/MADE'.

Diameter 185 mm, height 70 mm.
Reference: Newport 1976: R33.
Source: Newport, R.

744. 1980-676/200: Bowl of dark brown/buff/green mottled phenolic, with faceted edge. A Stadium Product, made in Britain, *c.*1930. Edges chipped. Trade mark moulded on base: 'A/STADIUM/PRODUCT/BRITISH'. 'STADIUM' in Italic script, whole contained in outline of house with pitched roof.

Diameter 185 mm, height 70 mm.
Reference: Newport 1976: R33.
Source: Newport, R.

745. 1980-676/201: Shallow circular dish moulded in mottled ochre and black phenolic, with screw fitting for foot, *c.*1930. Incomplete (foot missing).

Diameter 220 mm, height 15 mm.
Reference: Newport 1976: R34.
Source: Newport, R.

746. 1980-676/202: Large circular mottled green, brown, red, orange and black phenolic bowl on ring base with four supports, *c.*1930.

Diameter 225 mm, height 60 mm.
Reference: Newport 1976: R35.
Source: Newport, R.
Plate 12

747. 1980-676/203: Large circular multichrome mottled bowl in maroon, dark green and rust phenolic, on a circular pedestal attached by a threaded brass insert. Made by Birkby's Ltd, and marked: 'ELO/REGD/ MADE IN ENGLAND/ WARE'; first and last lines:

'ELO...WARE' in large letters curved around the top and bottom of the inscription. Early 1940s.

Diameter 226 mm, height 100 mm.
Reference: Newport 1976: R36.
Source: Newport, R.
Plate 12

748. 1980-676/204: Rectangular door finger-plate of dark brown mottled phenolic, made by Elliot of Birmingham, England, mid-twentieth century. Trade mark moulded in the centre of the back: 'MADE IN/.../ENGLAND'. First and third lines contained in circle, '...' represents trade mark which is an 'L' within a yacht motif.

Length 278 mm, width 70 mm, thickness 5 mm.
Reference: Newport 1976: R42.
Source: Newport, R.

749. 1980-676/205: Circular ashtray of black and multicoloured phenolic, surmounted with a metal cigarette holder placed in the centre, base of ashtray marked: 'Jaxonite', 1930s. Inscription moulded into base: 'JAXONITE'.

Diameter 85 mm, height 35 mm.
Reference: Newport 1976: R43.
Source: Newport, R.

750. 1980-676/206: Cream homogeniser, moulded of brown, mottled phenolic, with metal handle, whole screw-fitting to a conical glass container decorated with a raised check pattern, made by Bel Jubilee, in England, c.1934. Inscription cast into handle, left side: 'JUBILEE/MADE IN/ENGLAND' contained within oval. Second inscription cast on right side of handle: 'JUBILEE/ PROV.PAT NOS./ 28331-34.28332-34' contained within oval (see cat. no. 751).

Height 200 mm, diameter 97 mm, width 192mm (with handle).
Reference: Newport 1976: R46.
Source: Newport, R.

751. 1980-676/207: Lemon-juice extractor of brown, mottled phenolic, circular with lemon-shaped squeezer in centre, part of 1980-676/206 (cat. no.

750), made by Bel Jubilee, in England, c.1934.

Diameter 95 mm, height 60 mm.
Source: Newport, R.

752. 1980-676/208: Circular tobacco box with screw-fitting lid, of dark brown and light brown mottled phenolic, base and rim of lid decorated with row of oak leaves, made in Britain, 1920s? Inscription moulded on lid: 'Tobacco' witten in flowing script and underlined with stroke starting at 'o'. Second inscription moulded in base: 'BRITISH/MADE'.

Diameter 107 mm, height 120 mm.
Source: Newport, R.

753. 1980-676/209: Wunnup Baccyflap of dark brown phenolic with screw-on lid. Base inscribed: 'WUNNUP BACCYFLAP/ MADE IN ENGLAND' in moulded circle.

Diameter 95 mm, height 33 mm.
Source: Newport, R.

754. 1980-676/210: Tape measure with circular walnut-effect phenolic casing and steel tape, turned by push button in centre, measures inches, foreign, 1930s? Casing chipped. Scale printed on tape: '1(1) 39' inches; bluish-black figures, first inch divided into 22 parts, remainder into sixteenths. Second inscription printed on tape: 'Foreign'.

Diameter 40 mm, height 20 mm.
Source: Newport, R.

755. 1980-676/211: Photographic accessory in form of clip fitting with metal clip and dark brown phenolic handle and support, made in France, c.1930. Trade mark moulded on both sides of handle: 'GALLIA/...'. '...' signifies woman's head shown in right profile, in art deco style. Second trade mark moulded on both sides of clip: 'GALLIA/.ROLL AIR./MADE IN FRANCE'.

Length 65 mm, width 61 mm, thickness 36 mm.
Source: Newport, R.

756. 1980-676/212: Hexagonal fitting of black phenolic decorated with Gallia trade mark, metal hook protrudes from one corner, internal pulley mechanism, English, 1930s. Trade mark moulded on both faces: 'GALLIA/MADE IN ENGLAND'. These two lines form two sides of a triangle decorated with woman's head outlined by larger man's head.

Length 118 mm, width 45 mm, height 20 mm.
Source: Newport, R.

757. 1980-676/213: Smith 'Sectric' alarm clock and wall socket, electric, made of dark brown phenol formaldehyde, plug attached, c.1940. Made in England by Smith's English Clocks, Cricklewood, London. Scale painted on face: '1(1)12' hours; black figures on silver ground. Inscription painted on face: 'SMITH/ SECTRIC/ ALARM/ MADE IN ENGLAND' in black letters.

Pt. 1: Clock. Inscription on lower left-hand side of back: 'SMITH'S/ENGLISH CLOCKS/ CRICKLEWOOD/LONDON N.'. Second inscription moulded on left-hand side of back: 'TO SET/ HANDS PRESS &/TURN KNOB C./MADE UNDER ONE OR/MORE ENG.PATENTS/ 366710/ 369438/ 374713/ 402456/ 419767/ OTHERS/PENDING' in circle. Third inscription moulded on right-hand side of back: 'TO/PREPARE ALARM/SET DIAL A.&/PULL OUT KNOB B./TO STOP ALARM/PUSH IN KNOB B./CLOCK STARTS/AUTOMATICALLY/ WITH CURRENT' in circle. Scale moulded on back of alarm switch: '1(1)12' hours. Fifth inscription moulded on back: 'MADE I[N] ENGLAND'; 'N' missing, obscured by button.

Pt. 2: Inscription moulded on back of plug: 'E/MADE/IN/ENGLAND/WG/250V/13 AMPS/AC ONLY/BSS 1363/L/N/CORD GRIP/ SCREWS'. Second inscription moulded on front of plug: 'FUSED'.

Length 105 mm, width 64 mm, height 118 mm.
Source: Newport, R.

758. 1980-676/214: Smith 'Sectric' alarm clock connector made of dark brown phenol formaldehyde. Made in England by Smith's English Clocks, Cricklewood, London, c.1940. Inscribed: 'SECTRIC CLOCK CONNECTOR'.

Length 53 mm, width 47 mm, thickness 20 mm.
Source: Newport, R.

759. 1980-676/215: Vactric de-mothing attachment for a vacuum cleaner, cylindrical, moulded in two parts from black phenolic with copper mesh, probably late 1930s, made in Scotland.

Length 115 mm, diameter 71 mm.
Reference: Newport 1976: R22.
Source: Newport, R.

760. 1980-676/216: Sifta salt cellar with glass body and black phenolic cap trimmed with metal, body decorated with transfer of Sifta Sam, mid-twentieth century. Trade mark printed on body saying: 'JOLLY Good Salt' and showing Sifta Sam, a sailor, carrying telescope.

Diameter 46 mm, thickness 100 mm.
Source: Newport, R.

761. 1980-676/217: Circular ashtray of black phenolic, raised flat edge, centre decorated with raised concentric circles, made in England by the National College of Rubber Technology, c.1935. Inscription moulded around rim: 'NATIONAL COLLEGE OF RUBBER TECHNOLOGY/MADE ON A BRIDGE MACHINE'; lines separated by stars, one on either side of line.

Diameter 116 mm, height 18 mm.
Source: Newport, R.

762. 1980-676/218: Conical flowerpot with flat, pierced base, made of brown and black mottled phenolic, made by R.H. Bath Ltd, Wisbech for National Plastics, late 1940s. Inscription moulded in base: 'APPROVED AND HIGHLY COMMENDED BY THE/ROYAL HORTICULTURAL SOCIETY' curved round half the edge of the base. Trade mark moulded in the base: 'NP' contained within square and standing above two flowerpots?, letters interlinked inside circle. Third inscription moulded inside base: 'R.H. BATH Ltd./Wisbech' encircles central piercing.

Diameter 137 mm, height 132 mm.
Source: Newport, R.

763. 1980-676/219: Dark green moulded phenolic pepper pot, cylindrical, narrows towards top, marked with: 'GR' and a crown, symbolising George VI, made in England. Trade mark moulded in the base: '.../VI/GR'. 'GR' encircles 'VI', surmounted by crown; 'GR' in interlocked flowing script.

Diameter 51 mm, height 86 mm.
Source: Newport, R.

764. 1980-676/221: Darning mushroom of mottled dark and light brown phenolic, circular base, with central hollow tapering tubular rod, rounded at tip, which screws to base, made in England by Jay, *c.*1930s? Inscription inside base around central rod: 'MADE IN ENGLAND'. Trade mark inside base opposite other inscription: 'TRADE MARK/A/JAY...BRAND/PRODUCT/MADE IN ENGLAND'. Lines 1 and 5 form four sides of a diamond, 'JAY' and 'BRAND' are separated by the picture of a jay, lines 2–4 contained in a diamond.

Height 97 mm, diameter 62 mm.
Source: Newport, R.

765. 1980-676/222: Set of five stacking ashtrays in holder, circular, made of dark red mottled phenolic, marked as a Stadium Product, made in Britain, 1930s. Inscription moulded into base of holder and ashtrays: 'A/Stadium/PRODUCT/BRITISH' contained within outline of house with ridged roof, 'Stadium' slants to right.

Holder: height 68 mm, diameter 78 mm.
Ashtray: diameter 85 mm.
Reference: Newport 1976: R44.
Source: Newport, R.

766. 1980-676/281: Two-pin adaptor with two sockets and one two-pin plug, made of walnut-effect phenolic, made in England, *c.*1930. Inscription moulded on top: 'TOTAL LOAD/5 AMP. 250V.'. Second inscription moulded on sloping face: 'MADE IN ENGLAND/U.K. REG.DES. No.816367'.

Height 34 mm, width 34 mm, breadth 44 mm.
Source: Newport, R.

767. 1981-134/20: Triangular three-way electrical adaptor for one round three-pin plug and two square three-pin plugs, all sockets on one face, made of dark brown phenolic with red fuse lift flap (possibly polyethylene), moulded in two parts, mid-twentieth century. Front inscribed: 'Grelco/ LIST Nº/ K//15/513' and: 'MAX TOTAL LOAD 13 AMPS'. Back inscribed: 'Grelco', 'MADE IN ENGLAND' and: 'FUSE LIFT FLAP'.

Length 102 mm, width 95 mm, thickness 62 mm.
Source: Greenaway, F.

768. 1981-134/21: Electrical adaptor and switch for three-pin plug, rectangular, made of brown phenolic, moulded in two parts, made by MULTI-KONTACT, *c.*1930. Front inscribed with a trade mark: 'MK' in circle. Back inscribed: 'NDP 15 AMP 250V/ L E/AC/ONLY/ MK/ PATENT', 'MADE IN ENGLAND NSP'.

Length 89 mm, width 55 mm, thickness 50 mm.
Source: Greenaway, F.

769. 1981-134/22: Three-way electrical adaptor for three-pin plugs, made of dark brown phenolic, square, moulded in two parts, *c.*1930. Back inscribed: 'Grelco/ MADE IN ENGLAND' and: 'Grelco/ LIST Nº MW3/15/5/ MAX TOTAL LOAD/ 15 AMPS'.

Length 79 mm, width 55 mm, thickness 48 mm.
Source: Greenaway, F.

770. 1981-134/23: Two-way electrical adaptor for three sizes of three-pin plug, made of dark brown phenolic, rectangular, moulded in two parts, *c.*1930. Back inscribed: 'LOAD NOT TO/ EXCEED 15A 250V', painted in white letters, and two moulded inscriptions: 'PAT APP/FOR' and: 'MADE IN ENGLAND'.

Length 68 mm, width 68 mm, thickness 45 mm.
Source: Greenaway, F.

771. 1981-134/24: Two-way electrical adaptor for three-pin plugs, made of dark brown phenolic, of irregular trilobate form, moulded in one piece, *c.*1930. One side has three inscriptions (moulded): 'G<u>rel</u>co', 'UK REG N<u>O</u> 802954/ MADE IN ENGLAND', 'MAX TOTAL LOAD 15 AMPS'.

Length 85 mm, width 70 mm, thickness 42 mm.
Source: Greenaway, F.

772. 1981-134/25: Three-pin electrical plug made of dark brown phenolic, square with rounded corners, moulded in two parts, *c.*1930. Front inscribed with a trade mark: 'C' within a circle. Back inscribed: 'CRABTREE PATENT/ MADE IN ENGLAND/ Made to B.S. 546/15 AMP/ 250V'; lines 3 and 4 painted, rest moulded.

Length 55 mm, width 55 mm, thickness 51 mm.
Source: Greenaway, F.

773. 1981-134/27: Three-pin electrical plug made of dark brown phenolic, roughly trilobate, moulded in two parts, with part of flex remaining, made by MULTI-KONTACT, *c.*1930. Front inscribed with a trade mark: 'MK' in circle. Back inscribed with 'E' (earth), 'L' and 'N'; also: '15A/B.S./546' in circle; 'MADE IN ENGLAND/ GRIP/ SCREWS'.

Length 90 mm, width 54 mm, thickness 52 mm.
Source: Greenaway, F.

774. 1981-134/29: Three-pin electrical plug made of dark brown phenolic, trilobate, moulded in two parts, *c.*1920. Back inscribed with a trade mark: 'CONTACTUM', 'MADE IN ENGLAND', '5 AMP', 'E' (earth), 'L' and 'N'.

Length 45 mm, width 42 mm, thickness 41 mm.
Source: Greenaway, F.

775. 1981-289/9 (now 1980-676 pt) Circular dial of brown phenol-formaldehyde. Ribbed edge, *c.*1940.

Diameter 29 mm, thickness 21 mm.
Source: Newport, R.

776. 1984-1747: Black phenolic pin tray with hinged lid in the Bakelite Company's trefoil shape. Lower half is divided into three sections. Lid inscribed: 'WITH THE COMPLIMENTS OF/ BAKELITE LIMITED/ 12/16 GROSVENOR GARDENS/ LONDON S.W.1.'. Inside the lower half is moulded the Bakelite Limited trade mark: a trefoil containing a 'B' surmounting the infinity symbol with 'REGISTERED TRADE MARK' moulded below. Made by Bakelite Limited, *c.*1950.

Length and width 132 mm, height 34 mm.
Source: BXL Plastics.

777. 1985-180: Coffin made from wood-flour-filled phenol-formaldehyde resin, made in 1938, believed to be largest phenolic moulding, made in UK, lid broken and incomplete.

Length 1850 mm, width 540 mm, height 360 mm.
Source: Bakelite UK
Figure 38

778. 1985-841: Television cabinet moulded in dark brown phenolic, *c.*1950. Trade mark on front: 'SOBELL'.

Height 910 mm, width 385 mm, depth 425 mm.
Source: Bakelite Ltd.

779. 1985-849: Maroon phenolic ashtray made in Mouldensite moulding powder 160 at Darley Dale, Derbyshire. Inscription in four groups around the rim on the upper surface: 1: 'MOULDENSITE/MFG COMPANY/ WORKS/ DARLEYDALE DERBYSHIRE'; 2: 'PLASTIC MOULDING PREPARATIONS/ IMPREGNATING VARNISHES & /ENAMELS, LACQUERS,/ CEMENTS, LIG, ETC.'; 3: 'EXCELLING ALL OTHER PHENOLIC/ CONDENSATION PRODUCTS/ IN BI-ELECTRIC STRENGTH'; 4: 'ACID, OIL, STEAM & WATER RESISTANCE/ MOULDING & IMPREGNATING QUALITIES/ UNIFORMITY & EVENESS OF FINISH/ HEAT RESISTANCE.'

Diameter 118 mm, height 25 mm.
Source: Reboul, P.

780. 1985-850: Black phenolic match-box holder inscribed: 'BAKELITE/ REDMANOL/ FORMITE/ Mouldensite' made at Darley Dale, Derbyshire. Second inscription: 'BRITISH' below Bakelite Company trade mark in form of trefoil containing a 'B' surmounting the infinity symbol.

Diameter 95 mm, height 28 mm.
Source: Reboul, P.

781. 1985-851: Coronet 'Vogue' camera with dark brown phenolic body, with metal fillings and leather bellows; reputedly first off the production line, 1936. Front of camera inscribed: '"Coronet"/ BRITISH MADE/ PATENTS APPLIED FOR/"Vogue"'. Base moulded with the trade mark: 'Coronet/Vogue', 'Vogue' written vertically. Moulded by Elliott.

Length 155 mm, width 68 mm, height 72 mm.
Source: Reboul, P.
Plate 12

782. 1985-865: Circular ashtray moulded from mottled dark brown phenolic at the Science Museum, for the Plastics Industry Exhibition, 1933. The inscription on the base is contained within circle and reads: 'THE SCIENCE MUSEUM/THE PLASTICS INDUSTRY EXHIBITION/LONDON 1933.'

Diameter 77 mm, height 28 mm, thickness 2 mm.
Source: Plastics and Rubber Institute.

783. 1985-1384: Fascia from 1937 Hillman Minx made of dark brown phenolic. Various instructional marks on front and back.

Length 936 mm, width 325 mm, height 170 mm.
Source: Catto, G.

784. 1987-1037: Ormond electric hair-dryer made from dark brown phenolic. Dated purchase 24 October 1960, in original box with comb and mirror, with metal clips for attachment of the dryer and comb. Comb is tortoiseshell-effect cellulose acetate. Original guarantee and cardboard box packaging. Inscription on

metal plaque on side of dryer: 'E 1022/ ENGINEERING/ 'ORMOND'/ COMPANY LTD/ 230-250 VOLTS 2.2 AMP./ A.C. OR D.C./ MADE IN ENGLAND'. Plug inscribed: 'MADE IN ENGLAND'. Guarantee card gives the address of the company as: 'THE ORMOND ENGINEERING Cᵒ LTD;/ ORMOND HOUSE, ROSEBERY AVENUE, LONDON E.C.1'. The base of the box is inscribed: 'MADE IN ENGLAND'. The cardboard box is printed on the lid with: 'THE BETTER BUILT/ ORMOND/ ELECTRIC/ HAIR DRYER IN CASKET'. The first short side is inscribed: 'SUPRESSED/ Ormond/ HAIRDRYER/ IN CASKET' with: 'EASY CONTROL' written vertically on either side of inscription. The first long side is inscribed: 'FOR QUICK DRYING/ Ormond/ SAFE AND PLEASANT TO USE'. The second short side is inscribed: 'SUPRESSED/ Ormond/ HAIRDRYER/ IN CASKET' with: 'WALNUT' and: 'IVORY' written vertically on either side of inscription. The second long side is inscribed: 'WALNUT AND IVORY/ Ormond/ DUAL PLUG FOR EASY CONNECTION'.

Dryer: length 240mm, width 185 mm, depth 82 mm.
Comb: length 187mm, width 34 mm, depth 45 mm.
Source: Saunders. M.
Plate 12

CAST PHENOLICS

785. 1979-624/6: Pair of onyx-effect cast phenolic candlesticks, in form of rimmed cup-shaped candle holder mounted on cylindrical column which is mounted on square, stepped base, chrome mounts, 1930s. One cup chipped.

Height 126 mm, width 98 mm, breadth 98 mm.
Source: Jesse, J.

786. 1979-624/9: Pair of amber-coloured cast phenolic candlesticks, in form of cup-shaped candle holder mounted on long cylindrical column, which is mounted on square, stepped base, chrome mounts, 1930s.

Height 205 mm, width 98 mm, breadth 98 mm.
Source: Jesse, J.

787. 1979-624/10: Pair of candlesticks of green/yellow cast phenolic in stylised form of a budding plant, with square bases, 1930s.

Length 97 mm, width 97 mm, height 140 mm.
Source: Jesse, J.
Plate 12

788. 1979-624/11: Three-branch candlestick in stepped chrome and amber-coloured cast phenolic. Cast phenolic candle cups and base. Art deco design, 1930s.

Length 197 mm, width 51 mm, height 134 mm.
Reference: Hillier 1968 (illustrated); Hillier 1971: 176.
Source: Jesse, J.

789. 1979-624/12: Pair of candlesticks in form of cylindrical, cast phenolic stem, green in centre, enclosed by two mustard-yellow horizontal bands, chrome hemispherical base and cup, late 1930s. Inscription handwritten on base: 'eMx'?; illegible.

Height 120 mm, diameter 96 mm.
Reference: Hillier 1971: 176, 212 (no. 1397); Hillier 1968: 155.
Source: Jesse, J.

790. 1979-624/14: Pair of cast phenolic candlesticks with circular bases and candle-wax catcher, beaded column of warm brown phenolic, with black candleholder, and black top and lowest beads.

Height 193 mm, diameter 92 mm.
Source: Jesse, J.

791. 1979-624/17: Electric lamp of cast phenolic; shade is amber-coloured, in form of fluted tube which screws on to flat laminated brown disc (under bulb holder) of stand; stand has square amber-coloured base and green fluted stem, English, 1930. Inscription handwritten on base of stand is illegible.

Overall: height 157 mm.
Shade: height 90 mm, diameter 77 mm.
Stand: height 100 mm, width 100 mm.
Source: Jesse, J.

792. 1979-624/22: Circular fluted box of amber-coloured cast phenolic with ebony cast phenolic lid (stepped) and base, handle is amber-coloured in form of cylinder, English, *c.*1930.

Height 70 mm, diameter 104 mm.
Reference: Hillier 1971: 176, 212 (no. 1388).
Source: Jesse, J.

793. 1979-624/23: Circular box, the fluted sides of yellow/green cast phenolic, the lid and base in black. English, *c.*1930.

Diameter 104 mm, height 64 mm.
Source: Jesse, J.
Plate 12

794. 1979-624/24: Circular fluted box of onyx-effect cast phenolic, with lid and base of black cast phenolic, section of handle in form of fluted circle, English, *c.*1930. Base slightly chipped. Inscription moulded on base: 'A/Meritor/PRODUCT/.MAW OF BARNET'; gold letters contained in a rectangle.

Height 75 mm, diameter 77 mm.
Source: Jesse, J.

795. 1979-624/25: Circular fluted box of jade-effect cast phenolic with black inset lid and base, jade handle in form of convex strip, English, 1930.

Height 50 mm, diameter 80 mm.
Source: Jesse, J.

796. 1979-624/26: Circular box of amber-coloured cast phenolic, inset lid and base of mustard brown cast phenolic, handle of amber colour in form of concavely curved strip, *c.*1930.

Height 52 mm, diameter 77 mm.
Source: Jesse, J.

797. 1979-624/27: Circular container made of cast phenolic with orange base, and orange lid with black surround and black knob, with navy-blue felt base.

Height 67 mm, diameter 87 mm.
Source: Jesse, J.

798. 1979-624/28: Box of amber-coloured cast phenolic; body is a semi-circular, fluted tube, flat lid with octagonal handle, rectangular ends forming legs, English, 1930s.

Length 85 mm, width 82 mm, height 75 mm.
Source: Jesse, J.

799. 1979-624/38: Circular fluted box of amber-coloured cast phenolic, with lid and base of black cast phenolic, handle circular in section, English, 1930s.

Height 80 mm, diameter 77 mm.
Source: Jesse, J.

800. 1979-624/42: Circular fluted box of amber-coloured cast phenolic, with lid and base of black cast phenolic; lid has raised circle in centre on which rests handle in form of a cylinder, English, 1930.

Height 70 mm, diameter 65 mm.
Reference: Hillier 1971: 176, 212 (no. 1388).
Source: Jesse, J.

801. 1979-624/43: Box with hemispherical fluted body of amber-coloured cast phenolic, with flat sides, lid and diamond-shaped handle of yellow acrylic sheet, late 1930s.

Length 90 mm, width 97 mm, height 90 mm.
Source: Jesse, J.

802. 1979-624/44: Circular fluted box of marble-effect green cast phenolic, with lid and base of transparent green acrylic, cast phenolic handle in form of cross-cut cylinder, late 1930s, English. Handle slightly chipped.

Diameter 85 mm, height 90 mm.
Source: Jesse, J.

803. 1979-624/45: Circular fluted box of olive-green cast phenolic with lid and base of clear acrylic sheet, with clear

acrylic diamond-shaped handle, late 1930s.

Diameter 88 mm, height 70 mm.
Source: Jesse, J.

804. 1979-624/46: Circular fluted box of olive-green cast phenolic with lid and base of pale blue acrylic sheet, with clear acrylic diamond-shaped handle, late 1930s.

Diameter 88 mm, height 70 mm.
Source: Jesse, J.

805. 1979-624/64: Circular fluted box with inset lid, of green onyx cast phenolic, lid handle in form of a slightly curved strip, 1930s. Crack in base.

Height 77 mm, diameter 85 mm.
Source: Jesse, J.

806. 1979-624/65: Circular fluted box of green onyx cast phenolic with amber-coloured base and inset lid, handle in form of upright octagon, coloured green and screwed to lid, base made in two parts, comprising a flat circle standing on a flat outer rim, 1930s.

Height 90 mm, diameter 77 mm.
Source: Jesse, J.

807. 1979-624/66: Circular fluted box of amber-coloured cast phenolic with handle in form of upright hexagon, inset lid, base made in two parts, comprising a flat circle standing on a flat outer rim, English, 1930s.

Height 90 mm, diameter 78 mm.
Source: Jesse, J.

808. 1979-624/67: Circular fluted box of amber-coloured cast phenolic with inset lid; handle is circular in section, base made in two parts comprising a flat circle standing on a flat outer rim, made in England, 1930s.

Height 85 mm, diameter 78 mm.
Source: Jesse, J.

809. 1979-624/68: Circular fluted box of green marble-effect cast phenolic with lid and base of pale orange yellow, circular knob on lid in form of three superimposed discs, base is attached to box by three brass screws, 1930s.

Height 70 mm, diameter 80 mm.
Source: Jesse, J.

810. 1979-624/70: Circular fluted box of red marble-effect cast phenolic with flat hemispherical handle on lid, supported by two trapezoidal sheets of pale green acrylic, English, late 1930s.

Length 106 mm, width 80 mm, height 100 mm.
Source: Jesse, J.

811. 1979-624/97: Art deco scent bottle of amber-coloured cast phenolic in form of stylised leaf, edges ridged to suggest four superimposed leaves, contains cylindrical glass phial, probably French, 1930s.

Height 100 mm, width 60 mm.
Reference: Hillier 1971: 176, 212 (no. 1391); Bennett 1979: 17 (top row right).
Source: Jesse, J.

812. 1979-624/98: Pair of bookends of transparent amber-coloured cast phenolic surmounted by orange bears, cast, 1930s. Cracks in right-hand leg of each bear.

Height 100 mm, length 85 mm, width 70 mm.
Source: Jesse, J.

813. 1979-624/100: Tray and coaster set. 1930s.

Pt. 1: Flat rectangular tray of black phenolic, with two handles moulded from amber cast phenolic.
Length 343 mm, width 178 mm, height 37 mm, thickness 3.5mm (tray).

Pt. 2: Two circular coasters (set with tray) of cast phenolic, in form of flat, black base screwed to amber-coloured rim with fluted edges, *c*.1930. Incomplete (screw covers missing except for one which is half missing).
Diameter 103 mm, height 18 mm.
Source: Jesse, J.

814. 1979-624/102: Condiment set of cast phenolic, red salt and pepper pots and circular handle fitted into rectangular brown tortoiseshell-effect base, three parts, 1930s. Incomplete (one cork missing).

Length 129 mm, width 47 mm, height 90 mm.
Source: Jesse, J.

815. 1979-624/103: Condiment set, four parts, of orange and yellow marble-effect cast phenolic, comprises pepper, salt and mustard pots and plano-convex shaped tray with circular insets for pots, 1930s. Two chips in base.

Salt and pepper pots: height 55 mm, diameter 38 mm.
Mustard pot: height 27 mm, diameter 40 mm.
Tray: height 25 mm, width 129 mm, depth 49 mm.
Overall: height 65 mm.
Source: Jesse, J.

816. 1979-624/104: Six napkin rings, each of different-coloured cast phenolic, red, green, yellow, orange, peach, brown, octagonal in form with a central, circular hole, 1930s.

Diameter 47 mm, thickness 18 mm.
Source: Jesse, J.

817. 1979-624/105: Pepper and salt pots of amber-coloured cast phenolic, egg-shaped, supported on three black balls, 1930s.

Height 57 mm, diameter 35 mm.
Source: Jesse, J.

818. 1979-624/107: Pair of spherical pepper pots with flattened base and hollow interior, made of marble-effect green cast phenolic with black lids, 1930.

Height 33 mm, diameter 30 mm.
Source: Jesse, J.

819. 1979-624/108: Pair of pepper pots of marble-effect green cast phenolic, in form of step-cut cylinder; one has black lid, one has green lid, 1930.

Height 45 mm, diameter 25 mm.
Source: Jesse, J.

820. 1979-624/109: Two napkin rings moulded in the form of roosters, with central hole for napkin, made of brown cast phenolic resin, late 1930s.

Height 73 mm, width 68 mm, thickness 24 mm.
Reference: Pascale and Cernia 1983: 113, Fig. 103.
Source: Jesse, J.

821. 1979-624/110: Napkin ring moulded in the form of a fish, with central hole for napkin, of dark red cast phenolic resin, transparent eyes, late 1930s. Base damaged (hole gouged out of it).

Height 63 mm, width 70 mm, thickness 10 mm.
Source: Jesse, J.

822. 1979-624/111: Napkin ring moulded in the form of a fish, with central hole for napkin, of yellow cast phenolic resin, with green eyes, late 1930s. Incomplete (one eye missing).

Height 51 mm, width 58 mm, thickness 11 mm.
Source: Jesse, J.

823. 1979-624/112: Napkin ring moulded in the form of an elephant with central hole for napkin, made of marble-effect yellow cast phenolic resin, late 1930s. Small chip on one edge.

Height 53 mm, width 73 mm, thickness 17 mm.
Source: Jesse, J.

824. 1979-624/113: Three napkin rings moulded in the form of birds, with central hole for napkin, of yellow, red and green marble-effect cast phenolic resin, late 1930s.

Height 65 mm, width 80 mm, thickness 14 mm.
Source: Jesse, J.

825. 1979-624/114: Two napkin rings moulded in the form of rabbits, with central hole for napkin, of green and orange cast phenolic resin, late 1930s. Ear of green rabbit slightly chipped.

Height 60 mm, width 70 mm, thickness 15 mm.
Source: Jesse, J.

826. 1979-624/126: Electric light switch in different coloured cast phenolics: green and yellow with red and green switches.

Length 62 mm, width 28 mm, thickness 29 mm.
Source: Jesse, J.
Plate 12

827. 1979-624/129: Rectangular inkwell and holder of orange cast phenolic, with two parallel grooves at the front, stepped curves on each side and two inkwells with slide tops. Designed by Charles

Boyton of Carvacraft for John Dickinson and Co. Ltd, England, 1948.

Length 291 mm, width 175 mm, height 65 mm.
Source: Jesse, J.

828. 1979-624/130: Rectangular desk blotter of amber-coloured cast phenolic, with black phenolic convex base, stepped curves decorate the sides, designed by Charles Boyton of Carvacraft for John Dickinson and Co. Ltd, England, 1948.

Length 151 mm, width 81 mm, height 55 mm.
Source: Jesse, J.

829. 1979-624/131: Wedge-shaped stamp wetter of amber-coloured cast phenolic, square hollow in the middle, stepped curves decorate the sides, semi-circular in section, designed by Charles Boyton of Carvacraft for John Dickinson and Co. Ltd, England, 1948.

Length 102 mm, height 40 mm, width 79 mm.
Reference: Pascale and Cernia 1983: 117, Fig. 109.
Source: Jesse, J.

830. 1979-624/132: Desk note paper block of amber-coloured cast phenolic, sides decorated with stepped design, designed by Charles Boyton of Carvacraft for John Dickinson and Co. Ltd, England, 1948. Trade mark printed on base: 'Carvacraft/MADE IN GT. BRITAIN/.../A...'. Gold lettering. Penultimate line filled with drawing of hands holding a hammer and chisel.

Length 223 mm, width 135 mm, thickness 31 mm.
Source: Jesse, J.

831. 1979-624/133: Desk calendar of amber-coloured cast phenolic, plano-convex in cross-section, sides fan-shaped in design, designed by Charles Boyton of Carvacraft for John Dickinson and Co. Ltd, England, 1948.

Length 157 mm, width 31 mm, height 80 mm.
Source: Jesse, J.

832. 1979-624/134: Square letter rack with two trapezoidal uprights to hold letters, hexagonal pen holder with circular bore, made of translucent amber-coloured cast phenolic, concave groove runs along front, 1930s.

Length 194 mm, width 140 mm, height 100 mm.
Source: Jesse, J.

833. 1979-624/137: Inkwell consisting of a rectangular flat base with two square inkwells; made of veined orange cast phenolic, with brown feet, sides of well, handles and pen rest.

Length 152 mm, width 96 mm, height 73 mm.
Source: Jesse, J.
Plate 12

834. 1979-624/138: Desk holder of green cast phenolic, with flat square base, and fluted holder attached at angle to base, *c.*1930.

Length 80 mm, width 79 mm, height 75 mm.
Source: Jesse, J.

835. 1979-624/145: Amber-coloured cast phenolic valve radio, marked: 'FADA Radio' and: 'SHORT WAVE', American, 1940s.

Length 229 mm, width 140 mm, height 165 mm.
Source: Jesse, J.
Plate 13

836. 1979-624/150: Necklace of cylindrical beads of amber-coloured cast phenolic, threaded with gold and orange string, 1930s.

Length 195 mm.
Bead: diameter 13 mm, length 15 mm.
Source: Jesse, J.

837. 1979-624/162: Brooch of cast phenolic in form of an amber-coloured cactus in a maroon vase, edged with two strips of diamanté, cactus tipped with yellow acrylic? flower, designed by Digby Morton, 1940s. Incomplete (two diamanté are missing). Inscription incised in back: 'Designed by Digby Morton'; signed by designer in his own handwriting.

Length 75 mm, width 25 mm, thickness 10 mm.
Source: Jesse, J.
Plate 1

838. 1979-624/164: Ring of transparent, amber-coloured, cast phenolic with black disc inset in bezel; bezel is V-shaped in plan, with vertical grooves, late 1930s. Ring cracked and worn.

Length 27 mm, width 28 mm, height 17 mm.
Source: Jesse, J.
Plate 1

839. 1979-624/201 Brush and mirror set. English, 1930s.

Pt. 1: Brush (set with mirror) of amber-coloured cast phenolic, art deco fan design on back.
Length 198 mm, width 90 mm, height 35 mm.

Pt. 2: Mirror of amber-coloured cast phenolic, art deco fan design on back.
Length 260 mm, width 130 mm, height 15 mm.
Source: Jesse, J.

840. 1979-624/202: Rectangular inkwell with cover, both plano-convex in cross-section, of green onyx cast phenolic, with black cylindrical ink-pot, base stepped at sides and front, cover stepped at front, designed by Charles Boyton of Carvacraft, for John Dickinson and Co. Ltd, Great Britain, 1948. Inscription inlaid on base: 'Carvacraft/MADE IN GT BRITAIN/...../A DICKINSON/PRODUCT'; inscription blurred, trade mark before last two lines shows two hands holding a hammer and chisel, in gold.

Length 170 mm, width 163 mm, height 60 mm.
Reference: Pascale and Cernia 1983: 119, Fig. 111.
Source: Jesse, J.

841. 1979-624/239: Desk calendar of cast phenolic, flat, black rectangular base, the two green calendar slots are an upright rectangle and a disc, lower surface of base covered with green felt, 1930s.

Length 87 mm, width 34 mm, height 39 mm.
Source: Jesse, J.

842. 1979-624/249: Ashtray of veined brown cast phenolic, square, with two cigarette rests, bird of purple marble-effect plastic sits on edge of ashtray, 1950s? Bird's tail chipped.

Height 70 mm, width 75 mm, depth 70 mm.
Source: Jesse, J.

843. 1979-624/255: Sculpture of turtle dove in deep red cast phenolic with wooden base, twentieth century. Tail chipped.

Length 134 mm, width 66 mm, height 214 mm.
Source: Jesse, J.

844. 1979-624/266: Brown art deco-style clock of cast phenolic and acrylic. Orange circular dial with black markings, on flat base supported by two cylindrical columns, also orange, 1940s. Incomplete (hands and one winder missing).

Length 207 mm, height 160 mm, width 127 mm.
Source: Jesse, J.

845. 1979-624/274: Valve radio of maroon phenolic and orange cast phenolic, rectangular, made by the General Electric Company, Bridgeport, Connecticut, USA, 1940s. Incomplete (base screws missing). Inscription printed on front: 'GENERAL GE ELECTRIC/MADE IN U.S.A.'. Scale printed on face: '55(5)170 KILOCYCLES'; black on yellow, scale preceded by: 'BC' and followed by: 'KC', below scale is written: 'KILOCYCLES' at one end and: 'POLICE' at other. Second inscription printed on base: 'MANUFACTURED BY/GENERAL ELECTRIC CO./BRIDGEPORT. CONN. MADE IN U.S.A.'; blue print on white paper, denotes various patents. Third inscription printed on back: 'REMOVE SCREWS TO SERVICE TUBES'.

Length 235 mm, width 151 mm, height 190 mm.
Source: Jesse, J.

846. 1979-624/276: Rectangular pen holder, plano-convex in cross-section, of green onyx-effect cast phenolic, with two pen holders of black imitation obsidian on top, base stepped at sides and front, designed by Charles Boyton of Carvacraft for John Dickinson and Co. Ltd, Great Britain, 1948. Inscription printed on base: 'Carvacraft/MADE IN G.../...../A DICKINSON/PRODUCT'; inscription partially incised gold letters, second line is partially rubbed out, 'G...' not certain; above last two lines is a trade

mark which is a line drawing of two hands holding a hammer and chisel.

Length 170 mm, width 163 mm, height 70 mm.
Source: Jesse, J.

847. 1980-676/220: Child's spinning top of cast dark green phenolic, circular with pointed tip and central rod-shaped handle, early twentieth century?, made in England, 1920–50. Tip slightly chipped. Inscription moulded around tip: 'MADE IN ENGLAND'.

Diameter 60 mm, height 35 mm.
Source: Newport, R.

848. 1980-676/224: Circular button of brown cast phenolic, pierced centrally with two holes, mid-twentieth century?

Diameter 31 mm, depth 9 mm.
Reference: Newport 1976: S6.
Source: Newport, R.

849. 1980-676/225: Circular napkin ring of marble-effect ochre and green cast phenolic, *c.*1930.

Diameter 48 mm, height 29 mm.
Source: Newport, R.

850. 1980-676/226: Desk electric bell push of brown cast phenolic, square base, circular bell push with brass button, stands on four circular feet, 1920s.

Length 54 mm, width 54 mm, height 48 mm.
Source: Newport, R.

851. 1980-676/227: Circular fluted napkin ring of amber-coloured cast phenolic, 1930s.

Diameter 62 mm, thickness 22 mm.
Source: Newport, R.

852. 1994-656: Set of 20 amber-coloured cast phenolic beads, for a necklace (purchased in Burma in the 1920s).

Diameter 15 mm.
Source: George, A.D.

PHENOLIC MACHINERY

853. 1954-674: Compression mould for plastics. Plate on front: 'SUPPLIED BY FINNEY PRESSES LTD./

BIRMINGHAM/ VOLTS...
ELEMENTS.../LOAD... SUPPLY/
CYCLES/ BRITISH MADE'.

Length 296 mm, width 375 mm, height 428 mm.
Source: British Plastics Federation.

854. 1981-659: Resin kettle used in the
manufacture of 'Erinite', synthetic and
natural phenolic resins for the paint
industry, *c.*1936.

Length 1640 mm, width 1140 mm, height 2270 mm.
Source: BP Chemicals Ltd (Stroud).

855. 1989-503: Rod impact tester used in
cast phenolic testing and four samples of
cast phenolic. Tester is metal with
transparent acrylic points and scale in
inches: '0–160' and percentages: '0–100'.

Pt. 1: Tester: length 555 mm, width 153 mm, height
444 mm.

Pt. 2: Sample 1: transparent yellow cylinder with
rounded end.
Length 175 mm, diameter 27 mm.

Pt. 3: Sample 2: yellow cylinder with rounded end.
Length 172 mm, diameter 28 mm.

Pt. 4: Sample 3: Bark-effect handle with oval yellow
ends.
Length 106 mm, width 32 mm, thickness 21 mm.

Pt. 5: Sample 4: Bark-effect handle with yellow ends.
Length 88 mm, width 21 mm, thickness 17 mm.
Source: Catalin Ltd.

THIOUREA-UREA-
FORMALDEHYDE (THIOUREA-
FORMALDEHYDE)

856. 1979-624/101: Sugar caster of flame
and cream-coloured marble-effect
thiourea-urea-formaldehyde, with
stepped base. Marked: 'BANDALASTA
REGD 176 BGM/BANDA MADE IN
ENGLAND/ WARE'; first and last lines
in large letters and whole inscription
contained within a circle.

Diameter 72 mm, height 117 mm.
Source: Jesse, J.
Plate 14

857. 1980-676/238: Hexagonal Bandalasta
bowl no. 151, coloured cream with black
powder marks, made of thiourea-urea-
formaldehyde B. Base inscribed with

trade mark: 'BANDALASTA/REGD/
151/BANDA/MADE IN ENGLAND/
WARE'; first and last lines in large script
contained within in circle; 'BANDA' has
large '&' superimposed over 'N'.

Diameter 152 mm, height 55 mm.
Source: Newport, R.
Plate 14

UREA-FORMALDEHYDE (UF)

858. 1979-624/19: Pink geometric electric
wall light, of urea-formaldehyde, consists
of flat panel with stepped edge, from
which projects at right angles the light
fitting, made in England, late 1930s.
Inscription moulded on base and back of
light fitting: 'MADE IN ENGLAND'.

Length 250 mm, width 123 mm, height 135 mm.
Source: Jesse, J.

859. 1979-624/29: Oblong pipe box of
green/brown marble-effect urea-
formaldehyde, decorated with raised step
moulded around edges of base and lid;
parallel raised steps run across the top of
the lid. Art deco design. The base
impressed: 'The BRITISH BUTTNER
PIPE Cᵒ Lᵀᴰ', 1930s.

Length 190 mm, width 100 mm, height 77 mm.
Source: Jesse, J.

860. 1979-624/33: Circular box of
marble-effect green, red and yellow urea-
formaldehyde; base has sixteen legs, lid
faceted to continue legs, with black and
gold tassel, French, *c.*1930.

Diameter 128 mm, height 67 mm.
Source: Jesse, J.

861. 1979-624/34: Rectangular cigarette
box made for State Express Cigarettes,
with white lid made of urea-
formaldehyde moulded with classical
Greek dancers and musicians, with black
phenolic base, English, 1940s. Inscription
moulded in centre of base: 'STATE
EXPRESS/C1'; contained within
concave-cornered rectangle first line
bigger letters than second, and in ornate

scroll. Second inscription moulded on edge of base: 'MADE IN ENGLAND'.

Length 118 mm, width 84 mm, height 57 mm.
Source: Jesse, J.

862. 1979-624/51: Cream-coloured urea-formaldehyde circular box, the lid impressed with roses, with central raised dome. Stamped inside lid: 'EDITIONS E FORNELLS PARIS'. 1930s. Inside of base stamped: 'FRANCE'.

Diameter 128 mm, height 80 mm.
Source: Jesse, J.

863. 1979-624/52: Circular powder box of urea-formaldehyde, ivory in colour, lid decorated with stylised flowers, made in France by Editions Fornells, 1930s. Inscription moulded on base: 'FRANCE'. Second inscription moulded inside lid and base: 'EDITIONS ./-/PARIS/-/.E.FORNELLS'. Inscription contained within a circle; 'EDITIONS' and 'E.FORNELLS' form a circle inside this.

Diameter 120 mm, height 55 mm.
Source: Jesse, J.
Figure 39

864. 1979-624/53: Circular box of ivory urea-formaldehyde, lid decorated with stylised flowers and leaves, French, Editions Fornells, 1930s. Trade mark moulded inside handle: 'EDITIONS.1-/PARIS/-/.E.FORNELLS'; inscription contained within a circle; 'EDITIONS' and 'E.FORNELLS' form a circle inside this. Second inscription moulded on base: 'FRANCE'.

Diameter 137 mm, height 60 mm.
Source: Jesse, J.

865. 1979-624/55: Ten-sided box of green urea-formaldehyde, lid moulded and painted with stylised foliage picked out in gold and silver. Made by Editions Fornells, Paris, c.1930. Trade mark moulded on lid: 'FORNELLS PARIS' along edge of one leaf. Second inscription inside base: 'FRANCE' adjacent to edge.

Diameter 101 mm, thickness 38 mm.
Source: Jesse, J.

866. 1979-624/57: Octagonal box of ivory urea-formaldehyde, lid moulded in form of Arabian oasis scene, French, Editions Fornells, 1930s. Inscription moulded inside lid and base: 'EDITIONS./ - / PARIS/ -/.E.FORNELLS'; inscription contained within a circle; 'EDITIONS' and 'E.FORNELLS' form a circle inside this, almost rubbed out from base. Second inscription moulded inside base along one short edge: 'FRANCE'.

Length 150 mm, width 150 mm, height 50 mm.
Source: Jesse, J.
Figure 39

867. 1979-624/58: Octagonal box of black urea-formaldehyde; corners are shorter than sides and are fluted, lid moulded with relief of two female nudes and a fawn amid forest; relief is antiqued, French, Editions Fornells, 1930s. Trade mark moulded inside lid and base: 'EDITIONS./-/PARIS/-/.E.FORNELLS'; inscription contained within circle; 'EDITIONS' and 'E.FORNELLS' form a circle inside this.

Width 150 mm, length 150 mm, height 53 mm.
Source: Jesse, J.

868. 1979-624/60: Black circular container with lid, curved base; lid is domed and decorated with moulded flowers (poppies?), of black urea-formaldehyde, made by Editions Fornells, Paris, French, 1930s. Inscription moulded inside lid and base: 'EDITIONS./-/PARIS/-/.E.FORNELLS'; inscription contained within a circle; 'EDITIONS' and 'E.FORNELLS' form a circle inside this. Second inscription moulded on base: 'FRANCE'.

Height 60 mm, diameter 115 mm.
Reference: Bennett 1979: 17 (bottom row right).
Source: Jesse, J.

869. 1979-624/61: Circular powder box of cream urea-formaldehyde, lid decorated with moulded design of the head of

Artemis (Diana) and a leaping deer, English, 1930s, designed by H. Earland.

Diameter 110 mm, height 50 mm.
Reference: Katz 1978: 141; Newport 1976: T 50.
Source: Jesse, J.

870. 1979-624/62: Cream-coloured urea-formaldehyde Quickmix blender. Cylindrical with stepped design. Base stamped: 'BREVETE FRANCE & ETRANGER'. 1950s. Lid inscribed with trade mark: 'QUICKMIX'.

Diameter 78 mm, height 105 mm.
Source: Jesse, J.
Plate 14

871. 1979-624/69: Circular powder box with cream/yellow marble-effect lid of urea-formaldehyde moulded with flower decoration, cardboard and metal base, made in Paris, France, by Lancôme, *c*.1930. Inscription moulded inside lid: '2' within circle, in centre of lid. Second inscription printed on base: 'PH....'. Remainder unreadable, red print on white label. Lid chipped.

Pt. 1: Inscription printed on base of powder
    container: 'POUDRE/DE/LANCÔME/NO.2...
    DRÉ/LA MÊ... FAIT/ÉGALEN... ITES/CLA... SE/
    ROSE... ÈE/NO.6.../BISTRÉES.../FONCÉES: N.../
    N°21.../..../..../..../....../N°5 MAT CHAIR
    DORÉE./PARIS FRANCE'.
Diameter 92 mm, height 35 mm.
Source: Jesse, J.

872. 1979-624/87: Spherical ashtray with green marblised urea-formaldehyde lid and black phenolic base, with three black cigarette holders hinged open and close, made by Roanoid for Roxon, in England, 1930s. Inscription moulded inside lid: 'PAT NO 389426'. Inscription moulded inside base: 'PATENT APPLIED FOR – FOREIGN PATENTS PENDING – MADE FOR ROXON BY ROANOID'; arranged around tray.

Diameter 85 mm, height 85 mm.
Reference: Hillier 1968: 66–7; Bennett 1979: 14–15.
Source: Jesse, J.

873. 1979-624/88: Spherical ashtray with pink marblised urea-formaldehyde lid and black phenolic base, with three black cigarette holders hinged to open and close, made by Roanoid for Roxon and Dunlop, made in England, 1930s. Inscription moulded inside lid: 'PAT NO 389426'. Second inscription moulded inside base: 'PATENT APPLIED FOR – FOREIGN PATENTS PENDING – MADE FOR ROXON BY ROANOID'; arranged around tray.

Diameter 85 mm, height 85 mm.
Reference: Hillier 1968: 66–7; Bennett 1979: 14–15.
Source: Jesse, J.
Plate 14

874. 1979-624/89: Spherical ashtray of blue marblised urea-formaldehyde with three black phenolic cigarette holders hinged to open and close, made by Roanoid for Roxon, in England, 1930s. One holder chipped, crack in top. Inscription moulded inside lid: 'PAT NO 389426'. Second inscription moulded inside base: 'PATENT APPLIED FOR – FOREIGN PATENTS PENDING – MADE FOR ROXON BY ROANOID'; arranged around tray.

Diameter 85 mm, height 85 mm.
Reference: Hillier 1968: 66–7; Bennett 1979: 14–15.
Source: Jesse, J.

875. 1979-624/90: Spherical ashtray with green marblised urea-formaldehyde lid and black phenolic base, with three black cigarette holders hinged to open and close, made by Roanoid for Roxon and Dunlop, made in England, 1930s. Crack in lid. Inscription moulded inside lid: 'PAT NO 389426'. Second inscription moulded inside base: 'PATENT APPLIED FOR – FOREIGN PATENTS PENDING – MADE FOR ROXON BY ROANOID'; arranged around tray. Third inscription impressed on lid: 'DUNLOP' in orange letters.

Diameter 85 mm, height 85 mm.
Reference: Hillier 1968: 66–7; Bennett 1979: 14–15.
Source: Jesse, J.

876. 1979-624/91: Cigarette lighter of ivory urea-formaldehyde with black band around middle, pear-shaped with circular hand-piece, made by Dorset Light Industries Ltd, Bridport, Dorset, 1950s.

Inscription moulded on base: 'MADE IN ENGLAND/BY/DORSET LIGHT INDUSTRIES/LTD/ BRIDPORT, DORSET./ PROV. PAT.6105/ 50/ REG.DES./ 'D.L.I.'/FLINTLESS'; one of four inscriptions, last two lines contained in circle, 'BY' has Z-shaped motif on either side. Second inscription moulded on base: 'LIGHTER FUEL/..../ TO RE-FUEL OR REPLACE BATTERIES/ ..../BATTERIES/...'. Third inscription punched above band: 'G.C.G.' in black letters.

Height 110 mm, diameter 80 mm.
Source: Jesse, J.

877. 1979-624/92: Circular ashtray with square cigarette rest for two cigarettes attached; base is of yellow and brown marked urea-formaldehyde; interior is of brown phenolic, a British Buttner Product, 1930s. Cigarette rest base is cracked. Inscription moulded on base: '.British. Buttner. Products' in cursive script, arranged in circle.

Length 117 mm, width 101 mm, height 30 mm.
Source: Jesse, J.

878. 1979-624/93: Large circular ashtray with oblong cigarette rest for two cigarettes, two more rests in rim. Base is cream urea-formaldehyde, interior is black phenolic, c.1930.

Length 169 mm, width 148 mm, thickness 26 mm.
Source: Jesse, J.

879. 1979-624/94: HMS *Queen Mary* ashtray, with white urea-formaldehyde outer shell and dark brown phenolic inner shell. Inscribed: 'R.M.S./"Queen Mary"' in cursive script, c.1930.

Diameter 101 mm, width 118 mm, height 29 mm.
Source: Jesse, J.

880. 1979-624/95: Circular ashtray with oblong cigarette rest for two cigarettes attached. Base is cream urea-formaldehyde, interior is brown phenolic, c.1930.

Length 115 mm, width 98 mm, thickness 29 mm.
Source: Jesse, J.

881. 1979-624/115: Table dustpan and brush, made of green mottled urea-formaldehyde, made by Stadium, Great Britain, c.1930. Pan chipped at edge. Trade mark moulded on pan base: 'MADE IN/STADIUM/GREAT BRITAIN' contained in circle, 'STADIUM' in cursive hand, and bigger than rest of inscription.

Pt. 1: Crescentic dustpan with raised edge and flat semi-circular handle, pierced for hanging.
Length 222 mm, width 130 mm, thickness 24 mm.
Pt. 2: Rectangular brush, with flat handle, curved at top. Compression mould marks inside.
Length 127 mm, width 60 mm, thickness 13 mm.
Source: Jesse, J.
Plate 14

882. 1979-624/121: Circular powder compact with red urea-formaldehyde base and black phenolic lid with metal surround and hinge. Inner lid silvered gauze with metal surround inside base, c.1930. Base edge slightly chipped.

Diameter 62 mm, thickness 16 mm.
Source: Jesse, J.

883. 1979-624/147: Handbag of blue urea-formaldehyde. Rectangular with lid edge cut in convex curve. Collapsible, with blue silk lining, containing purse, mirror and bank note holder, c.1940. Inscription engraved on lower stud fastening: '.V...B....D...' around border.

Length 215 mm, width 135 mm, thickness 22 mm.
Source: Jesse, J.

884. 1979-624/187: Rectangular cigarette box of urea-formaldehyde, white lid, black base, made for the Parker Pen Company, in England, 1930s. Lid decorated with art deco design of parallel lines. Inscription moulded on base: 'PARKER PEN CIGARETTE BOX/ NO.220 B/MADE IN ENGLAND'.

Length 162 mm, width 78 mm, height 38 mm.
Source: Jesse, J.

885. 1979-624/189: Set of eight stacking cups and saucers in mottled colours, of urea-formaldehyde, made by ML, England, 1940s. Inscription moulded on base of cup: '6/ML/MADE IN ENGLAND'; 'M' superimposed over 'L'. Second inscription moulded on base of saucer: '8/ML/MADE IN ENGLAND'; 'M' superimposed over 'L'.

Cup: height 55 mm, diameter 75 mm, width 95mm
Saucer: height 20 mm, diameter 120 mm.
Source: Jesse, J.
Plate 14

886. 1979-624/192: Salt and pepper pots moulded in urea-formaldehyde, in form of pink flower with green leaves, made in England. Mid-twentieth century. Inscription moulded on base: 'MADE/IN/ENGLAND/REGD'. Second inscription inside base: 'T' and 'V' stamped within base of salt and pepper pots respectively.

Diameter 48 mm, height 59 mm.
Source: Jesse, J.

887. 1979-624/193: Square 'Kelvinator' jug of cream urea-formaldehyde, decorated with helmeted head (twice), mid-twentieth century. Trade mark moulded on bottom edge: 'KELVINATOR' repeated on each of four sides.

Width 94 mm, length 93 mm, height 150 mm.
Source: Jesse, J.
Plate 14

888. 1979-624/195: Egg cup in mottled colours of moulded urea-formaldehyde, with three cylindrical feet, made by London Moulders Ltd, England, 1940s.

Height 48 mm, diameter 42mm
Feet: height 22 mm, diameter 6 mm.
Reference: *British Catalogue of Plastics* 1947: 80.
Source: Jesse, J.

889. 1979-624/197: Set of six moulded plates, of cream urea-formaldehyde, decorated with mermaid seated in scallop shell, made by U.D.A. Plastics Ltd, English, 1950s. Inscription moulded on base: 'BRITISH MADE/Modern Stylists/SERIES/U.D.A. PLASTICS LTD.'; first and fourth lines curved round rim of base, second line is in flowing script.

Diameter 153 mm, height 20 mm.

Source: Jesse, J.
Plate 18 (2 pts)

890. 1979-624/198: Oval moulded serving dish of cream urea-formaldehyde, decorated with mermaid seated in scallop shell, made by U.D.A. Plastics Ltd, English, 1950s. Inscription moulded on base: 'BRITISH MADE/Modern Stylists/SERIES/U.D.A. PLASTICS LTD.'; second line is in flowing script and on the diagonal.

Length 285 mm, width 225 mm, height 38 mm.
Source: Jesse, J.
Plate 18

891. 1979-624/211: Sandy-coloured circular box in Indian style, probably urea-formaldehyde, fluted with knob on lid, *c.*1930.

Diameter 126 mm, height 90 mm.
Source: Jesse, J.

892. 1979-624/205: Handbag of cream urea-formaldehyde with red moulded handle. Rectangular and collapsible, with cream silk lining and purse. Made in France, *c.*1930. Inscription on edge of purse, under lid: 'MADE IN FRANCE', gold on cream.

Length 196 mm, width 142 mm, thickness 17 mm.
Source: Jesse, J.

893. 1979-624/206: Handbag of cream urea-formaldehyde. Trapezoidal, with lid edge cut out in form of a wave. Collapsible, with cream silk lining and purse. *c.*1930. Half of stud fastening missing. Inscription engraved on lower stud fastening: '.V...B...D...' around border.

Length 221 mm, width 125 mm, thickness 16 mm.
Source: Jesse, J.

894. 1979-624/209: Rectangular cigarette box with fluted sides, white base of urea-formaldehyde, black phenolic lid with rectangular depression in centre and four cigarette rests, one on each side, made in England, 1930s.

Inscription moulded on base: 'MADE IN ENGLAND'.

Length 114 mm, width 82 mm, height 58 mm.
Source: Jesse, J.

895. 1979-624/217: Rectangular cigarette box of green mottled urea-formaldehyde. Hinged lid decorated with two stylised birds in flight, art deco design with four feet. *c*.1930. Inscription moulded on base at short edge: 'AB-5'. 'A' and 'B' joined together.

Length 162 mm, width 80 mm, thickness 48 mm.
Source: Jesse, J.
Plate 14

896. 1979-624/225: Ten-sided box of white urea-formaldehyde, lid moulded with decoration of a head of Pan and a young girl, wreathed with ivy, French, Editions Fornells, 1930s. Outside of base cracked, lid chipped. Inscription moulded inside base: 'EDITIONS./—/PARIS/—/.E.FORNELLS'; inscription contained within a circle; 'EDITIONS' and 'E.FORNELLS' form a circle inside this. Second inscription moulded on base along edge: 'FRANCE'.

Diameter 118 mm, height 53 mm.
Source: Jesse, J.
Figure 39

897. 1979-624/227: Rectangular cigarette box base with ivory urea-formaldehyde hinged lid, lid decorated with moulded horseman spearing lion in Assyrian style, base of dark brown phenolic; box contains nineteen cigarettes, and was made by Birkby's Ltd, Yorkshire: Liversedge, England, 1930s, under the trade name 'Elo Ware'. Inscription die-stamped on base of box: 'ELO/REGD./MADE IN ENGLAND/WARE'; inscription contained in circle. Second inscription printed on side of cigarette: 'PLAYER'S/ "MEDIUM"/NAVY CUT' in blue print.

Box: length 168 mm, width 85 mm, height 60mm
Feet: diameter 12mm
Cigarettes: diameter 8 mm, length 69 mm.
Reference: Bennett 1979: 16–17 (bottom row centre).
Source: Jesse, J.

898. 1979-624/242: Pair of green urea-formaldehyde step-cut circular candlesticks mounted with chrome, with flat green felt base, art deco design, late 1930s. Incomplete (one chipped at base).

Diameter 102 mm, height 38 mm.
Source: Jesse, J.

899. 1979-624/243: Pair of step-cut, square candlesticks of ivory urea-formaldehyde, with four diagonal lines, one radiating from each corner, chrome candle holder, black felt base, 1930s.

Length 87 mm, width 87 mm, height 50 mm.
Source: Jesse, J.

900. 1979-624/256: Rectangular plaque of cream urea-formaldehyde, moulded with the figure of a naked male winged warrior, with raised arms, right arm holding a sword, and about to sever the three heads of a dragon. Signed: 'McM', with 'V' (for victory) repeated five times at base in Morse code. Details picked out in brown paint. Plaque designed to commemorate allied victory at the end of the Second World War, *c*.1945. Signature moulded in lower left-hand corner: 'M^cM' in Roman letters. Trade mark moulded on back: 'DE LA RUE PLASTICS'.

Length 383 mm, width 254 mm, thickness 13 mm,
  length 533mm (with hanging attachment).
Source: Jesse, J.

901. 1979-624/277: 'Geni' electric lamp stand, moulded from white urea-formaldehyde with black phenolic base, made by Lustro Distributors Ltd, England, *c*.1930. Trade mark moulded on base: 'Geni THE LAMP/ A KLAMPSHAYD PRODUCT/ BRITISH MADE BY/ LUSTRO DISTRIBUTORS LTD/ LONDON ENGLAND'. Inscription on base: 'PATENTS & DESIGN/ REGISTRATIONS PENDING'.

Length 138 mm, width 138 mm, height 185 mm.
Source: Jesse, J.

902. 1979-624/278: Oblong pipe box of blue marble-effect urea-formaldehyde.

Made by the British Buttner Pipe Company, 1930s. The base is moulded with the trade mark: 'THE BRITISH BUTTNER/ PIPE C⁰ L^TD' enclosed within an oblong box.

Length 190 mm, width 100 mm, height 80 mm.
Source: Jesse, J.

903. 1979-624/283: Circular trumps reminder with round window showing suits and 'no trumps' turned by black phenolic handle, of mottled urea-formaldehyde with black base and handle, 1930s. Inscription printed on disc showing at window: white disc with picture of suits of cards, clubs, hearts, spades, diamonds and no trumps, printed in black and red on white. Base chipped in two places.

Diameter 60 mm, height 20 mm.
Source: Jesse, J.

904. 1979-624/291: Display stand of plastics in different colours, with tear-shaped pieces of urea-formaldehyde, and conical pieces made of phenolic. Rod missing.

Pt. 1: Tear-shaped black phenolic with rounded edges, pierced centre.
Length 180 mm, width 153 mm, thickness 12 mm.

Pt. 2: Tear-shaped piece, now painted black, originally blue, pierced at narrow end, rounded edges, probably urea-formaldehyde.
Length 142 mm, width 94 mm, thickness 4 mm.

Pt. 3: Tear-shaped piece, now painted black, originally red, pierced at narrow end, rounded edges, probably urea-formaldehyde.
Length 144 mm, width 94 mm, thickness 3 mm.

Pt. 4: Tear-shaped piece, now painted black, originally green, pierced at narrow end, rounded edges, probably urea-formaldehyde.
Length 144 mm, width 94 mm, thickness 3 mm.

Pt. 5: Tear-shaped piece, now painted black, originally yellow, pierced at narrow end, rounded edges, probably urea-formaldehyde.
Length 144 mm, width 95 mm, thickness 3 mm.

Pts 6–14: Nine cones made of black phenolic, with flat top.
Diameter 28 mm, height 34 mm.

905. 1980-676/228: Picnic salt and pepper pot set which push together to form a seal for the contents, moulded of green urea-formaldehyde known as Scarab, by Streetly for Woolworth, designed by J. Butler, 1934, made in England. Pepper pot cracked on top. Inscription moulded on base of pots: 'MADE/IN/ ENGLAND/A.1.'. Second inscription moulded on top of pepper pot: 'BRIT.PAT.No.411660' around depression in centre of pot.

Length 66 mm (assembled), diameter 38 mm.
Reference: Newport 1976: T44.
Source: Newport, R.

906. 1980-676/229: Mottled green condiment set of urea-formaldehyde, moulded in eight parts, with an aluminium handle, with tray moulded with three steps, salt and pepper pots in six-step design, and mustard pot in three-step design with lid and spoon. Cream-coloured spoon decorated with three radial lines and inscribed: 'MADE IN ENGLAND'.

Pt. 1: Tray: length 168 mm, width 75 mm, height 100 mm.
Pt. 2: Salt pot: diameter 32 mm, height 55 mm.
Pt. 3: Pepper pot: diameter 32 mm, height 55 mm.
Pt. 4: Mustard pot: length 47 mm, width 38 mm, height 45 mm.
Pt. 5: Spoon: length 63 mm, width 16 mm, height 3.5 mm.
Reference: Newport 1976: T49.
Source: Newport, R.
Plate 14

907. 1980-676/230: Circular powder box of cream urea-formaldehyde, lid decorated with moulded design of the head of Artemis (Diana) and a leaping deer, English, 1930s, designed by H. Earland.

Diameter 110 mm, height 50 mm.
Reference: Katz 1978: 141 (illustrated); Newport 1976: T50.
Source: Newport, R.

908. 1980-676/231: Cream-coloured urea-formaldehyde clockwork alarm clock. Front moulded in an art deco fan-shaped design. The silver-painted dial inscribed: 'INGERSOL'. Various identifying and instructional marks; back inscribed: 'MADE IN ENGLAND'.

Length 196 mm, width 69 mm, height 143 mm.

Reference: Newport 1976: T83.
Source: Newport, R.
Plate 14

909. 1980-676/232: Rectangular 'Grosvenor' cigarette box with a hinged lid, lid decorated with parallel lines in band across centre and on hinges, ivory lid, black base, moulded in Beetle (urea-formaldehyde) by Streetly for Ardath, designed by A.H. Woodfull in 1937, made in England. Inscription moulded on base: 'MADE IN ENGLAND'.

Length 175 mm, width 126 mm, height 55 mm.
Reference: Newport 1976: T57.
Source: Newport, R.

910. 1980-676/233: Circular pin box with screw-fitting lid, moulded of translucent red Beetle (urea-formaldehyde), lid decorated with art deco design of circle cut by smaller circle and by parallel lines arranged in a V-shape, made in England, 1930. Trade mark moulded on base: 'A.1./ Beetleware/MADE/IN/ENGLAND/W.7 4'; second line in cursive script and underlined, whole contained within a circle.

Diameter 83 mm, height 45 mm.
Source: Newport, R.

911. 1980-676/234-6: Three circular beakers of apple green with white marble-effect urea-formaldehyde, raised rim, made by London Moulders Ltd, in England, 1940s. Trade mark moulded on base: '12/ML/MADE IN ENGLAND'. 'M' and 'L' superimposed over each other to form trade mark.

Height 94 mm, diameter 72 mm.
Source: Newport, R.
Plate 14

912. 1980-676/237: Yellow with white marble-effect Linga Ware beaker made of urea-formaldehyde. Base inscribed: 'MADE IN B'HAM/ REG/ LINGA/ WARE/ 1805/ ENGLAND'; middle four lines within trapezoid trade mark.

Diameter 74 mm, height 87 mm.
Source: Newport, R.

913. 1980-676/239: Thermos flask of grey and maroon urea-formaldehyde with arched handle, glass lining and cork stopper. Model no. 65, refill no. 14F, made in England by Thermos Ltd, 1950s. Inscription moulded on base: 'THERMOS LIMITED/ THERMOS/ REGISTERED TRADE MARK/ MODEL NO.65/REFILL NO.14F/ MADE IN ENGLAND'; first and last lines run round edge of base.

Height 255 mm, width 125 mm, diameter 95 mm.
Source: Newport, R.
Plate 14

914. 1980-676/240: Slydo rectangular cigarette case of blue mottled with white urea-formaldehyde, hinged lid slides open to reveal base fluted to contain cigarettes, lid decorated with moulded design of crossed bands, one of which is ridged, made by Stelloid Products Ltd, Mountsorrel, England, 1930s. Inscription moulded inside lid: 'BRITISH SLYDO MADE/PATENT APPLIED FOR/UK USA CANADA S AFRICA' contained within rectangle with rounded corners. Second inscription moulded inside edge of base: 'PAT.APPLIED FOR'.

Length 100 mm, width 81 mm, height 13 mm.
Source: Newport, R.

915. 1980-676/241: Slydo rectangular cigarette case of ivory-coloured urea-formaldehyde, hinged lid slides open to reveal base fluted to contain cigarettes, lid decorated with moulded design of crossed bands, one of which is ridged, made by Stelloid Products Ltd, Mountsorrel England, 1930s. Inscription moulded inside panel: 'BRITISH SLYDO MADE/PATENT APPLIED FOR/UK USA CANADA S AFRICA' contained within rectangle with rounded corners. Second inscription moulded inside edge of base: 'PAT.APPLIED FOR'.

Length 100 mm, width 81 mm, height 13 mm.
Source: Newport, R.

916. 1980-676/242 Cigarette case in original box.

Pt. 1: Rectangular Slydo cigarette case of green mottled urea-formaldehyde, hinged lid slides open to reveal base fluted to contain cigarettes, lid decorated with moulded design of crossed bands, one of which is ridged, made by Stelloid Products Ltd, Mountsorrel, England, 1930s. Inscription moulded inside lid: 'BRITISH SLYDO MADE/PATENT APPLIED FOR/UK USA CANADA S AFRICA' contained within rectangle with rounded corners. Inscription moulded inside edge of base: 'PAT.APPLIED FOR'.
Length 100 mm, width 81 mm, height 13 mm.

Pt. 2: Rectangular cardboard box with green lid and white base, lid has a marbled effect.
Length 103 mm, width 88 mm, height 15 mm.

Pt. 3: Instruction sheet for the Slydo cigarette case. Inscription printed on surface: 'THE/ "SLYDO"/ Cigarette case/TO OPEN:- Slide lid FORWARD /.../..../.../..../.../MADE IN ENGLAND by/Stelloid Products Ltd./Mountsorrel/Nr. Leicester'.
Length 85 mm, width 75 mm.
Source: Newport, R.

917. 1980-676/243: Egg cup in mottled red and pink urea-formaldehyde, with three cylindrical feet, slightly raised rim, probably made by London Moulders Ltd, England, 1940s. Inscription moulded inside base: '3'. Inscription painted on side: 'Roger' in cursive script.

Height 42 mm, diameter 45 mm.
Source: Newport, R.

918. 1980-676/244: Cylindrical mug of white urea-formaldehyde with decoration commemorating the coronation of Elizabeth II, 1953, made in England, 1953. Inscription moulded on base: 'MADE IN ENGLAND'. Transfer on side of mug reads: 'HONI.SOIT ...L.Y.PENSE/H.M.CORONATION.19 53' and consists of royal standard and Union Jack flying above royal coat of arms under which is a long banner with last line on it, in red, blue, white and gold.

Length 96 mm, width 73 mm, height 73 mm.
Source: Newport, R.

919. 1980-676/245: Glolite Midget key light of green and white urea-formaldehyde, fluted cylinder which unscrews centrally into two parts (one green and one white), internal spring mechanism for battery, made by the Glolite Corporation, New York, USA, 1930s. Trade mark moulded at both ends: 'GLOLITE CORP.N.Y./..../MIDGET'. '...' represents a man wearing a top hat and monocle, smoking a long cigarette.

Length 40 mm, diameter 14 mm.
Source: Newport, R.

920. 1980-676/246: Hexagonal napkin ring of mottled urea-formaldehyde, multicoloured. Trade mark moulded on edge: 'DODCA'.

Diameter 46 mm, height 24 mm.
Source: Newport, R.
Plate 14

921. 1981-134/1: Electrical adaptor and switch for three-pin plug, square, made of white urea-formaldehyde, moulded in two parts, made by MULTI-KONTACT, mid-twentieth century. Front inscribed with a trade mark: 'MK' in circle. Back inscribed: 'MADE IN ENGLAND'.

Length 87 mm, width 87 mm, thickness 46 mm.
Source: Greenaway, F.

922. 1981-134/2: Electrical adaptor and switch for three-pin plug, square, flat, made of white urea-formaldehyde, moulded in three parts, back has a brown phenolic and metal attachment, made by MULTI-KONTACT, mid-twentieth century. Front inscribed with a trade mark: 'MK' in circle. Urea-formaldehyde back inscribed: 'MADE IN ENGLAND'. Phenol-formaldehyde attachment marked: 'MK L/ 15A/ 250/N/ AC ONLY' and: 'MADE IN ENGLAND/ E/ 5298/ N'. Metal piece marked: 'BRIT PAT'.

Length 85 mm, width 85 mm, thickness 40 mm.
Source: Greenaway, F.

923. 1981-134/3: Electrical adaptor for three-pin plug, made of white urea-formaldehyde with inner casing of back made of brown phenolic, trapezoidal, mid-twentieth century. Front inscribed: 'FUSED SAFETY ADAPTOR/15-5 AMP/ Grelco / MADE IN ENGLAND/

USE CORRECT FUSE LINKS/ MAX TOTAL LOAD 15 AMP'. Back inscribed: 'Grelco/ LIST No.51/ USE 5AMP FUSES', 'PUSH & LIFT'.

Length 70 mm, width 64 mm, thickness 52 mm.
Source: Greenaway, F.

924. 1981-134/4: Electrical adaptor and switch for three-pin plug, rectangular, made of white urea-formaldehyde, moulded in two parts, mid-twentieth century. Back plate missing. Front inscribed: 'ACSA'. Back inscribed: 'E' (earth), 'L' and: 'N', '250 VOLTS/5 AMPS/ AC ONLY', 'PAT. NOS./772782/772785/ & OTHERS', 'BM 9727 2', ' MADE IN ENGLAND'.

Length 72 mm, width 47 mm, thickness 38 mm.
Source: Greenaway, F.

925. 1981-134/5: Three-way electrical adaptor for three-pin plugs, made of white urea-formaldehyde, moulded in two parts, mid-twentieth century. One side inscribed: '5A MAX' in circle. Back inscribed: 'MADE IN ENGLAND' in circle, 'REGD/ 878896/DES', and: 'PATENTS APPD FOR' in flattened oval.

Length 70 mm, width 50 mm, thickness 48 mm.
Source: Greenaway, F.

926. 1981-134/8: Three-pin electrical plug made of white urea-formaldehyde, moulded in two parts, c.1930. Front has trade mark: 'Seeboard'. Back inscribed with: 'E' (earth), 'L' and: 'N', 'EDISWAN/ MADE IN ENGLAND/ GRIP/SCREWS'.

Length 55 mm, width 50 mm, thickness 55 mm.
Source: Greenaway, F.

927. 1981-134/9: Three-pin electrical plug made of white urea-formaldehyde, square, with three raised ridges on front, moulded in two parts, c.1930. Back inscribed with 'E' [earth], 'L' and: 'N'; 'MADE IN ENGLAND' in circle; 'WG/5AMP/250V/FLEX GRIP', first line in circle (trade mark).

Length 50 mm, width 42 mm, thickness 38 mm.
Source: Greenaway, F.

928. 1981-134/10: Three-pin electrical plug made of white urea-formaldehyde, roughly oval, moulded in two parts, mid-twentieth century. Front inscribed with trade mark: 'EVER READY' contained within an oval capsule. Back inscribed with: 'E' (earth), 'L' and: 'N'; '15 AMP/ MADE IN ENGLAND'.

Length 55 mm, width 53 mm, thickness 52 mm.
Source: Greenaway, F.

929. 1981-134/11: Three-pin electrical plug made of white urea-formaldehyde, oval, with three raised ridges on front, moulded in two parts, c.1930. Back inscribed with: 'E' (earth), 'L' and: 'N'; '15AMP 250V/ No. 6051/ TW/ EMPIRE/ MADE'. 'TW' is contained within a shield and is a trade mark; the two letters are superimposed over each other.

Length 52 mm, width 50 mm, thickness 50 mm.
Source: Greenaway, F.

930. 1981-134/12: Three-pin electrical plug made of white urea-formaldehyde, roughly triangular, moulded in two parts, made by MULTI-KONTACT, mid-twentieth century. Front inscribed with a trade mark: 'MK' in circle. Back inscribed with: 'E' (earth), 'L' and: 'N'; also: '15A/B.S.546' in circle; 'MADE IN ENGLAND/ GRIP SCREWS'.

Length 57 mm, width 55 mm, thickness 53 mm.
Source: Greenaway, F.

931. 1981-134/16: Three-pin electrical plug made of white urea-formaldehyde, trilobate in form, moulded in two parts, c.1930. Front marked: 'MARBO' in diamond. Back inscribed with: 'E' (earth), 'L' and: 'N'; '5AMP/ MADE IN ENGLAND'.

Length 45 mm, width 40 mm, thickness 40 mm.
Source: Greenaway, F.

932. 1981-134/17: Three-pin electrical plug made of white urea-formaldehyde, roughly triangular, with three raised ridges on front, moulded in two parts, c.1930. Back inscribed with: 'E' (earth),

'L' and: 'N'; '15AMP. 250V/ Nᵒ 6310/EMPIRE'.

Length 54 mm, width 50 mm, thickness 46 mm.
Source: Greenaway, F.

933. 1981-134/22: Two-way electrical adaptor for three-pin plugs, made of white urea-formaldehyde, of irregular trilobate form, moulded in one piece, *c.*1930. One side has three inscriptions (moulded): 'Grelco', 'UK REG NO 802954/ MADE IN ENGLAND', 'MAX TOTAL LOAD 15 AMPS'.

Length 85 mm, width 70 mm, thickness 42 mm.
Source: Greenaway, F.

934. 1994-1078: Circular box of ivory urea-formaldehyde, lid moulded with 'Lisette' design showing young girl holding fan, and touching tree. Made by Editions Fornells, France, 1931.

Diameter 108 mm, height 52 mm.
Source: Gilbert Fornells Amat, M.

935. 1994-1079: Three billiard balls of urea-formaldehyde, two white (nos. 1 and 3) and one red (no. 2), in original cardboard box in imitation green crocodile. Made by Editions Fornells, France. Box lid inscribed: 'For.Match' in gold. Balls 1 and 2 inscribed: 'FORMATCH'.

Box: length 201 mm, width 74 mm, thickness 66 mm.
Balls nos. 1 and 2: diameter 61mm.
Ball no. 3: diameter 60.5 mm.
Source: Gilbert Fornells Amat, M.

936. 1994-1080: Replica seated Buddha of white urea-formaldehyde on black plastic base. Made from original 1934 mould by Fornells S.A., France, *c.*1992. Inscribed: 'fornells s.a. Paris' with trade mark of deer's head.

Length 83 mm, width 68 mm, height 90 mm.
Source: Gilbert Fornells Amat, M.

POLYVINYL CHLORIDE (PVC)

937. 1979-624/200: Boxed set of four PVC white 'cocktail mats' in imitation linen with moulded stitching forming red edging and black and red design. Cardboard box has cellophane lid. Made by Hedwin, *c.*1950. Inscription printed on box lid: 'NEW PLASTIC/ Cocktail mats/BY/HEDWIN/.4 original designs/. alcohol proof'. 'HEDWIN' is enclosed in grey scroll forming cross-bar of 'H' – trade mark. Rest of inscription in grey letters.

Length 230 mm, width 150 mm, thickness 13 mm.
Pt. 1: White cardboard rectangular box with clear cellophane lid.
Length 230 mm, width 150 mm, thickness 13 mm.
Pts 2–5: Four identical cream mats with red edging and black and red swirling design.
Length 220 mm, width 142 mm, thickness 1 mm.
Source: Jesse, J.

POLYETHYLENE (PE)

938. 1962-103: Specimen of polyethylene in form of curved rod, produced at the Wallerscote Pilot Plant of Imperial Chemical Industries Ltd, England, 22 December 1938.

Length 67 mm, diameter 12.5 mm.
Science Museum Negative No.: 1336/77.
Source: Freeth, F.A.
Plate 16

939. 1962-143: Walking stick made of cream-coloured polyethylene produced in the Wallerscote Pilot Plant of Imperial Chemical Industries Ltd, December, England, 1938.

Length 840 mm, width 102 mm, diameter 16 mm.
Science Museum Negative No: 1337/77.
Source: Cocksedge, E.N.
Figure 42

940–945. 1977-273: Collection of samples illustrating uses of low-density polyethylene, made by Imperial Chemical Industries Ltd, second half of the twentieth century.

Source: ICI (Plastics Division).

940. 1977-273/1: 1.47" diameter submarine telegraph cable. Triangular label stuck to cable marked: 'ICI/MADE FROM "ALKATHENE"/ AN ICI

PLASTIC'. Mid-twentieth century. 'ICI' is a trade mark contained within circle and surmounting two wavy lines. Second inscription on metal plaque affixed to side of base: 'B.P.O. 1.470/0 .368/ LIGHTWEIGHT SUBMARINE CABLE'.

Height 160 mm, diameter 82 mm.
Plate 16

941. 1977-273/2: Roll of polyethylene film, mid-twentieth century.

Length 301 mm, diameter 82 mm.

942. 1977-273/3: Squeezy bottle for DUFIX glue made of polyethylene, with red cap. Cracked at base. Mid-twentieth century. Front marked in purple writing: 'ICI/ DUFIX/ adhesive/ FOR THE HOME/ AND HANDYMAN/ strong • clean • dries clear'. 'ICI' is trade mark. Base stamped: 'REG DES: No2/ 931148', '2' inverted. Instructions for use on back.

Height 108 mm, width 62 mm, thickness 24 mm.

943. 1977-273/4: Blue book of colour master batches for ICI Alkathene film containing twelve samples, marked: 'ICI/ "ALKATHENE"/ COLOUR/ MASTERBATCHES/ FOR FILM/ IMPERIAL CHEMICAL INDUSTRIES LIMITED/ PLASTICS DIVISION • WELWYN GARDEN CITY • HERTFORDSHIRE'. 'ICI' is a trade mark in circle surmounting two wavy lines. Mid-twentieth century.

Film: maximum dimensions: length 210 mm, width 150 mm, thickness of paper.

944. 1977-273/5: Polyethylene granules, white. Mid-twentieth century.

Granule: diameter 5 mm.

945. 1977-273/6: Two master batch collections of coloured polyethylene, mid-twentieth century.

Pt. 1: Seventeen samples marked: 'Alkathene ICI'. Length 75 mm, width 50 mm, thickness 3 mm.
Pt. 2: Twenty samples in three graduated steps of thickness, marked: 'ALKATHENE ICI'. 'ICI' is a trade mark. Mid-twentieth century.

Length 56 mm, width 39 mm, thickness 3 mm, 2 mm and 1 mm.
Plate 16

946. 1977-622: Specimen of polyethylene made at Wallerscote Works of ICI on 22 December 1938. Labelled as part of the 1016th kg to be produced.

Length 40 mm, diameter 7 mm.
Source: Allberry, E.C.

947. 1979-304: Piece of early polyethylene, in form of rod (pierced at one end), c.1939.

Length 335 mm, diameter 18.5 mm.
Source: Walton, A.

948. 1979-624/120: Polyethylene handcream bottle squeezey, in form of pale green hand with black top, stamped 'Linc-o-lin' with instructions, made by Lincoln hair products Limited, London, England. Mid-twentieth century. Inscription on lower side: 'LINC-O-LIN/HAND CREAM/VERY HIGHLY CONCENTRATED HAND CREAM./USE LITTLE & OFTEN. IMMEDIATELY/BEAUTIFIES CHAPPED & WORK WORN HANDS./LINCOLN HAIR PRODUCTS LIMITED/LONDON, W.3.'. 'LINC-O-LIN' is a trade mark with ornate 'L's. Second trade mark near top edge: 'HOLCON'.

Length 103 mm, width 37 mm, thickness 18 mm.
Source: Jesse, J.

949. 1979-624/261: Night light of polyethylene, green base and white shade. Battery driven. Made in the USA, c.1940s. Inscription moulded on lower edge: 'MADE IN U.S.A'.

Length 144 mm, width 78 mm, height 325 mm.
Source: Jesse, J.

950. 1980-676/248: Square picnic cup and saucer of pale green polyethylene, 1940s.

Cup: length 90 mm, width 77 mm, height 55 mm.
Saucer: length 125 mm, width 121 mm, height 10 mm.
Source: Newport, R.
Plate 16

951. 1980-676/249: Square picnic cup and saucer of pale green polyethylene, 1940s.

Cup: length 90 mm, width 77 mm, height 55 mm.
Saucer: length 125 mm, width 121 mm, height 10 mm.
Source: Newport, R

952. 1980-676/250: Beaker of light bottle-green polyethylene, made by Twinco 'Table Talk', made in England, 1940s. Inscription moulded on base: 'Twinco Table Talk/MADE IN ENGLAND'; first line in slanting script.

Diameter 75 mm, height 95 mm.
Source: Newport, R.
Plate 16

953. 1980-676/251: Torch in shape of dog of red polyethylene, made by Ever Ready, in Britain, 1950s. Incomplete (bulb missing). Inscription moulded on rear end: 'EVER READY/MADE IN BRITAIN'.

Length 95 mm, width 23 mm, height 27 mm.
Source: Newport, R.
Plate 16

954. 1980-676/283: Spray of polyethylene flowers, yellow, white and pink, backed by fern. Mounted on white cardboard, *c.*1950.

Length 63 mm, width 68 mm, thickness 8 mm.
Source: Newport, R.

955. 1985-220: Two sandwich boxes with blue bases and white lids, made by Tupperware. Second half of the twentieth century.

Length 128 mm, width 115 mm, height 92 mm.
Source: Tupperware International.
Plate 16

956. 1985-562: 'Polythene-Film Store-Pak' in printed regenerated cellulose paper-backed wallet, early 1950s. Wallet now split. Pack marked: '"Store-Pak" The New Wonder American-Style "Polythene-Film" ALL PURPOSE STORAGE BAG/[six lines]/Essential Protection Against /INSECTS/DAMP/DUST/ 7'6ᴰ EACH/ A YANKY PACK PRODUCT'.

Length 205 mm, width 185 mm, thickness 9 mm.
Source: Goldong, N.

957. 1985-1565: Yellow 'Jif' lemon with green top. Lemon blow moulded in polyethylene December 1955, made by Cascelloid (now BXL Cascelloid Division). Inscribed: 'Jif/REAL/LEMON JUICE' and: 'PRESERVATIVE SULPHUR DIOXIDE/ CONTENTS 2.FL.OZ/ FOREIGN PRODUCT'. Label around neck reads: 'RECKITT & COLMAN LTD. NORWICH', 'Jif' and: 'PRICE 1ˈ- EACH'.

Length 79 mm, diameter 47 mm.
Source: BXL Cascelloid Division.
Plate 16

958. 1985-1566: 'Chocolate Whirl' proprietary blow moulded polyethylene bottle, in creamy white, March 1957, made by Cascelloid (now BXL Cascelloid Division). Inscribed on base: 'GAS' contained within a circle.

Diameter 50 mm, height 93 mm.
Source: BXL Cascelloid Division.
Plate 16

959. 1985-1567: Atkinson's talcum powder blow moulded yellow polyethylene bottle, *c.*1951, made by Cascelloid (now BXL Cascelloid Division). Inscribed on both sides: 'ATKINSONS/ PUFF-PUFF/...NDER/ TALCUM POWDER'. Floral decoration above and below. On one side inscription is red, on the other green.

Height 140 mm, width 50 mm, depth 45 mm.
Source: BXL Cascelloid Division.

960. 1985-1568: 'Squezy' bottle with two metal ends, the first squeeze-to-use detergent pack, 1958, made by Cascelloid (now BXL Cascelloid Division). Inscribed with various advertising logos including: 'Made by DOMESTOS Ltd'.

Height 155 mm, diameter 68 mm.
Source: BXL Cascelloid Division.
Plate 16

961. 1985-1569: Vinolia 'Baby Powder' Bear, blow moulded in blue polyethylene with white cap, second British blow

moulded bottle, 1950, made by
Cascelloid (now BXL Cascelloid
Division). Inscribed:
'Vinolia/BABY/POWDER'.

Height 140 mm, width 67 mm, depth 62 mm.
Source: BXL Cascelloid Division.
Plate 16

962. 1985-1670: Reel of gel-spun
Dyneema shiny white polyethylene fibre.
Inscription typed on label: 'DYNEEMA/
04.093,03 - 325/ 216', mid-twentieth
century.

Length 283.5 mm, diameter 61 mm.
Source: DSM Marketing Centre.

963. 1995-85: Triangular medallion made
from the first ton of polyethylene
produced at ICI, Wallerscote, in
December 1938. Medallion marked:
'DEC.1938 WALLERSCOTE', attached
to metal clip marked: 'FB' (Frank
Bebbington).

Length 52 mm, width 37 mm, thickness 17 mm.
Source: Bebbington, F.
Plate 16

964. 1995-86: Pill box made from the first
pound of polyethylene in 1936 at ICI,
Research Department. Presented to Mr
Frank Bebbington, one of the research
team. Lid decorated with upright lion
holding ICI logo.

Diameter 18 mm, height 12 mm.
Source: Bebbington, F.
Plate 16

POLYETHYLENE MACHINERY

965. 1977-259: Michels's mercury-sealed,
high-pressure ethylene compressor.
Designed in 1936 at Amsterdam
University under the direction of Dr A.
Michels at the request of ICI (Alkali) Ltd.

Length 1320 mm, width 920 mm, height 1730 mm.
Science Museum Negative No.: 355/78, 356/78.
Source: ICI (Plastics Division).

966. 1977-260: 9-litre reaction vessel, on
trolley, in which the first ton of
polyethylene had been produced by

December 1938. Sectioned. Designed in
1936 by W.R.D. Manning and S.G.
Marshall of ICI (Alkali) Ltd, Northwich
(see cat. nos. 963 and 967).

Length 1360 mm, width 950 mm, height 2660 mm.
Source: ICI (Plastics Division).
Figure 41

967. 1977-451: No. 2, 9-litre steel reaction
vessel for polyethylene
manufacture. Together with the no. 1
vessel (1977-260: cat. no. 966) it produced
the first ton of polyethylene during
1937–38 at ICI (incomplete and without
trolley or stirrer motor). One coil
broken. Stamped: 'HECLA 135'.

Length 1090 mm, width 415 mm, height 420 mm.
Source: ICI (Plastics Division).

968. 1983-1288: Ethylene compressor
from first full-scale polyethylene plant at
ICI Wallerscote, with sectioned valve and
five dials, c.1939.

Length 2400 mm, width 1320 mm, height
  2450 mm.
Source: ICI (Petrochemicals and Plastics Division).

969. 1991-379: High-pressure intensifier
pump for the manufacture of low-density
polyethylene. In operation at
Grangemouth, December
1957–December 1989.

Length 6960 mm, width 1200 mm, height
  1080 mm.
Source: BP Chemicals Ltd.

POLYMETHYL METHACRYLATE (PMMA, ACRYLIC)

970. 1974-571: Sample of Walkerite
(polymethyl methacrylate) plastic, used
in making dentures, c.1935. Salmon-pink
and now broken into more than 23 pieces;
with original cellophane wrapping and in
original maroon box. Box inscribed:
'THE NEW WALKERITE/ Reg. No.
482203/ Supersedes all other forms of
Walkerite/ Manufactured and supplied
under licence from/ H.M. Govt. dept. of
Scientific and Industrial Research by/
THE DENTAL MFG. Co. Ltd.,

LONDON, W.1., ENGLAND'.
Inscription inside box: '*IMPORTANT*/
keep in a dry place and do not touch/
WALKERITE with wet fingers or water/
THIS MATERIAL MUST BE USED
NOT LATER THAN / 12 APR 1940'.
Penultimate line in red and last line date-
stamped.

Box: length 132 mm, width 75 mm, depth 20 mm.
Walkerite: largest piece: length 63 mm, width 34 mm,
  thickness 3.5mm.
Source: British Dental Association Museum.

971. 1975-116: Four samples of ICI
'Diakon' master-batch acrylic plastic.

Pt. 1: Pearlescent. Marked: '"DIAKON" ACRYLIC/
  PEARLESCENT/ MASTERBATCH N./ICI'. ICI is
  trade mark surmounting two wavy lines, within a
  circle.
Length 62 mm, width 35 mm, thickness 4 mm,
  height 6 mm.
Pt. 2: Amber 304. Marked: '"DIAKON" ACRYLIC/
  AMBER 304/ ICI'. 'ICI' is trade mark surmounting
  two wavy lines, within a circle.
Length 62 mm, width 35 mm, thickness 4 mm,
  height 6 mm.
Pt. 3: Blue 710. Marked: '"DIAKON" ACRYLIC/
  BLUE 710/ ICI'. 'ICI' is trade mark surmounting two
  wavy lines, within a circle.
Length 62 mm, width 35 mm, thickness 4 mm,
  height 6 mm.
Pt. 4: Blue 755. Marked: '"DIAKON" ACRYLIC/
  BLUE 55/ ICI'. 'ICI' is trade mark surmounting
  two wavy lines, within a circle.
Length 62 mm, width 35 mm, thickness 4 mm,
  height 6 mm.
Source: Imperial Chemical Industries Ltd.

972. 1979-624/15: Pair of pink and black
acrylic candlesticks, with black circular
base, semi-circular stem; candle holder in
form of a flower. 1946.

Height 108 mm, width 75 mm, thickness 73 mm.
Source: Jesse, J.

973–974. 1979-624/40 Pts 1 and 2: Two
circular pink acrylic boxes with three
black rectangular flat feet, lid has chrome
finial resting on black circular plinth, late
1940s (set with cat. no. 975).

Diameter 71 mm, height 50 mm.
Source: Jesse, J.
Plate 17 (Pt. 1)

975. 1979-624/41: Rectangular cigarette
box of pink acrylic, with black, square,
flat feet and trim at the corners, with
chrome finial resting on black rectangular
plinth on lid, late 1940s (set with cat. nos.
973–974).

Length 140 mm, width 89 mm, height 57 mm.
Source: Jesse, J.
Plate 17

976. 1979-624/75: Model shoe of
transparent pale pink acrylic flecked with
gold glitter, moulded, *c.*1950.

Length 79 mm, width 26 mm, thickness 58 mm.
Source: Jesse, J.

977. 1979-624/86: Square ashtray of
marble-effect orange/yellow acrylic, with
transparent acrylic bowl supported by
maroon cast phenolic cigarette rests, with
brass feet. Made in France, second half of
twentieth century. Inscription in centre of
one edge: 'DÉPOSÉ'.

Length 109 mm, width 109 mm, height 28 mm.
Source: Jesse, J.

978. 1979-624/116: Acrylic ashtray of
roughly apsidal form, with black base and
pink border, with two cigarette rests, one
on each side, art deco design, 1940s.
Cover missing from one of fixing screws
on base.

Length 190 mm, height 27 mm, width 100 mm.
Source: Jesse, J.

979. 1979-624/156: Dress clip made of
two cylinders of cracked transparent
acrylic? or possibly cellulose acetate,
interspersed with two cylinders of black
phenolic. Metal clip. 1940s.

Length 44 mm, width 25 mm, height 16 mm.
Source: Jesse, J.
Plate 17

980. 1979-624/190: Eau-de-nil green
Champion 'Venus' acrylic four-valve
radio, in the form of a globe supported on
four twisted transparent acrylic arms and
square base, made by the Champion
Electric Corporation Ltd, 1947. Marked:
'VENUS'.

Diameter 238 mm, height 267 mm.

Source: Jesse, J.
Plate 17

981. 1979-624/194: Pair of pepper pots made of four square slabs of transparent acrylic, surrounding a chromed column which is stained blue, 1940s.

Length 60 mm, width 38 mm, breadth 38mm
Source: Jesse, J.
Plate 17

982. 1979-624/196: Large transparent acrylic fruit bowl, oval in shape with four curlicue legs and twisted handle, *c.*1950.

Length 485 mm, width 290 mm, height 225 mm.
Source: Jesse, J.
Plate 17

983. 1979-624/204: Oval ice bucket of transparent red acrylic, faceted sides, strip handle attached to black vertical strips down either side, pink rose glued to lid. Inscription inside rose: 'RO. NO/789391', *c.*1950.

Length 164 mm, width 126 mm, height 130 mm.
Source: Jesse, J.

984. 1979-624/207: Circular powder compact in clear acrylic; lid faceted with hexagonal design, made by Hampden. Mid-twentieth century. Inscription on outside of puff: 'hampden' in cursive script inlaid with gold.

Diameter 102 mm, thickness 23 mm.
Source: Jesse, J.
Plate 17

985. 1979-624/210: Circular fluted box, scalloped lid in clear acrylic, injection moulded. Lid has raised cylinder in centre as handle. Mid-twentieth century; bought in Australia in 1976.

Diameter 120 mm, height 120 mm.
Source: Jesse, J.

986. 1979-624/215: Pink acrylic box with flap on top on a fly-away piece of curved clear transparent acrylic, *c.*1950.

Length 160 mm, width 63 mm, height 85 mm.
Source: Jesse, J.

987. 1979-624/219: Rectangular box of transparent acrylic, inner surfaces painted with black lacquer surrounding leaves and roses carved in the transparent acrylic, circular handle, 1940s. Lacquer slightly chipped.

Length 165 mm, width 90 mm, depth 43 mm.
Source: Jesse, J.

988. 1979-624/240: Photograph holder of acrylic, cream and black stripes around frame, black rectangular base, 1940s.

Length 185 mm, width 152 mm, depth 50 mm.
Source: Jesse, J.
Plate 17

989–995. 1979-624/244: Pink and green acrylic table set comprising three rectangular boxes, three candlesticks and a tray, 1940s.

Source: Jesse, J.

989. 1979-624/244 Pt. 1: Candlestick with flat green base, striped pink, green and clear column, square in cross-section, surmounted by flat green disc, topped by four-sided pink and green candle holder. 1940s.

Length 68 mm, width 67 mm, height 145 mm.
Source: Jesse, J.
Plate 17

990. 1979-624/244 Pt. 2: Candlestick with flat green base, striped pink, green and clear column, square in cross-section, surmounted by flat green disc, topped by four-sided pink and green candle holder. 1940s.

Length 68 mm, width 67 mm, height 150 mm.
Source: Jesse, J.

991. 1979-624/244 Pt. 3: Candlestick with flat green base, striped pink, green and clear column, square in cross-section, surmounted by flat green disc, topped by four-sided pink and green candle holder. 1940s.

Length 63 mm, width 63 mm, height 145 mm.
Source: Jesse, J.
Plate 17

992. 1979-624/244 Pt. 4: Triangular green tray, rounded corners; feet are laminated pink and green; rim consists of four transparent acrylic strips supported each on two pink and green laminated rectangles. 1940s.

Length 320 mm, width 187 mm, height 20 mm.
Source: Jesse, J.

993. 1979-624/244 Pt. 5: Rectangular box with green lid and base, sides transparent acrylic with white criss-cross pattern painted on them; wedge-shaped handle is striped pink, green and clear, four square flat feet. 1940s.

Length 120 mm, width 68 mm, height 60 mm.
Source: Jesse, J.
Plate 17

994–995. 1979-624/244 Pts 6–7: Two acrylic boxes, same form as cat. no. 993. 1940s.

Length 88 mm, width 68 mm, height 60 mm.
Source: Jesse, J.

996. 1979-624/250: Rectangular cigarette box of pink acrylic with transparent acrylic edges, flip-top lid, late 1940s.

Length 94 mm, width 84 mm, depth 18 mm.
Source: Jesse, J.

997. 1979-624/251: Table lighter of pink and clear acrylic, in form of four rectangular slices, two pink, two clear, arranged in steps (Ziggurat), art deco design, surrounding chrome column, topped by square lid containing lighter, late 1940s.

Length 121 mm, width 38 mm, height 67 mm.
Source: Jesse, J.
Plate 17

998. 1979-624/257: Model giraffe, of transparent yellow acrylic?, possibly polyester, flecked with silver glitter, moulded, *c*.1950.

Length 49 mm, width 37 mm, height 116 mm.
Source: Jesse, J.

999. 1979-624/268: Electric, lemon-yellow acrylic clock with clear transparent acrylic face, gently curved in reverse S-bend, with phenolic back. Made by Clyde. Trade mark moulded on upper part of back: 'Clyde' in flowing, forward-slanting script. Inscription moulded on lower part of back: '200–250V./A.C./50

CYCLES/MADE IN SCOTLAND'. Scale moulded on face: '(1) 12' hours marked as black strokes, apart from '3', '6', '9' and '12', which are on circular white discs and painted in black. Fourth inscription moulded in middle, round switch 1: 'STARTER/TURN' curves round top of starter switch; arrow curves around to left, under switch. Fifth inscription moulded around middle, round switch 2: 'HAND SET' curves round top of hand-set switch; arrow curves around to left, under switch.

Length 297 mm, width 75 mm, height 179 mm.
Source: Jesse, J.

1000. 1980-676/269: Moulded bon-bon tray of acrylic, green square base with wavy edges, rounded corners and two roughly triangular indentations for bon-bons, twisted transparent acrylic handle, arranged diagonally across, 1940s.

Length 137 mm, width 136 mm, height 90 mm.
Source: Newport, R.
Plate 17

1001. 1980-676/270: Oil-filled television magnifier, transparent acrylic with glycerine infill and two PVC hanging straps, one on each top corner. Lens painted black on top and bottom surface.

Length 510 mm, width 290 mm, height 100 mm.
Source: Newport, R.

1002. 1980-676/271: Circular box of acrylic, made by Wilmot Breedon as a souvenir of the Coronation of Elizabeth II, 1953, made in England. Inscription moulded on base: 'DESIGNED AND PRODUCED BY WILMOT BREEDON LTD BIRMINGHAM ENGLAND/WB'; first line encircles base circumference, second line within square, 'W' superimposed on animal, possibly a cat. Monogram moulded on lid: 'HON SOIT QUI MAL Y NSE/DIEU ET MON DROIT/1953'; royal coat of arms, gold on red background; first line should read 'HONI' and 'PENSE'.

Diameter 80 mm, height 48 mm.
Source: Newport, R.

1003. 1984-249/1: Circular transparent acrylic window from Constellation aircraft, in hard rubber frame, pierced for screws, *c.*1947. Made by Lockheed in England.

Diameter 227 mm, thickness 7 mm.
Source: Aces High Ltd.

1004. 1984-249/2: Circular transparent acrylic window with cogged edges from Constellation aircraft, *c.*1947. Made by Lockheed in England.

Diameter 412 mm, thickness 10 mm.
Source: Aces High Ltd.

1005. 1989-117: Fourteen kitchen units constructed in steel and green acrylic with integrated sink, gas refrigerator and oven, by Weldall & Assembly Ltd, Birmingham, England, 1950.

Pt. 1: Length 3860 mm, width 565 mm, height 91 mm.
Pt. 2: Length 1720 mm, width 700 mm, height 825 mm.
Source: Halstead, G.

POLYMETHYL METHACRYLATE MACHINERY

1006. 1974-572: Walkerite oven, *c.*1930, made by Chas Hearson and Co. Ltd, London. Inscription on metal plaque on front of oven: 'WALKERITE OVEN/ MADE BY/ CHAS. HEARSON & C⁰ Lᵀᴰ/ - FOR -/ THE DENTAL MANUFACTURING C⁰ Lᵀᴰ/ LONDON'. Second plaque inscribed: '204 VOLTS .6 AMPS'. Third plaque below oven door inscribed: 'HEARSON'S/ PATENT ELECTRIC DRYING OVEN/ PAT. No. 27909/09'.

Length 475 mm, width 390 mm, height 685 mm.
Science Museum Negative No.: 82/76 A.
Source: British Dental Association Museum.

NYLON (PA, POLYAMIDE)

1007. 1965-480: Sample of first nylon knitted tubing. Knitted July 1935 from polyamide made from pentamethylenediamine and sebacic acid. Made by Du Pont Nemours Ltd, USA.

Length 118 mm, width 110 mm, thickness 2 mm.
Source: Du Pont de Nemours and Co.
Figure 43

1008. 1994-357: Sample of early British nylon (polyamide), resembling white cotton wool, made by British Nylon Spinners, 1951.

Length 85 mm, width 72 mm, thickness *c.*10 mm.
Source: Morris, P.

TERYLENE (PETP, POLYETHYLENE TEREPHTHALATE)

1009. 1953-33: Three spools of polyethylene terephthalate filaments produced at the Chemical Research Laboratory, Teddington (D.S.I.R) in 1943–44.

Pt. 1: Wooden reel with gold thread. Marked: 'CHEMICAL RESEARCH LABORATORY/ POLY-ETHYLENE TEREPHTHALATE/ FILAMENT (A)/Ref.No._Date_/ TEDDINGTON, MIDDLESEX'. Diameter 100 mm, height 64mm.
Pt. 2: Wooden reel with pale gold thread. Marked: 'CHEMICAL RESEARCH LABORATORY/ POLY-ETHYLENE TEREPHTHALATE/ FILAMENT (B) I.V., 0.24 /Ref.No._Date_/ TEDDINGTON, MIDDLESEX'. Diameter 98 mm, height 64mm.
Pt. 3: Wooden reel with ivory thread. Marked: 'CHEMICAL RESEARCH LABORATORY/ POLY-ETHYLENE TEREPHTHALATE/ FILAMENT (A) I.V., 0.245 /Ref.No._Date_/ TEDDINGTON, MIDDLESEX'. Diameter 100 mm, height 64 mm.
Source: DSIR.
Figure 45

1010. 1973-494: Collection of terylene fibres, seven specimens.

Pt. 1: Terylene in form of white thread on grey bobbin. Label: 'ICI/TERYLENE/167 dtex/ f30 S/TYPE 500/MERGE/11/ MADE IN UK'. 'ICI' is trade mark, with 'ICI' over two wavy lines and all contained within a circle.
Length 370 mm, diameter 95 mm.

Pt. 2: Terylene in form of white thread on grey
 bobbin. Label: 'ICI/TERYLENE/135-44Z/
 MERGE/04/ glänzend/trilobal'. 'ICI' is trade mark,
 with 'ICI' over two wavy lines and all contained
 within a circle.
Length 370 mm, diameter 105 mm.

Pt. 3: Terylene in form of white thread on blue
 spool. Handwritten label: 'Terylene/ 167f 30S
 /Type 500 (dull)/ (circular x-sect)'.
Length 230 mm, diameter 82 mm.

Pt. 4: Terylene in form of white thread on blue
 spool. Handwritten label: 'Terylene/ 150f 44Z
 /(bright)/ (trilobal x-sect)'.
Length 230 mm, diameter 82 mm.

Pt. 5: Crimplene, in form of white thread on blue
 spool. Handwritten label: 'Terylene/167f 30/
 circular/ dull/ False-twist bulked/ "CRIMPLENE"'.
Length 230 mm, diameter 82 mm.

Pt. 6: Crimplene, in form of white thread on blue
 spool. Handwritten label: 'Terylene/150f 44/bright/
 trilobal/ False-twist bulked'.
Length 230 mm, diameter 82 mm.

Pt. 7: Crimplene, in form of white thread on blue
 spool. Handwritten label: 'Terylene/150f 44/bright/
 trilobal/knit/de-knit/bulked'.
Length 230 mm, diameter 82 mm.
Source: ICI Fibres Ltd.

1011. 1977-285: First sample of 100 per
cent spun Terylene yarn, produced at the
Shirley Institute, *c.*1949. White thread on
brown spindle.

Length 262 mm, diameter 42 mm.
Source: ICI Ltd (Fibres Division).

GLASS-FIBRE-REINFORCED PLASTIC (GRP)

1012. 1983-1098: Early glass-fibre-
reinforced plastic model boat. Number
15 15 male moulding using 0.005 inch
fine weave glass cloth and Marco Resin
21C cured with 2 per cent benzoyl
peroxide and dimethyl aniline accelerator
at room temperature. Cloth laid on in
strips, 1950. Made by the Scott Bader
Company, England.

Length *c.*360 mm, width *c.*100 mm, height *c.*80 mm.
Source: Scott Bader Company.

1013. 1983-1104: Early glass-fibre-
reinforced plastic model boat. Male
moulding using fibreglass diamond mat

and Marco Resin 28C cured with 2 per
cent cyclohexanone peroxide and cobalt
naphthenate, sanded smooth, 1951, with
original wooden mould. Made by the
Scott Bader Company, England.

Pt. 1: Boat: length 662 mm, width 201 mm, height
 90 mm.
Pt. 2: Mould: length 642 mm, width 152 mm, height
 82 mm.
Source: Scott Bader Company.

POLYSTYRENE (PS)

1014. 1979-624/30: Novelty cigarette box,
roll top of cream polystyrene and mock
leather (PVC) sides. Roll top moves back
to reveal five cigarette holders. Box base
inscribed: 'A/ Rolinx/ PRODUCT/
MADE IN ENGLAND/ BRIT PAT.
NOS 593961 & 642536/ U.S. PATENT
18/4/52/OTHER FOREIGN PATS.
APP. FOR'. 1950s. Under roll top is a
coat of arms on the front of the box
marked: 'S.S. STRATNAVER'.

Length 145 mm, width 84 mm, thickness 61mm;
 length (extended) 224 mm.
Source: Jesse, J.

1015. 1979-624/35: Rectangular cigarette
box of polystyrene, black base, ivory lid
moulded with design of two running
stags, English, 1940s. Inscription
moulded on base: 'MADE IN
ENGLAND'.

Length 125 mm, width 90 mm, height 56 mm.
Source: Jesse, J.

1016. 1979-624/159: Brooch of pearlised
pink polystyrene in form of a woman's
head, with red flower in hair and red lips
painted on, *c.*1945.

Length 66 mm, width 35 mm, height 12 mm.
Source: Jesse, J.
Figure 47

1017. 1979-624/180: Set of white
polystyrene cutlery containing knife,
fork, spoon, *c.*1950.

Pt. 1: White plastic knife with serrated blade. Trade
 mark moulded on end of handle of knife: 'Twinco'.
Length 183 mm, width 15 mm, thickness 4 mm.

Pt. 2: White plastic fork. Trade mark moulded on back
  of handle of fork: 'Twinco 12', '12' at right angle to
  'Twinco'.
Length 170 mm, width 21 mm, thickness 4 mm.
Pt. 3: White plastic spoon. Inscription moulded on back
  of handle: 'J PM. TS.48'
Length 125 mm, width 28 mm, thickness 9 mm.
Source: Jesse, J.

1018. 1979-624/188: Rectangular cigarette
box of polystyrene, black base, ivory lid
moulded with design of three-masted
galleon on sea, English, 1940s. Inscription
moulded on base: 'MADE IN
ENGLAND'.

Length 124 mm, width 90 mm, height 54 mm.
Source: Jesse, J.

1019. 1979-624/213: Rectangular box in
Chinese style, green marble-effect
polystyrene with black base, lid
surmounted by exotic bird, and decorated
with four dragons. Probably 1940s.

Length 209 mm, width 108 mm, height 110 mm.
Source: Jesse, J.

1020. 1979-624/229: Rectangular box
with convex ends, made of walnut-effect
polystyrene, lid decorated with moulded
design of the forequarters of running
deer, and a tree, USA, 1940s. Monogram
moulded inside lid: '.../HICKOK';
'HICKOK' surmounted by coat of arms
consisting of bird's head (cock?) on top of
shield on which knight's helmet and
plume are separated by a diagonal line.
Second inscription moulded on base:
'MADE IN/U.S.A.'. Small chip on corner
of base.

Length 115 mm, width 80 mm, height 48 mm.
Source: Jesse, J.

1021. 1979-624/230: Square box of
burgundy polystyrene, lid open-work
decoration showing Greek warrior
holding spear and shield with hound,
made by Hickok, USA, *c.*1930. Trade
mark on inner centre of base:
'HICKOK'. Above the inscription is coat
of arms split in half showing helmet and
feather, surmounted by bird's head.

Length 96 mm, width 96 mm, height 43 mm.
Source: Jesse, J.

1022. 1980-676/252: Apple-green
moulded polystyrene egg cup, petal-
shaped rim, moulded in two halves,
1950s.

Height 48 mm, diameter 48 mm.
Source: Newport, R.

1023–1026. 1980-676/253–6: Four
circular cups of pale blue and clear
marble-effect polystyrene, waved profile,
curved handle with flat top, part of toy
coffee set, made in England by Projects,
mid-twentieth century. Inscription
moulded on base: 'PROJECTS/MADE
IN ENGLAND'; arranged around
circumference of base.

Diameter 73 mm, width 88 mm, height 45 mm.
Source: Newport, R.
Plate 18 (cat. nos. 1024, 1026)

1027–1030. 1980-676/257–60: Four
circular saucers of pale blue and clear
marble-effect polystyrene, waved profile,
part of toy coffee set, made in England by
Projects, mid-twentieth century.
Inscription moulded around base
circumference: 'PROJECTS/MADE IN
ENGLAND'.

Diameter 101 mm, height 12 mm.
Source: Newport, R.
Plate 18 (cat. nos. 1028, 1030)

1031–1034. 1980-676/261-4: Four circular
plates of pale blue and clear marble-effect
polystyrene, waved profile, part of toy
coffee set, made by Projects, mid-
twentieth century. 1980-676/261 chipped
along edge. Inscription moulded around
circumference of base:
'PROJECTS/MADE IN ENGLAND'.

Diameter 129 mm, height 12 mm.
Source: Newport, R.
Plate 18 (cat. nos. 1032, 1034)

1035. 1980-676/265: Circular milk jug
with spout, of pale blue and clear marble-
effect polystyrene, waved profile, curved
handle with flat top, part of toy coffee
set, made in England by Projects, mid-
twentieth century. Inscription moulded
on base: 'PROJECTS/MADE IN

ENGLAND'; arranged around circumference of base.

Diameter 76 mm, width 13 mm, height 58 mm.
Source: Newport, R.
Plate 18

1036. 1980-676/266: Circular sugar bowl, of pale blue and clear marble-effect polystyrene, waved profile, two stepped lugs on opposite sides of rim, part of toy coffee set, made in England by Projects, mid-twentieth century. Inscription moulded on base: 'PROJECTS/MADE IN ENGLAND'; arranged around circumference of base.

Diameter 85 mm, width 100 mm, height 47 mm.
Source: Newport, R.
Plate 18

1037. 1980-676/267: Circular spouted coffee pot of pale blue and clear marble-effect polystyrene, waved profile, curved handle with flat stepped top, snap-on lid with handle, part of toy coffee set, mid-twentieth century, made in England by Projects. Inscription moulded around circumference of base: 'PROJECTS/ MADE IN ENGLAND'.

Diameter 84 mm, width 120 mm, height 120 mm.
Source: Newport, R.
Plate 18

1038. 1981-136: Twelve polystyrene samples of different colours formed into boxes. Pt. 1: red; Pt. 2: pale blue; Pt. 3: pale pink; Pt. 4: pale green; Pt. 5: pale yellow; Pt. 6: translucent green; Pt. 7: white; Pt. 8: translucent pink; Pt. 9: acid green; Pt. 10: pale pink; Pt. 11: translucent orange; Pt. 12: white. Mid-twentieth century.

Length 56 mm, width 65.5 mm, height 27 mm.
Source: BP Chemicals Ltd.
Plate 18

1039. 1981-582: Two bottles containing polystyrene beads and moulding powders from the first commercial dispersion polymerisation in the UK, 14–15

October 1950. In wooden holder.

Bottles: height 100 mm, diameter 50 mm.
Source: University of Birmingham (Department of Chemistry). Prof. R.N. Haward.

1040. 1992-675: Bottle of small polystyrene granules made by Monsanto Chemicals Ltd, 1956. Label on bottle inscribed: 'Polystyrene/ SAMPLE OF Lustrex G.P. Crystal/ No N56/3475 DATE 29.11.56...MONSANTO CHEMICALS LIMITED VICTORIA STATION HOUSE VICTORIA STREET/ LONDON SW1'.

Length 101 mm, diameter 51 mm.
Source: Science Museum.

DECORATIVE LAMINATES

1041. 1985-837: Three doors from the boardroom of the Tyseley Factory of Bakelite Ltd made from Warerite decorative laminate, 1936.

Pt. 1: Length 2035 mm, width 772 mm, depth 42 mm.
Pt. 2: Length 2043 mm, width 760 mm, depth 42 mm.
Pt. 3: Length 2040 mm, width 810 mm, depth 50 mm.
Source: Bakelite Ltd.

1042. 1985-1987: Formica decorative laminate: Fifteen samples, *c.*1960.

Pt. 1: Brown marked: 'Formica Grade GP1'.
Pt. 2: Cream speckled marked: 'Formica Grade MF3'.
Pt. 3: Brown tweed marked: 'Formica Grade A20'.
Pt. 4: Black tweed marked: 'Formica Grade A40'.
Pt. 5: Brown marked: 'Formica Grade P3'.
Pt. 6: Brown fabric marked: 'Formica Grade F3'.
Pt. 7: Brown marked: 'Formica Grade Px1.'
Pt. 8: Thick black marked: 'Formica NOVAPANEL'.
Pt. 9: Brown marked: 'Formica Grade PP3'.
Pt. 10: Black marked: 'Formica Grade BX1BLK'.
Pt. 11: Black marked: 'Formica Grade P1'.
Pt. 12: Cream speckled marked: 'Formica Grade MF1'.
Pt. 13: Black marked: 'Formica/ Industrial laminates/ SWITCHPANEL GRADE/ CS675N' (stamped in red).

Pt. 14: Brown marked: 'Formica Grade P1' (typed).
Pt. 15: Brown fabric marked: 'Formica Grade F1'.
Length 150 mm, width 97 mm, thickness 1 mm.
Source: Formica Corporation.

MISCELLANEOUS PLASTICS

1043. 1957-89: Exhibit illustrating the history, manufacture and applications of synthetic fibres, *c.* 1955.

Pt. 1: Gear pump for viscose manufacture; steel with transparent acrylic body.
Length 111 mm, width 74 mm, height 149 mm.
Pt. 2: Silkworm head model showing silk filament emerging from spinneret.
Length 111 mm, width 105 mm, height 95 mm.
Pt. 3: Panel entitled: 'OTHER FIBRES FROM NATURAL PRODUCTS' shows specimens of 'Fibrolane' staple fibre, fabric woven with 'Ardil' staple fibre, casein from milk, groundnuts, alginate fibres and triacetate.
Height 922 mm, width 334 mm, thickness 26 mm.
Pt. 4: Sectioned spinning box marked: 'COURTAULDS'.
Diameter 196 mm, height 324 mm.
Science Museum Negative No.: 902/57, 903/57, 904/57, 905/67, 125/67.
Source: The Man-made Fibres Producers' Committee and Imperial Chemical Industries Ltd.

1044. 1977-824: First three fusible interlinings manufactured on a commercial scale by Staflex (January 1951).

Length 195 mm, width 140 mm, thickness 1 mm.
Source: Staflex International Ltd.

1045. 1977-825: Three samples representing stages in the development of Staflex fusible interlinings.

Pt. 1: Sample of canvas with widely spaced printed dots, produced on a laboratory scale (see French patent no. 1,156,033, June 1956).
Length 137 mm, width 125 mm, thickness 0.2 mm.
Pt. 2: Sample of cotton printed with dots from an engraved roller, produced on a pilot scale, July 1959.
Length 150 mm, width 155 mm, thickness 0.2 mm.
Pt. 3: Sample of cotton-based cloth covered with plastic dots in the form of braille using, as an experiment, a perforated cylindrical screen made by the Royal National Institute for the Blind, *c.* November 1960.
Length 150 mm, width 155 mm, thickness 0.5 mm.
Source: Staflex International Ltd.

1046. 1977-826/1: Specimen of silicone rubber stereo for experimental printing of dots for fusible interlining, 1959.

Length 212 mm, width 64 mm, thickness 2 mm.
Source: Staflex International Ltd.

1047. 1977-826/2: Specimen of vulcanised fibre matrix used to cast cat. no. 1012.

Length 64 mm, width 50 mm, thickness 5 mm.
Source: Staflex International Ltd.

1048. 1979-624/21: Wooden photograph frame on swing base decorated with geometric design of black laquer and cream pearlised polyvinyl acetate, American, 1935.

Length 396 mm, width 78 mm, height 350 mm.
Source: Jesse, J.

1049. 1979-624/214: Blue rectangular box with silver moulded decoration and feet, Assyrian influence, of unknown composition, made by 'EBENA' in Belgium, 1920s. Inscription on base: 'MADE IN BELGIUM/EBENA', 'EBENA' contained within oval.

Length 164 mm, width 95 mm, height 78 mm.
Source: Jesse, J.

1050. 1979-624/288: Necklace of silvered plastic and metal, beads in form of two flat plastic discs enclosed by metal, belt-shaped plates on either side, two circular plastic beads at either end within semi-circular plates, art deco design, 1930s.

Length 450 mm, diameter 22 mm.
Source: Jesse, J.

1051. 1988-436: Pair of men's brown 'Koolon' shoes, size 6, made of Utrilon by UIM, England, with open-weave front top. *c.* 1950. Sole marked: 'Koolon', 'MADE/BY/U.I.M./PIL', 'MADE OF UTRILON', 'UTRILON PLASTIC' and: 'PAT. PEND.'.

Length 292 mm, width 106 mm, height 100 mm.
Source: Voller, G.C.

1052. 1991-425: Two early long-playing records in vinyl copolymer produced commercially in Britain from 1950.

Pt. 1: *Peter and the Wolf*, produced by DECCA, in original sleeve. Record marked: 'MADE IN ENGLAND/ DECCA, REG^D/ LONG PLAYING / UNBREAKABLE MICROGROOVE/ full frequency range recording'.
Record: diameter 250 mm, thickness 2 mm.
Sleeve: length 258 mm, width 258 mm, thickness 4 mm.

Pt. 2: *Burl Ives* in original sleeve. Produced by Brunswick. Sleeve marked: 'LONG-PLAYING FLEXIBLE MICROGROOVE RECORD'. Record marked: 'Brunswick LONG PLAYING / UNBREAKABLE MICROGROOVE RECORD / MADE IN ENGLAND'. Record stamped: 'CT', 'CA', and: 'MG 1246-B'.
Record: diameter 251 mm, thickness 2 mm.
Sleeve: length 254 mm, width 254 mm, thickness 4 mm.
Source: Bridger, L.W.

1053. 1992-674: Bottle of crystalline (?) polyvinyl acetate made by Hopkin and Williams Ltd. Mid-twentieth century.

Height 155 mm, diameter 57 mm.
Source: Science Museum.

GENERAL PLASTICS MACHINERY AND EQUIPMENT

1054. 1975-526: An NV-10-H injection moulding machine for plastics, *c.*1935, with instruction card. Inscription on front: 'THE/ NENE VALLEY/ NV/ TOOL CENTRE LTD' on raised circular plaque. Inscription on black phenolic switch: 'ON/ SANTON LTD/ OFF/ NEWPORT ENG/ ON'. Sticky label on front marked: 'SUPPLIED BY/ 600/ GEORGE COHEN SONS & CO. LTD/ + LONDON . LEEDS . ETC. +'. At end of ram: 'Z001 6(?)'. Stamped on back: 'NV-1-11/62'.

Length 1770 mm, width 480 mm, height 871 mm.
Science Museum Negative No.: 352/78.
Source: Gregory, R.H.

1055. 1979-105: Iddon transfer press, water hydraulic, steam heated plattens. Nominally 30-ton load, without pressure accumulator. Accumulated pressure pumps and valves, pressure pump and electric motor. With valves and control gear.

Pt. 1: Length 1670 mm, width 540 mm, height 900 mm.
Pt. 2: Length 700 mm, width 550 mm, height 1020 mm.
Source: Chemical Defence Establishment.

1056. 1985-370: Cylinder from PECO injection moulding machine, inscribed: 'HEDIN LTD 230/250V 1250W', 1950. Rear end inscribed: 'M12 FO83°' and: 'M12 FOO8A'. Rear end cover marked: 'PCO^S'.

Length 1450 mm, width 600 mm, height 630 mm.
Screw: Length 1190 mm, diameter 55 mm.
Source: Norsk Hydro Polymers Ltd.

1057. 1985-672: Hand-operated compression moulding machine dating from the 1920s.

Length 1460 mm, width 880 mm, height 1990 mm.
Source: London College of Polymer Technology.

1058. 1985-1557/1: Two original wooden 12-inch rulers for trying out the 'Netlon' concept on mashed potatoes, 1956; both serrated along middle of one edge.

Length 156 mm, width 27 mm, thickness 3.5 mm.
Source: Netlon Ltd.

1059. 1993-1562: Catgut tester with two scales (horizontal curved and vertical), one marked: '0.05 to 10LBS', with 0.05 gradations; the second marked: '0.2 to 50LBS' with 0.2 gradations. Two weights with attachment rings. Plaque on front inscribed: 'GOODBRAND & Co. LTD./ MAKERS/ STALYBRIDGE/ MADE IN ENGLAND'. Below this is an oval plaque marked: '3098'. Inscription on scale 1: 'REF. N° 6017B'. Inscription on scale 2: '10LBS × .05/ 50LBS × .2'.

Tester: Length 660 mm, width 485 mm, height 2 145 mm.
Weights: 1: length 230 mm, width 122 mm, height 155 mm.
2: length 213 mm, width 122 mm, height 155 mm.
Source: Science Museum.

Bibliography

Anon.
1936   An American's View of Plastics in England. *British Plastics and Moulded Products Trader* January: 364–5.
1945   *Plastics Catalogue*. New York: Plastics Catalogue Corporation.

Art and Industry
1938   *Art and Industry* 24 (Jan.–June).
1948a   *Art and Industry* 45 (September).
1948b   *Art and Industry* 45 (November).

Ashlee, P.C.
1982   Tusks and Tortoiseshell: The Early Development of the British Xylonite Industry. BA dissertation, University of Nottingham, April.

Baekeland, L.
1909   *Journal of Industrial Engineering Chemistry*. 1: 149.

Baker, W.J.
1970   *A History of the Marconi Company*. London: Methuen.

Barrett, J. (ed.)
1982   *Taking Shape 1*. Darwen: 'Perspex' Group of ICI Pharmaceuticals and Plastics Division.

Barron, H.
1938   Plastics are Stealing the Market *Art and Industry* 24: 140–3.

Barthes, R.
1989   *Mythologies*. London: Paladin. (original edn 1957).

Bayley, S. (ed.)
1985   *The Conran Dictionary of Design*. London: Octopus Conran.

Baynes, K. and Pugh, S.
1981   *The Art of the Engineer*. Guildford: Lutterworth Press.

Bennett, I.
1979   Plastics – Art and Antiques. *Plastics Today*. 2 : 14–17.

Bereano, P., Bose, C. and Arnold, E.
1985   Kitchen Technology and the Liberation of Women from Housework. In *Smothered by Invention*, W. Faulkner and E. Arnold, eds. London: Routledge, 162–81.

Bertram, A.
1938   *Design*. London: Pelican.

Birmingham Times
1854   *Birmingham Times* 2: 1.

Bowers, B.
1982   *A History of Electric Light and Power*. London: Peter Peregrinus.

Breskin, C.A.
1945   *Plastics Catalogue: The 1945 Encyclopedia of Plastics*. New York: Plastics Catalogue Corporation.

Briggs, A.
1961–95   *The History of Broadcasting in the United Kingdom*. 5 vols. London and Oxford: Oxford University Press.

British Catalogue of Plastics
1947   *British Catalogue of Plastics*, ed. E. Molloy. London: National Trade Press.
1948   *British Catalogue of Plastics*, ed. E. Molloy. London: National Trade Press.

British Industrial Plastics Ltd
1951   *Beetle Bulletin* (July) 1. Oldbury: BIP Publicity Department.
1952   *Beetle Bulletin* (June) 2. Oldbury: BIP Publicity Department.

British Plastics (and Moulded Products Trader)
1932   *British Plastics (and Moulded Products Trader)* 4 (40) (September). London: Plastics Trade Press.

British Xylonite
1899a   Price list. Hale End: British Xylonite.
1899b   British Xylonite Company Catalogue.
1927   1927 Catalogue. Hale End: British Xylonite.

Brookes and Adams Ltd
n.d.   'Bandalasta' Ware (The Ideal Picnic and Dainty Table Ware). Birmingham: Brookes and Adams (undated, probably 1927).

Brown, D.
1994   Polymers in Dentistry. *Plastiquarian*, 13: 3–6, 17.

Brydson, J.A.
1982   *Plastics Materials*. 4th edn. London: Butterworth Scientific.
1991   *Plastics*. London: HMSO.

Bullivant, L.
1986   'Design for Better Living' and the Public Response to Britain Can Make It. In *Did Britain Make It? British Design in Context 1946–86*. London: Design Council, 145–55.

Byatt, I.C.R.
1979   *The British Electrical Industry, 1875–1914*. Oxford: Clarendon Press.

Catterall, Claire
1990   Perceptions of Plastics: A Study of Plastics in Britain 1945–1956. In *The Plastics Age*, P. Sparke, ed. London: Victoria & Albert Museum, 67–73.

Chandler, D.
1936   *Outline of History of Lighting by Gas*. London: South Metropolitan Gas Co.

Chartered Institute of Marketing
n.d.   A History of the Chartered Institute of Marketing. Typescript. Maidenhead: Chartered Institute of Marketing.

Clarke, A.
1990a   Tupperware – the Product as Social Relation. Paper given at the conference on 'Industry and Anti-Industry', Victoria & Albert Museum, 7–9 December.

1990b   The Tupper Echelons. *Guardian*, 27 September: 65.

Coates, A.
1987   *The Commerce in Rubber: The First 250 Years*. Oxford: Oxford University Press.

Coleman, D.C.
1969   *Courtaulds: An Economic and Social History. Vol. II: Rayon*. Oxford: Clarendon Press.

Collins, M.
1987   *Towards Post-Modernism – Design Since 1851*. London: British Museum.

Collins Baker, C.H.
1922   *Design and Modern Industry: The Year Book of the Design and Industries Association*. London: Benn Bros.

Dalton, H.
1945   *Hansard*, 19 December 1944. London: HMSO.

Davis, A. (ed.)
1950a   *Design* 17 (May). Council of Industrial Design.
1950b   *Design* 24 (December). Council of Industrial Design.

Design Congress
1951   *Design Policy in Industry as a Responsibility of High Level Management*. Conference papers, September. London: Council of Industrial Design.

Design Policy in Industry
1951   *Design Policy in Industry*. London: Council of Industrial Design.

Diderot, D.
1959   *A Diderot Pictorial Encyclopaedia of Trades and Industry*. Vol. 2. New York: Dover. (Original edn 1763.)

Doleman, I.
1985   Personal communication to S. Mossman.

Dormer, P.
1986   Home Rules. In *Our Domestic Landscape*, I. Bellow, P. Dormer *et al.* Manchester: Corner House, 12–13.
1991   *The Meanings of Modern Design*. London: Thames and Hudson.

Dreyfus, H.
1959   *The Measure of Man*. New York: Whitney Library of Design.

DuBois, J.H.
1943   *Plastics*. Chicago: American Technical Society.
1972   *Plastics History USA*. Boston: Cahners Books.
1981   *Plastics*. 6th edn. New York: Van Nostrand Reinhold.

DuCros, Sir Arthur
1938   *Wheels of Fortune: A Salute to Pioneers*. London: Chapman & Hall.

Dunlop, J.B.
1924   *The History of the Pneumatic Tyre*. Dublin: Alexander Thomas.

Edwards, L.
1990   Gutta Percha, the Plastic of its Time. *Plastiquarian*, 6: 14–15.
1991–2   Polyethylene – the New Insulating Material. *Plastiquarian* 9: 12.

Ekco
1939   Ekco Ltd. Catalogue 1939/40. Southend Museum Collection.
1955   Ekco Ltd. Brochure 1955. Southend Museum Collection.

Electricity Council
1982   *Electricity Supply in the United Kingdom. A Chronology*. 3rd edn. London: Electricity Council (original edn 1973).

Elias, T.E. (ed.)
1934   The Post-War Tradition 1919–1934. *British Commerce and Industry* 1. London: Russell Square Press, 30–8.

Eliot, T.S.
1972   A Cooking Egg. In *Selected Poems*. London: Faber.

Erinoid
n.d.   Casein Plastics, Trade Literature. Stroud: Erinoid Ltd. Science Museum technical files. (*c*.1935)

Everyday Things and their Story
n.d.   *Everyday Things and their Story*. London: Odhams Press (undated, probably 1944).

Ewing, E.
1978   *Dress and Undress*. London: Batsford.

Faraday, M.
1832   Experimental Researches in Electricity. Paper read to the Royal Society, 24 November 1831. *Philosophical Transactions* (1832) 122: 125–62.

Friedel, R.
1978   Men, Materials, and Ideas: A History of Celluloid. PhD thesis, Johns Hopkins University (submitted 1976).
1983   *Pioneer Plastic: The Making and Selling of Celluloid*. Wisconsin: University of Wisconsin Press.
1990   The First Plastic. In *The Plastics Age*, P. Sparke (ed.). London: Victoria & Albert Museum, 24–31.

GEC Moulded Plastics Division
1963   *Plastics by Design*. Birmingham: GEC (Engineering).

Gloag, J.
1945   *Plastics and Industrial Design*. London: George Allen & Unwin.

Glover, C.
1981   Colin Glover, former Managing Director of BX and BXL Ltd, taped interview with Percy Reboul, Plastics Historical Society, 29 July.

Going, T.
1990a   A Resounding Ekco: E.K. Cole Ltd. *Plastiquarian* 6: 12–13.
1990b   Ekco Coloured Cabinets. *British Vintage Wireless Society Magazine*.

Goldsmith, J.N.
1934   Alexander Parkes, Parkesine, Xylonite and Celluloid. Bound MS, Science Museum Library.

Good Housekeeping
1957   How to Shop for Home Plastics. *Good Housekeeping* July: 65–70.

Greenstock, H.
n.d.   "…Go on and Prosper": Reminiscences of the early days of the plastics industry. Brantham: BXL Plastics Ltd. (*c*.1981).

Gutta Percha Company
1852   Gutta Percha Company catalogue. London: Gutta Percha Co.

Hackney Archives
1869   D/B/XYL/14/1: Alexander Parkes and Another to the Xylonite Company Ltd – Assignment of Letters Patent, 23 June. Hackney Archives Department.
1873   D/X/XYL/14/2: Assignment of Letters Patent/The Liquidation of the

Xylonite Co. Ltd and the said Company to Mr Daniel Spill, 8 December. Hackney Archives Department.
1874   D/B/XYL/14/3: Mortgage of Letters Patent and Leasehold Premises at Homerton for Securing £700 and Interest, December 31 (from D. Spill to H.N. Palmer Esq.). Hackney Archives Department.

Hackney Archives no. 1
1869   D/B/XYL/2/1: Price list.

Hackney Archives no. 2
n.d.   D/B/XYL/19/1-3.

Hackney Archives no. 3
n.d.   D/B/XYL/1/18/1.

Hackney Archives no. 4
1918   D/B/XYL/1/1/4.

Hackney Archives no. 5
1894   D/B/XYL/1/1/1: Minutes of Directors' Meetings. Vol. 3.

Hackney Archives no. 6
1895   D/B/XYL/1/1/2: Minutes of Directors' Meetings.

Hackney Archives no. 7
1913   *Minutes of Evidence and Appendices of the Department Committee on Celluloid.* London: HMSO.

Hancock, T.
1857   *Personal Narrative of the Origin and Progress of the Caoutchouc or India Rubber Manufacture in England.* London: Longman, Brown, Green, Longmans, Roberts.

Hannah, L.
1979   *Electricity before Nationalisation.* London and Basingstoke: Macmillan Press; Baltimore, MD: Johns Hopkins University Press.

Hard, A.H.
1933   *The Romance of Rayon.* Manchester: Whittaker & Robinson.

Hardwick, P.
1981   *Discovering Horn.* Guildford: Lutterworth Press.

Harrods
1985   Catalogue (1929). London: David & Charles.

Haslett, C.
1934   *The Electrical Handbook for Women.* London: English Universities Press.

Hebdige, D.
1988   Towards a Cartography of Taste. In *Hiding in the Light.* London: Comedia, 45-76.

Hertz, H.
1888   On the Action of a Rectilinear Oscillation upon a Neighbouring Circuit. *Weidemann's Annalen* 34: 155.

Hill, J.
1986   *Radio Radio.* Bampton: Sunrise.

Hillier, B.
1968   *Art Deco of the 20s and 30s.* London: Studio Vista/Dutton Pictureback.
1971   *The World of Art Deco.* London: Studio Vista.

Hoggart, R.
1957   *The Uses of Literacy.* London: Pelican.

Houses of Parliament
1879   *Parliamentary Committee under the Chairmanship of Sir Lyon Playfair to Consider all Private Bills Seeking Powers to Supply Electricity.* Committee appointed 28 March 1879, reported 13 June 1879.

Hyatt, J.W.
1914   Address of Acceptance (of the Perkin Medal). *Journal of Industrial and Engineering Chemistry* 6: 158–61.

ICI
1939   *ICI POL.7 Annual Review, 1939.* Science Museum Library Archives.
1942   *ICI POL.7 Annual Review, 1942.* Science Museum Library Archives.
1944–5   *ICI POL.7 Annual Review, 1944–5.* Science Museum Library Archives.
1953   *ICI POL.7 Annual Review, 1953.* Science Museum Library Archives.
1954   *ICI POL.7 Annual Review, 1954.* Science Museum Library Archives.
1956   *ICI POL.8 Annual Review 1956.* Science Museum Library Archives.

ICI Plastics
c.1964   *Landmarks of the Plastics Industry.* London: ICI Plastics Division.

Jarvis, A.
1946   *The Things We See/Indoors and Out.* Harmondsworth: Penguin.

Jolly, W.P.
1972   *Marconi: A Biography.* London: Constable.

Jones, Y.
1981   *The Birmingham Japanning and Papier Maché Industries.* Birmingham: Birmingham City Museum.

Kahlbaum, G.W.A. and Darbishire, F.V.
1899   *The Letters of Faraday and Schönbein.* London: Williams & Norgate.

Katz, S.
1978   *Plastics: Designs and Materials.* London: Studio Vista.
1984   *Classic Plastics.* London: Thames & Hudson.
1986   *Early Plastics.* No. 168. Aylesbury: Shire Publications.

Kaufman, M.
1963   *The First Century of Plastics – Celluloid and its Sequel.* London: Plastics and Rubber Institute (reprinted 1980).
1967   *History of PVC.* London: McClaren & Sons.
1968   *Giant Molecules,* London: Aldus Books.
1980   The Origins of the IRI and PI. Science Museum Library, Kaufman Archive, 18 December.

Kennedy, C.
1986   *ICI: The Company that Changed Our Lives.* London: Hutchinson.

Kimberly Mumford, J.
1924   *The Story of Bakelite.* New York: Robert L. Stillson.

Krainik, C. and Krainik, M.
1989   *Union Cases.* USA: Privately published.

Littlewoods
1986   Mail Order Catalogues. Microfiche edn. London: Ormonde.

Lougee, E.F. (ed.)
1936   *Modern Plastics* 14 (2) (October). Philadelphia: Breskin & Charlton.
1939   *Modern Plastics* 17 (2) (October). New York: Breskin.

MacCarthy, F.
1972   *All Things Bright and Beautiful.* London: George Allen & Unwin.

Mark, H.F.
1975   *Giant Molecules.* New York: Time-Life Books.

Mark, H. and Whitby, G.S. (eds)
1940   *Collected Papers of Wallace H. Carothers on Polymerization.* New York: Interscience.

Martineau, H.
1851   Flower Shows in a Birmingham Hot-House. *Household Words* 4: unpaginated.

Maxwell, C.
1864   *A Dynamical Theory of the Electromagnetic Field.* Paper read to the Royal Society, 8 December.

Mechanics Magazine
1849   *Mechanics Magazine* 50.

Meikle, J.L.
1990   Plastics in the American Machine Age 1920–1950. In *The Plastics Age*, P. Sparke, ed. London: Victoria & Albert Museum, 40–53.

Merriam, C.P.
n.d.   Private journal. Science Museum Library, BXL Archive no. 6/2.

Merriam, J.
1976   *Pioneering in Plastics – The Story of Xylonite.* Ipswich: East Anglian Magazine.

Mitchell, R.G.B.
1993   History & Development of the Vinyl LP Record. *Plastiquarian* 11: 14–17.

Modern Plastics Encyclopedia
1947   *Modern Plastics Encyclopedia* 1. New York: Plastics Catalogue Corporation.

Moncrieff, R.W.
1975   *Man-Made Fibres.* 6th edn. London: Newnes-Butterworth.

Moore, G.
1968   The Paper King of Birmingham. *Warwickshire and Worcestershire Life* January 14 (11) : 24–5.

Morgan, J.
1989   Quality Control and Product Development, Erinoid, 1954–1961. *Plastiquarian* 2: 12–13.

1994   Personal communication to S. Mossman, March.

Morris, P.J.T.
1990   *Polymer Pioneers*. Philadelphia: Beckman Center for the History of Chemistry.

Mossman, S.T.I.
1994   Parkesine and Celluloid. In *The Development of Plastics*, S.T.I. Mossman and P.J.T. Morris, eds. Cambridge: Royal Society of Chemistry, 10–25.

Mossman, S.T.I. and Morris, P.J.T. (eds)
1994   *The Development of Plastics*. Cambridge: Royal Society of Chemistry.

Murrell, K.F.H.
1965   *Ergonomics*. London: Chapman & Hall.

Myers, K.
1986   *Understains: The Sense and Seduction of Advertising*. London: Comedia.

National Electrical Manufacturers Association
1946   *A Chronological History of Electrical Development from 600 B.C.* New York: NEMA.

NCR
1984   *1884–1922: The Cash Register Era*. Dayton, Ohio: NCR.

Newport, R.
1976   *Plastics Antiques*. Oldbury Warley: British Industrial Plastics.

Nicholson, J.W.
1991   *The Chemistry of Polymers*. Cambridge: Royal Society of Chemistry.

Oral testimony
1988   Taped interview by P. Reboul with Ron Greenstock.
1990   Market research on Touring Exhibitions commissioned by Yorkshire and Humberside Museums Council and the Museums and Galleries Commission. Responses to suggested plastics exhibition.
1991   Workshop held by Kathryn Ensall and Mark Suggitt to accompany the Yorkshire and Humberside exhibition 'Popular Plastics', Bankfield Museum, Halifax, 1 May.

Parkyn, B.
1953   *Polyester Handbook*. London: Scott Bader.
1994   Fibre-Reinforced Composites. In *The Development of Plastics*, S.T.I. Mossman and P.J.T. Morris, eds. Cambridge: Royal Society of Chemistry, 105–14.

Parsons, R.H.
1939   *The Early Days of the Power Station Industry*. Cambridge: Cambridge University Press.

Pascale, A. and Cernia, F.
1983   *Gli anni di Plastica*. Milan: Electa Editrice.

Pearce, J. (ed.)
1987   *Gardner's Chemical Synonyms and Trade Names*. Aldershot and Brookfield, VT: Gower Technical Press.

Pevsner, N.
1937   *An Enquiry into Industrial Art in England*. Cambridge: Cambridge University Press.

PHS
1881   Plastics Historical Society Archive, Parkes notes (with E10) titled E10 'Sutton Coldfield March 7th 1881', 3.

PHS N1
c.1881   Plastics Historical Society Archive, N1 Notes by Alexander Parkes, franked Kelch of Inverness.

Priestley, J.B.
1937   *Midnight on the Desert*. London: William Heinemann.

Ray, P. (ed.)
1949   *Designers in Britain* 2. London: Allan Wingate.

Reboul, P.
1991   Oral testimony, 27 January.

Roberts, R.
1980   *The Classic Slum*. London: Pelican.

Routledge, R.
1893   *Discoveries and Inventions of the Nineteenth Century*. 10th edn. London: George Routledge.

Smith, A.
1976   *An Inquiry into the Nature and Causes of the Wealth of Nations*. Oxford: Clarendon Press.

Smith, P.I. (ed.)
1947   *Practical Plastics Illustrated*. London: Odhams Press.

Société du Bois Durci
n.d.   Société du Bois Durci price list (undated, *c.*1860).

Sparke, P.
1983   *Consultant Design: The History and Practice of the Designer in Industry*. London: Pembridge Press.

Sparke, P. (ed.)
1990   *The Plastics Age*. London: Victoria & Albert Museum.

Suffolk Record Office no. 1
1877   *Wages Book, 1877*. BXL papers, no. HC410.

Suffolk Record Office no. 2
n.d.   BXL papers, no. HC410.

Suggitt, I.
1991   Oral testimony, 3 May.

Suggitt, M.
1991   Letter to S. Mossman, 11 July.

Swift, G.
1992   *Ever After*. London: Picador.

Telcon
1950   *The Telcon Story, 1850–1950*. London: Telegraph Construction & Maintenance.

Tilley, J.P.
1994   Versatility of Acrylics, 1934–1980. In *The Development of Plastics*, S.T.I. Mossman and P.J.T. Morris, eds. Cambridge: Royal Society of Chemistry, 95–104.

Tilson, B. (ed.)
1989   *Made in Birmingham: Design and Industry 1889–1989*. Brewin Books.

The Times
1934   *The Times Trade and Engineering Supplement*. 24 February: 37.

Turner, M.
1990   *Made in Hong Kong; A History of Export Design in Hong Kong*. Hong Kong: Hong Kong Museum of History.

Upholsterers' Handbook of Dunlopillo
1949   *Upholsterers' Handbook of Dunlopillo*. Birmingham: Dunlop Rubber.

Waugh, E.
1991   *The Ordeal of Gilbert Pinfold*. Harmondsworth: Penguin (original edn 1957).

Weil, D.
1986   Fluent in Plastics. In *Our Domestic Landscape*, I. Bellow, P. Dormer, *et al.* Manchester: Corner House, 30–1.

Williamson, C.
1988   *Plastiquarian* 1: 8.
1989   *Plastiquarian* 2: 8.
1994   Victorian Plastics – Foundations of an Industry. In *The Development of Plastics*, S.T.I. Mossman and P.J.T. Morris, eds. Cambridge: Royal Society of Chemistry, 1–9.

Wilson, G.
1994   Polythene: The Early Years. In *The Development of Plastics*, S.T.I. Mossman and P.J.T. Morris, eds. Cambridge: Royal Society of Chemistry, 70–86.

Workers of the Writers' Program of the Work Projects Administration in the Commonwealth of Pennsylvania
1945   *Plastics*. Chicago: Albert Whitman.

Xylonite Magazine
1955a   *Xylonite Magazine* 12 March, 6.
1955b   *Xylonite Magazine* June, 113.

Yarsley, V.E. and Couzens, E.G.
1941   *Plastics*. London: Pelican.

Yorkshire Post
1950   *Yorkshire Post*, 28 April.

Index

Note: page numbers indicated in **bold** type are associated with objects in the Catalogue.